MODERN ACCOUNTING IN FINANCIAL SERVICES

ACCOUNTANCY FOR BANKING STUDENTS 5TH EDITION

To Sandie and Penny

MODERN ACCOUNTING IN FINANCIAL SERVICES

ACCOUNTANCY FOR BANKING STUDENTS

5TH EDITION

by

J. R. Edwards, MSc(Econ.); FCA; FCIB; ATII

and

H. J. Mellett, MSc(Econ.); FCA; FCIB

FINANCIAL WORLD Publishing

THE CHARTERED INSTITUTE OF BANKERS

Financial World Publishing
4-9 Burgate Lane
Canterbury
Kent
CT1 2XJ
United Kingdom

T   01227 818687
F   01227 479641
E   editorial@ifslearning.com

Financial World Publishing publications are published by The Chartered Institute of Bankers, a non-profit making registered educational charity.

The Chartered Institute of Bankers believes that the sources of information upon which the book is based are reliable and has made every effort to ensure the complete accuracy of the text. However, neither CIB, the author nor any contributor can accept any legal responsibility whatsoever for consequences that may arise from errors or omissions or any opinion or advice given.

Typeset by John Smith

Printed in the UK

ISBN 0-85297-610-0

Contents

CHAPTER 2   Frameworks for Financial Reporting

CHAPTER 3   Form and Content of Company Accounts

CHAPTER 4 Reporting Fixed Assets in Company Accounts

CHAPTER 5 Reporting Other Assets and Liabilities in Company Accounts

CHAPTER 6 Group Accounts

CHAPTER 7 Capital Reduction, Reorganization and Reconstruction

CHAPTER 8   Share and Business Valuation

CHAPTER 9   Interpretation of Accounts: Traditional Ratio Analysis

CHAPTER 10   Interpretation of Accounts: Cash Flow

CHAPTER 11 Business Decision Making: Cost behaviour

CHAPTER 12 Business Decision Making: Investment Appraisal

CHAPTER 13   Forecasts and Budgets

Preface

Accountancy is a practical subject concerned with the measurement of useful financial information and its communication to interested parties. There are many groups of individuals who use financial information as the basis for resource allocation decisions; these include management, shareholders, bankers, trade suppliers and employees. Because of this common interest in financial information as a basis for decision making, much of the material contained in this book is of equal relevance to each of these groups. Different user groups require financial information for different types of resource allocation decisions however, and this book is primarily written to meet the needs of bankers and, more specifically, to help banking students prepare for and pass the *Accounting, Analysis and Planning* paper of The Chartered Institute of Bankers. However, this text contains a farily full coverage of accounting theory and practice relating to the preparation and use of financial reports and is therefore suitable reading for the second and third year of degree courses and for the examinations of other professional bodies.

The book naturally assumes a basic knowledge of accountancy, particularly the ability to prepare final accounts from either a trial balance or incomplete records, and is organized in such a way as to enable students to proceed from preliminary studies of accounting to the standard required in the *Accounting, Analysis and Planning* examination in a series of logical stages. The book contains a full coverage of syllabus topics, and a student who acquires a good understanding of the various matters discussed can be confident of success in the examination. Each chapter is self-contained, and together they comprise a comprehensive treatment of topics at the appropriate level for that examination. Teachers and students can therefore choose to study topics in whichever order they consider suitable, although we recommend the order followed in the text.

Financial services managers come into contact with the accounting process primarily as users of financial information but we believe that, in order to assess the significance of the information they receive, they must understand both why and how it is prepared. The principal feature of this book is that it combines an examination of these three major facets of accountancy as a process of communication, namely why particular types of financial information are provided, how the information is prepared, and the significance of the data that is made available. Questions in the *Accounting, Analysis and Planning* examination reflect this emphasis. The majority of questions contain at least two parts. The first of these calls for the preparation of financial information, while the second part requires the student to explain why it is prepared and/or what the information means.

Modern Accounting in Financial Services makes extensive use of examples, within each chapter, both for explanatory purposes and to test the student's understanding of the points discussed. In addition, each chapter contains a final section that consists of a number of questions which students are expected to work through. Many of the examples and most of the questions are taken from past examination papers and, in all cases, solutions are provided. Sometimes the numerical solutions do not represent the only possible arrangement of the figures; also, the comments are not necessarily exhaustive in all cases. This is in the nature of the accounting process: figures mean different things to different people and, as examiners, we look for logical argument rather than conformity to a prescribed model. Students are strongly urged to work through the questions before they look at the solutions. Striving to prepare answers is an essential part of the learning process, and little is gained by simply comparing the question with the solution provided without first working through the question.

Acknowledgements
We wish to thank The Chartered Institute of Bankers for permission to reproduce questions from past examination papers.

1

THE NATURE AND USE OF ACCOUNTING STATEMENTS

1.1 INTRODUCTION

The Chartered Institute of Bankers celebrated its centenary in 1979 while the Institute of Chartered Accountants in England and Wales (ICAEW), perhaps the best-known British professional accounting body, reached the same historic landmark just one year later. Both accounting and banking have a much longer history, of course, but each recognized the need to establish a formal institute to fulfil a wide range of important functions at about the same time. These functions include, among others, the establishment of educational standards (with examinations leading to universally recognized qualifications), and the provision of a focal point to discuss professional matters. Both professions have flourished over the last one hundred years or more, and have made valuable contributions to British economic development. The activities of the banks and the accounting firms complement one another, but there is also some overlap which produces an element of competition – for example, in the field of advice on taxation – and this is healthy and in the customers' interests.

The financial services manager, who is an important user of financial information, must achieve a thorough knowledge of the nature of the accounting process and the scope and limitations of accounting reports. It is the purpose of this book to equip them with some of the tools needed for their chosen profession. The purposes of Chapter 1 are to reintroduce readers to the main accounting reports, which were the subject of their earlier studies in accountancy, and to examine the relationship between these accounting reports.

1.2 THE ACCOUNTING PROCESS

Accounting is essentially concerned with recording, measuring and communicating financial facts to interested parties. The process begins with a transaction, or economic event, such as the delivery of goods, the supply of services, or the receipt or payment of cash. The process ends when this economic event is embodied in a financial statement designed to enable the prospective user to make well-informed decisions, e.g. a bank statement which informs a customer that his bank balance has fallen to a low level might indicate that he should take steps either to reduce the level of his expenditure or to make a formal application for an overdraft facility. The various stages in the accounting process are presented diagrammatically in Figure 1.1.

Figure 1.1 shows that the accounting process is divided into two basic elements, namely recording and reporting financial information. In terms of the development of

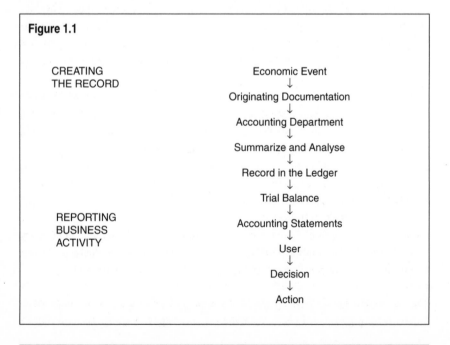

Figure 1.1

CREATING
THE RECORD

Economic Event
↓
Originating Documentation
↓
Accounting Department
↓
Summarize and Analyse
↓
Record in the Ledger
↓
Trial Balance
↓

REPORTING
BUSINESS
ACTIVITY

Accounting Statements
↓
User
↓
Decision
↓
Action

accountancy, the book-keeping function has the far longer history, and evidence exists which shows that accounting records were kept thousands of years ago for control purposes, i.e. to provide records of amounts owed, amounts to be collected and properties owned at a particular point in time. In more recent times accounting records have been used increasingly as a basis for preparing accounting reports. Indeed the present-day accountant devotes much more time to the preparation and interpretation of accounting reports than to book-keeping. Part of the reason for this is that the book-keeping function has been reduced to a fairly routine process, both as the result of computerization, and because of the introduction of more effective systems of internal control. The result is that book-keeping makes few demands on the accountant's professional skill and this leaves him/her free to devote more time to the reporting function which has grown immensely in importance.

The emergence of the large-scale limited liability company has been the single most important factor stimulating the need for financial reports. In the one-man (woman) business there is little need for the development of reporting procedures; the owner/manager retains close contact with all aspects of business activity, and is able to assess progress simply by examining the bank balance and from direct contact with customers, suppliers, and employees. In this situation, accounting reports provide the owner with little additional information to help manage business affairs. They are prepared only for tax purposes and, in the case of the small limited company, to comply with the requirements of the Companies Acts. This changes as businesses increase in size, because it results in the separation of the ownership and managerial functions; it causes top management to become more remote from the 'shop floor', and it increases companies' reliance on trade credit, the bank and other forms of loan finance. The result is an increase in the demand for accounting information as a basis for investment and credit-granting decisions. The various users of accounting reports are considered further in section 1.3 of this chapter.

1.3 USERS OF ACCOUNTING INFORMATION
1.3.1 Internal and External Users
Users of accounting information are conventionally classified as either internal or external to the company. Internal users consist of a single group, namely management, and their access to the company's accounting records is unrestricted. Indeed, it is their responsibility to ensure that the accounting system is suitably designed to make available the range of financial information that management needs as a basis for decision making. If the required information is unavailable, it is fair to

say that management has only itself to blame. The position of external users of accounting reports is different. Shareholders are legally entitled to receive a copy of the annual accounts, but that is all. It must be remembered, however, that in the majority of UK limited companies the directors hold the majority of the shares and, in those cases, management and ownership coincide. Creditors, on the other hand, have access to the public information filed with the Registrar of Companies, although they sometimes put pressure on management to disclose more.

It was not so long ago that shareholders and creditors were regarded as the only important external users of accounting reports, but that is no longer the case. In more recent years there has developed an increased appreciation of the fact that there exists a large number of groups who possess a legitimate interest in company performance. In 1975 the accounting profession published a document, called *The Corporate Report*, in an attempt to stimulate discussion concerning the scope and aims of published financial reports in the light of modern needs and conditions. This report lists the following seven user groups who are thought to have a reasonable claim to corporate financial information:

- The equity investor group, including existing and potential shareholders and holders of convertible securities, options or warrants.

- The loan creditor group, including existing and potential holders of debentures and loan stock, and providers of short-term secured and unsecured loans and finance.

- The employee group, including existing, potential and past employees.

- The analyst-adviser group, including financial analysts and journalists, economists, statisticians, researchers, trade unions, stockbrokers and other providers of advisory services such as credit rating agencies.

- The business contact group, including customers, trade creditors and suppliers and, in a different sense, competitors, business rivals, and those interested in mergers, amalgamations and takeovers.

- The government, including tax authorities, departments and agencies concerned with the supervision of commerce and industry, and local authorities.

- The public, including taxpayers, consumers and other community and special interest groups such as political parties, consumer and environmental protection societies and regional pressure groups.

Each of the above groups has a common interest in company accounts, but they use the financial information available to them as the basis for often quite different decisions. For instance, the equity investor group, i.e. shareholders, wants help in reaching share trading decisions: whether to retain their present investment, whether to increase it, or whether to dispose of their shareholding. Employees, on the other hand, require financial information to help them to assess employment prospects and for the purpose of collective bargaining. There are significant variations in the quantity of financial information made available to each of these groups, and this is caused by different legal requirements, voluntary decisions by management to make financial information available to particular users, and the ability of certain individuals to succeed in demanding additional disclosure.

1.3.2 Bankers as Users of Accounting Information

Bankers are substantial users of accounting information, both to help them to reach an initial loan decision and to monitor progress after the advance has been made. In the past, finance provided by the clearing banks invariably took the form of an overdraft or short-term loan, although in practice these facilities were in many cases effectively transformed into long-term finance as the result of periodic renewal. Nevertheless, the advances remained technically subject to repayment on call or at short notice. More recently, the banks have become willing to make a longer-term commitment, both in recognition of the changing nature of companies' financial requirements and as a result of increased competition from other financial institutions. Whether the advance is short-term, medium-term or long-term, the banker needs to be satisfied on the following points:

- the company will be able to meet the interest payments accruing during the period of the loan;

- the company will be able to repay the capital sum at the end of the loan period;

- the company is able to offer adequate security, e.g. the assets owned by the company are expected to remain sufficient to cover the amount of the loan after first meeting all prior claims;

- the loan does not contravene any restrictive covenants contained in the company's articles of association, e.g. these may provide that loans are not to exceed a certain percentage of the shareholders' equity.

Although the above features are common to all loan appraisals, the banker is likely to emphasize different aspects of his investigation depending on the expected duration of the loan. For a short-term loan, the banker is interested in estimates of the net cash flow over the next few months, whereas for a longer-term advance the banker needs to be convinced that the company is financially stable and that adequate profits will be earned throughout the foreseeable future. The ability of a borrower to repay both the interest and capital sum is the banker's prime consideration, and if forecasts indicate that these conditions cannot be met the advance will not be made. However, even the best laid plans may be thwarted by unexpected events, and adequate security should be obtained. Prospective borrowers are expected to meet this latter condition, irrespective of whether the loan is short- or long-term, but the degree of risk increases with the duration of the loan, and this will be in the banker's mind when assessing whether the security offered is acceptable (i.e. an asset that might be expected to retain its value in the short term only would not be acceptable as security for a long-term advance).

The bank manager normally requires a copy of the company's most recent annual accounts to help in reaching a loan decision.

In general, however, the annual accounts satisfy the banker's information requirements only to a limited extent. This is because:

- They are out of date. If the accounts are prepared on a calendar year basis, they are unlikely to be available until March or April of the following year. These are of limited use to a banker who is asked for money in April and even less useful when the loan request is made later in the year. For instance, the accounts may list an asset that would be considered ideal security, but this information is of no use to the bank if the asset has since been sold.

- The annual accounts are past history, whereas the banker wants to know what is likely to happen to the company in the future. Last year's accounts may show a good profit and a steady financial position, but trading conditions are subject to constant change, and a series of setbacks may result in heavy losses and a rapid deterioration in the company's financial structure.

Both these criticisms point to the need for additional, more relevant, accounting information. Fortunately the bank is usually in a good position to ensure that appropriate data is provided, because failure or refusal to make available the required information results in rejection of the request for finance. The banker usually requires special-purpose reports which enable an appraisal of the future prospects of the company to be made, including its ability to make the necessary interest and loan repayments. These reports often consist of an up-to-date statement of the company's financial position, and forecast accounts which set out estimates of future cash flows and profitability. The period covered by these forecasts should coincide with the expected duration of the loan so that the banker can make a rational assessment of the company's ability to meet the conditions imposed for repayment.

Much of the accounting information that the banker requires is often readily available. For example, where finance is required for a new project, the kind of estimates referred to above should already have been prepared in order to enable management to decide whether the proposed course of action is worthwhile. This is not always the case, however, particularly where the customer is a small business which does not operate a formal management accounting system. In this situation, relevant financial estimates must nevertheless be obtained from the business, although professional advice may need to be obtained either from an accountant or from the bank in order to comply with this requirement. The banker must, however, guard against making unnecessary demands for information, because compliance might prove unduly costly and cause the potential customer to look towards alternative sources of finance. This is not to suggest that the banker should 'make do' where inadequate financial details are supplied, but it does point to the need to make a realistic assessment of requirements in the light of the customer's request. In all cases the financial services manager should be on the lookout for any display of excessive optimism on the part of management, and must consider the likely effect of actual results falling significantly below expectations. In this context, particular attention is given to the accuracy of any past forecasts prepared by management, and to the banker's assessment of a customer's personality. Many of the management accounting techniques which are used to assess future prospects, and are therefore of interest to bankers, are considered in Chapters 9 to 13.

After the advance has been made, it is important to ensure that progress is properly monitored. Again the annual accounts do not normally satisfy the banker's information requirements; it will be necessary to insist that the borrower prepares and submits regular, perhaps quarterly, accounts which show profit earned to date and the developing financial condition of the company. Quite possibly the accounts will show that results are coming up to expectations, or at least that they are sufficiently favourable to enable the borrower to meet the conditions of the loan. In either case repayment will take the expected course. Alternatively, trading conditions may prove unfavourable with the result that the accounts show large losses and a rapidly deteriorating financial condition. Whether the loan can be 'called in' depends on the terms and conditions of the advance, but wherever possible the banker should take prompt action to obtain repayment before the company's assets are reduced even further by continuing losses.

1.4 REVISION OF PRINCIPAL ACCOUNTING STATEMENTS

Readers should be familiar with the nature of the profit and loss account and balance sheet from their earlier studies, and they should also have had a great deal of practice in preparing these two accounting statements. Final accounts questions typically involve either one of the following two possibilities:

- Candidates are given a trial balance, together with a list of necessary adjustments, and are required to prepare final accounts (Example 1.1 and Question 1.1).

- Candidates are given lists of assets and liabilities at the beginning and end of an accounting period, together with details of cash transactions during the year, and asked to prepare final accounts (Question 1.2).

Readers are strongly urged to work Example 1.1 and to compare their answer with the solution provided. They should also work Questions 1.1 and 1.2, in order to make sure that they possess the basic accounting skills required by candidates beginning a course leading to the Accounting, Analysis and Planning examination. Any student who fails to produce satisfactory solutions to these questions requires further revision of final accounts preparation using a suitable text, such as *Introduction to Accounting* by Marriott, Edwards and Mellett, published by Sage.

Example 1.1

The following trial balance was extracted from the books of Lingford Ltd as at 31 December 20X1:

	£	£
Share capital		50,000
Share premium		8,000
Motor vans at cost	40,000	
Provision for depreciation at 1 January 20X1		14,800
Purchases	129,938	
Sales		179,422
Rent and rates	2,500	
General expenses	5,842	
Wages	19,876	
Bad debts	542	
Provision for doubtful debts at 1 January 20X1		684
Directors' salaries	16,000	
Trade debtors and trade creditors	16,941	11,171
Stock at 1 January 20X1	28,572	
Bank balance	24,921	
Profit and loss account as at 1 January 20X1		21,055
	£285,132	£285,132

You are given the following additional information:
(i)   the authorized and issued share capital is 50,000 ordinary shares of £1 each;
(ii) wages due but unpaid at 31 December 20X1 amounted to £264;
(iii) the provision for doubtful debts is to be increased by £102;
(iv) stock at 31 December 20X1 was £38,292;
(v)   rent and rates amounting to £300 were paid in advance at 31 December 20X1;
(vi) depreciation on motor vans is to be charged at the rate of 20 per cent per annum on cost;
(vii) it is proposed to pay a dividend of £5,000 for the year 20X1.

Required
A trading and profit and loss account for the year 20X1, not necessarily in a form for publication, and a balance sheet as at 31 December 20X1.

Note:
Ignore taxation.

Solution

Workings:
The journal entries given below may be used to incorporate the effect of the adjustments required by the additional information (ii)-(vii). Students may alternatively prefer to omit journal entries and make the adjustments on the face of the trial balance given in the question.

Journal entries (narrative omitted)		£	£
(ii)	Wages	264	
	Accrued expense		264
(iii)	Bad and doubtful debts	102	
	Provision for doubtful debts		102
(iv)	Stock	38,292	
	Purchases		38,292
(v)	Prepaid expense	300	
	Rent and rates		300
(vi)	Depreciation expense	8,000	
	Provision for depreciation		8,000
(vii)	Dividend	5,000	
	Proposed dividend		5,000

Trading and Profit and Loss Account of Lingford Ltd for 20X1	£	£
Sales		179,422
Less: Stock at 1 January 20X1	28,572	
Purchases	129,938	
Stock at 31 December 20X1	(38,292)	
Cost of goods sold	_____	120,218
Gross profit		59,204
Less: Depreciation	8,000	
Rent and rates (2,500-300)	2,200	
General expenses	5,842	
Wages (19,876 + 264)	20,140	
Bad and doubtful debts (542 + 102)	644	
Directors' salaries	16,000	52,826
Net profit		6,378
Add: Profit and loss account at 1 January 20X1		21,055
		27,433
Less: Dividend		5,000
Retained profit		22,433

Balance Sheet of Lingford Ltd as at 31 December 20X1	£	£
Fixed Assets		
Motor vans at cost		40,000
Less: Provision for depreciation		22,800
		17,200
Current assets		
Stock	38,292	
Trade debtors, less provision for doubtful debts (16,941-786)	16,155	
Prepaid expense	300	
Bank balance	24,921	
	79,668	
Less: Current Liabilities		
Creditors and accruals (11,171 + 264)	11,435	
Proposed dividend	5,000	
	16,435	
Working Capital		63,233
		80,433
Financed by:		
Authorized and issued ordinary share capital (£1 shares)		50,000
Share premium account		8,000
Retained Profit		22,433
		£80,433

1.5 DIFFERENT MEASURES OF BUSINESS ACTIVITY

The balance sheet and the profit and loss account are quite different accounting statements, both in terms of the form that they take and the information that they are designed to communicate. The balance sheet is a summary of the assets belonging to a company and the various ways in which these assets are financed, i.e. it is a document which might be regarded as setting out the financial 'state of play' as at a particular date. It has been described as an instantaneous photograph of the business, and this is an apt metaphor, but like all photographs it does not tell the whole story, merely the situation at a particular point in time. A day later, or a day earlier, the financial photograph might look quite different. For example, a medium-term loan raised on the last day of an accounting period might immediately transform the apparent short-term financial position of a company from weak to healthy. Fraudulent manipulation of accounting information is unusual, but 'window-dressing' is more common and users of accounts should keep an eye open for procedures that improve the apparent profitability or financial condition of a company.

The profit and loss account, on the other hand, is intended to supply information concerning events which have occurred during an accounting period. The relationship between the two statements is indicated by Figure 1.2.

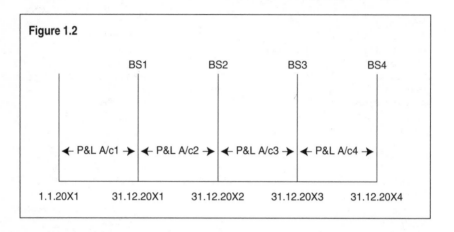

Figure 1.2

The company is formed on 1 January 20Xl and the first year's accounts deal with the year to 31 December 20Xl. These consist of a profit and loss account covering the period from formation to December 31, and a balance sheet which sets out the financial position at the year end. Balance sheets are subsequently prepared, as a minimum, at twelve-monthly intervals during the life of the company, while profit and loss accounts report trading transactions that have occurred between the date of the previous balance sheet and the date of the current balance sheet.

The drawback of the profit and loss account is that, although it provides certain useful information concerning progress made during a particular accounting period, it does not tell us all that we want to know, e.g. it does not tell us how much the company has spent on fixed assets during the year. To provide a view of financial progress during the year, a cash flow statement should also be prepared.

The contents of the profit and loss account and cash flow statement are illustrated and contrasted in the following example.

Example 1.2

The following information is provided in respect of Sprouse Ltd:

Summarized Profit and Loss Account for 20X1

	£000	£000
Sales		2,200
Less: Stock at 1 January 20X1	500	
Purchases	1,500	
Stock at 31 December 20X1	(600)	
Cost of goods sold		1,400
Gross Profit		800
Less: Depreciation	350	
Other expenses	170	
		520
Net Profit		280

Balance Sheet as at 31 December 20X1

20X0			
£000		£000	£000
2,200	Fixed assets at cost	3,400	
350	*Less*: Provision for depreciation	700	
1,850			2,700
	Current Assets		
500	Stock	600	
300	Trade debtors	360	
250	Bank balance	140	
1,050		1,100	
	Less: Current Liabilities		
500	Trade creditors	520	
550	Working capital		580
2,400			3,280
	Financed by		
1,400	Share capital		2,000
1,000	Retained profit		1,280
2,400			3,280

'Other expenses' are paid for in cash immediately. The company issued 600,000 £1 shares at par during the year and purchased fixed assets costing £1,200,000.

Required:
The following financial statements for 20X1:
(i)   the profit and loss account;
(ii) the cash flow statement.

Solution

Financial Statements for 20X1		Profit Flows £000	Cash Flows £000
Revenue transactions:			
Inflows	Sales	2,200	
	Receipts from customers		2,140 (WI)
Outflows	Purchases	(1,500)	
	Increase in stock	100	
	Cost of goods sold	(1,400)	
	Payments to suppliers		(1,480) (W2)
	Depreciation	(350)	
	Other expenses	(170)	(170)
		(1,920)	(1,650)
Internally-generated net flow		280	490
Capital transactions:			
Inflows	Share capital		600
Outflows	Fixed assets		(1,200)
Net flow		280	(110)

W1. £2,200,000 (sales) + £300,000 (opening debtors) – £360,000 (closing debtors)
W2. £1,500,000 (purchases) + £500,000 (opening creditors) – £520,000 (closing creditors)

Each of the above accounting statements is based on the transactions undertaken by Sprouse Ltd during 20X1, but they contain different information and report widely divergent net 'flows'. The differences can be explained numerically by means of the following reconciliation:

Net profit reconciled with the reduction in cash

	£000	£000
Profit earned		280
Add: Depreciation		350
Issue of shares		600
Increase in trade creditors		20
		1,250
Less: Purchase of fixed assets	1,200	
Increase in stock	100	
Increase in debtors	60	
		1,360
Reduction in bank balance		110

The items in the reconciliation may be explained as follows:
Additions:
- Depreciation must be added back to profit because it is a 'book entry' and it does not represent an outflow of cash (see Chapter 10.2.1).

- The issue of shares produces additional cash but, because it is a capital transaction, it does not affect profit and so must be added to profit to arrive at the change in the cash balance.
- Sprouse made purchases totalling £1,500,000, which appear in the profit and loss account, but payments to suppliers of only £1,480,000 appear in the cash statement, and so the £20,000 not yet paid is a temporary source of finance.

Deductions:
- The purchase of fixed assets is a capital transaction which does not affect profit in the year the acquisition takes place, but it results in an outflow of cash and so must be deducted in arriving at the cash balance.
- Similarly, increases in the amount invested in stocks and debtors represent applications of cash which must be deducted in order to arrive at the final cash balance.

The financial totals contained in each of the two 'flow' statements differ, but this is because each document is designed to focus attention on contrasting aspects of the company's progress. These objectives are examined below, and illustrated by reference to Example 1.3.

1.5.1 The Profit and Loss Account
The three functions of this document are:

- *To show how much profit has been earned.* The importance traditionally attached to the profit and loss account (the term is used here to cover the manufacturing account, trading account, general profit and loss account and appropriation account) is attributable to the fact that the wellbeing of a company substantially depends on whether sufficient profits are generated for the following two purposes:

  (a) Dividends. A company must be able to pay shareholders a reasonable return on their investment. Alternatively, in the case of an unincorporated enterprise, profits must be sufficient to cover the owners' drawings.

  (b) Expansion. Management normally wishes to expand the level of business activities and, although some of the finance required is likely to be raised externally, the remainder must be provided out of retained profit.

- *To explain how the reported balance of profit was computed.* Users wish to assess the adequacy of reported profit, and for this reason the calculation of profit, by matching expenditure with revenue, is given 'above the line' in the manufacturing account, trading account and general profit and loss account. This information enables the user to compare profit with sales and also calculate the gross profit mark-up. Additional information, such as the balance sheet figure for net assets and the results achieved by other firms, is of course needed to make a more comprehensive assessment of the company's performance.

- *To show the disposition of reported profit.* The allocation of profit between retention and distribution, is shown 'below the line' in the profit and loss appropriation account.

1.5.2 The Cash Statement

Cash has been described as the 'life blood' of a business, and it is fair to say that a company can only survive and prosper, in the long run, if it is able to generate sufficient cash inflows to cover cash outflows. It does not necessarily follow, of course, that cash inflows must match cash outflows in every individual accounting period, and, moreover, it is quite possible for a company to report a substantial profit for a year during which the cash balance has fallen, and vice versa. For example, Sprouse (Example 1.2) earned a satisfactory profit during 20Xl, but cash went down by £110,000, mainly as the result of heavy expenditure on fixed assets. This may not turn out to be a cause for concern, but it is an important financial development and its significance must be carefully assessed. The purposes of the cash statement are, therefore. to report the net change in the cash balance and to help to explain how the surplus or deficit arose by listing the cash inflows and cash outflows that occurred during the accounting period. Important differences between the two statements concern the scope they provide for error and bias:

- The preparation of the profit and loss account allows considerable scope for manipulation, because it requires valuation decisions to be reached for most balance sheet assets and liabilities.

- The cash statement has the advantage of being based on 'hard facts', because its preparation requires no valuation decisions whatsoever to be made.

The purpose of the above discussion is to show that each of the two flow statements has different rather than conflicting objectives. Neither of the documents should be considered inherently superior, and they should be used to complement each other when an attempt is made to assess financial developments.

Readers should test their understanding of the calculations and concepts discussed so far by working Example 1.3.

Example 1.3

The balance sheet of Chadwick, a trader, as at 1 January 20X4, was as follows:

BALANCE SHEET

	£	£
Plant and machinery at cost		27,500
Less: Accumulated depreciation		9,600
		17,900
Current assets:		
Stock	7,800	
Trade debtors	5,300	
	13,100	
Current liabilities:		
Trade creditors	3,500	
Bank overdraft	800	
	4,300	
Working capital		8,800
		£26,700
Financed by:		
Capital		£26,700

The following information is provided for 20X4:

	£
Receipts from customers	63,500
Payments to suppliers	37,600
Depreciation charged	6,100
Loan from friend	2,000
Interest paid on loan	150
Purchase of plant	8,000
General expenses paid in cash	7,300
Cash drawings	12,000

At 31 December 20X4, £3,950 was owing to trade creditors and £5,900 owed from trade debtors. Stock on hand amounted to £ 11,000.

Required:
(a) Prepare the following financial statements for 20X4:
   (i) receipts and payments of cash (the statement should reveal the net increase or decrease in the cash balance);
   (ii) trading and profit and loss account;

(b) Explain, by means of a numerical reconciliation, the difference between the profit (loss) for the year and the net change in the cash balance.

(c) Discuss the respective merits and demerits of the profit and loss account and the cash account as bases for assessing the performance of a business.

Solution

(a) (i) *Receipts and Payments for 20X4*

		£	£
Receipts:	Customers		63,500
	Loan		2,000
			65,500
Payments:	Suppliers	37,600	
	Loan interest	150	
	Plant	8,000	
	General expenses	7,300	
	Drawings	12,000	65,050
Net increase in cash			450

(ii) *Trading and Profit and Loss Account for 20X4*

	£	£
Sales (63,500-5,300 + 5,900)		64,100
Less: Purchases (37,600-3,500 + 3,950)	38,050	
Opening stock	7,800	
Closing stock	(11,000)	
Cost of goods sold	———	34,850
Gross profit		29,250
Less: Depreciation charged	6,100	
Loan interest	150	
General expenses	7,300	13,550
Net profit		15,700

(b)

		£	£
Net profit			15,700
Add:	Extra credit from suppliers		450
	Depreciation		6,100
	Loan		2,000
			24,250
Less:	Additional investment in: Debtors	600	
	Stock	3,200	
	Plant	8,000	
	Drawings	12,000	23,800
Net increase in cash			450

(c) Discussion should be centred on the following matters:
   Cash statement:
   1. It is a statement of objective facts (cash flows) and its preparation provides less scope for error and bias than other accounting statements.
   2. It reports the financial effect of all transactions undertaken during an accounting period.
   3. It mixes capital and revenue transactions and is entirely backward-looking. It is therefore of little use as a basis for predicting likely future results.

Profit and loss account:
1. Its preparation requires subjective judgements to be made concerning such matters as the amount of debts likely to be collectible and the value to the firm of fixed assets. As a result, the scope for error and bias is considerable.
2. Where no adjustment is made for the effects of inflation, reported profits include 'holding gains' (see Chapter 2.2.2).
3. It concentrates on revenue transactions and, therefore, provides useful information for assessing past corporate and managerial performance.
4. By separately identifying non-recurring transactions, it provides some help for users when attempting to predict likely future developments.

1.6 SOME COMMON MISCONCEPTIONS AND ERRORS

It is clear from the discussion in 1.5 that there is not necessarily a close correspondence between profit and the net increase or decrease in cash. Questions are sometimes asked (see Question 1.4) that test the candidate's understanding of the effect of a number of proposed transactions and adjustments on various financial magnitudes which include, in addition to profit and cash, such items as working capital or net current assets (i.e. the balance of current assets less current liabilities), the working capital ratio (i.e. current assets expressed as a ratio of current liabilities) and the liquidity ratio (liquid assets: liquid liabilities). Readers who have followed a preliminary course of accounting will be familiar with each of these items; other readers will find them described fully in chapter 9.

Some of the common misconceptions revealed and errors made when answering this type of question are discussed below.

1.6.1 Bonus Issues of Shares

Profits earned and retained within a business remain legally available for distribution, although in practice this is normally impossible because reinvestment in business assets is likely to have taken place, i.e. the resources are used to finance expansion. A bonus issue (sometimes called a capitalization issue or scrip issue) recognizes this fact and is accounted for by making an appropriate transfer from reserves to the share capital account.

Example 1.4

Balance Sheet Extract

	£
Authorized Share Capital. £1.000,000, divided into ordinary shares of £1 each	
Issued Share Capital. 300.000 ordinary shares of £1 each fully paid	300,000
Reserves	650,000
	950,000

Required:
The revised balance sheet extract, assuming the company makes a bonus issue of two for one, thereby capitalizing £600,000 of the balance on reserves.

Solution

Revised Balance Sheet Extract

	£
Authorized Share Capital. £1,000,000, divided into ordinary shares of £1 each	
Issued Share Capital. 900,000 ordinary shares of £1 each fully paid	900,000
Reserves	50,000
	950,000

The term 'bonus issue' is something of a misnomer because no one receives any tangible benefit, neither the company nor the shareholders. In the company's books an entry is made to record the transfer from reserves to share capital, but that is all. As far as the shareholders are concerned, they have three times as many shares, but the book value of their equity interest remains unchanged at £950,000 and the market value of each share will fall to approximately one third of the former price. The issue therefore affects neither profit, nor working capital, nor cash. (Bonus issues are examined in detail in Chapter 7.2.)

1.6.2 Varying the Depreciation Charge

A popular misconception is that the quantity of funds available to a business can be altered by varying the depreciation charge, and that a company's cash difficulties can therefore be solved by increasing the amount deducted in the profit and loss account. It seems likely that the reason for this misunderstanding is that depreciation is added back to profit in order to compute 'net cash flow from operating activities' for the purpose of preparing cash flow statements complying with the provisions of Financial Reporting Standard 1 (see Chapter 10). Readers will also have noticed that depreciation was treated in the same way for the purpose of preparing the reconciliation between the net profit and net cash flow of Sprouse Ltd for 20X1.

Example 1.5

Extract from a Cash Flow, Statement

	£
Net profit	325,000
Add: Depreciation	200,000
Profit before depreciation	525,000

Required:
The revised extract assuming the depreciation charge is increased to £300,000.

Solution

Revised Extract from a Cash Flow Statement

	£
Net profit	225,000
Add: Depreciation	300,000
Profit before depreciation	525,000

Depreciation is a deduction in the profit and loss account and, if the charge is increased to £300,000, profit is reduced to £225,000 but cash generated in the form of profit before charging depreciation remains unchanged at £525,000. The important point which the student should therefore grasp is that cash available is increased as the result of profitable trading activity: the depreciation charge earmarks a proportion of cash generated for retention in the business but cannot affect its volume.

1.6.3 Revaluation of Fixed Assets

Fixed assets are usually reported in a company's balance sheet at their original cost less accumulated depreciation to date. As time goes by it is possible that a large discrepancy will arise between the original cost of a fixed asset and its present-day value. Management might therefore decide to remove the undervaluation, perhaps because it intends to raise a loan and wishes to show the assets available as security at their true value. Freeholds are the most likely subject for this type of adjustment, partly because they are ideal security for a loan and partly because the excess of current value over book value is likely to be much greater than for other fixed assets.

Example 1.6

Balance Sheet Extract

	£
Freehold property at cost	500,000
Less: Accumulated depreciation	100,000
	400,000

Required:
The revised balance sheet extracts assuming the freehold property is revalued professionally at £1,000,000.

Solution

Revised Balance Sheet Extract

	£
Freehold property at professional revaluation	1,000,000
Share Capital	xxxxxxx
Revaluation reserve	600,000

The freehold is now reported at £1,000,000, and the revaluation surplus of £600,000 is credited to 'Revaluation reserve' which appears immediately after share capital in the company's balance sheet.

We can see that once again the adjustment is merely a book entry, and in this case affects neither reported profit, nor working capital (net current assets) nor cash.

1.6.4 Change in Credit Periods Allowed or Received

The period of credit allowed to customers may be increased as part of a strategy designed to improve the attractiveness of buying a company's products. Alternatively, or in addition, a company may pay its trade creditors more quickly in order to obtain discounts for prompt settlement. Changing the period of credit allowed or received has direct implications for cash flow, but affects neither working capital (net current assets) nor profit unless discounts are involved.

Example 1.7

Balance Sheet Extracts

Current Assets:	£
Stock	90,000
Trade debtors	60,000
Bank balance	70,000
	220,000
Less Current Liabilities:	
Trade creditors	40,000
Working capital (net current assets)	180,000

Required:
The revised balance sheet extracts assuming that twice the period of credit had been allowed to customers, so that the year-end balance for trade debtors becomes £120,000, i.e. it is assumed for simplicity that the level of sales is not affected by the new policy.

Solution

Revised Balance Sheet Extracts

Current Assets:	£
Stock	90,000
Trade debtors	120,000
Bank balance	10,000
	220,000
Less: Current Liabilities	
Trade creditors	40,000
Working capital (net current assets)	180,000

Notes:
The extra credit allowed to customers results in a reduction of £60,000 in the amount of cash collected. Working capital and profit remain unchanged.

1.6.5 Change of Accounting Policy

Students should be familiar with the fact that a number of different methods exist for valuing business assets. Fixed assets may be depreciated on the straight-line basis, reducing-balance basis, or in accordance with usage, while stock may be valued, for internal reporting purposes, on the marginal cost or total cost basis, and purchases may be matched with sales using the last in first out (LIFO) or first in first out (FIFO) cost flow assumption. This is not an exhaustive list of the alternatives available, even for fixed assets and stocks, but it demonstrates the fact that a wide range of options exists, and it is management's job to choose between them. Sometimes management changes its mind and decides to adopt a new method of valuation, e.g. it may decide to change from the marginal cost to the total cost method of stock valuation. This requires closing stock to be revalued upwards, but the important point for students to grasp is that the whole of the increase should not be reported as profit arising during the current accounting period. There will have been stocks on hand at the beginning of the accounting period, and these must also be restated at a total cost valuation and the increase recorded as profit arising in prior accounting periods.

Example 1.8

Trading Account for 20X1

		£000	£000
Sales			1,400
Less:	Opening stock valued at marginal cost	200	
	Cost of goods manufactured during 20X1	900	
	Less: Closing stock valued at marginal cost	(280)	
Cost of goods sold			820
Gross Profit			580

Required:
Produce the revised trading account for 20X1 assuming that stock is to be accounted for on the total cost basis and the following valuations are obtained:

At 1 January 20X1	£250,000
At 31 December 20X1	£360,000

Solution

Revised Trading Account for 20X1

		£000	£000
Sales			1,400
Less:	Opening stock valued at total cost	250	
	Cost of goods manufactured during 20X1	900	
	Less: Closing stock valued at total cost	(360)	
	Cost of goods sold		790
Gross Profit			610

Notes:
1. Closing stock has been revalued upwards by £80,000 (£360,000-£280,000), of which £50,000 (the difference between the opening figure for stock on the two valuation bases) is attributable to prior accounting periods and should be added to profit brought forward. The remaining £30,000 is reported as additional profit for the current accounting period, and increases gross profit from £580,000 to £610,000.
2. Stocks are included in the balance sheet at £360,000 and the reported value of working capital therefore increases by £80,000.
3. Cash is not affected by changing the method of stock valuation.

1.6.6 Reserves

Where an examination question shows a company in financial difficulties and under pressure from its creditors, students often suggest that the company can solve its cash problems by using the reserves to pay outstanding liabilities. This is, of course, quite wrong, and reveals a total misunderstanding of the relationship that exists between sources of finance and assets as exhibited in a company's balance sheet.

Example 1.9

Summarized Balance Sheet as at 31 December 20X1

ASSETS	£	SOURCES OF FINANCE	£
Fixed assets at net book value	210,000	Share capital	200,000
Stock	100,000	Reserves	135,000
Debtors	90,000		
Cash	10,000*		335,000
		Current liabilities	75,000
	410,000		410,000

*This amount is needed to meet day-to-day operating requirements.

The above balance sheet, presented in horizontal format to help illustrate the point being made, shows that the company has been successful and has built up substantial reserves as a result of generating and retaining profits over the years. It is also clear that these reserves have been reinvested in fixed assets, stock and debtors, and no cash surplus to operating requirements now remains. It is therefore a company's assets that must be examined to discover whether there are liquid resources available to meet an existing or future liability, and not the sources of finance which merely list the book value of the various claims against those assets.

1.7 QUESTIONS

Question 1.1

Thinker Ltd is a company that runs a wholesale warehouse. Its trial balance at 30 June 20X3 was:

	£000	£000
Sales		11,260
Ordinary shares of £1 each		3,000
Freehold land at cost	1,500	
Freehold buildings at cost	1,600	
Accumulated depreciation on freehold buildings at 1 July 20X2		100
Stock of goods for sale at 1 July 20X2	1,250	
Fixtures and fittings at cost	300	
Accumulated depreciation on fixtures and fittings at 1 July 20X2		146
Purchases	9,000	
Salaries and commissions	750	
Heat, light, maintenance and other expenses	700	
Profit and loss account at 1 July 20X2		2,468
Rates	175	
Bank interest and charges	27	
Overdraft		240
Debtors	2,670	
Cash	2	
Provision for bad and doubtful debts at 1 July 20X2		20
Creditors		740
	17,974	17,974

You are given the following additional information:
(1) The value of stock at 30 June 20X3 was £1,375,000.
(2) The buildings are depreciated on the straight-line basis, assuming a life of 50 years and a zero residual value.
(3) The fixtures and fittings are depreciated on the reducing-balance basis using a rate of 20%.
(4) On 30 June 20X3 the land was professionally valued at £2,100,000 and the directors have decided to incorporate this revaluation in the accounts at that date.
(5) A bad debt of £35,000 is to be written off, and the provision for bad and doubtful debts reduced to £10,000.
(6) The entry for rates in the trial balance includes a payment of £60,000 made in April 20X3 in respect of the six months to 30 September 20X3.
(7) The directors recommend that a dividend of 10p per share be provided for.

Required:
Prepare the trading and profit and loss account of Thinker Ltd for the year to 30 June 20X3 and a balance sheet at that date.

Notes:
(1) Work to the nearest £000.
(2) Ignore taxation.
(3) The accounts do not necessarily have to he in a form suitable for publication, but should be presented in good form.

Question 1.2

The following information is extracted from the books of Denston, a trader, at 31 December 19Xl:

Total bank account for 19Xl:

	£		£
Opening balance	821	Cash paid to suppliers	18,624
Cash received from		Salaries	2,249
customers	24,264	Rent and rates	824
Closing balance	1,030	Lighting and heating	168
		General expenses	1,781
		Drawings	2,469
	£26,115		£26,115

	31 Dec. 19X0	31 Dec. 19Xl
	£	£
Stock in trade	2,141	2,648
Debtors	3,219	3,388
Creditors for:		
purchases	1,842	1,891
lighting and heating	31	42
Rent and rates paid in advance	100	120
Fixed assets	2,200	*see note*

Required:
(a) Denston's balance sheet at 31 December, 19X0.
(b) Denston's trading and profit and loss account for 19Xl and her business balance sheet at
     31 December 19Xl.

Note:
Depreciation, for 19Xl, is to be charged on fixed assets at the rate of 10 per cent per annum on the
opening balance.

Question 1.3

The following information is provided for Turquand Ltd, a trading company, in respect of 20X8:

(1) BALANCE SHEET AT 1 JANUARY 20X8

	£000	£000
Fixed Assets		
Tangible fixed assets at cost		200
Less: Accumulated depreciation		35
		165
Intangible asset: Development expenditure		12
Current Assets		
Stock	63	
Debtors	51	
Cash at bank	13	
	127	
Current Liabilities		
Trade creditors	35	
Net current assets		92
Total assets less current liabilities		269
15% loan repayable 31 December 20X10		60
		209
Capital and Reserves		
Called-up share capital		100
Retained profit		109
		209

(2) TRANSACTIONS DURING 20X8 INCLUDE:

	£000
Receipts from customers	362
Payments to suppliers	214
Bad debts written off	5
Administration and distribution expenses	62
Development expenditure amount paid	11
Tangible fixed assets owned on 1 January 20X8, revalued at	375
Purchase of fixed assets	39
Loan repaid (early) on 31 December 20X8, including interest due	69

(3) DETAILS AT 31 DECEMBER 20X8

	£000
Stock in hand	75
Debtors	52
Trade creditors	42

(4) ACCOUNTING POLICIES

Tangible fixed assets, which were revalued on 1 January 20X8, are written off on the straight-line basis over their estimated useful life. On this basis, a charge of £42,000 must be made for the year.

Development expenditure is carried forward to the extent its recovery out of related revenues is reasonably assured. It has been decided that, of the expenditure to date, £15,000 is recoverable at 31 December 20X8.

Required:
(a) The trading and profit and loss account for 20X8.
(b) A cash account for 20X8.
(c) The balance sheet at 31 December 20X8.
(d) An assessment of the financial progress of Turquand Ltd during 20X8. This assessment should include a comparison of the respective merits of the statements prepared under (a) and (b) as indicators of performance during the year.

Note: Ignore taxation and dividends.

Question 1.4

The directors of Rowland Ltd are considering the company's estimated financial position at the end of July 20X1. The following information has been prepared:

FORECAST PROFIT AND LOSS ACCOUNT YEAR TO 31 JULY 20X1

	£000	£000
Sales		6,000
Less: Purchases	3,600	
Increase in stock	(100)	
Cost of goods sold		3,500
Gross profit		2,500
Less: Depreciation of plant	300	
Other overhead expenses	2,000	2,300
Operating profit		200

FORECAST BALANCE SHEET AT 31 JULY 20X1

	£000	£000
Goodwill		400
Freehold property		1,000
Plant and machinery at cost less depreciation		600
		2,000
Current Assets		
Stock	500	
Trade debtors	750	
Bank balance	50	
	1,300	
Less: Trade creditors	300	
Net current assets		1,000
Total Assets less Current Liabilities		3,000
Debenture repayable 20X-11		500
		2,500

Financed by:

Share capital (50p shares)	1,000
Retained profit	<u>1,500</u>
	<u>2,500</u>

It is to be assumed that a year consists of twelve months, each of 30 days, and that transactions take place at an even rate throughout the year.

The directors require finance for a planned expansion of activities and have heard that, when deciding to make an advance, it is normal practice for a potential lender to examine certain key financial measurements and performance indicators. The directors are therefore interested in the financial effects of the following actions on the above forecast accounts:

(1) Making a bonus (capitalization) issue of three ordinary shares for every one share held at present. The issue to be made on 1 June 20X1.
(2) Reducing the depreciation charge for the year to £200,000.
(3) Showing the freehold property in the accounts at its recent professional valuation of £3,500,000.
(4) Writing the balance of goodwill off against retained profit.
(5) Offering customers a cash discount of 8% for payment within 30 days. This offer to take effect for sales made on or after 1 June 20X1. All the company's customers are expected to take advantage of the offer with the volume of sales remaining unaffected.
(6) Extending the period of credit taken from suppliers to two months for purchases made on or after 1 June 20X1.

Required:
Taking each of these six courses of action separately, set out a statement showing the following:

Course of Action	*Operating profit 20X0-1*	*Bank balance 31 July 20X1*	*Working capital 31 July 20X1*	*Debt:Equity ratio 31 July 20X1*
1				
2				
3				
4				
5				
6				

For any items unaffected by a course of action, show the original figures derived from the accounts.

2

FRAMEWORKS
FOR FINANCIAL
REPORTING

2.1 INTRODUCTION

The purpose of this chapter is to review the attempts made since the late 1960s to improve the usefulness of financial reports for the purpose of decisions made by the user groups identified in Chapter 1.3. The present chapter contains two main sections comprising:

- an analysis of the proposed alternative financial reporting frameworks to historical cost designed to take account of changes in general and/or specific price indices (section 2.2);

- a study of attempts made to establish a theoretical basis for financial reports through the issue of FRS 18 (2000) entitled 'Accounting policies' and *The Statement of Principles for Financial Reporting* (1999) (section 2.3).

2.2 ALTERNATIVES TO HISTORICAL COST ACCOUNTING – CPP AND CCA

A significant upturn in the general rate of inflation has, on a number of occasions since World War II, caused businessmen and investors to question the continued use of historical cost accounting (HCA) as the basis for financial reports. The divergence that emerges between reported values and real values, in such circumstances, raises justifiable doubts about whether published financial statistics provide relevant data for decision making. The solution is usually seen as the introduction of some system of accounting for price level changes. The methods that have been proposed are, for convenience, given the general description 'inflation accounting' in this chapter, although this label is technically imprecise because relative price changes may well occur, and almost certainly will occur, in a period of overall price stability. In the following sub-sections we:

- examine the theoretical roots of systems of accounting for price changes and review attempts to introduce such methods in the UK (see section 2.2.1);

- compare the HCA model with the main alternatives – current cost accounting (CCA) and current purchasing power accounting (CPP). In doing this, attention will be focused on basic principles (rather than complex calculations) so as to provide students with a clear understanding of their objectives and respected merits (see section 2.2.2);

- summarize the strengths and limitations of each of the three schemes (see section 2.2.3)

2.2.1 Theoretical Roots and Origins of Schemes

The 1920s saw the development of a substantial interest in inflation accounting in continental Europe. Much of the literature originated from France and Germany, which is not surprising in view of the high rates of inflation in each of those countries, particularly the hyperinflation that caused the collapse of the German mark in 1923. Much of this early literature dealt with the adjustment of accounts for changes in the general price level. However, German writers also supported the restatement of assets at their replacement (or current) cost or value, and this approach was advocated by authors in the Netherlands and in the USA. The best known interwar publication was the American H. W. Sweeney's *Stabilized Accounting* (1936) which is acknowledged as the authoritative early work on CPP.

Britain showed little interest in inflation accounting until prices rose rapidly in the early 1950s, at the time of the Korean War. The ICAEW examined the problem and issued *Recommendation on Accounting Principles* (these were the forerunners of the SSAPs and FRSs) 12 which gave unreserved support for the continued use of historical cost accounting. Following criticism of the reactionary tone of Recommendation 12, Recommendation 15 (1952) stressed the limitation of HC profit in times of inflation and the desirability of setting aside amounts from profit to recognize the effects of inflation, but it made no clear recommendation. Certain other professional accountancy bodies were more sympathetic to the need for change; a report by the research committee of what is now called the Association of Chartered Certified Accountants, for example, recommended the use of replacement costs. The more conservative attitude of the ICAEW prevailed, however, partly because it was then regarded as the leading professional accounting body, and partly because of the return to relatively low rates of inflation. The inflation accounting issue was shelved for nearly two decades and the opportunity of experimenting with new methods, in a period of relative price stability, was lost.

The 1970s saw a revival of interest in inflation accounting with prices rising at just over 7% per annum. Businessmen soon voiced their criticism of accounts which contained asset numbers that were clearly out of touch with their commercial reality. The Accounting Standard Committee's response was to issue Exposure Draft 8 which advocated the use of CPP. At that stage the government joined the debate by appointing its own committee on inflation accounting, chaired by Sir Francis Sandilands, in June 1974. The rumoured explanation for this appointment is that Prime Minister Harold Wilson's Labour Government was uneasy with the possible introduction, for businesses, of a scheme of accounting that might imply the need for the general indexation of government debt. This move placed the accounting profession in a quandary; whether to proceed with the implementation of Exposure Draft 8 and risk collision with the government, or to await the outcome of the Sandilands committee's deliberations? Heroically, but perhaps ill-advisedly, the former course was followed and SSAP 7 entitled *Current Purchasing Power Accounting* was issued in 1974. This provided for the publication of supplementary statements based on CPP. There was, almost immediately, a strong reaction against the new standard.

The business community disliked the requirement to recognize, as profit, the unrealized gains deemed to accrue from holding debt during a period of inflation. The way in which this worked is illustrated in Example 2.1.

Example 2.1

A trading company is formed with an initial share capital of £15,000 and an interest-free loan of £5,000. The company immediately acquires property costing £20,000. No further purchases or sales occur during the company's first accounting period when the general price index rises by 10%.

Requirement:
The profit and loss account for period 1, and the balance sheet at the end of period 1.

Solution

Profit and Loss Account

	£
Profit from operations	0
Gain on borrowing	500 W1
	500

Balance Sheet

	£
Share capital	16,500 W2
Gain on borrowing	500
	17,000
Loan	5,000
	22,000
Property	22,000 W3

W1 (5,000 x 110/100) – 5,000
W2 15,000 x 110/100
W3 20,000 x 110/100

The method of inflation accounting, called CPP, required non-monetary assets (in this example property) and non-monetary claims (shareholders' equity) to be adjusted upwards for changes in the general index. Monetary claims (the loan) and monetary assets (of which there are none in this example) remain unadjusted on the grounds that the amounts payable and recoverable are unaffected by changes in the price level. The result is that property is increased by £2,000 and equity is adjusted upwards by £1,500 in order to protect its purchasing power during a period when prices have risen by 10%. The interest-free loan remains unchanged at £5,000, and so one quarter of the increase in the value of property, i.e. £500, instead accrues to the shareholders as a 'gain on borrowing'.

The effect of applying these rules is, therefore, to show a company making money from holding debt during a period of inflation, on the grounds that the loan is repaid in due course with £s possessing a lower value. This approach, although theoretically supportable, came in for a great deal of understandable criticism later in 1974 when highly-geared property companies, apparently very profitable when their accounts were prepared in accordance with SSAP 7, were in reality on the verge of bankruptcy as the result of the property crisis.

The 'death-knell' for SSAP 7 came when the Sandilands Committee reported in 1975. The essence of its criticism was that merely to adjust historical cost figures for the effect of inflation provides no real protection for shareholders. Effective protection can only be provided, it argued, by producing relevant information for decision making. In the Committee's view, balance sheets which showed current values and profit and loss accounts which distinguished between operating gains (the measure of management efficiency) and holding gains (windfalls) were best suited to achieving this objective. They therefore favoured the development of a system of CCA.

The task of implementing these proposals was given to the ASC which issued Exposure Draft 18 in 1976. This was in due course rejected by the ICAEW's own members as unnecessarily complex and unworkable. A cynical contemporary comment was that backwoodsmen accountants simply could not understand it. But, to be fair, if they could not understand it, what chance the general public? The 'Hyde Guidelines' were an interim step superseded by SSAP 16 entitled 'Current Cost Accounting', itself based on Exposure Draft 24. It was initially fairly well received but, against a background of falling inflation rates, compliance began to decline. Explanations put forward by company chairmen to justify its discontinued use included: a lack of demand on the part of user groups; the cost of producing the figures; and the need for subjective judgement. ED 35 was issued in 1984 as a proposed revision to SSAP 16 but was taken no further. The compulsory status of SSAP 16 was removed in 1986 and the standard was withdrawn altogether in 1988.

The series of schemes recommended met with varying measures of approval. The ICAEW's annual survey of 300 quoted companies shows that 2% adopted some method of inflation accounting in 1973 (see Table 2.1). Under encouragement from the ASC, this proportion rose to 58% by 1980 when inflation was running at 18%. At the height of its popularity, in 1982, SSAP 16 was implemented by 94% of the sample. Reaction set in swiftly and the collapse of interest is demonstrated by the fact that the 1988 survey showed just 1% of quoted companies adopting SSAP 16 and 1% providing the information recommended by Exposure Draft 35.

What were the reasons for the failure of the inflation accounting experiment? The following suggest themselves as possibilities:

- The initial emphasis on CPP, in the UK, probably got the inflation accounting experiment off to a bad start. It is conceptually more difficult to grasp and it produces balance sheet figures that have no obvious economic significance.

- The solutions were too complex. The ASC attempted to do too much too quickly. History shows that accounting progresses in an evolutionary rather than a revolutionary manner, and this is something now recognized by the Accounting Standards Board. Changes need to be made gradually; a more promising approach might be to start by encouraging periodic valuations of fixed assets and, in this context, recent regulatory developments (considered in Chapter 4) are to be welcomed.

- The ASC was too rigid in insisting on a particular method, i.e. CPP and then CCA. There was a need to allow more flexibility based on the view that any method which took some account of changes in the price level must be better than a system which ignored them altogether.

- The failure to educate producers and users as to the importance of the problem and the need to find a solution.

- The fall in the rate of inflation caused most parties to lose interest in devising a system of inflation accounting.

2.2.2 HCA, CPP and CCA Compared

Probably the best known and most widely accepted definition of income is that produced by Sir John Hicks to describe the income of the individual as:

the maximum value which he can consume during a week, and still expect to be as well off at the end of the week as he was at the beginning.

The analogous definition of company profits formulated by the Sandilands Committee was:

the maximum value which the company can distribute during the year, and still expect to be as well off at the end of the year as it was at the beginning.

Table 2.1 Percentage of companies producing different types of price level statements 1968 to 1988

Year to 30/6	68	73	74	75	76	77	78	79	80	81	82	83	84	85	86	87	88
No. of companies	100	300	300	300	300	300	300	300	300	300	300	300	300	300	300	300	300
Price level statements CPP	–	2	3	16	13	5	1	1	–	–	–	–	–	–	–	–	–
CCA/ED 18	–	–	–	–	2	5	5	2	1	–	–	–	–	–	–	–	–
CCA/Hyde	–	–	–	–	–	–	35	46	24	6	–	–	–	–	–	–	–
CCA/ED 24	–	–	–	–	–	–	–	5	22	–	–	–	–	–	–	–	–
CCA/SSAP 16	–	–	–	–	–	–	–	–	10	72	94	80	59	26	4	2	1
CCA/ED 35	–	–	–	–	–	–	–	–	–	–	–	–	–	8	1	1	1
Other	–	–	1	3	10	20	4	2	1	–	1	1	2	–	1	–	1
Total	–	2	4	19	25	30	45	56	58	78	95	81	61	34	6	3	3
No price level statements	100	98	96	81	75	70	55	44	42	22	5	19	39	66	94	97	97
	100	100	100	100	100	100	100	100	100	100	100	100	100	100	100	100	100

Source: Hanson, J. D. (1989) 'Developments in financial reporting practice over the last twenty years', in Tonkin, D. J. and Skerratt, L. C. L. (eds) *Financial Reporting 1988-89. A Survey of UK Reporting Practice*, London: The Institute of Chartered Accountants in England and Wales, p. 22.

Under both definitions the entity is considered to be as 'well off' if its capital has been maintained intact. This raises the crucial question of how capital is to be measured, with any increase in value at a later date as compared with an earlier date regarded as the surplus which may be termed 'profit'. The possibilities will now be contrasted both diagramatically (Figure 2.1) and numerically (example 2.2). To help to underline the significance of the calculations, we shall assume that reported profit is the same as distributable profit, i.e. that the profit appearing in the accounts could be paid out in dividends if it was so desired.

Figure 2.1 measures £s on the vertical axis and the passage of time on the horizontal axis. t_0 is the beginning of an accounting period and t_1 the end of that period. It is a new company and AO measures opening capital (t_0) and DC the value of the business at t_1. The question is how to allocate the value, measured by DC, between capital and

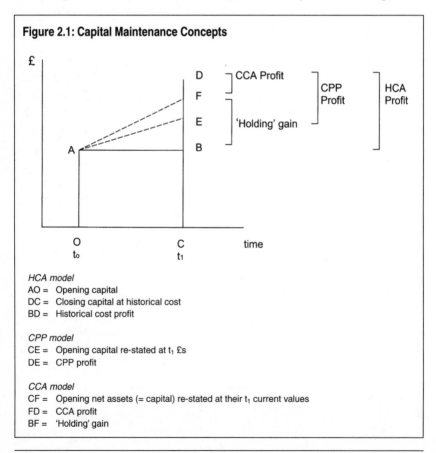

Figure 2.1: Capital Maintenance Concepts

HCA model
AO = Opening capital
DC = Closing capital at historical cost
BD = Historical cost profit

CPP model
CE = Opening capital re-stated at t_1 £s
DE = CPP profit

CCA model
CF = Opening net assets (= capital) re-stated at their t_1 current values
FD = CCA profit
BF = 'Holding' gain

profit. The three approaches may be summarized as follows:

HCA capital is the cash sum raised at the outset and this is represented at t_1 by BC, i.e. the same money value as at the beginning of the year. Any increase in the net worth of the firm, over and above BC, may therefore be treated as profit and is available for distribution. BD is therefore historical cost-based profit and, if it is all distributed, legal (money) capital nevertheless remains intact.

CPP capital, invested by shareholders, is here regarded as a pool of purchasing power units whose value must be maintained intact so that, when the firm closes down, a sum of money, possessing an equivalent amount of purchasing power, can be returned to the shareholder. Figure 2.1 shows that the general price level has risen because CE (at t_1) represents purchasing power equivalent to AO at t_0. Under this approach, a CPP profit of DE is available for distribution and, if distributed, leaves the purchasing power of the shareholders' capital intact in real terms.

CCA treats capital as the operating capacity of the assets purchased with funds invested in the firm. It is these assets that generate income, so nothing must be distributed until sufficient resources have been retained in the business to enable the replacement of assets which are sold or have been worn out. In Figure 2.1, it is assumed that the average price of assets owned by the firm is rising more quickly than the general rate of inflation, and FC (at t_1) must be retained in the business in order to maintain intact productive capacity. Current cost profit available for distribution is DF, while FB is the 'holding gain', i.e. it is the 'gain' that arises from holding assets during a period of rising prices and, because replacement costs are now that much higher, this additional amount must be retained in the business in order to maintain intact operating capacity.

These relationships are now illustrated, numerically, in Example 2.2.

Example 2.2: HCA, CPP AND CCA

Lakeside was incorporated on 1 January with an issued share capital of £1,000. The £1,000 was immediately invested in 5 units of stock costing £200 each. The current replacement cost of stock rose to £230 per unit on 20 January and remained at that figure for the rest of the month. The entire stock was sold on 31 January for £1,400 in cash. The retail price index moved from 100 to 104 between the date the stocks were purchased and sold. All other costs and taxation are to be ignored.

Required.
(a) The HCA, CPP and CCA balance sheets as at 20 January
(b) The HCA, CPP and CCA profit and loss accounts for January and the respective balance sheets at 31 January.

Solution

(a) *Balance Sheets at 20 January*

	HCA £	CPP £	CCA £
Share capital	1,000	1,040*	1,000
Holding gain	–	–	150
	1,000	1,040	1,150
Stock	1,000	1,040*	1,150

(b) *Profit and Loss Account for January*

	HCA £	CPP £	CCA £
Sales	1,400	1,400	1,400
Less: Cost of Sales	1,000	1,040*	1,150
Net Profit	400	360	250

Balance Sheets at 31 January

	HCA £	CPP £	CCA £
Share capital	1,000	1,040*	1,000
Holding gain	–	–	150
Net profit	400	360	250
	1,400	1,400	1,400
Cash	1,400	1,400	1,400

* 1,000 x 104/100

The balance sheets prepared at 20 January show:

HCA – no change; the stock remains unrealized and, in accordance with the accruals concept, continues to be recorded at historical cost.

CPP – stock is restated at the figure that must be charged against revenue to maintain intact the real value of the shareholders' investment.

CCA – stock is restated at current replacement cost and a 'holding gain' of £150 has been recognized.

The significance of the information contained in the accounts prepared at the end of the month are next discussed on the assumption that the entire reported profit is to be distributed to Lakeside's shareholders.

HCA The distribution of reported profit, £400, leaves £1,000 in the business. The money capital has been maintained intact but there is insufficient cash available to enable stock to be replaced (five units now cost £1,150) and so the level of activity must be curtailed or additional finance must be raised from the shareholders or from creditors.

CPP The reported profit is in this case £360 and, if distributed, leaves the purchasing power of shareholders' capital intact at £1,040, i.e. the stated amount of shareholders' capital is matched by an equivalent amount of cash in the bank. Again, however, cash is insufficient to replace stock and enable operations to continue at existing levels.

CCA The accounts split the historical cost profit of £400 between current cost profit of £250 and a holding gain of £150. Even if the company decides to distribute the entire reported profit, the measurement process ensures that sufficient resources are retained within the business to maintain intact operating capacity.

It might be mentioned, at this stage, that CPP and CCA may be combined to get 'the best of both worlds' and show, in one set of accounts

- the amount which must be retained in the business to protect the value of the shareholders' investment, and

- assets at their real values rather than in terms of 'funny money'.

Taking the above CCA balance sheet for the purpose of illustration, the holding gain of £150 would then be split into the £40 required to maintain purchasing power and the £110 that represents a real increase in the value of the shareholders' investment.

The different concepts of capital have different objectives. HCA and CPP are both concerned with maintaining intact the value of the shareholders' investment. The difference is that HCA maintains capital intact in money terms whereas CPP protects capital's purchasing power. The purpose of CCA, by way of contrast, is to help ensure that operating capacity is safeguarded. Because they have different objectives, it is not surprising to discover that they are considered relevant to different user groups. HCA and CPP are seen as principally concerned with protecting the shareholders' investment, i.e. accounting statements are seen as stewardship documents designed to explain to shareholders whether or not the value of their investment remains intact.

CCA, on the other hand, by focusing on current costs, is seen to produce balance sheet figures more relevant to an assessment of a company's overall financial position. Moreover, by charging against sales proceeds the true cost of resources being consumed, CCA provides a better measure of managerial performance and more relevant data for resource allocation decisions.

Where either CPP or CCA are adopted, reported figures for gross assets, capital employed and reported profit are each materially affected during a period of rising (or falling) prices (Figure 2.2). Assuming prices are rising, the adoption of CPP or CCA will result in lower reported profits and higher balance sheet values. Whether CPP profit will be lower or higher than CCA profit, however, depends on the relationship between movements in the general price level and movements in the price of assets belonging to the company.

Figure 2.2

Effect on profit and capital employed of changing from HCA to CPP or CCA

	Profit	*Capital employed*
CPP	lower	higher
CCA	lower	higher

NB: Assuming prices are rising

What is certain is that few companies can therefore be expected, in a competitive environment, to adopt either of these schemes voluntarily. The comment made in the 1986 directors' report of Pilkington Brothers plc is particularly illuminating in this context. This company had been an enthusiastic supporter of CCA but reverted to the use of HCA because 'the directors believe that the present policy places the group at a disadvantage when its reported results are compared with the majority of UK companies which account for tangible assets on the historical cost basis'. Also revealing is the directors' further assertion that 'within the company, the directors will continue to assess performance in inflation accounting terms'.

2.2.3 Strengths and Limitations of HCA, CPP and CCA Summarized

HCA – Strengths

- HCA has stood the test of time. It has been the basis for financial reporting for centuries and, given the premise that accounting evolves to meet user needs, this would appear to be strong evidence of its utility to external users.

- HCA is insisted upon by the Inland Revenue for taxation purposes. A refusal of the tax authorities to accept an alternative basis for taxation was one of the reasons for the failure of the inflation accounting experiment of the 1970s and 1980s.

- It is recognized that historical cost accounting suffers from a number of limitations – for example, the figures in the balance sheet may be totally unrelated to current values – but these weaknesses are fully understood and adjusted for by users of financial information.

- HCA is based on facts. The fixed asset figures, for example, represent the price paid. This objectivity reduces the scope for subjective judgement and manipulation of financial data and increases the reliability of published financial information.

- Following on from the fact that the accounts are based on established facts, HCA is attractive to the external auditors because it provides an objective basis for establishing the accuracy of reported information.

- The data to be reported is readily available. The initial record of transactions must be on the basis of prices ruling at that date, that is the numbers which are subsequently referred to as the 'historical costs'. It is therefore convenient to use HCA also for the purpose of financial reporting.

- In a period of rising prices, the HC-based profit figure includes an inflationary element. The result is that HCA reports a higher profit figure than alternative methods that take account of changing prices.

HCA – Limitations
- The continued use of HCA is principally attributable to 'inertia'. The information is used simply because it is readily available rather than because it is relevant to external users.

- HCA results in a company reporting only realized profits. The value of an organization is also affected by unrealized profits. A method of accounting which also reports these changes in value to external users is to be preferred.

- HCA mixes together different generations of £s in the profit and loss account and the balance sheet. For example, in the profit and loss account, sales revenue is expressed in prices representing values during the current accounting period whereas the depreciation charge may be based on the historical cost of a fixed asset purchased, perhaps, 20 years ago. This process of mixing different generations of £s has been likened to preparing consolidated accounts without first taking the precaution of translating the results of an overseas subsidiary into sterling.

- HCA involve a great deal of subjectivity and does not represent objective facts as is sometimes claimed. For example, in the case of fixed assets, the calculation of the depreciation charge requires estimates to be made concerning useful life and residual value. In addition, the choice between different methods of depreciation, such as straight line and reducing balance, involves judgements being made.

CPP – Strengths
- CPP identifies the amount of money that must be generated and retained within the business to maintain intact the purchasing power of the shareholders' capital.

- CPP identifies the increase in shareholders' wealth by removing from monetary profit the inflationary element due only to the rise in the general price level. It is therefore considered a better measure of the real increase in shareholders' wealth generated during an accounting period.

- CPP expresses the items appearing in the accounts in comparable values, i.e. in £s representing current purchasing power. This avoids mixing together £s of different generations as does HCA.

- The statement of incomes, expenses, assets and liabilities in terms of a stable monetary value improves comparisons with (a) other companies and (b) previous years, provided those accounts are also re-stated.

- Because it is a relatively simple, year-end, adjustment to HCA data, CPP attracts similar advantages: relatively cheap, objective, and easy to verify (the level of the retail price index is factual).

CPP – Limitations
- It may be questioned whether the re-stated asset values mean anything – they are neither the original price paid, nor the asset's current value. CPP is sometimes dismissed as being based on 'funny money'.

- The method may result in virtually no adjustment to the information contained in the accounts despite significant changes in the company's asset values, i.e. the price of a particular company's assets may have moved significantly up or down, but they will not be changed if the general price level remains stable.

- The quality of the price index. These are merely averages and will probably not match exactly the expenditure pattern of any single shareholder.

- The problem of comprehension on the part of users of accounting data; the current purchasing power concept is not the easiest one to grasp.

- Because CPP simply re-states historical costs, rather than creating totally new figures, it suffers from a number of similar drawbacks to HCA.

CCA – Strengths

- CCA produces more realistic asset values. This is particularly the case with fixed assets which, under HCA, are often reported at only a fraction of their real value.

- CCA matches like items with like. Price indices and asset revaluations are used to re-state original costs in terms of current costs for the purpose of measuring periodic profit.

- CCA identifies 'true' profits, by distinguishing holding gains that must be retained in the business to maintain intact operating capacity.

- CCA provides a better basis for levying taxes which, otherwise, erode operating capability by requiring payment to the government of a proportion of both the capital and 'true' profit element of HC profit.

- Because it is based on the opportunity cost concept, CCA brings to the attention of management, and others, the full costs of continuing to use resources for their existing purpose rather than transferring them to an alternative use.

- Following on from the previous point, CCA is thought to provide better information for a variety of decisions, including the following:

    - for dividend policy, by making sure that distributions are confined to real profits;

- for the purpose of management performance assessment, by focusing on the real costs and revenues arising from business activity; and

- as a basis for pricing policy, by helping to ensure that all costs are covered.

• By making use of specific price indices, prepared by the government, it is possible to prepare current cost accounts relatively cheaply and easily.

CCA – Limitations

• CCA involves a great deal more subjective judgement than do the alternative accounting models.

• CCA is based on the assumption that assets are going to continue in their existing use, whereas a successful business will have to be continually modifying its range of activities in the light of competition and new business opportunities.

• The maintenance of operating capacity is a pointless task where the demand for the company's products is diminishing.

2.3 CONSTRUCTING A THEORETICAL BASIS FOR PUBLISHED FINANCIAL REPORTS

2.3.1 Growing Criticism of Published Financial Reports

The way in which assets are valued has direct implications for the level of reported profit. If assets are overvalued at the end of an accounting period, profits will be overstated; if assets are undervalued, profits will be understated. In either case, users of the accounts will be provided with misleading financial information and decisions that lead to an optimum allocation of resources are less likely to be taken. It must of course be recognized that valuation errors cancel out over time. For instance, the closing stock of one accounting period is the opening stock of the next, and so, if overvaluation occurs at the end of period one, reported profits will be too high for period one and too low for period two. However, in neither accounting period does reported profit give a fair reflection of the company's actual performance.

In the mid-1960s, the British accountant's ability to prepare, for publication, entirely reliable factual statements of a company's financial position was rarely questioned. The popular view was that the accounting process was time-consuming, painstaking, meticulous, and boring, but that it was all worthwhile because the result of the accountant's labours was an absolutely accurate statement of a company's financial position. Accountants no longer enjoy immunity from public criticism and the quality of their work is constantly being challenged, as are the standards prevailing in many of the other established professions.

In accountancy, the more critical attitude stems from a series of events in the late 1960s, among which the GEC/AEI takeover is perhaps the best known. In October 1967, GEC (The General Electric Company) made a takeover bid for the shares of AE1 (Associated Electrical Industries). Often the directors of a company which is the subject of a takeover bid wish to repel the attack, and that was the case on this occasion. One of the defensive tactics, employed by the directors of AEI, was to circulate to its shareholders a document explaining the advantages of retaining their present investment, and informing them that the company's forecast profit for 1967 was £10m. In the event, the takeover bid was successful and the accounts of AEI for 1967 were eventually published in April 1968, but instead of reporting a profit of £10m they revealed a loss of £4½m. An obvious explanation for this massive discrepancy might have been that substantial errors were made when preparing the forecast, but an investigation showed that this was not the case. The 'forecast' for 1967 was prepared late in the year (October) so that only a small element of estimating was required, and this function was efficiently performed. The investigation instead revealed that the discrepancy was mainly caused by the new management team taking a different (less optimistic) view regarding the value of AEI's assets.

The general public was shocked to discover that accounting was not the precise science they had believed it to be, and that the level of reported profit was substantially a matter of opinion rather than objective fact. For instance, it was widely recognized, for the first time, that the amount of the depreciation charge, and therefore the balance sheet value of fixed assets, could differ enormously depending on such matters as estimates of the asset's useful life and the depreciation method considered appropriate. Prompt action was required to prevent any further erosion of the accountant's reputation.

2.3.2 SSAP 2 and FRS 18

The accounting profession's response was to establish The Accounting Standards Committee (ASC), in 1970, in the endeavour to restore public confidence. The job identified for this committee was to prepare Statements of Standard Accounting Practice, designed to achieve the following objectives.

- To encourage the adoption of best accounting practices.

- To ensure, as far as possible, that companies adopt similar procedures.

- To disclose the procedures that have actually been adopted.

The key accounting standard issued by the ASC was SSAP 2 entitled 'Disclosure of accounting policies'. It was the key standard in the sense that it was the only standard designed to provide user groups with a broad understanding of the underlying nature of published financial reports. It was not the first standard issued because the introduction of an acceptable method of accounting for the results of associated companies was perceived to be a more pressing priority. The aims of SSAP 2 were to ensure that:

- Companies prepared their accounts in accordance with certain 'fundamental accounting concepts' specified in the statement (any deviation from these concepts to be disclosed).

- Companies reported which 'accounting policies' they have chosen from the 'accounting bases' available for the purpose of valuing the assets and liabilities which appear in their accounts. The statement did not specify the permissible accounting bases – that was left to the individual accounting standards. For example, FRS 16 entitled 'Tangible fixed assets' approves a number of different 'bases' for charging depreciation which include the reducing-balance basis and the straight-line basis. It is then left to each company to choose what it judged to be the appropriate accounting policy for depreciating a particular category of fixed asset.

SSAP 2 was superseded by FRS 18 entitled 'Accounting Policies' in December 2000. The reason for the change was to bring the foundational accounting standard into line with the conceptual framework for financial reporting contained in the *Statement of Principles* (issued 1999) considered later in this chapter.

The objective of FRS 18 is to ensure that:

1. an entity adopts the accounting policies for valuing assets and liabilities most appropriate for the purpose of ensuring that the accounts give a true and fair view.

2. the accounting policies adopted are reviewed regularly to ensure that they

remain appropriate, and are changed when a new policy becomes more appropriate to the entity's particular circumstances and,

3. sufficient information is disclosed in the financial statements to enable users to understand the accounting policies adopted and how they have been implemented. (para. 1)

It continues to be the job of most other accounting standards, as indicated above, to identify the range of acceptable accounting policies from which particular entities make their selection. The following extracts from the accounts of the Beecham Group are typical examples of how companies disclose the accounting policies used for valuing stocks and for calculating depreciation:

Stocks
Stocks are stated at the lower of cost and net realizable value generally using the first in, first out method of valuation. The cost of finished goods and work in progress comprises raw materials, direct labour and expenses, and related production overheads.

Depreciation
The cost of fixed assets, except freehold land, is written off in equal annual instalments over the estimated useful lives of the assets. The average lives for each major asset category are:

Freehold buildings	50 years
Leasehold land and buildings	Term of lease
Plant and equipment	10/15 years
Vehicles – motor cars	5 years
lorries and other vehicles	7 years

FRS 18 identifies two underlying accounting 'concepts' (compared with four previously), and these are concepts that are considered to play a pervasive role in financial statement preparation and, therefore, the choice of accounting policies to be employed. The two concepts are:

The going concern concept This assumes that the company will continue in business for the foreseeable future. The main effect of this assumption is that the liquidation value of fixed assets, which may be significantly different from book value, can be ignored because there is no intention to discontinue business activity. An entity should prepare its financial statements on the going concern basis unless

a.   the entity is being liquidated or has ceased trading, or

b.   the directors have no realistic alternative but to liquidate or cease trading.

Where it is clear that the entity is no longer a going concern, assets and liabilities may need to be reported on a liquidation basis.

The accrual concept This requires:

a.   revenues to be matched with related expenses when measuring profit

b.   revenues and expenses to be included in the profit and loss account as they are earned and incurred rather than when they are received and paid.

An entity should prepare its financial statements, other than cash flow information, on the accruals basis of accounting.

There are four further criteria or 'objectives' against which an entity should judge the appropriateness of accounting policies to its particular circumstances. These are: relevance; reliability; comparability; and understandability. We shall see that these tests feature prominently in the *Statement of Principles*.

The suitability of an accounting policy must also be assessed in light of the following constraints.

a.   The need to balance the four 'objectives'. For example, a policy may appear to provide relevant information but may be rejected if the message it conveys is incomprehensible.

b.   The need to balance the cost of providing information with the likely benefit of such information to the users of the entity's financial statements.

2.3.3 The Need for a Theoretical Framework

We have noted above that concern with the quality of published financial reports is a recurrent theme in the UK, with shareholders and other groups naturally in uproar when their company unexpectedly collapses. Maxwell Communications, Polly Peck and BCCI are further well-known examples of corporate collapse where the failure of either the previously published financial reports or the company's auditors to alert investors to the nature and extent of the company's financial problems has been the subject of strong criticism. The perceived deficiencies of published financial reports, despite the welter of accounting standards (for example, 25 SSAPs were issued by the Accounting Standards Committee between 1970 and the late 1980s when the above financial catastrophes made banner headlines) has sometimes been attributed to the lack of a generally accepted accounting theory. This line of argument is naturally dear to the hearts of academic accountants but it has traditionally received little sympathy from accounting practitioners who are often characterised as more concern with 'getting things done' than 'thinking about them'.

It is part of the problem of accountancy that the important linkages between accounting theory and accounting practice are rarely fully recognized, but this is not entirely surprising in view of the fact that such connections are often difficult to describe and demonstrate. The broad relationship between accounting theory and accounting practice has been usefully described by the US academic E. S. Hendriksen, as a system of logical reasoning which takes the form of a set of broad principles that:

- provide a general frame of reference by which accounting practice can be evaluated, and

- guide the development of new practices and procedures.

More specifically, the idea is that the broad set of principles should provide the basis for enabling decisions to be made concerning the valuation of assets and liabilities, what to report in the accounts and how to present it. That is, accounting practice is constructed on a coherent theoretical foundation. The need for a theory of accounting is alternatively expressed as the quest for the development of a conceptual framework of accounting, and this has been defined by the US standard-setting body, the Financial Accounting Standards Board (FASB), as:

a constitution, a coherent system of interrelated objectives and fundamentals that can lead to consistent standards and that prescribes the nature, function and limits of financial accounting and financial statements. (Scope and Implications of the Conceptual Framework Project, FASB, 1976)

The conceptual framework can therefore be seen to reflect a need to underpin the standard setting process so as to produce the following advantages:

- To move away from the 'fire fighting' approach that characterized the development of standard accounting practice at least until the end of the 1980s, with standards often dismissed as representing little more than attempts to combat current criticisms of financial reporting practices and for ignoring the broader picture.

- To reduce the potential number of accounting standards by placing emphasis on general principles rather than specific rules.

- To provide the basis for justifying procedures to user groups and combating the threat of government interference by demonstrating the fact that accounting practice is derived from sound theoretical foundations.

- To help to avoid inconsistencies between accounting standards, by providing a basis for resolving issues such as substance vs. form and accruals vs. prudence.

- To help to decide whether profit should be measured through the balance sheet approach or by matching costs against revenues.

The significance of the last matter will benefit from further elaboration. A fundamental decision that needs to be made is whether the correct conceptual basis for measuring profit should focus on the profit and loss account approach or the balance sheet approach. In a paper prepared for the Research Board of the ICAEW, David Solomons warned that, as in many areas of accounting, 'there is no prospect of proving that one of these views is right and the other wrong, [but] it is possible to find reasons for preferring one view to the other' *(Guidelines for Financial Reporting Standards* (1989, p .17). The profit and loss approach sees the balance of earnings arrived at as the difference between the revenues for a period and the expenses incurred in earning that revenue. This is, of course, the essence of the traditional historical cost model that remains largely in place in Britain today. The balance sheet approach sees earnings as the difference between net assets (assets minus liabilities) at the beginning and the end of the period under review, after making adjustments for the capital introduced and withdrawn.

Looked at another way, the question is whether the figures in the balance sheet should be the 'bits left over' (unallocated costs and deferred credits) – as happens under the profit and loss approach – or whether the valuation of assets and liabilities for inclusion in the balance sheet should be seen as central to the profit measurement process. Solomons favours the balance sheet approach which, he believes, should be constructed to report, in broad terms, assets at their current values (as advocated by the Sandilands Committee and the ill-fated SSAP 16 entitled 'Current Cost Accounting') and the adjustments required to maintain intact real financial capital (as advocated by SSAP 7 entitled 'Current Purchasing Power Accounting'). The twin outcomes are seen, by Solomons, to be accounts that provide a better measure of shareholder wealth creation, which is after all the objective of profit making enterprises, and help to preserve the integrity of the balance sheet as a statement of values. The present conflict and confusion between the profit and loss account approach and the balance sheet approach may be illustrated by reference to the content of two UK standards:

- SSAP 15, entitled 'Accounting for Deferred Taxation', requires the balance sheet provision for deferred taxation to be based on the liability method, with the difference between the balance brought forward and carried forward simply dumped in the profit and loss account. That is, the balance sheet approach prevails.

- FRS 15, entitled 'Tangible Fixed Assets', focuses to a substantial extent on the allocation of past expenditure to the profit and loss account, thereby giving precedence to the accruals principle, leaving the unallocated expenditure on fixed assets as a residual balance to be reported in the balance sheet. That is, the profit and loss account approach prevails.

Part of the purpose of a conceptual framework is to help to make a choice between the two approaches based on logical reasoning. It should also help to resolve other inconsistencies, such as the fact that SSAP 13 gives precedence to the prudence concept over the accruals concept in the treatment of research and development expenditure.

2.3.4 In Search of the 'Holy Grail'
A promising initiative designed by the ASC to move matters forward was the issue of

The Corporate Report (1975) – a discussion paper which advocated a user decision-oriented framework for the development of financial reporting practices. This framework places user requirements centre stage by:

- emphasizing the wide range of potential users, in sharp contrast to the earlier focus on only shareholders and creditors;

- identifying the desirable characteristics of corporate reports, namely relevance, understandability, reliability, completeness, objectivity, timeliness and comparability;

- drawing attention to additional statements that should be published in the corporate report – a value added statement, an employment report, a statement of money exchanges with government, a statement of transactions in foreign currency, a statement of future prospects and a statement of corporate objectives.

Unfortunately, this important initiative was soon overshadowed by the inflation accounting debate and controversy surrounding the publication of the Sandilands Report considered earlier in this chapter.

In the USA, the FASB spent millions of dollars a year on its 'conceptual framework project' in the 1970s and 1980s, and the topic was placed high on the agenda of the ASC, in 1978, when it published *Setting Accounting Standards: A Consultative Document*. The ASC acknowledged recurrent criticism of its failure to develop such a framework, but pointed out that, 'while such a foundation would be a great advantage, it is unavailable at present' (para. 7.2.).

A revival of interest in the construction of a theoretical basis for financial reports followed the replacement of the ASC by the Accounting Standards Board (ASB) in 1990.

2.3.5 The Accounting Standard Board's Statement of Principles

The ASB has, since its formation, placed upfront its determination to pursue the idea of a conceptual framework to underpin the standards that it issues, with the expectation that this will help to prevent some of the errors made by its predecessor body. Indeed, its *Forward to Accounting Standards* (issued June 1993) states that FRSs are to be based on the *Statement of Principles for Financial Reporting* which address the concepts underlying the information presented in financial statements.

Following a long gestation period, the *Statement of Principles* was finally issued in 1999.

The ASB, in drafting the *Statement of Principles*, acknowledged that it drew heavily on previous projects in other countries, including the work of the FASB and the International Accounting Standards Committee. This element of overlap should help towards the international harmonization of financial reporting practice.

The Statement consists of the following seven chapters:

1. The objective of financial statements;

2. The reporting entity;

3. The qualitative characteristics of financial information;

4. The elements of financial statements;

5. Recognition in financial statements;

6. Measurement in financial statements;

7. Presentation of financial information.

The objective of financial statements (Chapter 1) emphasizes the need to display the results of the stewardship of management and to provide information which will be helpful to a wide range of users in making economic decisions. The statement takes the view that all user groups have a common interest in the financial position, performance and financial adaptability of the enterprise as a whole. However, investors are judged to be 'the defining class of user' (para. 1.10) and the provision of financial statements that meet their needs, it concludes, will 'also be focusing on the common interest that all users have' (para. 1.11). This is an important assertion and establishes the idea that general-purpose financial statements, where the format is principally dictated by the requirements of investors, are to be preferred to special-purpose statements for separate user groups. This is clearly a convenient conclusion; companies can continue to publish a single annual report and thus avoid a spiralling of the cost of administering the financial reporting function. At the same time, an important benefit will be the avoidance of the confusion and uncertainty that might result from the publication of two or more sets of accounts containing different information.

Chapter 2 identifies the conditions that must be met in order for a particular reporting entity to be required to publish financial statements, i.e. where 'there is a legitimate demand for the information that its financial statements would provide and it is a cohesive economic unit'.

The qualitative characteristics of financial information (Chapter 3) are handily summarized in a diagram which is reproduced here as Figure 2.3. The content and role of this diagram is to a great extent self-explanatory, but a few additional comments may be helpful. Relevance, reliability, comparability and understandability are identified as the primary characteristics of financial reports, with materiality as the over-arching 'threshold quality'; if the information is not material, it is by definition not useful and can therefore be disregarded. Relevant information is seen to be that which aids decision making by either helping to predict the future value of the entity or to confirm its existing value. Reliable information is seen to be that which is free from error or bias. Comparability focuses, in particular, on the need for the careful application of accounting standards over time, thereby ensuring a consistent treatment and a common basis for assessing the performance of two or more enterprises. Understandability requires attention to be paid to presentation and the capabilities of user groups, although information should not be omitted simply because it might be too difficult for certain groups to comprehend, particularly where its value to others can be demonstrated. The chapter also recognizes the existence of 'trade offs' in the need to achieve a balance between desirable characteristics, to ensure the information is timely and that a fair balance is maintained between costs and benefits.

Chapter 4 identifies seven elements of financial statements (assets, liabilities, equity, gains, losses, contributions from owners, and distributions to owners) and makes it clear that any item that does not fall within one of the definitions of these elements should be excluded from financial statements.

Chapter 5, which deals with the recognition of items in financial statements, states that new assets and liabilities or changes in assets and liabilities should be recognized and reported in the accounts if:

- there is sufficient evidence of their existence, and

Figure 2.3: The qualitative characteristics of financial information

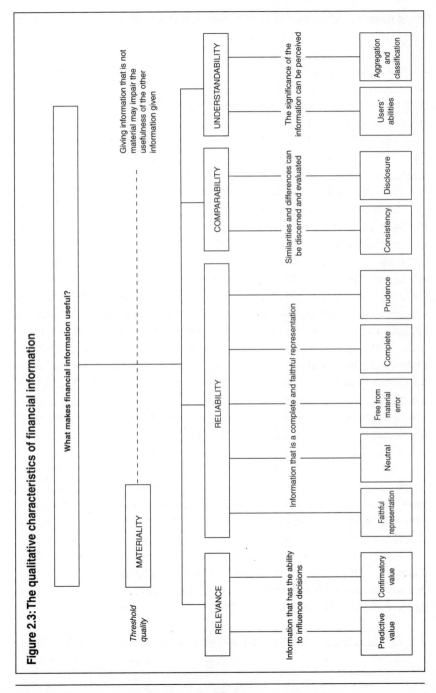

- the item can be measured at a monetary amount with sufficient reliability.

The criteria for ceasing to recognize assets and liabilities (derecognition) are the converse of the above.

We can here see that the linkage between underlying theory and the standard setting process is being forged. For example, the concept of recognition is given specific application in FRS 5 which deals with the 'substance of transactions' (discussed more fully in chapters 4 and 5), and where:

> Assets are – rights or other access to future economic benefits controlled by an entity as a result of past transactions or events.

> Liabilities are – an entity's obligation to transfer economic benefits as a result of past transactions or events.

For illustrative purposes, let us take consignment stock, which is an arrangement whereby stock is in the possession of one party but is owned by another. This situation typically arises in the motor trade where the distributor has possession of vehicles that the manufacturer continues to own. In order to determine the appropriate accounting treatment, the crucial question is one of identifying the point at which the distributor acquires the rights and obligations associated with ownership of the asset rather than simply when legal title actually passes. The 'application notes' attached to FRS 5 set out a number of tests which may be applied in order to decide whether or not the stock should be regarded as becoming the property of the distributor at the date of delivery rather than at the time when legal transfer takes place, usually invoice date. The stock will be regarded as becoming the property of the motor vehicle distributor at the date of delivery (the substance of the arrangement) rather than invoice date (the legal form of the arrangement) where the following types of condition apply;

- The manufacturer cannot require the distributor to return the stock.

- The distributor has no right to return the stock or is commercially compelled not to exercise that right because, for example, penalties would be imposed.

- The price charged by the manufacturer is based on prices ruling at the date of delivery.

- Obsolete stock cannot be returned to the manufacturer and no compensation is paid for losses due to obsolescence.

In these circumstances the vehicles and related liability should appear in the balance sheet of the distributor, despite the fact the distributor is not the owner, and should be removed from the balance sheet (derecognition) when, for example, the distributor sells the stock and discharges the liability.

This basis for financial reporting, which focuses on the identification of assets and liabilities to be reported in the balance sheet (the balance sheet approach), if given widespread application, would signal a significant departure from the existing framework which is primarily concerned with recording and identifying past revenues and expenditures to be recorded in the profit and loss account (the profit and loss approach). Taken to its extreme conclusion, it might mean that all transactions would be recorded in the accounts on the basis of effective contractual commitments rather than, at present, the earlier of the date when the transaction is performed or consideration passes. The approach implied by Chapter 5 is therefore seen, by some, to be part of the move towards making the balance sheet a valuation document, which idea receives further support from the contents of Chapter 6.

'Measurement in financial statements' (Chapter 6) recognizes that assets purchased or liabilities incurred should initially be recorded at historical cost but, in accordance with the provisions of Chapter 5 relating to recognition in financial statements, makes provision for 're-measurement' at current value.

Chapter 7 sets out the ASB's views concerning the presentation of financial information and these ideas have been given practical application in, for example, the content of the generally highly-acclaimed FRS 3 entitled *Reporting Financial Performance*.

2.3.6 Review
The potential role of a conceptual framework and therefore, in Britain, the Statement of Principles, has been described as follows by Ross M. Skinner.

> *Attempts to state conceptual frameworks are unlikely to result in great flashes of illumination that instantly resolve areas of controversy in financial reporting. It is only if standard setters are prepared to take an explicit framework seriously and allow its influence to guide their*

*resolution of individual issues that it will, little by little and from precedent to precedent, gain in power and utility'. (*Accounting Standards in Evolution, 1987, p.649)

This sets the position out fairly well. A conceptual framework can provide a useful underpinning for the standard-setting process, but one should not expect too much from it. The accounting environment is constantly changing and history has shown us that standards need to be revised periodically to fit new circumstances. This is perhaps less likely to be required in a case of a conceptual framework in view of the fact that the principles which it sets out are rather more broad-based and their purpose is to remain relevant in different times and places. It is here that one of the difficulties with the construction of the *Statement of Principles* becomes evident: it must be sufficiently broad to remain relevant over time but sufficiently focused to help to direct the standard-setting process at any point in time.

We can finish this chapter by listing the specific reasons given by the ASB for developing the *Statement of Principles*:

- To assist the ASB by providing a basis for reducing the number of alternative accounting treatments permitted by accounting standards and company law

- To provide a framework for the future development of accounting standards

- To assist auditors in forming an opinion as to whether financial statements conform with accounting standards

- To assist users of accounts in interpreting the information contained in them

- To provide guidance in applying accounting standards

- To give guidance on areas that are not yet covered by accounting standards

- To inform interested parties of the approach taken by the ASB in formulating accounting standards

2.4 FURTHER READING

Baxter, W. (1999) 'The ASB on principles', *Accountancy*, October, pp. 75-6.

Davies, M., Paterson, R. and Wilson, A. (1999), UK GAAP. *Generally Accepted Accounting Practice in the United Kingdom*, sixth edition, Longman, Chapter 2.

Ebling, P. (2000) 'An ever stronger influence', *Accountancy*, February, p. 81.

Elliott, B. and Elliott, J. (2000) *Financial Accounting and Reporting*, fifth edition, Hemel Hempstead: Prentice Hall, Chapter 7.

Lewis, R. and Pendrill, D. (2000), *Advanced Financial Accounting*, sixth edition, Pitman, Parts 1 and 4.

Statement of Principles for Financial Reporting, ASB, 1999, *Accountancy*, March 2000, pp. 109-38.

'Statement of Principles. Its evolution, not revolution', *Accountancy*, April, 1999, p. 5.

2.5 QUESTIONS

Question 2.1

(a) Explain the capital maintenance concepts underlying each of the following accounting methods:
- Historical cost accounting
- Current cost accounting
- Current purchasing power accounting

(b) Identify and discuss any two advantages claimed for each of the three methods.

Question 2.2

The following information is provided in respect of Cornwell Ltd.

(i) The company was incorporated on 1 January 19X1 and immediately issued 75,000 shares of £1 each for cash.

(ii) On 1 January 19X1, the company purchased, for cash, plant costing £50,000 and ten 'Grommets' (items of stock) for £2,500 each.

(iii) On 1 January 19X1, the company sold five 'Grommets' for cash, £4,000 each. On 31 December 19X1, the company sold the remaining five 'Grommets' for cash, £4,000 each.

(iv) On 31 December 19X1, the company paid operating expenses, in cash, amounting to £6,000.

(v)   The directors plan to pay out in dividends the maximum amount legally distributable.

Movements in the retail price index are as follows:

1 January 19X1	100
30 June 19X1	110
31 December 19X1	120

Required:
(a)   Prepare separate profit and loss accounts of Cornwell Ltd for the year ended 31 December 19X1 and balance sheets at that date on each of the following bases
    (i)   Historical cost accounting (HCA)
    (ii)   Current purchasing power accounting (CPP)

(b)   Discuss four advantages of current purchasing power accounting (CPP), and illustrate these advantages, where possible, by reference to the accounts you have prepared.

Note:
Ignore depreciation of plant.

Question 2.3

Pendrill plc uses historical cost accounting (HCA) for the purpose of its published accounts and employs current (replacement) cost accounting (CCA) for the purpose of management decision making. The following summarized financial statements have been prepared from the two accounting systems in respect of the year to 30 September 19X9.

Profit and Loss Accounts year ended 30 September 19X9

	HCA £ million	CCA £ million
Sales	120	120
Cost of sales	70	74
Depreciation	20	25
Running costs	16	16
Total operating costs	106	115
Operating profit	14	5
Interest payable	4	4
Net profit	10	1

Balance Sheet at 30 September 19X9

	HCA £ million	CCA £ million
Tangible fixed asset	90	110
Current assets	25	26
Current liabilities	−15	−15
	100	121
Shareholders' equity	60	81
Long-term loans	40	40
	100	121

Required:

(a) Define 'holding gains'. Explain why it is considered important to identify holding gains under a system of current cost accounting and indicate where amounts for holding gains are reflected in the balances shown in the above accounts.

(b) Compute the following accounting ratios from the information contained in each set of accounts for Pendrill Ltd reproduced above.
   - Net profit percentage
   - Total asset turnover
   - Return on shareholders' equity
   - Debt:equity ratio

(c) Explain for each ratio computed under (b) the reason for any difference between the figures computed on the basis of the two sets of accounts.

Note: Ignore taxation.

Question 2.4

Rowse Ltd commenced business on 1 January 1999 to produce and market a single product, designated RMT. The following information is provided relating to the first year of business operations:

1. Commenced business operations with a capital of £200,000 in the form of cash.

2. Produced 2,000 completed items of RMT at a cost of £160,000 paid in cash.

3. Received orders from customers for 1,800 items of RMT to be supplied at the normal market price of £100 each.

4. Fulfilled, on credit, orders for 1,700 items of RMT from the orders referred to in 3 above. The remaining orders were fulfilled after the end of the year.

5. Collected cash from debtors for 1,200 items of RMT. All remaining debts were expected to be settled.

The company is run by four directors who have different views concerning profit recognition:

- The Production Director is of the view that there is a ready market for RMT and so it is appropriate to recognize profit when production is complete.

- The Sales Director believes that obtaining orders from customers is the key to business success and argues that profit should be recognized when this occurs.

- The Managing Director takes the view that the delivery of RMT to customers is the appropriate stage for profit recognition.

- The Finance Director believes that it would be a mistake to recognize profit before "cash is in the bank".

Required:

(a) Prepare four separate profit calculations for the year to 31 December 1999 on the assumption that profit should be recognized in accordance with the views of each of the four directors. You should comment on the vested interests, if any, of each director in the profit recognition method he/she prefers. *[8 marks]*

(b) State which one of the four bases of profit recognition should be applied in practice and prepare the balance sheet based on this point of recognition. *[4 marks]*

(c) Examine and evaluate the criteria by which the point of revenue recognition adopted in (b) above is determined. *[8 marks]*

[Total – 20 marks]

Question 2.5

The Finance Director of Branshaw Ltd retired in December 1998 before he had time to prepare a set of draft accounts. His replacement has not yet been appointed. The two remaining directors have prepared the following draft balance sheet at 31 December 1998 based on their own assessments and on advice received:

Draft Balance Sheet at 31 December 1998

	£000	£000	£000
Fixed assets	*Cost*	*Depreciation*	*Book Value*
Machine 1	4,100	4,000	100
Machine 2	4,100	1,600	2,500
	8,200	5,600	2,600
Current assets			
Stock of Product 1		700	
Stock of Product 2		540	
Debtors		800	
Cash		40	
		2,080	
Current liabilities			
Creditors		1,000	
Net current assets			1,080
			3,680
Financed by			
Ordinary shares of £1 each			1,400
Profit and loss account:			
Balance at 1 January 1998		1,780	
Profit for 1998		500	
			2,280
			3,680

Notes:

1. The figures brought forward from last year's balance sheet were calculated in accordance with generally accepted accounting practice and were the subject of an unqualified audit report.

2. The valuations in the draft closing balance sheet were prepared by the two remaining directors in the following manner:

(i) Machine 1 has an effective productive life of 10 years and was judged to be halfway through its useful life at 31 December 1998. The Works Director takes the view that it should be immediately written down to its residual sale value of £100,000. In previous years, straight-line depreciation has been used.

(ii) Machine 2 has an effective productive life of 10 years and was halfway through its useful life on 31 December 1998. The Works Director is of the view, in this case, that there is no need to charge depreciation in 1998 as the machine has been well maintained and is still working as well as when it was new. In previous years, straight-line depreciation has been used on the assumption of a residual sale value of £100,000.

(iii) The stock of Product 1 cost £600,000 and will be sold for £900,000. The Stores Manager's advice is that it should be valued at £700,000 to 'allow for the fact that it is going up in value'.

(iv) The stock of Product 2 cost £600,000 and is expected to be sold for £800,000. Advice from the buyer was to 'take 10% off its cost just to be on the safe side'.

(v) The company has never experienced bad debts before 1998. The directors are positive that a customer who owes £72,000, which is included as part of the debtors of £800,000 in the year end balance sheet, will not be able to pay. However, they have decided not to make any provision for this, as 'we will know the exact position in 1999, and so any bad debt will be accounted for next year'.

(vi) In November 1998 an employee suffered an accident at work and sued Branshaw Ltd for compensation. A payment of £20,000 was agreed on 2 January 1999, but the directors decided not to make any allowance for this in the draft balance sheet on the grounds that the payment will not be made until the following financial year.

(vii) During 1998, 200,000 ordinary shares of £1 each were issued for cash. A total of £600,000 was received, all of which is included in the balance on the ordinary share account.

Required.

(a) Identify and define the accounting concepts central to FRS18 entitled 'Accounting Policies'.

[4 marks]

(b) Prepare a revised balance sheet for Branshaw Ltd at 31 December 1998, making any adjustments you consider necessary. You must show clearly the necessary adjustments to the draft profit for 1998.

[12 marks]

(c) Give, with brief explanation, one example of the application of each of the accounting concepts when calculating the balances for fixed assets included in the balance sheet prepared under (b).

[4 marks]

[Total – 20 marks]

Question 2.6

A conceptual framework of accounting has been defined by the US standard-setting body, the Financial Accounting Standards Board (FASB), as: 'a constitution, a coherent system of interrelated objectives and fundamentals that can lead to consistent standards and that prescribes the nature, function and limits of financial accounting and financial statements'. (*Scope and Implications of the Conceptual Framework Project*, FASB, 1976)

Required:
(a) Examine the purpose of a 'conceptual framework'.

(c) Identify and discuss briefly each of the seven chapters contained in the *Statement of Principles*.

3

FORM AND CONTENT
OF COMPANY
ACCOUNTS

3.1 SOURCES OF DISCLOSURE REQUIREMENTS

Under the Companies Act directors have a legal responsibility to prepare and publish accounts that give a 'true and fair view' of their company's financial affairs. The contents of the balance sheet, profit and loss account, cash flow statement, and directors' report are each subject to disclosure requirements prescribed by the following: company law, the Accounting Standards Board and, in the case of quoted companies, the International Stock Exchange.

Company Law The legal requirements currently in force are contained in the Companies Act 1985, which is the statute referred to in the remainder of this book unless otherwise stated.

Accounting Standards Board The accountancy profession assumed a large measure of responsibility for the form and content of company accounts. In 1970, following press criticism of accounting practices and the threat of detailed legal regulation of company accounts, the profession took steps to 'put its house in order'. The Accounting Standards Committee was established and issued 25 Statements of

Standard Accounting Practice (SSAPs) up to the date of its replacement by the Accounting Standards Board (ASB) in 1990. The ASB has to date (August 2001) issued 19 Financial Reporting Standards (FRSs) which are the successors to SSAPs. Nevertheless, SSAPs remain in force until withdrawn by the ASB or replaced by FRSs. There is a requirement for the directors to disclose and explain significant departures from accounting standards. In addition, the financial effects of such departures should normally be estimated and disclosed.

A number of accounting requirements, initially contained in SSAPs, are now incorporated in the Companies Act and have the force of law. The standards affected have not been withdrawn, however, and remain relevant because it is necessary to refer to these more detailed documents to interpret the brief instructions contained in the Act. An increasing number of SSAPs existing when the ASB was established have now been replaced with FRSs.

Stock Exchange Companies whose shares are listed (quoted) on the International Stock Exchange must also comply with the regulations imposed by that institution. These oblige quoted companies to disclose extra information in their accounts, although many of the requirements that the Stock Exchange first introduced have since been extended to all limited companies by either the accountancy profession or the legislature. Regulations that apply only to quoted companies are published in *The Stock Exchange Listing Agreement* and are outside the scope of the this book.

3.2 CONTENT OF THE ANNUAL REPORT

The directors are responsible for keeping proper accounting records that disclose at any time, and with reasonable accuracy, the transactions undertaken by the company and its financial position. The records are used as the basis for preparing the annual accounts and enable the directors to ensure that the financial statements, that they are legally obliged to prepare each year, comply with the Companies Act. These accounts must be laid before the company at the annual general meeting (AGM), and they must be circulated beforehand to all shareholders, debenture holders and any other persons entitled to attend the meeting. In addition, the directors must file a copy of the company's accounts with the Registrar of Companies, where they are available for public inspection. The accounts are normally included in a document called 'The Annual Report and Accounts' which contains a wide range of financial and general information. For a large company, it is an extensive document; to take an example, the 1999 annual report of BG Group plc covers 112 pages. A typical annual report includes the following main items:

1. The directors' report.

2. The report of the auditors.

3. The statement of accounting policies.

4. The financial statements: the profit and loss account; the balance sheet; the cash flow statement.

5. The notes to the accounts.

To illustrate various topics discussed in the text, a pro forma set of accounts, for Illustrative Company Ltd, are reproduced below. You may well find it useful to refer to these accounts when examining topics later in the book and, to help identification of this information, a grey tint has been used to identify the relevant pages.

Some additional comments on the information contained in the accounts of Illustrative Company Ltd are as follows:

(1) *The directors' report (pp. (1)-(3))*. The content of the directors' report is laid down by the Companies Act and the report of Illustrative Company Ltd contains many of the items one would expect to see in a typical set of accounts. Further items that must be disclosed, where appropriate, include: transfers to and from reserve; where the number of employees exceeds 250, the company's policy regarding the employment of disabled persons, and arrangements made to increase employee involvement, e.g. by providing them with regular information on matters of concern, by consulting them, and by operating employees' share schemes; and acquisitions made by a company of its own shares during the year.

(2) *The report of the auditors (p. (3))*. This report covers the information contained in the three principal financial statements: the profit and loss account; the balance sheet; and the cash flow statement. In preparing their report, the auditors are also required to consider whether the information contained in the directors' report is consistent with the accounts and, if it is not, they are required to say so. The auditors are appointed by, and responsible to, the members of the company and must report to them on the accounts prepared by the directors.

The audit report informs shareholders of the scope of the audit, i.e. that work done complies with the instructions issued by the Auditing Practices Board for the guidance of auditors. It also sets out the auditors' findings. Notice that it does not certify the accuracy of the accounts, but instead expresses the opinion that the accounts show a true and fair view. The auditor of a limited company must be professionally qualified, however, and would be expected to exercise appropriate skill and judgement in reaching his or her conclusions. Readers may also have noticed that the specimen audit report does not state that the accounts comply with relevant SSAPs or FRSs, but it is reasonable to assume that there has been compliance unless there is a statement to the contrary. If the auditor has any reservation regarding the truth and fairness of the accounts, this must be referred to in the report. Details of any qualification normally precede the second sentence. Where, for example, a report is qualified because provision has not been made for the loss likely to result from the liquidation of a major customer, the following wording is appropriate:

No provision has been made against an account of £150,000 owing by a company which has been placed in liquidation since the year end. The liquidator has indicated that unsecured creditors are unlikely to receive any payment and in our opinion full provision should be made.

Except for the failure to provide for the amount described above, in our opinion...

In the case of listed and large unlisted companies, a qualified audit report is not a common feature. Many qualifications are not necessarily of major importance to bankers and other users of accounting reports. For instance, the failure of a company to depreciate its freehold buildings contravenes FRS15 and, quite properly, results in a qualified audit report. However, this qualification is unlikely to be of very great concern to anyone who is interested in the asset primarily as security for a loan which has been made, when it is clear that the property could easily be sold for a figure significantly in excess of its original cost.

An audit qualification is much more common for small businesses because of shortcomings in their systems of internal control. Many of the 'checks and balances' which are needed in a large company are neither practical, appropriate nor necessary in a small enterprise. The most effective form of security for many of these organizations is the close involvement of the directors in all aspects of business activity, but this may produce auditing problems. For example, a company may operate primarily on a cash basis but, because cash transactions are handled entirely by the directors, a high degree of security is assured. However, in the absence of independently verifiable evidence to support these transactions, it is not possible for the auditor to confirm the complete reliability of the company's records and the following qualification is made:

> *Except for any adjustments that we might have found necessary had we been able to obtain sufficient evidence about cash sales, in our opinion the financial statements give a true and fair view of the company's position at 31 December 20X3 and of its profit and cash flows for the year ended on that date and have been properly prepared in accordance with the Companies Act 1985.*

(3) *The statement of accounting policies (pp. (5)-(6)).* There are various methods available for valuing different business assets. In order to help investors to assess the financial results reported by their company, it is therefore important for them to know which policies have in fact been employed.

(4) *The financial statements (pp. (6)-(9)).* Historically, it was broadly left to the directors to decide how the information should be presented in British company accounts. This naturally resulted in a great deal of diversity and made comparisons between individual companies difficult. It was partly to meet this criticism, but more immediately to help to harmonize accounting procedures throughout the European Union, that standardized methods of presentation were introduced by the Companies Act 1981 (now included in the Companies Act 1985).

Companies may choose from two balance sheet formats and four profit and loss account formats. Both balance sheets contain the same headings and the only difference is the method of presentation: format 1 uses a vertical layout and format 2 a horizontal layout. The profit and loss account offers a choice between two alternative approaches, each of which may be presented in vertical or horizontal format. The essential difference between these two approaches is in the method used to classify items of expenditure. Formats 1 (vertical) and 3 (horizontal) analyse expenses by function, and therefore disclose figures for costs of sales, distribution costs and administrative expenses. Formats 2 (vertical) and 4 (horizontal) analyse expenses by type, and therefore show figures for raw materials, staff costs and depreciation. The vertical format is most popular in practice, i.e. companies use balance sheet format 1 and profit and loss account format 1 or 2.

(5) *The notes to the accounts (pp. (10)-(17))*. These are cross-referenced to the accounts themselves and go into particular matters in more detail. Again the content of the notes is dictated by requirements contained in the Companies Acts as supplemented by the provisions of relevant Accounting Standards. The notes for Illustrative Company Ltd by no means show all possibilities but they do cover most of the items likely to arise in a typical set of accounts.

There are two further matters that need to be mentioned before we leave this discussion of the form and content of published accounts.

(1) *The chairman's review*. This is usually prepared only by large public companies and, in such circumstances, normally appears as the first item in the annual report. It is one area which is not subject to any regulations regarding content. The chairman is free to say exactly what he or she wishes, but comments generally cover the following broad areas:

- An assessment of the year's results.

- An examination of factors influencing those results, e.g. the economic and political climate or the effect of strikes.

- A reference to major developments e.g. takeovers or new products.

- Capital expenditure plans.

- An assessment of future prospects.

The Chairman's message usually conveys a fair amount of optimism even if the financial facts published later in the report make depressing reading. A strong point in favour of the chairman's review is that it is readable and readily comprehensible to the layman. A major drawback is that, with regard to future prospects, it must be based on opinion rather than fact, but it is useful background material when attempting to assess progress by an interpretation of the financial information contained in the accounts.

(2) *Modified accounting requirements*. The general rule is that all companies, irrespective of their size, must present their shareholders, debenture holders, and other persons entitled to attend the AGM, with accounts that comply, in full,

with the requirements of the Companies Acts. However, listed companies are permitted to provide members with summary financial information rather than full accounts, although full accounts must be provided when specifically requested. Small and medium-sized private companies (see below) are released from the obligation to prepare consolidated accounts (see Chapter 6), while private companies may pass a resolution to the effect that the following requirements be dispensed with: to lay accounts and reports before the AGM; to hold an AGM; to appoint auditors annually. The effect of the last change is that auditors remain in office until they, or the company, decide otherwise.

There are also certain possible modifications to the requirements applying to accounts filed with the Registrar of Companies. In the case of 'small' and 'medium-sized' companies, these may be abridged versions of the accounts presented to the AGM. The identification of small and medium-sized companies is done by reference to the level of turnover, the figure for total assets, and the average number of employees. The reduction in disclosure requirements is not substantial in the case of medium-sized companies but, in the case of small companies, neither a profit and loss account nor directors' report need be filed, the information to be disclosed by way of notes is significantly reduced and a condensed balance sheet may be prepared. Further, a parent company (see Chapter 6.3) is in general exempt from the requirement to prepare consolidated financial statements if its group falls into the small or medium-sized category.

The reason for these concessions is that medium and small private companies are often essentially family concerns which, it is thought, should not be subjected to the close public scrutiny considered desirable in the case of larger companies. Not everyone agrees with this view, and continued opposition to the exemptions granted is based on the argument that it is reasonable to demand full disclosure from all companies, in exchange for the privilege of limited liability. It must be remembered, however, that small and medium-sized companies have to prepare full accounts for shareholders, and others, so the price of confidentiality is the extra cost of preparing the modified accounts. For this reason, the directors often ignore the exemptions offered and instead file full accounts with the Registrar.

Illustrative Company Ltd

DIRECTOR'S REPORT

The directors submit their report and accounts for the year ended 31 December 20X2.

Results and dividends The operating profit for the year, after taxation, was £571,000.

The directors recommend a final ordinary dividend of £160,000 amounting to £200,000 for the year which leaves a profit of £371,000 to be retained.

Review of the business The company's principal activity during the year was the manufacture of components for prefabricated buildings and the construction of prefabricated buildings.

Turnover has increased by 7.6% from £9,765,000 to £10,502,000. The directors believe that the trend will continue. The market for prefabricated accommodation is rising steadily and the company is in a good position to take advantage of any opportunities which may arise in the future.

Market value of land and buildings The freehold properties were revalued at 1 January 20X2. The valuation of £500,000, which was £394,000 higher than the former net book value, has been incorporated in these accounts.

Fixed assets The company has continued to improve plant and machinery during the year, involving expenditure of £335,130.

Research and development The company continues to increase its commitment to research and development because work in this area is vital if the company is to retain its present strong position in the market.

(1)

Illustrative Company Ltd

Future developments The directors consider that 20X3 will be another successful year which will build on the recent fruitful links concerning the sale and construction of primary schools for local authorities.

Events since the end of the year The company has sold one of its trade investments for £231,000. The proceeds will be used to modernize the plant located at Swanbridge.

Directors and their interests The directors at 31 December 20X2 and their interests in the share capital of the company (all beneficially held except those marked with an asterisk which are held as trustee) were as follows:

	At 31 Dec. 20X2	At 1 Jan. 20X2 or subsequent date of appointment
	Ordinary shares	*Ordinary shares*
P Waters (Chairman)	20,000	20,000
M Phipps	180.000	180.000
	60,000*	60,000*
J R Cowdell	500	500
R McArthur (appointed 1 July 19X2)	250	—

In addition P White served as a director until 30 June 20X2 when he resigned. J R Cowdell retires from the board at the Annual General Meeting and, being eligible, offers himself for re-election.

Political and charitable contributions During the year the company made a political contribution of £20,000 to the Conservative Party and various charitable contributions totalling £3,500.

(2)

Illustrative Company Ltd

Auditors A resolution to re-appoint as auditors Edwards, Mellett & Co. will be put to the members at the Annual General Meeting.

By order of the Board
H Less
Secretary
15 May 20X3

STATEMENT OF DIRECTORS' RESPONSIBILITIES

Company law requires the directors to prepare financial statements for each financial year that give a true and fair view of the state of affairs of the company as at the end of the financial year and of the profit or loss of the company for that period. In preparing those financial statements, the directors are required to:

- Select suitable accounting policies and then apply them consistently;

- Make judgements and estimates that are reasonable and prudent; and

- Prepare the financial statements on the going concern basis unless it is inappropriate to presume that the company will continue in business.

The directors are responsible for keeping proper accounting records that disclose with reasonable accuracy at any time the financial position of the company and to enable them to ensure that the financial statements comply with the Companies Act. They are also responsible for safeguarding the assets of the company and hence for taking reasonable steps for the prevention and detection of fraud and other irregularities.

(3)

Illustrative Company Ltd

REPORT OF THE AUDITORS
to the members of
Illustrative Company Ltd

We have audited the financial statements on pages 6 to 17 which have been prepared under the historical cost convention [as modified by the revaluation of certain fixed assets] and the accounting policies set out on pages 5-6.

Respective responsibilities of directors and auditors The company's directors are responsible for the preparation of financial statements. It is our responsibility to form an independent opinion, based on our audit, on those statements and to report our opinion to you.

Basis of opinion We conducted our audit in accordance with Auditing Standards issued by the Auditing Practices Board. An audit includes examination, on a test basis. of evidence relevant to the amounts and disclosures in the financial statements. It also includes an assessment of the significant estimates and judgments made by the directors in the preparation of the financial statements, and of whether the accounting policies are appropriate to the company's circumstances, consistently applied and adequately disclosed.

We planned and performed our audit so as to obtain all the information and explanations which we considered necessary in order to provide us with sufficient evidence to give reasonable assurance that the financial statements are free from material misstatement, whether caused by fraud or other irregularity or error. In forming our opinion we also evaluated the overall adequacy of the presentation of information in the financial statements.

Opinion In our opinion the financial statements give a true and fair view of the state of the company's affairs as at 31 December 20X2 and of its profit for the year then ended and have been properly prepared in accordance with the Companies Act 1985.

Edwards Mellett & Co.
Registered auditors
15 May 20X3   (4)

Illustrative Company Ltd

ACCOUNTING POLICIES

Accounting convention The accounts are prepared under the historical cost convention, modified to include the revaluation of freehold land and buildings.

Depreciation of fixed assets Depreciation is provided on all fixed assets, other than freehold land, at rates calculated to write off the cost or valuation, less estimated residual value, of each asset evenly over its expected useful life, as follows:

Freehold buildings — over 25 years
Plant and machinery — over 6 to 10 years
Goodwill — over 12 years

Stocks The basis of valuation is the lower of cost and net realizable value. The figure for cost is arrived at by computing the amount involved in bringing each product to its present location and condition:

Raw materials — purchase cost on a first-in, first-out basis

Work in progress and — cost of direct materials and labour plus attributable
finished goods overheads based on the normal level of activity

Net realizable value is based on estimated selling price less further costs expected to be incurred to completion and disposal.

Long-term contracts Profit is recognized on the basis of work completed and invoiced to customers at the balance sheet date. Incomplete work is stated at cost less provision for any known or anticipated losses and payments on accounts received or receivable.

Research and development Research and development expenditure is written off as incurred.

(5)

Illustrative Company Ltd

Deferred taxation Deferred taxation is provided in accordance with the liability method on all short-term timing differences. Provision is also made for long-term timing differences, except for those which are not expected to reverse in the foreseeable future.

PROFIT AND LOSS ACCOUNT
for the year ended 31 December 19X2

	Notes	19X2 £000	19X1 £000
Turnover	1	10,502	9.765
Cost of goods sold		8,406	7,801
Gross profit		2.096	1,964
Administrative expenses	2	723	645
Distribution costs		407	474
Operating profit		966	845
Income from investments		20	15
Interest payable		(135)	(90)
Profit on ordinary activities before taxation	3	851	770
Tax on profit on ordinary activities	4	280	258
Profit after taxation		571	512
Dividends	5	200	200
Retained profit for the year		371	312
Retained profit brought forward		325	13
Retained profit carried forward		696	325

(6)

Illustrative Company Ltd

STATEMENT OF TOTAL RECOGNIZED GAINS AND LOSSES

	20X2 £000	20X1 £000
Profit for the financial year	571	512
Unrealized surplus on revaluation of freehold properties	394	–
Total gains and losses recognized since last annual report	965	512

RECONCILIATION OF MOVEMENTS IN SHAREHOLDERS' FUNDS

	20X2 £000	20X1 £000
Profit for the year	571	512
Less: Dividends	200	200
	371	312
Recognized gain on revaluation of fixed assets	394	–
Net addition to shareholders' funds	765	312
Opening shareholders' funds	925	613
Closing shareholders' funds	1,690	925

(7)

Illustrative Company Ltd

BALANCE SHEET (at 31 December 20X2)

	Notes	20X2 £000	20X1 £000
Fixed assets			
Tangible assets			
Land and buildings		484	106
Plant and machinery		1,854	1,627
	6. 7	2,338	1,733
Intangible assets	8	72	80
Investments	9	50	50
		2,460	1,863
Current assets			
Stocks	10	652	610
Long-term contract balances	11	106	38
Debtors and prepayments	12	307	284
Short-term investments		30	30
Cash at bank and in hand		9	1
		1,104	963
Creditors: amounts falling due within one year			
Bank overdraft		(106)	–
Current instalment due on debentures	13	(100)	(100)
Trade creditors		(355)	(443)
Current corporation tax		(235)	(199)
Other taxes and social security costs		(95)	(86)
Proposed dividend		(200)	(200)
Other creditors		(57)	(43)
Accruals		(7)	(4)
Net current assets (liabilities)		(51)	(112)
Total assets less current liabilities		2,409	1,751
Creditors: amounts failing due after more than one year			
Debentures	13	(700)	(800)
Provision for liabilities and charges			
Deferred taxation	14	(19)	(26)
		1,690	925
Capital and Reserves			
Called-up share capital	15	500	500
Share premium account		100	100
Revaluation reserve	7	394	–
Profit and loss account		696	325
		1,690	925

P Waters Director,   J R Cowdell Director,   15 May 20X3

(8)

Illustrative Company Ltd

CASH FLOW STATEMENT
for the year ended 31 December 20X2

	Notes	20X2 £000	20X1 £000
Net cash inflow from operating activities	16	878	885
Returns on investment and servicing of finance			
Interest received		20	15
Interest paid		(135)	(90)
Net cash flow from returns on investment and servicing of finance		763	810
Taxation			
Tax paid		(246)	(207)
Investing activities			
Payments to acquire tangible fixed assets		(335)	(308)
Receipts from sale of tangible fixed assets		20	30
		202	325
Equity dividends paid		(200)	(200)
		2	125
Financing			
Repayment of debentures		(100)	(100)
Increase in cash and cash equivalent		(98)	25

(9)

Illustrative Company Ltd

NOTES TO THE ACCOUNTS
at 31 December 20X2

1. Turnover Turnover represents the invoiced amount of goods sold, stated net of value added tax, trade discounts, and, in the case of long-term contracts, the value of work completed and invoiced to customers during the year. The turnover and pre-tax profit is split between the following classes of business.

Sales	20X2	20X1
	£	£
Manufacture of components	6,301,500	6,502,800
Construction of prefabricated buildings	4,200,660	3,262,075
	10,502,160	9,764,875
Profit		
Manufacture of components	534,760	542,550
Construction of prefabricated buildings	316,340	227,500
	851,100	770,050

2. Exceptional items Administrative expenses include £96,150 written off in respect of debts due from a major customer, Colum Ltd, which was placed in the hands of a receiver on 28 January 20X3. This amount requires disclosure as an exceptional item in view of its abnormal size.

3. Profit This is stated

	20X2	20X1
	£	£
after charging:		
Directors' remuneration (see below)	183,500	169,100
Staff costs (see below)	3,140,090	2,745,160
Hire of plant and machinery	106,300	82,100
Auditors' remuneration	32,600	29,800
Depreciation	118,310	97,600
Research and development	8,100	7,200
Interest payable on:		
Bank overdraft	55,160	–
Other loans	80,000	90,000
and crediting:		
Rental income (less outgoings)	7,500	7,000
Income from investments		
Listed	5,100	6,200
Unlisted	14,950	9,090

(10)

Illustrative Company Ltd

Directors' remuneration consists of:	20X2	20X1
	£	£
Fees	16,000	16,000
Other emoluments (including pension contributions)	156,500	142,100
Pensions to former directors	11,000	11,000
	183,500	169,100
Emoluments of chairman	9,000	9,000
Emoluments of highest paid director	62,000	57,000
Number of directors (excluding the above) whose emoluments are in the range:		
£25,001-£30,000	1	1
£45,001-£50,000	–	1
£55,001-£60,000	1	–
Staff costs consist of:		
Wages and salaries	2,752,170	2,405,800
Social security costs	296,300	272,100
Other pension costs	91,620	67,260
	3,140,090	2,745,160
Number of employees whose emoluments exceeded £30,000 were in the range:		
£30,001-£35,000	2	2
£35,001-£40,000	1	–
The average number of employees during the year was made up as follows:		
Manufacture	86	87
Construction	85	63
Selling, distribution and administration	29	29

(11)

Illustrative Company Ltd

4. Tax on profit on ordinary activities

	20X2 £	20X1 £
Based on the profit for the year:		
Corporation tax	285,580	249,160
Tax credits attributable to dividends received	5,010	3,820
Deferred taxation	(7,040)	12,160
	283,550	265,140
Taxation over-provided in previous years	(3,160)	(7,150)
	280,390	257,990

If full provision had been made for the potential amount of deferred tax, the tax charge for the year would have been increased by £6,590 (20X1-£2,360).

5. Dividends

	20X2 £	20X1 £
Ordinary: interim paid	40,000	40,000
final proposed	160,000	160,000
	200,000	200,000

(12)

Illustrative Company Ltd

6. Tangible fixed assets

	Freehold land and buildings £	Plant and machinery £	Total £
Cost or valuation:			
At 1 January 20X2	150,000	2,270,150	2,420,150
Additions	–	335,130	335,130
Surplus on revaluation	350,000	–	350,000
Disposals	–	(15,620)	(15,620)
At 31 Dec. 20X2	500,000	2,589,660	3,089,660
Depreciation:			
At 1 Jan. 20X2	44,000	643,050	687,050
Provided during the year	16,000	102,310	118,310
Surplus on revaluation	(44,000)	–	(44,000)
Disposals	–	(9,650)	(9,650)
At 31 Dec. 20X2	16,000	735,710	751,710
Net book amounts			
At 1 Jan. 20X2	106,000	1,627,100	1,733,100
At 31 Dec. 20X2	484,000	1,853,950	2,337,950

7. Freehold land and buildings included at valuation
The following information is provided:

	£
Historical cost:	
At 1 Jan. 20X2 and 31 Dec. 20X2	150,000
Depreciation based on cost:	
At 1 Jan. 20X2	44,000
Charge for the year	4,000
At 31 Dec. 20X2	48,000
Net historical cost value:	
At 1 Jan. 20X2	106,000
At 31 Dec. 20X2	102,000

(13)

Illustrative Company Ltd

The freehold properties were valued at 1 January 20X2, by 0. Terry & Co. Chartered Surveyors, on an open market basis at an amount of £500,000 including £100,000 in respect of land. The surplus of £394,000 has been credited in revaluation reserve. The depreciation charge has been increased by £12,000 per annum to reflect the higher valuation.

8. Intangible fixed assets

Goodwill	£
Cost:	
At 1 Jan. 20X2	96,000
Depreciation:	
At 1 Jan. 20X2	16,000
Provided during the year	8,000
At 31 Dec. 20X2	24,000
Net book value at 1 Jan. 20X2	80,000
Net book value at 31 Dec. 20X2	72,000

9. Investments

	20X2	20X1
	£	£
Listed investments at cost	12,600	12,600
Unlisted investments at cost	37,500	37,500
	50,100	50,100
Valuation:		
Listed investments: market value	32,000	26,000
Taxation on potential capital gain if sold at valuation	6,400	4,400

The listed investments are dealt with on a recognized stock exchange.

The company owns 12% of the issued ordinary share capital of Millbrook Ltd, an unlisted company registered in England.

(14)

Illustrative Company Ltd

10. Stocks

	20X2	20X1
	£	£
Raw materials	123,590	118,770
Work in progress	109,320	126,500
Finished goods	419,620	365,090
	652,530	610,360

Finished goods would amount to £603,500 (20X1-£491,750) if valued at replacement cost at 31 December 20X2.

11. Long-term contract balances

	20X2	20X1
	£	£
Net cost to date less provision for foreseeable losses	128,450	44,050
Payments received on account	22,100	6,500
	106,350	37,550

12. Debtors and prepayments

	20X2	20X1
	£	£
Trade debtors	225,600	230,810
Amounts recoverable on contracts	76,550	46,100
Prepayments	5,160	7,350
	307,310	284,260

The amounts recoverable on contracts represent the excess of recorded turnover over payments received on account.

13. Debenture
The debenture loan bears interest at 10% per annum and is repayable in annual instalments of £100,000.

	20X2	20X1
	£	£
Amounts repayable within five years	500,000	500,000
Amounts repayable after five years	300,000	400,000
	800,000	900,000

The current portion of the loan amounting to £100,000 (20X1-£100,000) is shown in current liabilities. The loan is secured on the freehold property.

(15)

Illustrative Company Ltd

14. Deferred taxation Deferred taxation provided in the accounts and the potential amounts, including the amounts for which provision has been made, are as follows:

	Provision		Potential	
	20X2	*20X1*	*20X2*	*20X1*
	£	£	£	£
Capital allowances in advance of depreciation and amortization	–	–	37,850	31,260
Other differences in recognising revenue and expense items in other periods for taxation purposes	59,100	66,200	59,100	66,200
	59,100	66,200	96,950	97,460
Less: Advance corporation tax on proposed dividend	40,000	40,000	40,000	40,000
	19,100	26,200	56,950	57,460
Taxation on valuation surplus	–	–	6,400	4,400
	19,100	26,200	63,350	61,860

15. Share capital

	Authorized		Allotted issued, and fully paid	
	20X2	*20X1*	*20X2*	*20X1*
	£	£	£	£
	No.	No.	£	£
Ordinary shares of £1 each	1,500,000	1,500,000	500,000	500,000

16. Reconciliation of operating profit to net cash inflow from operating activities

	19X2	*19X1*
	£000	*£000*
Operating profit	966	845
Depreciation charge	126	106
Loss (profit) on disposal of tangible fixed assets	(14)	5
Increase in stocks	(42)	(58)
Increase in long-term contract balances	(68)	(39)
Increase in debtors and prepayments	(23)	(27)
Increase in creditors, accruals etc.	(67)	53
Net cash flow from operating activities	878	885

(16)

Illustrative Company Ltd

17. Sale of investment subsequent to year end The company sold its trade investment in Millbrook Ltd on 31 March 20X3 and realized a gain on disposal of £129,645 (after providing for taxation of £43,850), which will be credited to the profit and loss account in 20X3.

18. Capital commitments

	20X2	20X1
	£	£
Contracted	107,500	79,500
Authorized but not contracted	237.600	206.000

19. Contingent liabilities

	20X2	20X1
	£	£
Guarantee of the bank overdraft of a supplier	10.000	10,000
Bills discounted	1,250	1,000

20. Transactions with Related Parties

a) During the year, consultancy fees of £27,500 (20X1 – £25,000) were paid to Cowdell Consultants Ltd, a company owned and run by J R Cowdell.

b) P Waiters is a director of Component Traders Ltd. Illustrative Company Ltd has guaranteed £10,000 (20X1 – £10,000) in favour of this company.

(17)

3.3 COMPARABILITY OF PUBLISHED ACCOUNTS

The general purpose of financial reports is to convey information to people who are interested in assessing the past performance and future progress of business entities. The specific uses of the profit and loss account can be summarized as follows. To help:

- understand past performance;

- predict future profit and losses; and

- forecast the resulting cash flows.

In practice, it is forecast accounts that are often of most interest to decision makers, but this information is not generally available. Where it is, it must be examined and evaluated in the light of the content of the firm's audited annual accounts. However, users of accounting information usually have to rely entirely on the annual accounts for the purpose of reaching commercial decisions. The purpose of FRS3, entitled 'Reporting Financial Performance', is to help to improve the interpretive value of the annual accounts.

To be able to assess how well a company is doing, and how it is likely to perform in the future, it is necessary to interpret financial figures in the light of the company's business situation. For example, the nature of its trading activity will have implications for the levels of liquidity and gearing deemed desirable. Of equal relevance is size; if it is a large organization, it is likely to trade in a number of different products and geographical areas, and so, to understand its overall results, the contribution made by each segment of activity must be studied. In addition, firms do not remain static, and some activities may stop and new ones start. The impact of new activities on reported results is likely to be especially marked if they come from the acquisition of an existing company.

The logic behind FRS3 is that, where the annual accounts are used as the basis for prediction and assessment, it is necessary to distinguish between recurrent and non-recurrent transactions and between continuing and discontinued operations. There are two obvious reasons for this:

- If the aim is to estimate future profits or losses, it is necessary to exclude the impact of non-recurrent transactions and the results achieved by parts of the undertaking that the company no longer owns or runs.

- If the aim is to compare actual reported results with last year's results or with the forecasts made for the current period, the impact of non-recurrent transactions and any contribution made by companies acquired during the year must be eliminated to ensure that like is being compared with like.

Non-recurring transactions are considered further in section 3.3.1 and new and discontinued operations in section 3.3.2.

3.3.1 Non-Recurring Profits and Losses

The profits earned and losses suffered by a business either arise from normal operating activities or accrue as a result of non-recurrent transactions or events outside the normal scope of a company's trading activities. The problem is how to account for these non-recurrent transactions, e.g. an unusually large bad debt that results in the removal of the debtor from the total collectable shown in the balance sheet and an equivalent charge in the profit and loss account. A case can be made that non-recurring transactions should be excluded from the profit and loss account as their inclusion distorts the true trend of operating results and therefore causes wrong conclusions to be drawn regarding a company's past performance and likely future prospects.

Example 3.1

The following information is provided in respect of the affairs of Parlock plc which made a non-recurring gain of £1,500,000 in 19X3.

Annual profits for	Including non-recurring gain £000	Excluding non-recurring gain £000
20X1	2,400	2,400
20X2	2,600	2,600
20X3	3,500	2,000
20X4	1,400	1,400

Inclusion of the non-recurring gain might cause individuals examining the accounts for 20X3 to assume that annual profits are still rising, whereas in reality recurring profits have begun to fall.

On the other hand, there are strong arguments for including non-recurring transactions in the profit and loss account. These are:

- Non-recurring transactions have exactly the same effect on the financial position of a business as normal operating transactions, and for this reason they should be given equal prominence.

• Allocation of individual transactions either to the profit and loss account or directly to reserves is a matter of judgement, and this provides scope for both error and the manipulation of financial information. In either case the result may be that the wrong conclusions are drawn regarding a company's performance.

• Exclusion could cause users to overlook the effect of a non-recurrent transaction when assessing corporate performance.

• It is the directors' job to manage all aspects of business activity, whether they give rise to recurrent or non-recurrent profits and losses, and the reported profit figure should therefore measure management's overall performance.

These arguments led to the introduction of the requirement, contained in FRS3, for almost all non-recurrent profits and losses to be reported in the profit and loss account with full disclosure of their effect. This ensures that readers do not overlook the financial effect of important transactions, but, at the same time, it enables them to identify recurring profits which might be considered more relevant when attempting to predict likely future results. FRS3 distinguishes three categories of non-recurring profits and losses, and the accounting treatment of a particular item depends on the category into which it falls:

(i) Exceptional items. Broadly speaking, these are items which are abnormal as regard their size but which result from the ordinary activities of the business. Examples include:

(a) abnormal charges for bad debts, write-offs of obsolete stock and work in progress and abortive research and development expenditure;

(b) abnormal provisions for losses on long-term contracts;

(c) under- or over-provisions of tax on normal operating profits in respect of previous years;

(d) fundamental reorganization or restructuring of operations;

(e) the profit or loss on the sale of fixed assets or investments not acquired with the intention of resale;

(f) writing off intangibles, including goodwill, because of unusual developments during the year which cause them to lose value;

(g) the profit or loss on the sale or termination of an operation.

These items relate to ordinary operating activities and should therefore appear 'above the line', i.e. they should be taken into account in calculating post-tax reported profit on ordinary activities for the year. Exceptional items must be separately disclosed, either on the face of the profit and loss account or by way of a note (see Example 3.2).

(ii) Extraordinary items. These arise as the result of events outside normal trading activities; they are material in amount and are not expected to recur. Such items are not associated with normal operations, and they are therefore brought into the profit and loss account (less attributable taxation) after post-tax profits arising from ordinary activities have been computed. Because of the extreme rarity of such items, no examples are provided in the standard.

(iii) Prior period adjustments. These consist of only:

(a) Material adjustments applicable to prior years arising from changes in accounting policies, e.g. where a company changes from capitalizing development costs to writing them off as they are incurred.

(b) The correction of fundamental errors made when preparing earlier years' accounts, e.g. where the directors forget to count the stocks in one of the warehouses and, as a result, materially understate profit.

Prior year items (net of any related tax) are adjusted against retained profits brought forward from previous years (see Example 3.2). FRS3 makes it clear that any adjustments to incorrect estimates, made in earlier years, must not be accounted for as prior year items and must be shown on the face of the profit and loss account. For example, a major customer may go into liquidation, owing £1,000,000, and the company may make a bad debt provision of £600,000 in anticipation of an ultimate payment of 40p in the £ to unsecured creditors. This optimism may prove unfounded, in which case the remaining balance of £400,000 has to be written off in the following year. When this happens, the additional write-off is not accounted for as a prior year item, despite the fact that it was caused by a liquidation which occurred in a previous year. Instead, it must be accounted for as an exceptional item provided the amount is material. Similarly, material adjustments to wrongly estimated extraordinary items must be accounted for as extraordinary items when the correction is made.

Example 3.2

The following balances relating to 20X1 have been extracted from the books of Rockingham plc:

	£000
Turnover .	11,170
Cost of sales	7,721
Profit on the sale of shares in Postbridge Ltd	500
Administration expenses	621
Distribution costs	133
Interest payable	26
Interim dividend paid	250
Retained profit at 1 January 20X1	3,875

The following additional information is provided:

1. Shares in Postbridge Ltd were sold during the year. These shares were purchased ten years ago and were the only investments owned by the company. It is estimated that attributable tax payable will be £ 150,000.

2. The company's cost of sales includes a £200,000 write-off of uninsured stocks damaged by fire.

3. After the above balances were extracted, the directors decided to adopt the policy of depreciating the company's freehold building which has been owned for some years. This decision requires the opening book value of the building to be reduced by £700,000, and a charge for 20X1 of £114,000 must be added to cost of sales.

4. Corporation tax on profits from normal trading operations is estimated at £1,200,000.

5. The directors propose to pay a final dividend of £600,000.

Required:
The profit and loss account and statement of retained profits of Rockingham plc for 20X1 in 'good form' and complying with the provisions of FRS3 so far as the information permits.

Solution

Workings	£000
Cost of Sales	7,721
Add: Additional depreciation	114
Adjusted cost of sales	7,835

Profit and Loss Account of Rockingham plc for 20X1

	£000	£000
Turnover		11,170
Less: Cost of sales (note 1)		7,835
Gross profit		3,335
Less: Distribution costs	133	
Administrative expenses	621	
		754
Operating Profit		2,581
Less: Interest payable		(26)
Add: Income from investments (note 2)		500
Profit before taxation		3,055
Tax on profit from ordinary activities		1,350
Profit for the year attributable to the shareholders		1,705
Less: Dividends paid and proposed		850
Retained profits for the year		855

Statement of Retained Profits

	£000	£000
Retained profit for the year		855
Retained profit at 1 January 20X1	3,875	
Prior year adjustment arising from change of accounting policy (note 3)	(700)	
		3,175
Retained profit at 31 December 20X1		4,030

Notes:
1. Cost of sales includes a £200,000 write off of uninsured stock damaged by fire. Amount requires disclosure as exceptional in view of abnormal size.

2. During the year the company realized £500,000 on the sale of its shareholdings in Postbridge Ltd purchased some years ago.

3. The directors have decided to depreciate the company's freehold building, purchased some years ago, in order to give a fairer presentation of the results and financial position of the company.

3.3.2 New and Discontinued Operations

The importance of understanding changes in the range of activities that make up the whole of the company is illustrated in Figure 3.1.

Figure 3.1 Changing activities over time

Segment	20X1	20X2	20X3
1	Operational	Disposed	Operational
2	Operational	Operational	Operational
3	Operational	Operational	Acquired
4			Operational

This shows that in 20X1 the company had three main segments of activity – 1, 2 and 3, but predictions for 20X2 based on the results of 20X1 would be wrong to the extent that activity 1 is no longer contributing. In the same way, segment 4 is added by acquisition in 20X3, and so comparisons with 20X2 are invalid unless the results of segment 4 are ignored.

It is for this reason that FRS3 requires the profit and loss account to be split so as to show separately the results of continuing operations and those of discontinuing operations, including in both cases the effect of any exceptional items, where:

- Discontinuing operations are those operations of an entity which are sold during the accounting period or have been ceased permanently. The sale or termination must materially reduce the scale of operations in terms of classes of business, geographical spread, or turnover.

- Continuing operations are any not satisfying the conditions necessary to make them discontinued.

Using these definitions, the form of profit and loss account to be used in such circumstances is outlined in Figure 3.2.

Readers should note how the results of continuing and discontinuing operations are separated and that, within continuing operations, the impact of any companies acquired during the year must be shown separately. Also, up to three classes of exceptional items have to be shown on the face of the profit and loss account in the circumstances of a discontinuance of operations:

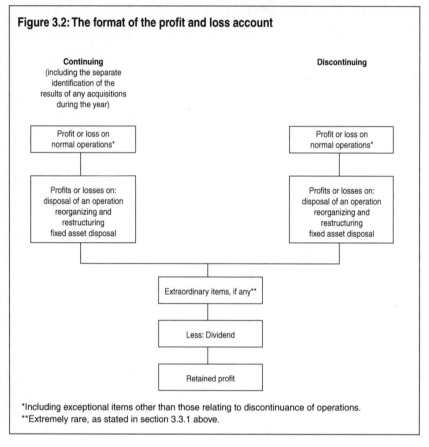

Figure 3.2: The format of the profit and loss account

Continuing
(including the separate identification of the results of any acquisitions during the year)

Discontinuing

Profit or loss on normal operations*

Profit or loss on normal operations*

Profits or losses on:
disposal of an operation
reorganizing and restructuring
fixed asset disposal

Profits or losses on:
disposal of an operation
reorganizing and restructuring
fixed asset disposal

Extraordinary items, if any**

Less: Dividend

Retained profit

*Including exceptional items other than those relating to discontinuance of operations.
**Extremely rare, as stated in section 3.3.1 above.

- Profits or losses on the sale or termination of an operation

- Costs of a fundamental reorganization or restructuring

- Profits or losses on the disposal of fixed assets (illustrated in Example 3.3)

The retained profit arrived at in the profit and loss account shown in the diagram is transferred to a statement of retained profits (as in Example 3.2) where it is added to the balance of profit brought forward from the previous year.

Example 3.3 shows a possible method of presenting the profit and loss account so that it complies with both FRS3 and the Companies Act 1985.

Example 3.3 The Profit and Loss Account

	Continuing operations	Acquisitions	Discontinued operations	Total
	£million	£million	£million	£million
Turnover	750	100	50	900
Cost of sales	(500)	(75)	(45)	(620)
Gross profit	250	25	5	280
Operating expenses	(125)	(10)	(4)	(139)
Operating profit	125	15	1	141
Profit on sale of property	13			13
Profit on ordinary activities	138	15	1	154
Interest payable				60
Profit on ordinary activities before tax				94
Taxation				27
Profit after tax				67
Dividend				30
Retained profit				37
Earnings per share, based on issued share capital of 149 million ordinary shares (£M67/149M)				45p

Notes:

(1) In practice, comparative figures for the previous year would be given.

(2) Any extraordinary items would be included after the profit after tax.

It can be seen that the presentation uses conventional headings down the left-hand side, with the new aspect being the way in which transactions are analysed across the page into continuing and discontinuing operations. This analysis stops at the line prior to the interest charge, and all further adjustments are made in the total column.

The profit on the disposal of fixed assets is shown as a separate entry on the face of the account. FRS3 specifies that the profit on disposal of fixed assets (to be included in the profit and loss account of the accounting period when the disposal takes place) must be calculated as the difference between the sale proceeds and the amount at which the asset is carried in the books. Therefore, if an asset has been revalued, the profit is calculated as proceeds less the revalued amount. For example, a piece of freehold land which was bought as a fixed asset cost £M10 in 20X0, was revalued upwards to £M15 in 20X5 and sold for £M28 in 20X8. The accounts for 20X8 would show a profit on disposal of £M28 − £M15 = £M13 profit. The £M5 revaluation surplus arising in 20X5 would have been entered in the revaluation reserve and is non- distributable.

Example 3.4

Fluid plc is a public quoted company which carries on a range of activities throughout the United Kingdom. The following information is made available in respect of Fluid plc and its subsidiary companies:

(1) *Year ending 31 March 20X4*

	£m
Sales	805
Surplus on revaluation of property	–
Loss on sale of property	22
Cost of sales	471
Operating expenses	253

(2) The company closed down one of its factories on 31 March 20X4. The results for the year to 31 March 20X4 contain the following figures in respect of the discontinued operation:

	£m
Sales	150
Cost of sales	120
Operating expenses	80

(3) The company purchased the entire share capital of one of its competitors on 1 April 20X3. The results for the year to 31 March 20X4 contain the following figures in respect of the new acquisition:

	£m
Sales	207
Cost of sales	140
Operating expenses	30

Required:
The profit and loss account of Fluid plc and its subsidiary companies for the year to 31 March 20X4 prepared in accordance with the requirements of FRS3, entitled 'Reporting Financial Performance'.

Solution

Profit and Loss Account, year to 31 March 20X4

	Continuing operations	Acquisitions	Discontinued operations	Total
	£m	£m	£m	£m
Turnover	448	207	150	805
Cost of sales	211	140	120	471
Gross profit	237	67	30	334
Operating expenses	143	30	80	253
Operating profit	94	37	(50)	81
Loss on sale of property	22	−	−	22
Profit on ordinary activities	72	37	(50)	59

3.3.3 Statement of Total Realized Gains and Losses (STRGL) and Reconciliation of Movements in Shareholders' Funds

The gains and losses that affect a company during the year can be divided into those that are included in the profit and loss account and those that are taken directly to reserves. FRS3 requires all gains and losses to be taken to the profit and loss account unless the law or another accounting standard counters this. All of a company's gains and losses for a year should be considered when assessing its financial performance, and the STRGL brings together all such movements in value. FRS3 considers that this additional statement enhances financial reporting by providing information that, in conjunction with the other accounting statements, is useful for assessing the return on investment.

The value of shareholders' funds can be affected not only by realized and unrealized gains and losses but also by other factors such as dividends or injections or withdrawals of capital. The purpose of this statement, required by FRS3, is to highlight these movements.

Both of these statements are useful when comparing performance, over time and between companies, because they provide a comprehensive insight into managerial performance. The STRGL shows how well management is husbanding all of the company's assets and not only those acquired for trading purposes. The total value of equity indicates the amount invested in a company by its ownership, and so examining the elements that have caused it to move over the year shows how any growth has been generated or reduction caused. These statements should also be used when carrying out comparisons because this will reveal whether there are significant differences in the factors contributing to overall movements.

3.3.4 Segmental Reporting

It is usual nowadays for many large companies to undertake different types of business and operate in several geographical areas. These are known as product or geographical segments, and each may have its own rate of profitability, opportunities for growth and degrees of risk. The Companies Act requires disclosure of both turnover and profit for different classes of business and only turnover for geographical areas; SSAP25 'Segmental Reporting' extends the requirements for large companies and those that are plcs. A company covered by SSAP25 must disclose turnover, profit and net assets for each product and geographical segment.

The provision of segmental information aids comparability because it allows the users of financial statements to better understand the company's past performance. By seeing the relative contribution of the different aspects of the undertaking it is possible to assess its future prospects. Also, it aids an appreciation of the impact that changes in significant parts of the business are likely to have on the firm as a whole. For example, knowledge of the relative contribution of different geographical areas enables the possible effects of currency exchange rate movements to be better appreciated.

3.4 DISTRIBUTABLE PROFIT

The rules for the calculation of distributable profits differ between private and public limited companies. Identification of the particular category a company falls into is a simple matter: public limited companies are identified by the designatory letters plc, whereas Ltd after a company's name indicates that it is a private company. There are many differences between these two types of company; perhaps the most notable is that public companies have a minimum share capital requirement of £50,000, and private companies are not allowed to make a public issue of shares or debentures.

The 1985 Act defines distributable profits of private companies as: accumulated realized profits minus accumulated realized losses, where:

- accumulated realized profits are realized profits that have not already been distributed as dividends or capitalised;

- accumulated realized losses are realized losses that have not been previously written off in either a reduction or reorganization of capital;

- profits or losses may be either capital or revenue in their origin.

The effect of these rules is that a company is legally entitled to declare a dividend out of realized profits brought forward but, if there are accumulated realized losses brought forward, these losses must be made good before a dividend can be paid. A company, with large accumulated realized losses, may therefore find it convenient to undertake a reduction of capital if it wishes to avoid a long delay before it can pay a dividend out of the profits accruing as the result of an improvement in trading conditions.

The Act does not define realized and unrealized profits and losses, but it does provide some guidance regarding the treatment of particular items.

- Provisions as defined by the Companies Act (i.e. 'any amount written off by way of providing for depreciation or diminution in value of assets [or] retained as reasonably necessary for the purpose of providing for any liability or loss which is either likely to be incurred, or certain to be incurred but uncertain as to amount or as to the date on which it will arise') are to be treated as realized losses, except that private companies need not provide for an unrealized loss arising on revaluation of all a company's assets.

- Any additional depreciation, which is charged as the result of an upward revaluation of fixed assets, may be added back to reported profits for the purpose of computing distributable profits. This provision was introduced to avoid discouraging companies from revaluing their assets where they considered such a course appropriate.

- Development expenditure, shown as a fixed asset, is to be treated as a realized loss for the purpose of computing distributable profit, unless there are 'special circumstances' justifying capitalization, in which case the expenditure may be carried forward. Special circumstances are not defined in the Act, but the capitalization of development expenditure which complies with the conditions laid down in SSAP13 is probably acceptable.

In those circumstances not specifically covered by the Act, the determination of whether a profit or loss has been realized must be made in the light of prevailing generally accepted accounting principles. This would suggest that profit should be computed in accordance with the fundamental concepts specified in FRS18 and the rules contained in other accounting standards.

Example 3.5

The following summarized information is provided relating to the affairs of Gold plc, Silver plc, both public limited companies, and Bronze Ltd, a private limited company.

1. *Summary, Balance Sheets at 31 December 20X4*

	Gold plc £000	Silver plc £000	Bronze Ltd £000
Share capital	12,000	6,000	2,000
Reserves	10,000	(2,600)	640
	22,000	3,400	2,640
Net assets	22,000	3,400	2,640

2. *Build up of Reserves at 31 December 20X4*

	Gold plc £000	Silver plc £000	Bronze Ltd £000
Retained realized profit (loss) at 1 Jan. 20X4	3,800	(4,600)	840
Realized profit for 20X4	2,600	2,000	500
Unrealized loss on revaluation of all fixed assets	–	–	(700)
Realized capital profit	1,200		
Unrealized profit (see 3)	2,400	–	–
	10,000	(2,600)	640

3. Gold owns a freehold property which cost £1,000,000 (including land at £200,000) some years ago. It was revalued at £3,400,000 (including land at £800,000) on 1 January 20X4. Since that date the building has been depreciated at 5% per annum based on the revalued figure in arriving at realized profit for the year.

Required:
(a) Define distributable profit in accordance with the provisions of the Companies Act 1985.

(b) Calculate the maximum distribution that can be legally made by Gold plc, Silver plc, and Bronze Ltd, on the basis of the above information, and explain any adjustments you make to the figures given above.

(c) What difference would it make to your answer under (b) if Gold plc made a bonus issue, at par, of 1 new ordinary share for every 2 shares held in December 20X4?

Solution

(a) The Companies Act 1985 defines distributable profits as accumulated realized profits minus accumulated realized losses, where accumulated realized profits have not already been distributed as dividends or capitalized, and accumulated realized losses are realized losses which have not been previously written off in either a reduction or reorganization of capital. Profits or losses may be either capital or revenue in their origin.

(b)

	Gold	Silver	Bronze
	£000	£000	£000
Retained profit (loss) at 1 January	3,800	(4,600)	840
Profit for 20X4	2,600	2,000	500
Realized capital profit	1,200	–	–
Depreciation relating to revaluation	180		
Maximum distribution	7,780	(2,600)	1,340

Explanation of treatment:

Gold: Unrealized profits are not distributable.
Additional depreciation, relating to the upward revaluation of the building, remains distributable, i.e. £2,600,000 (revised value of building) – £800,000 (historical cost) x 5% x 2 years.

Silver: No adjustment necessary; this company is unable to make a distribution.

Bronze: In the case of private companies, provision need not be made for an unrealized loss arising on the revaluation of all fixed assets.

(c) The bonus issue results in the capitalization of profits amounting to £6,000,000. The maximum distribution is therefore reduced to £1,780,000.

3.5 RELATED PARTY DISCLOSURES

It is assumed that items reported in the accounts are based on arm's length transactions. This means that the terms are those established with an external party with both sides bargaining freely and unaffected by any relationship between them. However, companies exist in a web of relationships and it is possible for a transaction to be influenced by their connection. Either the transaction may not have been undertaken or the terms may have been different if the parties were not related. The knowledge that two parties are related would alert the user of the accounts to the fact that they may be affected by the relationship, and a full appreciation of the impact requires disclosure of the value of the transactions.

FRS8 deals with 'Related Party Disclosures' and defines related parties as when one party has control of the other or they are both under common control. This encompasses holding and subsidiary companies along with associates and joint ventures and the management of these companies. Where transactions take place with related parties, FRS8 requires the disclosure of the names of the parties, the value of transactions that have taken place during the accounting period and amounts due at the balance sheet date. Disclosure is not required about transactions between companies included in a set of consolidated accounts or in a subsidiary entity's accounts where it is more than 90% owned.

3.6 FURTHER READING

Lewis, R. and Pendrill, D. (2000), *Advanced Financial Accounting*, sixth edition, Pitman, pp. 133-7; 155-70;411-5.

Alexander, D and Britton, A (2000) *Financial Reporting*, fifth edition, Thomson, chs. 13; 23; 26.

3.7 QUESTIONS

Question 3.1

The following is the draft trading and profit and loss account of Parnell Ltd for the year ending 31 December 1997:

	£m	£m
Turnover		563
Cost of sales		310
		253
Distribution costs	45	
Administrative expenses	78	
		123
Profit on ordinary activities before tax		130
Tax on profit on ordinary activities		45
Profit on ordinary activities after taxation-all retained		85
Profit brought forward at 1 January 1997		101
Profit carried forward at 31 December 1997		186

You are given the following additional information, which is reflected in the above trading and profit and loss account only to the extent stated:

1. Distribution costs include a bad debt of £15 million which arose on the insolvency of a major customer. There is no prospect of recovering any of this debt. Bad debts have never been material in the past.

2. The company has traditionally consisted of a manufacturing division and a distribution division. On 31 December 1997, the entire distribution division was sold for £50 million, its book value at the time of sale was £40 million. The surplus on disposal was credited to administrative expenses. (Ignore any related corporation tax.)

3. During 1997, the distribution division made sales of £100 million and had a cost of sales of £30 million. There will be no reduction in stated distribution costs or administration expenses as a result of this disposal.

4. The company owns offices which it purchased on 1 January 1995 for £500 million, comprising £200 million for land and £300 million for buildings. No depreciation was charged in 1995 or 1996, but the company now considers that such a charge should be introduced. The buildings were expected to have a life of 50 years at the date of purchase, and the company uses the straight-line basis for calculating depreciation, assuming a zero residual value. No taxation consequences result from this change.

5. During 1997, part of the manufacturing division was restructured at a cost of £20 million to take advantage of modern production techniques. The restructuring was not fundamental and will not have a material effect on the nature and focus of the company's operations. This cost is included under administration expenses in the profit and loss account.

Required:
(a) State the objective of FRS3 entitled 'Reporting Financial Performance'. *[2 marks]*

(b) State how each of the items 1-5, above, must be accounted for in order to comply with the requirements of FRS3. *[8 marks]*

(c) Redraft the trading and profit and loss account of Parnell Ltd for 1997, taking into account the additional information so as to comply, as far as possible, with relevant standard accounting practice. Show clearly any adjustments you make. Notes to the accounts are not required. *[10 marks]*

[Total – 20 marks]

Question 3.2

The following information is provided in respect of Makeup plc for the year to 30 September 1996:

	£m
Sales	250
Cost of goods sold	130
Administrative expenses	70
Distribution costs	24
Loss on disposal of plant relating to continuing operations	5
Reorganization costs	7
Taxation	5

The following further information is provided in respect of the above items:

1. The reorganization costs relate to a division closed down during the year. The above totals include the following relating to the division: sales £46 million; cost of goods sold £38 million; administrative expenses £7 million; distribution costs £3 million.

2. Makeup plc acquired the assets and liabilities of a local business on 1 January 1996. The above totals include the following arising in respect of the business taken over: sales £41 million; cost of goods sold £21 million; administrative expenses £6 million; distribution costs £2 million.

Required:
(a) Explain what you understand by the terms 'exceptional item' and 'extraordinary item'. Give, if possible, an example of each and explain their treatment in company accounts in order to comply with standard accounting practice.   [6]

(b) The profit and loss account of Makeup plc for the year to 30 September 1996 prepared in accordance with the requirements of FRS 3 entitled 'Reporting Financial Performance'.   [10]

(c) Outline the new features introduced by FRS 3 and explain the reason for their introduction. [4]

                                                                            [Total – 20]

Question 3.3

The final accounts of Pavin Ltd are in the process of being prepared. The following information is provided:

Profit and Loss Account for the year ended 31 December 20X5

	£000
Turnover	3,620
Franked investment income (amount received)	88
	3,708
Cost of goods sold	2,105
Administrative expenses	526
Distribution costs	317
Profit	760

Statement of Movement on Reserves

Retained profit brought forward	560
Retained profit for 20X5	760
Retained profit carried forward	1,320

Balance sheet as at 31 December 20X5

Plant and machinery at cost	2,108
Less: Accumulated depreciation to 31 December 20X4	1,000
	1,108
Development expenditure	190
Stocks	351
Debtors and prepayments	410
Cash at bank and in hand	7
	2,066

Capital, Reserves and Liabilities

Called-up share capital (£0.50 shares)	500
Profit and loss account	1,320
	1,820
10% debentures	120
Trade creditors	126
	2,066

1.   The development expenditure ledger account showed the following movements during 20X5:

	£000
Balance 1 January 20X5	88
Expenditure during 20X5	102
Balance 31 December 20X5	190

The directors have now decided that it would give a fairer view of the company's performance and financial position if development expenditure was written off immediately it was incurred.

2. The directors have previously valued stock on the first in, first out (FIFO) basis. The directors have now decided that the average cost (AVCO) basis should be used. The following valuations are provided:

	20X4 £000	31 December 20X5 £000
FIFO	316	351
AVCO	292	321

3. The company's manufacturing plant was purchased on 1 January 20X0 and has been depreciated to 31 December 20X4 on the straight-line basis at 10% per annum assuming a residual value of £108,000. The remaining useful life was re-assessed at three years on 1 January 20X5 and the residual value at the end of that period was estimated to be £148,000.

4. The figure for debtors and prepayments includes £90,000 due from one of Pavin's customers which went into receivership on 5 January 20X6. It is not thought that any of the debt will be recovered.

5. The debentures were raised on 1 January 20X5. The directors have decided to make an annual transfer of £12,600 to debenture redemption reserve in anticipation of repayment at the end of 10 years. Provision is to be made in the accounts for the interest due.

6. The corporation tax charge for the year (excluding tax credits) is estimated at £40,000.

7. The directors propose to pay a final dividend of 8 pence per share. The rate of advance corporation tax is 20/80ths.

Required:
(a) Define the following terms and, where possible, provide an example:
   (i)   exceptional item;
   (ii)   extraordinary item;
   (iii) prior year adjustment.   [6]

(b) Prepare for Payin Ltd:
   (i)   a profit and loss account for 20X5   [7]
   (ii)   a statement of movement on reserves for 20X5   [7]
   (iii) a balance sheet as at 31 December 20X5   [10]

The accounts should give effect, as appropriate, to the information provided in 1-7 above. The accounts need not be presented in accordance with the precise provisions of the Companies Acts but should be presented in good form and comply with relevant standard accounting practice so far as the information permits.

Note:
All items are to be considered material for disclosure purposes.
Notes to the accounts are not required.   [Total – 30]

Question 3.4

Filios Products plc brews beers, owns and manages pubs and hotels, manufactures and supplies alcoholic and soft drinks, and is a supplier and operator of amusement machines and other leisure facilities.

The accounts for 1997 contain the following information:

Balance Sheet of Filios Products

	£m
Fixed assets at book value	1,663
Current assets	
Stocks and debtors	381
Bank balance	128
	509
Less: Creditors falling, due within one year	193
Net current assets	316
Total assets less current liabilities	1,979
Less: 10% debentures	140
	1,839
Capital and reserves	
Share capital	800
Retained profit	1,039
	1,839

Profit and Loss Account of Filios Products

	£m	£m
Turnover		1,028
Less: Cost of sales	684	
Administration expenses	110	
Distribution costs	101	
Interest charged	14	909
Net profit		119

The following breakdown is provided of the company's results into three divisions and head office:

	Beer and pub operations	Hotel business	Other drinks & leisure	Head office
	£m	£m	£m	£m
Turnover	508	152	368	–
Cost of sales	3 16	81	287	–
Administration expenses	43	14	38	15
Distribution costs	64	12	25	–
Interest charged	10	–	–	4
Fixed assets at book value	890	332	364	77
Stocks and debtors	230	84	67	–
Bank balance	73	15	28	12
Creditors	66	40	56	31
10% debentures	100	–	–	40

The following information is obtained for competitor companies: Dean, which brews beer and manages pubs; and Clarke, which is in the hotel business:

	Dean	Clarke
	£m	£m
Turnover	600	150
Operating profit	80	60
Net assets	1,300	300

Required:

(a) Outline the nature of segmental reports and explain the reason for presenting such information in the published accounts. *[5 marks]*

(b) Prepare a segmental statement for Filios Products plc for 1997 complying, so far as the information permits, with the provisions of SSAP25 entitled 'Segmental Reporting', so as to show for each segment and the business as a whole:
    – turnover;
    – profit;
    – net assets. *[9 marks]*

(c) (i) Examine the relative performance of the operating divisions of Filios Products; and

    (ii) Compare the performance of the operating divisions of Filios Products, where appropriate, with that of the competitor companies.

The examination and comparison should be based on the following accounting ratios:
    – operating profit percentage;
    – net asset turnover;
    – return on net assets. *[16 marks]*

[Total – 30 marks]

Question 3.5

Gurney Ltd was incorporated on 1 January 20X4 with an authorized share capital of £1,000,000 divided into ordinary shares of £1 each. On the same date 400,000 shares were issued at par for cash. Long-term prospects are excellent, but profits are expected to fluctuate due to changes in trading conditions. The estimated profits (loss) and planned dividend per share for each of the next six years are as follows:

	Profits (Loss)	Dividend
	£000	pence
20X4	110	15
20X5	20	16
20X6	95	17
20X7	30	18
20X8	200	19
20X9	(20)	20

The dividend to be paid each year is the lower of the planned payment for the year and the maximum legal distribution.

The directors plan to finance a modest rate of expansion over the next six years out of retained profit and, for this reason, they have decided to capitalize the balance of undistributed profits at the end of 20X9.

Required:
(a) Calculate the planned dividend payment for each of the years 20X4-X9.   [3]

(b) For each of the years 20X4-X9 prepare a statement showing the profit available for distribution, the amount of the distribution and the amount of retained profits carried forward. You should give effect to any legal restrictions on the amount of dividend payable in the year in question. You should explain the treatment you adopt.   [15]

(c) Indicate the amount of the capitalization issue on 31 December 20X9.   [2]

Note: Ignore taxation.   [Total – 20]

4

REPORTING FIXED
ASSETS IN COMPANY
ACCOUNTS

4.1 INTRODUCTION

Accounting statements are used by a variety of different groups as the basis for reaching resource allocation decisions, although their usefulness must be judged according to their relevance to the matter under consideration. In the case of financial service managers, the principal concern is whether customers can meet their financial obligations. This mainly involves a consideration of whether payments for interest on loans, service charges and loan repayments will be made when due. Published accounts are useful for this and other purposes, but users must be aware of the fact that they do suffer important limitations.

Accounting statements have a comforting appearance of complete accuracy because: precise figures are given for each of the items reported in the profit and loss account and balance sheet; and the use of double entry causes the principal accounting statements to articulate with one another and balance. The reality is very different. Many of the balances reported in the accounts involve a large measure of estimation and subjective judgement. When calculating depreciation, for example, accountants and managers must estimate how long the asset will last, what it will then sell for, in perhaps ten years time, and whether to use the straight-line basis, reducing-balance basis or one of a number of other alternative depreciation methods. These are areas of great uncertainty and different choices result in different figures for reported profit. Users must therefore be aware of the fact that the figures contained in the accounts are the result of decisions made and opinions held by the people responsible for making the calculations, and that different individuals, all acting with the best of intentions, would be unlikely to produce the same results. The only major comfort is that, provided care is taken when making the calculations, and valuation procedures are consistently applied, the extent of the variation should not be great.

4.2 THE REGULATORY STRUCTURE

The ASC did much to raise the standard of financial reporting but was the subject of increasing criticism during the 1980s due to its failure to devise a satisfactory system of inflation accounting (see Chapter 2) and because of a growing tendency to issue standards that were sufficiently flexible to gain acceptance by the business community rather than insisting on what it considered to be best practice. For example, SSAP 22 permitted companies either to write-off purchased goodwill immediately against reserves or to capitalize it and amortize it through the profit and loss account over its estimated useful economic life.

The Review Committee chaired by Sir Ron (now Lord) Dearing was appointed by Consultative Committee of Accounting Bodies in 1987 to review and make recommendations on the standard setting process. It reported in 1988 and its recommendations found favour with the government which, on 26 February 1990, announced the establishment of the Financial Reporting Council under Dearing's chairmanship. The Financial Reporting Council has two 'subsidiaries': the Financial Reporting Review Panel and the Accounting Standards Board (ASB) (see Figure 4.1). The job of the Review Panel is to examine published accounts where there is evidence that the requirements of the Companies Act have been breached, particularly where it appears that they fail to show a true and fair view. The Review Panel may apply to the Court to issue revised accounts where those previously issued have been shown to be defective. This was done in the case of Trafalgar House which was forced to issue revised accounts for 1991 showing a loss of £38.5m compared with a profit of £122.4m in the earlier version.

The function of the ASB is to issue new accounting standards and withdraw any that are considered out of date. It is therefore the successor of the Accounting Standards

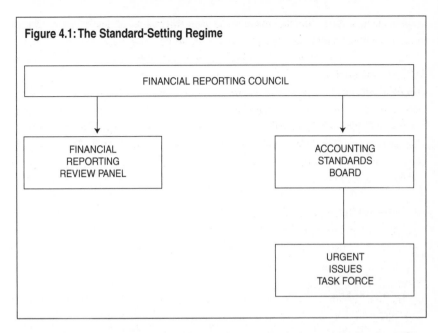

Figure 4.1: The Standard-Setting Regime

FINANCIAL REPORTING COUNCIL

FINANCIAL
REPORTING
REVIEW PANEL

ACCOUNTING
STANDARDS
BOARD

URGENT
ISSUES
TASK FORCE

Committee. The ASB is assisted by the Urgent Issues Task Force to deal with conflicts between accounting standards and statutory provisions which possibly lead to different interpretations.

Although the ASB may be seen as the successor to the ASC, it is different in a number of important respects. The ASB owes its existence to statutory edict and may issue accounting standards in its own name, whereas the ASC merely prepared standards to be issued by the professional accounting bodies. The independence of the ASB is underlined by the fact that it is financed, not only by the accounting profession (as was the ASC), but also by the financial community and the government. The fact that there is now a requirement for companies to disclose and explain any material departures from accounting standards further increases its authority.

The ASB published its *Statement of Aims* in 1991. This publication (as shown below) also explained how it would go about 'achieving the aims' and listed the 'fundamental guidelines' to be followed when going about its work.

Aims
The aims of the Accounting Standards Board are to establish and improve standards

of financial accounting and reporting, for the benefit of users, preparers and auditors of financial information.

Achieving the aims

The Board intends to achieve its aims by:

1. Developing principles to guide it in establishing standards and to provide a framework within which others can exercise judgement in resolving accounting issues.

2. Issuing new accounting standards, or amending existing ones, in response to evolving business practices, new economic developments and deficiencies being identified in current practices.

3. Addressing urgent issues promptly.

Fundamental guidelines

1. To be objective and to ensure that the information resulting from the application of accounting standards faithfully represents the underlying commercial activity. Such information should be neutral in the sense that it is free from any form of bias intended to influence users in a particular direction and should not be designed to favour any group of users or preparers.

2. To ensure that accounting standards are clearly expressed and supported by a reasoned analysis of the issues.

3. To determine what should be incorporated in accounting standards based on research, public consultation and careful deliberation about the usefulness of the resulting information.

4. To ensure that, through a process of regular communication, accounting standards are produced with due regard to international developments.

5. To ensure that there is a consistency both from one accounting standard to another and between accounting standards and company law.

6. To issue accounting standards only when the expected benefits exceed the perceived costs. The Board recognizes that reliable cost/benefit calculations are seldom possible. However, it will always assess the need for standards in terms of

the significance and extent of the problem being addressed and will choose the standard that appears to be most effective in cost/benefit terms.

7. To take account of the desire of the financial community for evolutionary rather than revolutionary change in the reporting process where this is consistent with the objectives outlined above.

On formation, the ASB adopted the 22 SSAPs issued by the ASC and still extant at the date of the latter's demise. The new body issues Financial Reporting Standards (FRSs). These cover new areas and are also gradually replacing the 22 SSAPs; for example, FRS 1 entitled 'Cash Flow Statements' replaced SSAP 10 entitled 'Source and Application of Funds'.

The SSAPs and FRSs included in the Accounting, Analysis and Planning syllabus are listed in Table 4.1, together with a record of where they are principally dealt with in this book.

Table 4.1

Regulation	Title	Chapter	Star
SSAP 4	Accounting for government grants	4	*
SSAP 9	Stock and long-term contracts	5	**
SSAP 13	Accounting for research and development	5	**
SSAP 15	Accounting for deferred tax	5	*
SSAP 17	Accounting for post balance sheet events	5	*
SSAP 19	Accounting for investment properties	4	*
SSAP 21	Accounting for leases and hire purchase contracts	4	**
SSAP 25	Segmental reporting	3	**
FRS 1	Cash flow statements	10	**
FRS 2	Accounting for subsidiary undertakings	6	**
FRS 3	Reporting financial performance	3	**
FRS 4	Capital instruments	5	*
FRS 5	Reporting the substance of transactions	5	**
FRS 6	Acquisitions and mergers	6	**
FRS 7	Fair values in acquisition accounting	6	**
FRS 8	Related party disclosures	3	*
FRS 9	Associates and joint ventures	6	**
FRS 10	Goodwill and intangible assets	4	**
FRS 11	Impairment of fixed assets and goodwill	4	**
FRS 12	Provisions, contingent liabilities and contingent assets	5	**
FRS 14	Earnings per share	9	**
FRS 15	Tangible fixed assets	4	**
FRS 16	Current taxation	5	**
FRS 17	Retirement benefits	5	*
FRS 18	Accounting policies	2	**

*   Students will be expected to have a working knowledge of the main content of these standards. Any examination of these standards will be limited to a layman's guide to the content and main coverage of the standard. Major questions will not applied to these standards and the examination of such standards will be limited to a short essay-type discussion forming part of a question and carrying no more than 4/5 marks.

**   These standards could form the basis of either quantitative or essay/note questions including the compulsory question in Section A of the examination paper. Students will be expected to have a detailed knowledge of the main principles of the standards, the reason for their introduction, the practical applications of the standards to the Profit and Loss Account, Balance Sheet, Cash Flow Statement and the effects of the standards on key financial ratios such as EPS, gearing, return on capital employed etc.

4.3 ACCOUNTING STANDARDS – A BOON OR CURSE?

The valuation of assets and liabilities reported in a company's published accounts is controlled, to a considerable extent, by accounting standards. By no means everyone is convinced of the usefulness of these Standards, or of their effectiveness, or that they should be given widespread application. It is therefore important for users of accounting information to be aware of the scope and limitations of standards so that they can make a rational assessment of the validity of the published accounts on which they are based.

4.3.1 Purposes of Accounting Standards

The main reason for setting up the Accounting Standards Committee and its successor, the ASB, was to reduce the wide variety of accounting practices employed by companies. It was believed that this 'plethora of principles' destroyed comparability between the accounts of one business and another. The functions of the ASB are to carry out a careful investigation of existing practices, to identify best practices, and to impose these on companies employing inferior procedures so as to improve their published reports. Naturally, it is sometimes difficult to obtain agreement about which is the best practice, and the solution is either to allow some flexibility or justify the favoured procedure with the argument that it is better to have second-rate figures prepared on a uniform basis than first-rate figures that are not comparable.

Standard practices also hold some appeal to the accountant who uses them as 'handy' rules to follow when preparing accounts. For example, he or she does not have to spend time considering how to report a non-recurring profit or loss, but can instead refer to FRS3 for instruction. The position of the accountant, as auditor, is helped when faced by an obdurate director wishing to adopt unconventional procedures to paint a picture of glowing success not justified on the basis of results actually achieved. In such circumstances the auditor can refer to accounting standards for authoritative support for more realistic procedures. Compliance with accounting standards has also been shown to be an effective defence for auditors faced with accusations of misconduct based on alleged failure to ensure that accounts show a true and fair view. A typical example is where a buyer believes he (or she) has paid too much for a company because he has relied on accounts which he considers misleading.

A final role for accounting standards is that they pave the way for new legislation. Standards may be issued and withdrawn more easily than a new Companies Act if it becomes clear that the provisions do not work well. It is therefore important that new regulations should be issued as Standards before they receive the full force of legislative support. This procedure has worked well; the Companies Act 1985 incorporated the main provisions of a number of standards, issued earlier, which had gained general acceptance.

4.3.2   Drawbacks of Accounting Standards

It is acknowledged that standards fulfil a valuable role in the short run, by ensuring that all companies adopt the best procedures currently used, but it is believed, in some quarters, that they may prove detrimental in the long run. Over the years considerable improvements have been made in the form and content of published accounts and much of this has occurred as the result of voluntary experiment and innovation. To place financial reporting procedures in a standardized straitjacket might therefore be to the longer-term detriment of users of financial statements. In a nutshell, a major potential hazard of Standards is that, although they may be intended as a floor, they end up as a ceiling.

A second problem is that, as industry itself is not standard, it seems unlikely that the figures they produce are amenable to a large degree of standardization. The tendency is therefore to enforce standards that are suitable for the average firm (the majority) but not for those on the margin. Related to this is the further problem that, in many areas, there is disagreement about which method should be used, e.g. whether to use average weighted cost or FIFO to value stock, or whether to use the deferral method or liability method to account for deferred taxation. The ASB should be careful not to attempt to stifle healthy controversy by choosing a particular method for widespread adoption unless it is sure that its decision will receive widespread support.

A further criticism of standards is that they surpress the need for accountants to exercise judgement which is a crucial feature of their status as professionals. Concern is expressed that the accountant will be relegated to the role of a mere technician who does no more than slot figures, calculated in accordance with accounting standards, into their appropriate location in the accounts. This seems to be an exaggerated view for, although numerous matters are standardized, there is still plenty of scope and need for the accountant to exercise professional judgement. Indeed, an important drawback of standardization is that it gives an illusion of complete precision and comparability which is totally unjustified in view of the wide range of subjective decisions that still have to be made.

A final criticism directed at the standard-setting process is that there are too many regulations. Forty-three standards have so far been issued (July 2001) and more are in the pipeline. One suggestion is that a 'plethora of principles' has been replaced by a 'surfeit of Standards'.

4.3.3 Scope of Accounting Standards

Limited companies range from the huge multinational to the local businessman who has registered his firm under the Companies Act for the sole purpose of obtaining a tax advantage, i.e. he is able to reinvest profits after paying corporation tax at 20% or so, rather than income tax at, perhaps, the top marginal rate of 40%. Clearly there are significant differences in the extent to which the outside world has a legitimate interest in the affairs of these two contrasting enterprises. The multinational may have thousands of shareholders, creditors and employees, and its activities may affect the lives of millions of individuals spread throughout the world. Whereas the small business may be entirely run by an owner/manager known personally by the limited range of individuals living in the locality who enter into transactions with his company.

The question arises whether it is appropriate to apply similar accounting standards to all these organizations. Most agree that a much heavier degree of accountability should be demanded from the multinational, and some would even argue that standards have no relevance whatsoever for the small company. In practice a surprisingly small amount of differentiation is made in the application of accounting standards to different sized businesses. Examples include FRS1, entitled 'Cash Flow Statements', which does not apply to 'small companies' as defined in the Companies Act, and FRS 14, entitled 'Earnings per Share', which applies only to listed companies. Because accounting standards are, by and large, for general application, there is probably too much regulation of the small company and, arguably, too little regulation of the large concern.

4.4 REMEASUREMENT OF ASSETS AND LIABILITIES

The broad content of the *Statement of Principles* was considered in Chapter 2. At this point, however, we need to consider more fully the messages contained in Chapter 6 of the Statement, namely 'Measurement in financial statements'. The content of Chapter 6 has proved highly controversial but is increasingly being given effect in FRSs issued by the ASB.

Chapter 6 begins by drawing attention to the fact that assets and liabilities may be reported in published accounts at either historical cost or current value. The basis for financial reports was traditionally historical cost and the accounts of most sole traders and partnerships and many limited companies continue to be prepared entirely on that basis. In recent decades, however, particularly when asset values have increased rapidly, we have seen a growing tendency for larger companies, including the majority of companies listed on the stock exchange, to revalue at least some of their assets on one or more occasions. This has resulted in accounts prepared on the basis of 'modified historical cost' or what the Statement calls the 'mixed measurement system'. The Statement 'envisages' that the mixed measurement system will be the basis for the standard setting process. The meaning of this assertion is not entirely transparent but presumably signifies the expectation that all entities subject to standard accounting practices will be required or permitted to adopt current values for the purpose of measuring at least some of their assets and liabilities. Where the Statement is rather more forthright is in ruling out the single restatement of any asset at current value which is then retained in the books indefinitely:

> *such measures will usually soon cease to be up-to-date current values and will then be neither a historical cost nor a current value. As such, they disturb the comparability and consistency of accounting measurement and are not consistent with the principles contained in the Statement.*

The Statement examines the main principles involved in measuring assets and liabilities on the basis of historical cost or current value, thereby providing guidance on these matters for the formulation of relevant FRSs (not all accounting standards are, of course, explicitly concerned with measurement issues, for example FRS 8 entitled 'Related party disclosures').

The selection by the ASB of historical cost or current value to report a particular asset or liability will depend on which approach best satisfies the qualitative characteristics of financial reports detailed in Chapter 3 of the Statement, principally: relevance, reliability, comparability and understandability (see Chapter 2.3.5 of this book).

Assets and liabilities will normally be initially recognized in the accounts at the value of the transaction at the time the asset is acquired or the liability is incurred. The reason for using the transaction value is that historical cost and current value (or the 'fair value' of the consideration paid or received as it is often described) are likely to coincide at that time. That is, the transaction will normally be undertaken at fair value and, subsequently, this is the amount referred to by the label historical cost.

The Statement requires subsequent remeasurement in the following circumstances:

• Where a company adopts historical cost to account for a particular asset, remeasurement will be necessary where recoverable amount (see below) is less than carrying value based on historical cost;

• Where a company adopts current value accounting for some or all of its assets, periodic remeasurement will be required in order to ensure that those assets are reported at the up-to-date current value.

Reflecting in particular the qualitative requirements of relevance and reliability, such remeasurements should only be made where:

• There is sufficient evidence that the monetary amount of the asset or liability has changed; and

• The new amount of the asset or liability can be measured with sufficient reliability.

The initial identification of historical cost is usually non-problematic, although the Statement goes to some length to draw attention to the fact that the common assumption that historical cost accounting measures 'involve little estimation' is invalid (para. 6.28). Indeed, the Statement continues, making allowances for bad and doubtful debts 'involves a degree of estimation that is not dissimilar to that involved in estimating current values not derived from an active market – and the results are often of broadly similar reliability'. The ASB is clearly keen to get over the message

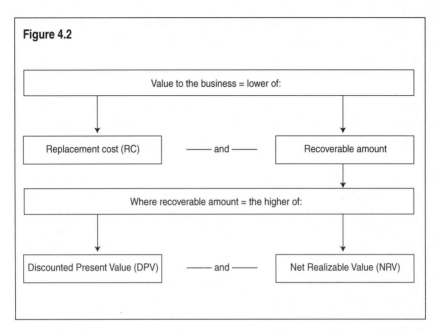

Figure 4.2

that companies need not, and should not, 'shy away' from current value accounting on the grounds that it presents insurmountable difficulties.

In a current value system of accounting, assets and liabilities are remeasured regularly so that changes in value are recorded as they occur, rather than simply when they are realised as is the case under historical cost accounting. The principles to be followed when remeasuring assets and liabilities are discussed below and illustrated by reference to the contents of Figure 4.2.

Where assets are to be remeasured at their current value, this is determined by identifying the asset's value to the business at the present point in time. Current value or 'value to the business' are synonymous labels and their amount may be determined in one of three ways:

• At entry value to the business – that is, the replacement cost (RC) at the present point in time

• At exit value to the business – that is, the net realizable value (NRV) if the item was sold

- At value in use – that is, the discounted present value (DPV) of the cash flows expected to arise from continued use and eventual sale by the present user

Where assets are to be accounted for at current value, remeasurement takes place 'to ensure that the assets or liabilities involved are measured at an up-to-date current value' (para 6.19). In such circumstances, the "value to the business" to be selected for remeasurement purposes is the maximum loss that a company would suffer if deprived of the asset. It is for this reason that the term "deprival value" is widely used to describe the relevant figure.

In the case of a going concern, assets will normally be in profitable use. The present value expected to arise from their continued use (DPV) is therefore likely to exceed replacement cost (RC). In such circumstances, the economically-rational business person, if deprived of the asset, would replace it in order to maximize the value of the business and, therefore, the shareholders' wealth. In the majority of circumstances, therefore, the appropriate deprival value of an asset will be RC.

If, however, the company is unable to replace the asset, or if RC exceeds the recoverable amount, the asset's deprival value will be its recoverable amount. The appropriate recoverable amount will then be the higher of discounted present value (DPV) and net realizable value (NRV) because:

- Where discounted present value exceeds net realizable value, the economically-rational businessperson will choose to retain and use the asset in order to generate the expected future cash flows;

- Where net realizable value exceeds discounted present value, the economically rational business person will immediately dispose of the asset.

Example 4.1

The following information is provided in relation to four assets owned by a business:

Asset	I	II	III	IV
	£	£	£	£
Discounted present value	200	50	200	150
Replacement cost	100	100	300	300
Net realizable value	50	200	150	200

Required:
For each asset, identify the relevant 'value to the business', or 'deprival value', and indicate the action that should be taken.

Solution

Asset	I	II	III	IV
	£	£	£	£
Replacement cost	100	100	300	300
Recoverable amount: higher of DPV and NRV	200	200	200	200
Value to the business:				
Lower of replacement cost and recoverable amount	100	100	200	200
Action to be taken	Use	Sell	Use	Sell

If the company was deprived of the asset, it would be worthwhile replacing only asset I and asset II.

In two important respects (Problem areas I and II), the Statement remains a little vague about the precise significance of the ideas it puts forward. However, the focus is intended to be on 'principles' and it is the precise content of the various standards (particularly FRS's 10, 11 and 15) that needs to be examined in order to discover how the ideas have been and will be given practical effect.

Problem area I The measurement procedures to be adopted when assets are recorded at current value, as summarized above, are reasonably clearly expressed in the Statement. The relationship between these procedures and the remeasurement procedures to be adopted where the company's policy is to use pure historical cost accounting, however, is left to implication. The Statement does tell us that assets

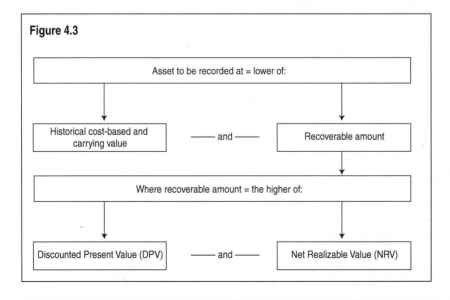

Figure 4.3

accounted for on the historical cost basis will need to be remeasured (the circumstances in which remeasurement might be necessary are set out in section 4.10 of this chapter) to ensure that they are 'not reported at amounts greater than their recoverable amounts' (para. 6.18). The relevant comparison, confirmed by FRS 11, is therefore between the asset's historical cost-based carrying value and its recoverable amount as set out in Figure 4.3.

If we rework the numbers in example 4.1 on the assumption that the figures for 'replacement cost' are instead historical cost-based carrying values of the same amounts, the actions to be taken are as follows:

Asset	I	II	III	IV
	£	£	£	£
Carrying value	100	100	300	300
Recoverable amount: higher of DPV and NRV	200	200	200	200
Value to the business:				
Lower of carrying value and recoverable amount	100	100	200	200
Action to be taken	Continue to use	Sell	Write down to 200 and continue to use	Write down to 200 and sell

Problem area II. The Statement sometimes switches between references to assets and liabilities to references only to assets. The specific references made to liabilities in the Statement are also not entirely helpful.

Paragraph 6.1 states that liabilities could be stated at:

- historical cost; or

- the cost of discharging the liability by the most economical means available; or

- in some cases (e.g. loans), the amount the entity could currently raise by issuing a similar debt security.

Within the nomenclature used in Figures 4.2 and 4.3, we might conclude:

1. Historical cost is the carrying value of the liability

2. The cost of discharging the liability by its most economical means is the liabilities' equivalent of net realizable value

3. The amount which the entity could currently raise by issuing a similar debt security is its replacement cost.

One might therefore reasonably assume that, where appropriate, the historical cost-based carrying value (1 above) should be revised downwards to net realizable value (2 above) or replacement cost (3 above), whichever is the lower.

Paragraph 6.32 of the Statement merely states that a liability should be carried at historical cost (1 above) or the lowest amount at which it could be settled (2 above). Perhaps the explanation for the slight inconsistency with paragraph 6.1 is that those responsible for drafting the Statement had here left aside the special case where the liability is in the form of a debt security.

Note: In the case of asset and liability measurements and remeasurements based on future cash flows, the relevant cash flows should be adjusted by a discount rate to take account of the time value of money and the associated risk.

4.4.1 Continuing Controversy

The *Statement of Principles* project generally and the valuation proposals in particular saw a period of gestation that lasted throughout most of the 1990s. A strong and persistent campaign against its contents was waged by the accountants Ernst & Young, mainly through the arguments presented by the authors of their highly acclaimed publication UK GAAP. Referring to the unsuccessful experiment with CCA discussed in Chapter 2 of this book, Mike Davies, Ron Patterson and Allister Wilson urged UK businesses to take action against the Statement before 'some version of current cost accounting is with us once again'. In a possible reference to the academic background of the ASB chairman, Sir David Tweedie (a former professor of accounting), Ernst & Young stated: 'We do not believe that the ASB should use British industry as a test-bed for academic theories on accounting, and we question whether it has a mandate to do so'. The ASB received a record 175 responses to the issue of the first draft of the Statement published in 1995. UK GAAP put this down to the fact that 'the Draft sought to alter the most fundamental of accounting methods and reporting practices' (1999, p. 125). Ernst & Young, in common with others, thus favoured retention of principally historical cost-based financial reporting on grounds that include objectivity, verifiability, comprehensibility and cost.

It was perhaps a response to the concerns expressed by business that the final version of the Statement toned down some of the early enthusiasm shown for current values.

'Measurement in financial statements' (Chapter 6) was published initially, in 1993, as a discussion paper entitled *The Role of Valuation in Financial Reporting*. This was much more forceful in its advocacy of current values, and justified its recommendation for their more widespread adoption on the following grounds that remain, in the present authors' views, entirely valid.

- Current value is relevant to users for the purpose of assessing the current state or recent performance of their business.

- Under current value, changes in shareholder wealth are recognized and recorded as they occur rather than only when they are realized which, in many cases, involves significant delay.

- Under current value, a distinction is made between holding gains (gains arising from holding assets during a period of rising prices) and current operating profit, thereby enabling users to select the particular information that they regard as relevant for their decisions.

The first full version of the Statement (issued 1995) continued to promote actively a measurement system based on current values as superior to historical cost and concluded: 'practice should develop by evolving in the direction of greater use of current values to the extent that this is consistent with the constraints of reliability and cost' (para. 5.38).

Although the final version of the Statement proved to be rather less forthright, we have seen that significant steps have been taken to implement requirements for the use of the concept of deprival value when measuring assets and liabilities for inclusion in the published accounts of UK companies. This is acknowledged by UK GAAP in the following words, which also address the ASB's insistence, in response to criticism, that the introduction of a system of current cost accounting has never been on its agenda:

*Since current cost accounting is merely historical cost accounting updated to current prices, there is no question of the ASB going down that road. What is not in doubt, however, is the fact that the ASB is clearly advancing rapidly down the road of current **value** accounting, as evidenced by its penchant for fair values and the notion of value in use. (1999, p. 135)*

The remainder of this chapter, together with Chapter 5:

- Explains how assets should be computed for inclusion in company published accounts in order to comply with standard accounting practice;

- Identifies a number of problems involved in the valuation of assets and liabilities;

- Shows how the regulators have attempted to reduce the scope for subjective judgement and the variety of accounting practices available for the valuation of assets and liabilities; and

- Draws attention to a number of unresolved issues.

4.5 TANGIBLE FIXED ASSETS

The method of accounting for tangible fixed assets is the subject of FRS 15. Table 4.2 summarizes the main issues and requirements and identifies the section of this chapter in which each matter is examined in greater depth.

Table 4.2: Main issues addressed by FRS 15

Issue	Main requirements	Section
Initial measurement	Record at cost	4.5.1
Capitalization of finance costs	Capitalize or write off immediately	4.5.1
Subsequent expenditure on fixed assets	Write off immediately (three exceptions)	4.5.1
Revaluation	Optional	4.5.2
Depreciation	Required, except for land or where immaterial	4.5.3
Remeasurement at recoverable amount	Obligatory	4.5.3
Gains and losses on disposal	Various	4.5.4

4.5.1 Initial Measurement

Tangible fixed assets are defined by FRS 15 as 'Assets that have physical substance and are held for use in the production or supply of goods or services, for rental to others, or for administrative purposes on a continuing basis in the reporting entity's activities.' (para. 2) The formats for financial reporting laid down by the Companies

Acts expect tangible fixed assets to be classified under the following headings:

- Land and Buildings

- Plant and Machinery

- Fixtures, fittings, tools and equipment.

Consistent with the provisions of the *Statement of Principles*, tangible fixed assets are initially measured and recorded at their transaction cost at the date of acquisition – that is, purchase price. Companies normally acquire tangible fixed assets from third parties but, sometimes, an entity constructs the fixed asset itself. In such circumstances, the initial measurement should include 'any costs directly attributable to bringing it into working condition for its intended use' (para. 8). This would justify the inclusion of direct materials, direct labour and any overheads related to the construction process – general overheads, however, should be excluded.

In some cases, companies finance construction through borrowing and the question then arises whether the cost of servicing the borrowing in the form of interest charges should or should not be capitalized. The effect of the alternative treatments is illustrated in example 4.2.

Example 4.2

Saux Ltd constructed an item of machinery with an expected five year life. The cost, including materials, labour and identifiable overheads, amounted to £10 million and was incurred over a two-year period ended 31 December 20X5. The company borrowed £2 million at 10% over the two-year period to finance the construction. The company makes up its accounts on the calendar year basis.

Required:
(a) Show the figure at which the machine would be reported in a balance sheet prepared at 31 December 20X5 on the separate assumptions that the company (i) expenses and (ii) capitalizes the interest cost.

(b) Discuss the effect on reported profit of each of the two methods used under (a) to account for construction finance costs.

Solution

(a)

Balance sheet entry for machine at 31 Dec. 20X5	(i) £ million	(ii) £ million
Materials, labour and overheads	10.0	10.0
Finance cost during construction	—	0.4
Transaction cost	10.0	10.4

(b) Under assumption (i), interest of £200,000 per annum is charged against profit in each of the years 20X4 and 20X5. The result is that the profits for each of those two years is correspondingly lower than under assumption (ii). If, however, the capitalization route is followed, there will be an additional depreciation charge of £400,000 over the 5-year period of ownership and use 20X6-20X-10.

Prior to the issue of FRS 15, directors were free to choose whichever option best suited their company's financial reporting objectives. Thus, if the directors of Saux Ltd wished to maximize reported profit for 20X4 and 20X5, they would naturally choose to capitalize finance costs incurred during the construction period. FRS 15 allows this freedom of choice to continue and the opportunity to standardize financial reporting practice in this area has been missed. The application of the accruals concept would seem to require the capitalization of finance costs but the introduction of such a requirement was seen to raise a bigger problem than the one that it resolved. The fact is that some companies raise loan finance to fund construction; others issue share capital or choose to finance the work out of internally generated resources. Companies relying on their own resources might then reasonably argue that a notional interest charge should be included as part of the cost of construction. This would raise at least two problems:

- What should the rate of interest be?

- Where should the corresponding credit entry be recorded? If in the profit and loss account, a company might choose to undertake construction of a substantial asset at least partly because it would help to boost reported profit in the short term.

The ASB therefore decided to leave this 'contentious issue' to the International Accounting Standards Board. FRS 15 does, however, tighten up accounting practice in one important respect. That is, capitalization of finance charges must cease on physical completion of the asset. Previously, property investment companies frequently continued to capitalize interest well beyond that date, often until the property was substantially let and income-producing.

Moving on in time, a company, having purchased or constructed a tangible fixed asset, is likely to incur 'subsequent expenditure' on the asset. The question that must then be addressed is whether such expenditure should be capitalized, and added to the recorded value of the fixed asset, or written off against profit. FRS 15 has decided that all subsequent expenditure should be written off except where one of the following three tests is satisfied:

1   Where the subsequent expenditure provides an enhancement of the economic benefits of the tangible fixed asset in excess of the previously assessed standard of performance. In other words, the normal capital-revenue test applies. If the expenditure looks like repairs or maintenance, it should be written off; if it improves the asset compared with its initial service potential, it should be capitalized.

2   Where a component of the tangible fixed asset, that has been treated separately for depreciation purposes and depreciated over its individual useful life, is replaced or restored.

3   Where the subsequent expenditure relates to a major inspection or overhaul of a tangible fixed asset that restores the economic benefits of the asset that have been consumed by the entity and have already been reflected in depreciation.

In other words, (2) and (3) allows the capitalization of expenditure which replaces or restores to its original condition an asset or component of a fixed asset which has been fully written off.

4.5.2 Revaluation

It has always been permissible for British companies to revalue their fixed assets; indeed, restatement at current valuation is specifically envisaged by the 'alternative accounting rules' contained in the Companies Act 1985. It is perfectly permissible (and common practice), however, for companies to retain a fixed asset in the books at its historical cost. This is despite the fact that historical cost may no longer bear any relationship whatsoever to the asset's current worth and, in such circumstances, is of no relevance whatsoever for the purpose of assessing, for example, the asset-backing for a secured loan.

Company directors are therefore in the position that they can choose whether or not to revalue fixed assets and have usually done so only when it matched corporate objectives. The majority of companies, particularly listed companies, have at some time in the past revalued some of their fixed assets. Indeed, FRS 15 reports the fact that 65% of companies included in the 1997 company reporting database had carried out revaluations. However, for half of these companies, the valuations had been made at least 5 years earlier and, in the majority of cases, only certain fixed assets had been restated at current value. Thus, it can be seen that there has been, over the years, considerable inconsistency in revaluation practices and this inconsistency was, to some extent, addressed by the issue of FRS 15.

Hannah King, Project Director of the ASB, summarized the purpose and content of FRS 15 as follows:

> *Cherry-picking is to be outlawed ... Until now, companies could freely pick and choose which of their assets they wish to revalue and when. This has allowed companies to flatter their balance sheet figures through the inclusion of meaningless out-of-date valuations, thereby hindering comparability between companies from year to year. FRS 15 puts a stop to this. (Accountancy, March 1999, p. 94)*

FRS 15 allows but does not require companies to revalue fixed assets so, in a substantial sense, inconsistency will continue. What FRS 15 does try to do is to introduce more consistency in the practices followed by companies who do decide to re-measure their assets at current value.

Companies opting for a policy of revaluation must revalue whole classes of tangible assets and not 'cherry-pick' those that suit management purposes. If, for example, management wished to bolster a company's apparent financial strength, it might wish to revalue only those properties that have gone up in value.

As indicated in section 4.5.1 of this chapter, there are three classes of tangible fixed assets recognized for financial reporting purposes. Companies may base their revaluations on these but 'may, within reason, adopt...narrower classes' (para. 62). An example of a narrower class would be a sub-set of land and buildings, such as freehold property, but the rather vague wording employed will undoubtedly open up other possibilities.

Where a company chooses to make revaluations, a full valuation must be performed at least every 5 years. There must also be an interim valuation (where the qualification requirements are less onerous) and further revaluations where there is 'a material change in value'.

The revaluation must be undertaken by a qualified valuer who may be internal or external to the firm. Where the valuation is undertaken internally, the work must be reviewed by a qualified external valuer. The one exception to these requirements is that, where there exists an active second-hand market or suitable indices so that a reliable figure can be obtained with reasonable certainty, the revaluations can be made by the directors. One example of a healthy second-market for fixed assets would be the case of car fleets.

Much of the specialist valuation information used to inform the content of FRS 15 was prepared by the Royal Institute of Chartered Surveyors whose report is reproduced as an appendix to the standard. The linkage between material contained in the appendix, the content of the standard itself, and the relationship with the valuation framework contained in the *Statement of Principles* is not always clear-cut, but the following seems to be broadly the situation.

The principal, but not only, focus of FRS 15 is the valuation of land and buildings and attention is drawn to the fact that other properties are rarely revalued. Land and buildings are divided into three categories:

1. Non-specialized properties. Examples are residential properties, shops, offices, standard industrial and warehouse buildings, public houses and petrol filling stations. These should be valued on the basis of existing use value (EUV), with the addition of notional directly attributable acquisition costs where material. The concept behind EUV is that of net current replacement cost, i.e. 'the cost of purchasing, at the least cost, the remaining service potential of the asset at the balance sheet date'. The requirement to use EUV therefore basically results in the application of the replacement cost valuation method which, within the context of the *Statement of Principles*, would be the appropriate method to use on the assumption that the assets are being profitably employed and recoverable amount is greater than EUV.

2. Specialized properties. These are properties which, 'due to their specialized nature, are rarely, if ever, sold on the open market for single occupation for continuation of their existing use, except as part of a sale of the business in occupation'. Examples are oil refineries, chemical works, power stations, dock installations, schools, colleges, universities, hospitals, museums, and libraries. Such properties should be valued on the basis of depreciated replacement cost, defined as:

The aggregate amount of the value of the land for the existing use or a notional replacement site in the same locality, and the gross replacement cost of the buildings and other site works, from which appropriate deductions may then be made to allow for the age, condition, economic or functional obsolescence and environmental factors etc.; all of these might result in the existing property being worth less to the undertaking in occupation than would a new replacement.

3. Properties surplus to an entity's requirements. In this case there would be no expectation to replace, neither is there a 'value in use' (DPV). Therefore, open market value (OMV) less attributable selling costs is equivalent to net realizable value within the *Statement of Principles* valuation framework, and would be the appropriate figure to use.

Having obtained an appropriate valuation for the type of property under consideration, this amount must then be compared with carrying value (whether based on historical cost or current value) to discover whether there is a revaluation gain or loss.

Where the comparison shows a gain, it must be credited to revaluation reserve and reported in the STRGL. The exception to this general rule arises where a revaluation gain reverses an earlier revaluation loss that has been recognised and charged to the profit and loss account. In these circumstances, the amount of the gain, up to but not exceeding the amount of depreciation charged to the profit and loss account at the time of the earlier downward revaluation after adjusting for any subsequent reduction in the depreciation charge resulting from that revaluation, may be credited back to the profit and loss account (see Example 4.4).

Where the comparison shows a deficit, its treatment in the accounts depends on the circumstances causing it to occur:

• Revaluation losses that 'are caused by a clear consumption of economic benefits should be recognized in the profit and loss account' (para. 65). Losses falling under this heading are those which might be regarded as akin to depreciation such as its physical deterioration or obsolescence.

• All other losses should usually be reported in the STRGL. However, where the asset has been previously revalued and the present revaluation requires a write-down to below the figure for depreciated historical cost (had the asset never been revalued), that part of the revaluation loss must be charged against profit.

Example 4.3

The following information is provided in relation to five assets owned by a business:

Asset	I	II	III	IV	V
Carrying value at 31 December 20X0	£	£	£	£	£
Depreciated historical cost	200	200			
Depreciated replacement cost			300	300	300
Memorandum record of depreciated					
historical cost at 31 December 20X0			200	200	200
Revaluation at 31 December 20X0	150	150	250	250	150

You discover that:
- Assets I and III need to be restated at recoverable amount due to reductions in their estimated service potential.
- Assets II, IV and V need to be restated at recoverable amount due to a general fall in the values of these kinds of assets.

Required:
(a) For each asset, identify the amount to be written off and indicate where it should be recorded in the accounts for the year ended 31 December 20X0.

(b) Explain your treatment of each asset

Solution

(a) Asset	I	II	III	IV	V
	£	£	£	£	£
Carrying value	200	200	300	300	300
Revaluation	150	150	250	250	150
Write off	50	50	50	50	150
Profit and loss account	50		50		50
STRGL		50		50	100

(b) For Assets I and III, the fall in value below carrying value of 50 is due to circumstances akin to depreciation and should be written off in the profit and loss account.

Assets II and IV have fallen in value due to a decline in the general value of these kinds of assets and the difference between carrying value, whether depreciated historical cost or depreciated replacement cost, must be written off to STRGL.

In the case of Asset V, the decline is due to a general fall in the value of the asset and, prima facie, should be written off against STRGL. However, the extent to which the write-down is to a figure below the carrying value, had it never been revalued (that is, depreciated historical cost), must be written off to the profit and loss account.

There is one further possibility to consider. Assume that the revalued figure for Asset I is the replacement cost and the recoverable amount (whether the value in use or net realizable value) is 170, then 20 of the deficit would be recorded in STRGL and only the remaining 30 would need to be written off against profit and loss account.

Example 4.4 provides the opportunity to further test your understanding of aspects of the material covered in this section.

Example 4.4

Mans Ltd purchased a property on 1 January 20X0 for £6 million. Annual depreciation of £150,000 was charged from 20X0 to 20X5 inclusive and on 1 January 20X6 the carrying value of the property was £5.1 million. The property was revalued at £4.5 million on 1 January 20X6 and a loss of £600,000 recognized in the profit and loss account. Following the revaluation the annual depreciation was reassessed at £126,000 and this amount was charged from 20X6 to 20X9 inclusive. On 1 January 20X-10, when the carrying value of the property was £3,996,000 the property was revalued again and the revalued amount was £5,400,000.

Required:
Calculate and explain the treatment of the revaluation surplus.

Solution

The revaluation surplus is £1,404,000 (£5,400,000 – £3,996,000). This is allocated between the profit and loss account and revaluation reserve as follows:

- £504,000 (£600,000 – [4 x (£ 150,000 – £126,00]) is credited to the profit and loss account.*

- £900,000 (the balance) is credited to a revaluation reserve.

* The amount of depreciation charged to the profit and loss account at the time of the earlier downward revaluation, adjusted for the subsequent reduction in the depreciation charge resulting from that revaluation, is credited back to the profit and loss account.

It is worth noting that, had the 20X6 valuation not taken place, the carrying value of the property at 1 January 20X-10 would have been £4.5 million (£6 million – [10 x £150,000]). Revaluing the property to the 20X-10 amount would therefore have generated a surplus of £900,000.

4.5.3 Depreciation

Depreciation can be defined as the decline in the value of a fixed asset to a company; it is normally caused by a combination of usage, the passage of time and obsolescence. There are two reasons for charging depreciation in the accounts:

- To ensure that the revenue recognized during a particular accounting period bears the full cost of resources used up during the same time period. If depreciation were omitted, profit would be overstated and wrong assessments might be made of a company's performance.

- To maintain intact the company's capital base by earmarking, for retention within the business over a fixed asset's useful life, a quantity of resources equal to its original cost. It is quite usual for these resources to be immediately reinvested in operating assets and so they will not be available, in the form of cash, to finance replacement when the asset wears out. In these circumstances, it is management's job to arrange an alternative source of finance when the need arises (this matter is discussed further in Chapter 10.7.1).

To compute the annual depreciation charge, the disposal value and expected useful life of the fixed asset must first be estimated. The difference between the cost and the estimated disposal value of the asset, called the depreciable amount, gives the balance to be written off, while the estimated life of the asset determines the period over which the write-off is to take place. It is important that estimates of both the asset's disposal value and useful life are accurate, since errors will result in too high or too low a depreciation charge, and the consequent under- or overstatement of reported profit.

Where the high disposal value was not anticipated at the outset, excessive charges will have been made in the accounts, and profit will have been understated. Turning to estimates of an asset's useful life, an overoptimistic assessment, not compensated for by an unexpected rise in the disposal value, results in the overstatement of profit during the asset's life, while reported profits are unduly depressed in the year that the item is sold and the balance remaining is written off.

Example 4.5

Tintern Ltd was incorporated on 1 January 19X1 and purchased a single fixed asset for £120,000. It was estimated that the fixed asset would last six years and then possess a negligible disposal value. It was decided to depreciate the asset on the straight-line basis, and this resulted in an annual charge of £120,000 ÷ 6 = £20,000. Trading activity was at a steady level and the annual profits before depreciation, for the first four years, were £50,000. At the end of 19X4 it was discovered that the fixed asset was worn out and in need of replacement.

Required:
Calculate reported profit for each of the years, 19X1-X4, and comment on the results.

Solution

Year	Profit before depreciation	Depreciation	Reported profit
19X1	50,000	20,000	30,000
19X2	50,000	20,000	30,000
19X3	50,000	20,000	30,000
19X4	50,000	60,000 (WI)	(10,000)

WI This comprises two elements: the annual depreciation charge of £20,000; plus the loss on disposal of £40,000, being the balance remaining in the books at the end of 19X4 when the asset was scrapped. This is a material revision of an incorrect estimate and should be separately disclosed in the accounts as an exceptional item.

We are told that the annual level of trading activity was steady, and this is borne out by the fact that profit before depreciation was £50,000 in each of the years 19X1-19X4. If the fixed asset's useful life had been accurately forecast, the annual depreciation charge would have been £120,000 ÷ 4 = £30,000, and reported profit, after charging depreciation, would also have been steady at £20,000 per annum. The effect of the forecasting error was to overstate reported profit in each of the first three years by £10,000, and to understate profit by £30,000 in 19X4. The result was that published profit figures were an unreliable measure of Tintern's trading performance, and users of the company's accounts are likely to have been misled.

The straight-line method of depreciation is used in Example 4.5, but readers will be aware of the fact that there exist many other methods which can be used to spread the depreciable amount (original cost minus scrap value) over the asset's estimated useful life. The main alternatives are the reducing-balance basis, the sum of the digits method, the usage basis and the annuity method.

Whichever method is used, the total amount written off is the same, but the distribution of the depreciable balance over the asset's life varies a great deal. The straight-line basis results in an equal annual charge, the reducing-balance basis and sum of the digits method each produce relatively high charges in the early years of an asset's life and relatively low charges in later years, the usage method results in a variable charge depending on the level of production, while the annuity method produces a charge that increases over the asset's life. It is management's job to make a fair allocation of the depreciable amount between accounting periods expected to benefit from using the fixed asset, and they should select the method which is most appropriate bearing in mind the type of asset and the way it is used in the business. The choice of method is important because it will affect the level of reported profit.

Example 4.6

Larchmont Ltd was established on 1 January 19X3 to manufacture a single product using a machine which cost £400,000. The machine is expected to last four years and then have a scrap value of £52,000. The machine will produce a similar number of goods each year and annual profits before depreciation are expected to be in the region of £200,000. The financial controller has suggested that the machine should be depreciated using either the straight-line method or the reducing-balance method. If the latter method is used, it has been estimated that an annual depreciation rate of 40% would be appropriate.

Required:
(a) Calculations of the annual depreciation charges and the net book values of the fixed asset at the end of 19X3, 19X4, 19X5 and 19X6 using:
   (i)   the straight-line method;
   (ii) the reducing-balance method.

(b) A discussion of the differing implications of these two methods for the financial information published by Larchmont Ltd for the years 19X3-19X6 inclusive. You should also advise management which method you consider more appropriate bearing in mind expected profit levels.

Note: Ignore taxation

Solution

(a)

	Straight-line method		Reducing-balance method	
	Depreciation	*Net book*	*Depreciation*	*Net book*
Year	*charge*	*value*	*charge*	*value*
19X3	87,000	313,000	160,000	240,000
19X4	87,000	226,000	96,000	144,000
19X5	87,000	139,000	57,600	86,400
19X6	87,000	52,000	34,560	51,840
	348,000		348,160	

(b) The discussion should cover the following main points:

The reducing-balance method, using a 40% rate of write-off, produces a marginally higher total depreciation charge and a marginally lower net book value at the end of 19X6, but the differences are not material. Both methods succeed in reducing the book value of the machine to its expected scrap value by the end of four years.

The allocation of the total depreciation charge between the four years differs significantly under the two methods. In 19X3 the reducing-balance method produces a charge which is £73,000 higher than under the straight-line method; the situation is substantially reversed in 19X6 when the reducing-balance charge is £52,440 lower.

The effect of the different rates of asset write-off has significant implications for the level of reported profits and the balance sheet figures for capital employed. If the straight-line basis is used, reported profit is expected to be stable at £113,000 (£200,000-£87,000), while the reducing-balance basis will result in a reported profit of £40,000 in 19X3, increasing to £165,440 in 19X6. In the balance sheet, the book value of fixed assets will initially decline much more quickly under the reducing-balance method.

The level of activity is expected to remain unchanged over the four years and so the straight-line basis, which produces an equal annual charge, is preferred.

FRS15 contains the following requirements relating to fixed assets and depreciation:

- Companies must depreciate all fixed assets, other than freehold land, over their expected useful life (see Example 4.7). There are two exceptions to this rule:

  1. Investment properties need not be depreciated (see section 4.7 below).

  2. Freehold land should be depreciated where it is acquired for extractive purposes, for example in the case of a quarry where useful economic life expires with the extraction of the contents.

- Where fixed assets are revalued, depreciation must be provided on the revalued figure (see Example 4.7).

- If it becomes apparent that the remaining book value will not be recovered in full out of future profits, the asset should be immediately written down to the estimated recoverable amount which should then be written off over the asset's remaining useful life (see Example 4.8).

FRS 15 contains the following additional requirements:

- Where there is a revision of an asset's estimated useful life, the remaining balance should be written off over the revised period (see Example 4.8).

- When a new depreciation method is adopted, with the objective of providing users with a fairer presentation of the financial results and position of the company, the remaining book value must be written off over the asset's remaining useful life on the new basis.

  For example, using the reducing-balance basis, an item of plant may have been written down to £30,000 by the end of 19X1. In 19X2, management may decide to change to the straight-line basis in order to give a fairer presentation of the results and financial position of the company. Assuming a remaining useful life of 4 years and a disposal value of £2,000, at the end of that period, the annual charge will be (£30,000-£2,000) ÷ 4 = £7,000. The effect of the change must be disclosed, if material.

- The accounts should disclose, for each category of fixed asset, the depreciation methods used and the useful life or depreciation rates used.

Example 4.7

Gibside Ltd purchased a freehold property for £600,000, including land, £100,000, on 1 January 19X1. On 1 January 19X6 the property was revalued by R. Jones & Co., Chartered Surveyors, at £2,000,000, including a figure of £400,000 for land. It is the company's policy to depreciate its buildings on the straight-line basis over 25 years. No adjustment to the expected life of the asset was required when the revaluation took place.

Required:
(a) Calculations of the depreciation charge for each of the years 19X1-19X6.

(b) The balance sheet figures for freehold property at 31 December 19X5 and 19X6. and the transfer to revaluation reserve arising from the revaluation on 1 January 19X6.

Solution

(a) Depreciation charge:
19X1-19X5: 4% of £500,000 (£600,000 – £100,000) = £20,000
19X6: 5%* of £1,600,000 (£2,000,000 – £400,000) = £80,000
*20 years life remains.

(b) Balance sheet figures, freehold property:

19X5: Cost	600,000
Less: Accumulated depreciation (5 x £20,000)	100,000
	500,000
19X6: As revalued by R. Jones & Co., Chartered Surveyors	2,000,000
Less: Accumulated depreciation	80,000
	1,920,000
Transfer to revaluation reserve:	
Freehold property revaluation on 1 January 19X6	2,000,000
Less: Book value of property at 1 January 19X6	500,000
	1,500,000

Example 4.8

Kinross Ltd, which makes up its accounts on a calendar year basis, purchased plant for £200,000 on 1 January 19X1, to manufacture goods for export. Management decided to write off the plant on the straight-line basis over 10 years, assuming a nil residual value. In December 19X4 there was a change of government in the main country to which goods were exported, and all imports were banned with immediate effect. The directors of Kinross have estimated that plant utilization will decline to 30% of its previous level. As a result, the plant is worth only £50,000 on 31 December 19X4 and this amount is to be written off by 31 December 19X6 when production will cease.

Required:
(a) Calculations of the amount of depreciation written off against profit for each of the years 19X1-19X6, based on the above information.

(b) The balance sheet figures for plant at 31 December 19X4.

Solution

(a) Depreciation charge: £
19Xl-19X4: 10% of £200,000   <u>20,000</u>

	£
19X4: Additional write off computed as follows:	
Book value of plant: Cost	200,000
Less: Accumulated depreciation	<u>80,000</u>
	120,000
Revised figure	<u>50,000</u>
	70,000
19X5-19X6: 50,000 ÷ 2	<u>25,000</u>

(b) Balance sheet extract, 31 December 19X4   £
Plant and machinery at cost   200,000
Less: Accumulated depreciation   <u>150,000</u> (WI)
     <u>50,000</u>

WI(4 x £20,000) + £70,000

An important objective of FRS 15 is to ensure that, specified exceptions aside, companies depreciate their fixed assets whether or not revaluation has taken place. There had been a tendency for the directors of some companies to engage in opportunistic behaviour in order to maximize the financial appearance of their company as reported in the profit and loss account and balance sheet. The upward revaluation of properties was favoured in order to improve the apparent financial strength of the company, asset-backing for loans and the gearing ratio. At the same time and in a variety of different ways, efforts were sometimes made to avoid the related increase in the depreciation charge that would diminish reported profit. As Hannah King pointed out, it had

> *become the norm in particular industries not to depreciate certain properties. As well as the hotel and brewing sector, examples can be found in the accounts of some retailers and retail banks. It is argued that because the properties are continually maintained and refurbished to a high standard, their useful economic lives are extended almost indefinitely, or the residual values of the assets at the end of their useful economic lives to the entity are not materially less than the carrying amount, so that no depreciation is necessary.*

The standard rejects these arguments on the grounds that it will eventually become uneconomic to maintain and restore buildings and that they will then only have a scrap value. However, FRS 15 does permit the non-depreciation of tangible fixed assets where one of the following two conditions are met.

1. The charge would be immaterial either because of the length of the estimated remaining useful life or because the estimated residual value of the tangible fixed asset is not materially different from the present carrying value.

2. The estimated remaining economic life of the tangible fixed asset exceeds 50 years.

There is a significant 'sting in the tail', however, namely the requirement for annual impairment reviews (see section 4.10, below).

It has been suggested – for example by Ron Paterson – that by requiring depreciation of revalued assets to be based on the revalued amount FRS 15 may be 'inadvertently regulating its preferred practice out of existence' (*Accountancy*, July 1999, p. 84). The reason for reaching this conclusion is that, in Paterson's view, many of the companies 'who have most enthusiastically valued their assets in the past tended to be those who did not depreciate them'. This is probably a touch pessimistic but there are companies that behave in the way Paterson predicts. The pub group, Regent Inns, for example, decided not to continue with a policy of annual valuation of its trading assets in the accounts for the year ended 3 July 1999. As a result, properties were included at their historical cost of £77 million compared with the directors' valuation of £110 million, and the consequential reduction in the depreciation charge boosted profits by £260,000. At the same time, the greater insistence of FRS 15 on charging depreciation is having its effect. For example, Pizza Express changed its accounting policy for the year ended 30 June 1999 in order to amortize the cost of freehold and long leasehold properties over the lesser of 50 years or the outstanding term of the lease. Group operating profit was reduced by £50,000 as the result of the policy change (*Accountancy*, November 1999, p. 96).

4.5.4 Gains and Losses on Disposal

Where a company has previously revalued its fixed assets, an important question is how any profit (or loss) on ultimate disposal should be reported in the accounts. For example, assume a company purchases a fixed asset for £100 in year 1, revalues the asset to £136 in year 2 (with the surplus of £36 credited to revaluation reserve), and sells the asset for £150 in year 3. Ignoring depreciation, the following are possible calculations of the profit arising on disposal:

(1) Profit £14. This is the difference between book value and selling price. The previous upward revaluation of £36 remains to the credit of revaluation reserve.

(2) Profit £50. This is the difference between original cost and selling price and is arrived at by adding back the revaluation surplus (£36) to the profit actually arising on disposal (£14).

FRS3 makes it clear that the calculation should be based on the difference between sales proceeds and carrying value, i.e. method (1). The outcome is that companies that revalue fixed assets will, over time, report lower profits than those who adhere strictly to the historical cost concept. To improve comparability, where there is a material difference between stated profits and those that result from the strict application of the historical cost concept, FRS3 requires a note to be added to the accounts which adjusts the profit figure to remove the effects of any revaluations.

4.6 GOVERNMENT GRANTS
Their treatment is the subject of SSAP 4 entitled 'Accounting for government grants'. Such grants are made in order to persuade or assist enterprises in pursuing courses of action which are deemed to be socially or economically desirable. The range of grants is very wide and includes financial encouragement for firms to move to areas that are relatively deprived economically. Grants may be treated as falling into either of two categories for accounting purposes:

Revenue grants These are grants made to give immediate financial support or assistance to an enterprise, to reimburse costs previously incurred to finance the general activities of an enterprise, or to compensate for a loss of current or future income. An example of a revenue grant would be one made to offset part or the whole cost of a company's training programme.

Capital grants These are specific contributions towards expenditure on fixed assets.

Grants, whether capital or revenue, must be accounted for in accordance with the accruals concept. In other words, the grant should be offset against the costs that it is intended to defray in the period that such costs are recognized in the profit and loss account. In the case of compensation for losses, the grants should be recognized to offset the losses as and when they are incurred.

There are two permissible methods available for matching capital grants with the related expenditure on fixed assets, each of which complies fully with the accruals concept:

1. Show the grant as deferred income in the balance sheet and transfer it to the profit and loss account over the life of the asset on a basis consistent with the company's depreciation policy.

2. Reduce the cost of the asset and hence the related annual depreciation charges.

Example 4.9

A company purchases a fixed asset for £25,000 on 1 January 20X2; the asset has a three-year life and an expected residual value of £1,000. The company's policy is to charge depreciation on the straight-line basis. The company received a government grant of £9,000 on the same date. It makes up its accounts on the calendar year basis. Annual profits before charging depreciation are £12,000.

Required:
Separate profit and loss account and balance sheet entries to reflect the above information in the company's accounts for each of the years 20X2-20X4 assuming the company:

(a) Credits the government grant to deferred income

(b) Credits the government grant to the fixed asset account

Solution

(a)	20X2	20X3	20X4
Profit and Loss Account extract	£	£	£
Operating profit before depreciation	12,000	12,000	12,000
Depreciation	−8,000	−8,000	−8,000
Grant released	3,000	3,000	3,000
Operating profit	7,000	7,000	7,000
Balance sheet extracts			
Fixed asset at cost	25,000	25,000	25,000
Accumulated depreciation	8,000	16,000	24,000
	17,000	9,000	1,000
Deferred credit:			
Government grant	6,000	3,000	–

(b)	20X2	20X3	20X4
Profit and Loss Account extract	£	£	£
Operating profit before depreciation	12,000	12,000	12,000
Depreciation (net)	−5,000	−5,000	−5,000
Operating profit	7,000	7,000	7,000
Balance sheet extracts			
Fixed asset at cost (net)	16,000	16,000	16,000
Accumulated depreciation	5,000	10,000	15,000
	11,000	6,000	1,000

4.7 INVESTMENT PROPERTIES

For the purpose of SSAP 19, an investment property is an interest in land /or buildings

(a) in respect of which construction work and development has been completed, and

(b) which is held for its investment potential, any rental income being negotiated at arm's length.

When SSAP 12 (the forerunner of FRS 15) was being developed in the mid-1970s, the property industry successfully lobbied against investment properties becoming subject to depreciation under the new standard. The result was the eventual introduction of a separate accounting standard, SSAP 19 entitled 'Accounting for investment properties', issued in 1981. A statement issued by the ASC on publication of ED 26, 'Accounting for investment properties', justified their special treatment on the grounds that it had been persuasively argued that a different treatment is required for a fixed asset that is not held for 'consumption' in the business operations of an enterprise but is held as a disposable investment. In such a case the current value of the investment, and changes in that current value, are of prime importance rather than a calculation of systematic annual depreciation.

SSAP 19 therefore stipulated that investment properties should be shown in the balance sheet at their open-market value on the grounds that such information is more relevant to users of financial statements, for example to shareholders in assessing the value of their investment and to bankers in evaluating available security for advances requested or made. Such evaluation should normally be carried out:

1. annually by persons holding a recognized professional qualification and having recent post-qualification experience in the location and category of properties concerned; and

2. at least every five years by an external valuer.

Any difference arising on revaluation, which is seen to take account of any depreciation, should be carried to an investment revaluation reserve.

An exception to these rules is that depreciation should be charged on investment properties that consist of leaseholds with an unexpired term of 20 years or less.

Investment properties may be held by a property investment company or by a company whose main activity is not the holding of such properties. The latter provision naturally produces a grey area where some companies argue that particular properties which they own or lease are investment properties and therefore need not be depreciated.

4.8 LEASING

'A lease is a legal agreement between a lessor and a lessee whereby the lessee obtains the right to use an item or some other asset owned by the lessor in exchange for periodic payments.' The length of a lease will naturally reflect the priorities of the two parties involved.

Typical matters requiring attention when negotiating a lease are:

- The period of the lease, which may vary from a day, or even less, to the entire life of the asset.

- The amount and timing of the lease payments.

- Whether the lease is cancellable.

- What is to become of the asset at the end of the lease period.

- Whether the lessee is to be liable for the difference, if any, between the residual value of the lease and the amount it is sold for.

- Who is to be responsible for the payment of maintenance and repairs, insurance, taxes and other operating costs.

In the case of short-term leases, most of the terms will be fixed by the lessor and the lessee is merely left with the 'take it or leave it' option. In longer-term contracts, there may be negotiation on most of these matters.

There have been a number of events responsible for the growth of leasing in the UK. One major factor was a consequence of the high profitability of companies within the financial sector and the poor performance of manufacturing industry in the late 1970s/early 1980s. In the endeavour to encourage manufacturing companies to re-equip with modern machinery, the British government allowed the purchaser immediate tax relief on the entire cost of a newly acquired fixed asset. This apparently generous arrangement was of no benefit to many manufacturing companies who wished to acquire new machinery because they were suffering losses during a series of economic recessions. To secure tax relief, therefore, the fixed asset was instead purchased by a friendly financial institution on behalf of its corporate client. The financial institution could then obtain the benefit of tax relief and share the resulting financial saving with the client in the form of lower lease rentals.

It was soon noticed, however, that the lease contract produced important, and welcome, effects from the viewpoint of financial reporting.

Example 4.10

The following are extracts from the balance sheet of Tournon Ltd at 31 December 20X1.

Balance Sheet at 31 December 20X1

	£000
Shareholders' equity	2,000
Loans	1,000
Total assets less current liabilities	3,000

The following further information is provided:

• At 31 December 20X1, Tournon required the use of a fixed asset with a five-year life costing £1 million.

• Money can be borrowed by Tournon at 10%.

• The fixed asset may be leased for £264,000 (paid in arrears) over a period of 5 years.

Required
(a) The revised balance sheet of Tournon assuming it purchases the asset using borrowing.

(b) The revised balance sheet of Tournon assuming it leases the asset.

(c) The debt:equity ratio based on the information in the balance sheet above and those prepared under (a) and (b).

(d) The profit and loss account for 20X2, so far as the information permits, under the separate assumptions indicated under (a) and (b), and further assuming that the profit before interest on the new loan, depreciation and lease rental is £800,000

Solution

(a)-(c)
Balance Sheets

	Original	Revised, assuming:	
		Borrowing	Leasing
	£000	£000	£000
Shareholders' equity	2,000	2,000	2,000
Loans	1,000	2,000	1,000
Net Assets	3,000	4,000	3,000
Debt/Equity ratio	1:2	1:1	1:2

(d)
Profit and Loss Account for the following year

	Borrowing	Leasing
	£000	£000
Profit before interest on new loan, depreciation and lease rental	800	800
Less: Interest on Loan	(100)	
Depreciation on new asset	(200)	
Lease rental	–	(264)
Profit	500	536

The message conveyed by the above example, soon grasped by some company directors, was that leasing an asset rather than financing it through borrowing avoided damaging effects on the company's gearing ratio and, as a result, reduced the company's apparent financial exposure.

The arrangement of a long-term lease as an alternative to acquisition represented an early example of a variety of arrangements, developed by corporate management and its advisers in the 1970s and 1980s, which became labelled 'special purpose transactions' (SPTs). An SPT is a transaction organized in such a way that, when reported in accordance with its precise legal form, its apparent effect differs significantly from the underlying commercial reality. The creation of 'off-balance sheet finance' is the principal objective of SPTs when a company wishes to raise loan capital but does not want to show a higher level of gearing in its balance sheet. In such a case, the SPT succeeds in excluding the asset and its related finance from one company's balance sheet (Company A) by arranging ownership through a second company (Company B) in such a way that Company A nevertheless enjoys effective control over the use of the asset.

The general position where ownership is separated from use and benefit in this way is shown in figure 4.4.

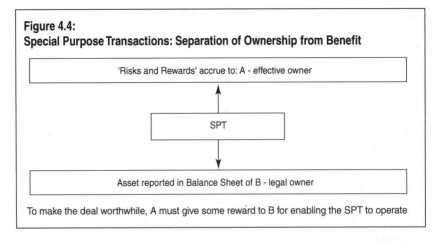

Figure 4.4:
Special Purpose Transactions: Separation of Ownership from Benefit

'Risks and Rewards' accrue to: A - effective owner

SPT

Asset reported in Balance Sheet of B - legal owner

To make the deal worthwhile, A must give some reward to B for enabling the SPT to operate

This is a manifestation of the age-old problem of whether accounting information is being used as a means of education or deception. The problem arises because of the potential conflict between the goals and priorities of preparers (the directors) and the users (for example, the shareholders and the trade and loan creditors). The directors will usually wish to convey an impression of profitability and financial security in the published accounts, and there is no doubt that these are the signals welcomed by user groups. If the actual results achieved by the company convey these images, the objectives of preparer and user coincide and one might imagine that the actual results will also be the published results. Where, however, the actual results promise to be less favourable than the market would wish to see, producing possibilities such as a down-grading of market price, criticism of management and resistance to enhanced remuneration packages, there is an incentive for the directors to devise financial accounting practices designed to achieve damage limitation. Such practices have been countered by a number of accounting standards including SSAP 21.

4.8.1 SSAP 21. Accounting for Leases and Hire Purchase Transactions

The purpose of this standard was to address the situation where loan capital remained off balance sheet as the result of a leasing arrangement. The potential significance of the problem was brought starkly to the attention of the business community and the regulators as early as 1974 when the package holiday business, Court Line Ltd, collapsed. The directors had leased aircraft to operate the company's package holiday business, and the investigation of its affairs following the collapse showed there to be undisclosed obligations relating to leased assets of £40 million. This was of course over a quarter of a century ago and the magnitude of this undisclosed financial obligation is demonstrated by the fact that it dwarfed the figure for shareholders' equity of £18 million reported in the last balance sheet published before the company collapsed. Both the shareholders and the creditors whose debts were reported in the balance sheet were astonished and dismayed to discover that the generally accepted accounting procedures of the day permitted the omission of vast liabilities from the balance sheet and, moreover, that such a company could get a clean audit report. Following their investigation of Court Line's affairs, the Department of Trade and Industry's inspectors reported that 'the amounts involved were material and should have been disclosed'.

The fact was, of course, that the financial reporting procedures followed by Court Line were entirely justified on a strict legal interpretation of its leasing agreements. The lessors were the owners of the aircraft not Court Line. However, the substance of the arrangement was that Court Line had acquired the aircraft for its exclusive use with finance provided by the lessor; an arrangement which, in commercial terms, was no different from Court Line buying the aircraft outright on credit terms. In other words there was a discrepancy between the legal form and the economic substance of the transaction, with Court Line choosing to comply with the former and ignore the latter.

It is an indication of the complexity of the topic and probably also effective lobbying from the leasing industry that it was not until 1984 – ten years later – that the problem was addressed through the issue of an accounting standard.

The standard was faced with the need to

- distinguish between leasing arrangements that resulted in off-balance sheet financing and those that did not and,

- determine the appropriate accounting treatment for each of them.

These objectives were achieved by devising and defining the terms 'finance lease' and 'operating lease' and specifying an accounting treatment for each of them. The key definitions contained in SSAP 21 are as follows:

Finance lease: A lease which transfers substantially all the risks and rewards of ownership to the lessee.

Operating lease: Any lease other than a finance lease.

Risks and rewards: These are presumed to be transferred from the lessor to the lessee where the present value of the minimum lease payments amounts, substantially, to the fair value of the leased asset.

Present value: Calculated using the interest rate implicit in the lease.

Implicit rate: Interest rate that equates the amounts of the lease rentals with present value.

Fair value: Price in an arm's length transaction.

Substantially: Normally 90% or more of fair value.

The essence of SSAP 21, therefore, was to draw a distinction between finance leases where the asset is leased to a particular party for all, or substantially all, of its useful life and operating leases where the asset is leased for a relatively short period to a succession of individuals (for example, hire cars). The distinction is based principally on the concept of the 'risks and rewards' of ownership. These have been referred to above in relation to Figure 4.4 but here require further elaboration.

Risks and rewards normally attach to the owner of an asset. For example, a company buys an asset on the expectation that it will produce future financial benefits. In terms of the labels discussed above, in relation to the *Statement of Principles*, the expectation is that the discounted present value of the future cash flows generated from the use of the asset will exceed the fair value of the asset at acquisition date. In the case of an arm's length transaction, this will be the amount actually paid. If these expectations are fulfilled, the rewards of ownership accrue to the owner. However, if the acquisition proves to have been a mistake – e. g. the market for the product disappears immediately the fixed asset is acquired – the risks and related loss are suffered by the owner. In an extreme case, therefore, the loss incurred will be equal to the entire cost of the asset.

In the case of a finance lease arrangement, however, the risks and rewards normally associated with ownership are instead transferred, through the lease contract, from the lessor to the lessee. For example, the contract may stipulate that, if the lessor wishes to end the leasing arrangement prematurely, there must be paid, as a penalty, a sum of money equal to the amount of the lease rentals outstanding.

The essence of the accounting requirements relating to finance leases, therefore, is to oblige the lessee (that is, the party possessing the risks and rewards and ownership) to report the asset in its balance sheet, with the present value of the rental payments outstanding under the lease contract reported as a liability. At the date the lease contract is entered into, these amounts will be identical but, as time goes by, they will diverge as the asset is depreciated in accordance with the company's accounting policies and the liability is reduced by the value of the capital element of lease rentals paid.

4.8.2 Accounting for Operating Leases

The treatment of operating leases is entirely straightforward and was the method used for all lease rental transactions before the requirements of SSAP 21 came into force.

As far as the lessor is concerned, the fixed asset is held as a source of future income and must be capitalized and amortized in the normal way. The lease rentals receivable are credited to the profit and loss account, as and when they fall due, with the counter-entry made to cash or lease debtor. In the books of the lessee, the lease rental paid is debited to the profit and loss account in line with usage of the asset, with the corresponding credit entry made to cash or lease creditor. The usual accruals or prepayment adjustments need to be made where a lease rental overlaps the end of an accounting period.

Example 4.11

Penn plc purchased a machine for £100,000 on 1 January 20X1. The machine has a five-year life and zero expected residual value. The machine is leased out as follows during 20X1:

| Agen Ltd | 6 months from 1 January for £20,000 |
| Cahors Ltd | 9 months from 1 July for £27,000 |

Rental payments are made at the start of each rental period.

Required:
The appropriate entries in the profit and loss account and balance sheet prepared for 20X1 by
(a) Penn plc and

(b) Cahors Ltd

Each company makes up its accounts on the calendar year basis.

Solution

(a) Penn plc – lessor	Workings	20X1
Profit and Loss Account extracts	£	£
Depreciation charge	100,000/5	20,000
Lease rental income	20,000+(27,000 x 2/3)	38,000
Balance Sheet extracts		
Fixed asset at cost		100,000
Accumulated depreciation		20,000
		80,000
Current liabilities		
Deferred income – lease rental	27,000/3	9,000
(b) Cahors Ltd – lessee	Workings	20X1
Profit and Loss Account extract	£	£
Lease rental expense	27,000 x 2/3	18,000
Balance Sheet extracts		
Current assets		
Lease rental prepayment	27,000/3	9,000

4.8.3 Accounting for Finance Leases

Books of the lessee

The 'fair value' of the asset (usually the price of the asset if purchased outright) is capitalized (debit entry) and recorded also as a liability (credit entry).

The problem concerns the accounting treatment of the lease payments, because these comprise two elements:

- The payment of the cash price.

- The interest charged by the lessor (the 'interest rate implicit in the lease').

That is, the lessor will charge rentals that are sufficient to cover repayment of the capital, in stages, and interest at a given rate on the balance of capital outstanding. As lease payments progress, the interest element therefore diminishes and the capital repayment element increases – it works like a repayment mortgage or an annuity.

The allocation of lease payments is shown diagrammatically in Figure 4.5.

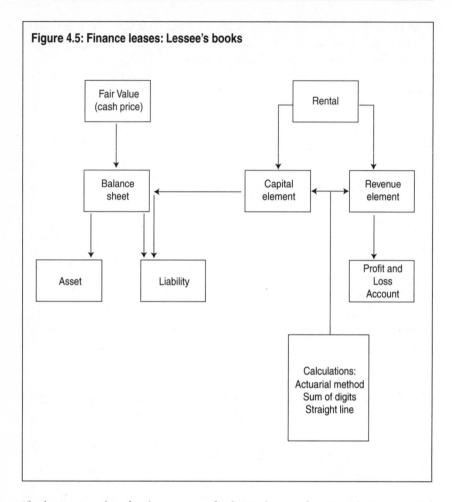

Figure 4.5: Finance leases: Lessee's books

The basic procedure for the purpose of splitting the rental payment between capital and interest may therefore be described as follows:

- Calculate the interest element in the rental payment as: total rental payments minus fair value.

- Allocate the interest element over the period of the lease using the 'interest rate implicit in the lease' (the actuarial method). This achieves the objective of producing a constant periodic rate of charge on the remaining balance of debt outstanding.

In practice, the interest rate implicit in the lease will have to be calculated. This calculation is easy enough to make using compound interest tables or a calculator but will, anyway, be given in any examination question on the topic.

Example 4.12

A Ltd. leases a machine to B Ltd. on 1 January 20X1.

B Ltd. makes four annual payments of £35,000 commencing 1 January 20X1.

A Ltd. sells the machine also for cash, £108,720.

The life of the fixed asset is estimated at four years and the residual value as zero.

The rate of interest implicit in the rental payments is 20%.

Required:
Show how these transactions are to be recorded in the books of:
(a)   the lessee; and
(b)   the lessor.

Solution

(a)   *Books of the Lessee – B Ltd.*

The rental payments may be split between interest and capital as follows:

		20X1	20X2	20X3	20X4
		£	£	£	£
1.	Total outstanding, 1 January	108,720	88,470	64,170	35,000
2.	Rental paid, 1 January	35,000	35,000	35,000	35,000
		73,720	53,470	29,170	–
3.	Interest charge for year, 20%	14,750	10,700	5,830	–
4.	Total outstanding, 31 December	88,470	64,170	35,000	–

Profit and Loss Account Entries

	20X1	20X2	20X3	20X4
	£	£	£	£
Depreciation charge	27,180	27,180	27,180	27,180
Interest charge	14,750	10,700	5,830	–

Balance Sheet Entries, 31 December

	20X1	20X2	20X3	20X4
	£	£	£	£
Fixed Asset at cost	108,720	108,720	108,720	108,720
Less: Accumulated depreciation	27,180	54,360	81,540	108,720
	81,540	54,360	27,180	–
A Ltd. – lease creditor	88,470	64,170	35,000	–

(b) *Books of the Lessor – A Ltd.*

Using the data from the previous example, the profit and loss account and balance sheet entries in A's books will be:

Profit and Loss Account Entries

	20X1 £	20X2 £	20X3 £	20X4 £
Lease income	14,750	10,700	5,830	–

Balance Sheet Entries

	20X1 £	20X2 £	20X3 £	20X4 £
B. Ltd – lease debtor	88,470	64,170	35,000	–

The actuarial method of spreading the interest payments is technically most desirable because the amount charged represents a constant rate of return on the outstanding balance of capital. However, companies are permitted to use, instead, the sum of the digits method (rule of 78) because this spreads the total interest charge in a similar pattern over the life of the leased asset, i.e. larger charges in the earlier years when there is more capital outstanding and lower charges later on. Applying the sum of the digits method to the information given in Example 4.12, the interest charge for the year is obtained by using the formula:

$$\text{Total interest charge} \times \frac{\text{Number of instalments outstanding in any year}}{\text{Sum of the digits of the years over which interest is paid}}$$

Total interest charge: Instalments, £35,000 x 4   £140,000
                Less: cash purchase price   108,720
                                         31,280

Allocated as follows:

Year 1 $31,280 \times \dfrac{3}{1+2+3}$ 15,640

      2     $31,280 \times \dfrac{2}{6}$ 10,427

      3     $31,280 \times \dfrac{1}{6}$ 5,213
                                           31,280

A third method for spreading the interest cost envisaged by SSAP 21 is the straight-line method which produces the following charge for each of the three years:

Straight line: $31,280/3 = £10,427$

This produces an equal interest charge each year and thus fails to reflect or even approximate the true financing cost. It is therefore acceptable to use this method only where the amounts are immaterial relative to the scale of business operations.

In the case of a manufacturer or trader leasing an asset to a customer, the lease rentals will include a profit element relating to the goods supplied as well as interest to cover the financing service. Where such a transaction qualifies as a finance lease, the 'risks and rewards' of ownership will have passed to the lessee and the profit element can be recognized in the profit and loss account of the lessor at the inception of the lease.

4.8.4 Sale and Leaseback
SSAP 21 also covers the sale and leaseback transaction which is an arrangement where the owner of the property (vendor/lessee) sells it to another entity and simultaneously leases it back from the new owner (purchaser/lessor). The need to base financial reporting on the 'economic substance' of the transaction, together with the provisions in the standard relating to 'risks and rewards', must be applied in the usual way. To make an appropriate classification, it is therefore necessary to consider the arrangements in light of the provisions in SSAP 21 relating to the identification of a finance lease or an operating lease. Such transactions are usually prompted by the desire to raise cash, rather than actually to sell the asset. In such circumstances, the property will be leased back on a long-term basis. The agreement will therefore usually, but not always, qualify to be accounted for as a finance lease.

There is the further question of the treatment of any profit or loss arising on the initial sale of the property. Where the arrangement qualifies as a finance lease, the profit or loss should be treated as a deferred revenue or expense and amortized in the accounts of the vendor/lessee over the period of the lease or the useful life of the asset, whichever is the shorter. In the case of an operating lease, any profit or loss is recognized immediately.

4.8.5 Lesson
The experience of leasing demonstrates how the usual relationship between the occurrence of an economic event and the accounting for the event can be reversed. The usual situation is that a transaction is undertaken independently of its accounting significance. The accountant then observes the economic event and records and

reports its financial effects. The history of leasing shows that business persons do not necessarily engage in a commercial transaction unaware or unconcerned with its financial reporting implications. The result is that business arrangements are sometimes structured in a manner intended to achieve desired financial reporting objectives – in this case off balance sheet finance. It then becomes the job of the regulators to counter such opportunistic behaviour on the part of management. SSAP 21 has attempted with some success to do just this but management has, in turn, worked hard to keep its financial reporting options open. Action has centred around devising leasing contracts that satisfy SSAP 21's definition of an operating lease but are, in reality, finance leases.

Illustration

Tours Ltd leased to Nantes Ltd a machine costing £20,000 and having an estimated residual value after three years of at least £6,000. The present value of the lease rentals paid by Nantes Ltd is £14,000. The arrangement is that, at the end of the three-year leasing period, the machine is sold to a third party. If the sales proceeds exceed £6,000, Tours receives £6,000 and Nantes (the lessee) retains any profit. If the machine is sold for less than £6,000, Nantes bears the first £2,000 of the loss after which Tours (the lessor) bears any further loss.

Looking at this arrangement from the point of view of SSAP 21, the lessee effectively guarantees £14,000 of rentals plus £2,000 of residual value, together less than 90% of the initial fair value. The lease would therefore qualify as an operating lease rather than a finance lease. (The transaction might, however, be captured by the 'all embracing' FRS 5 entitled 'Reporting the substance of transactions', introduced ten years later in 1994 – see Chapter 5.)

The results of empirical research suggest that it will prove very difficult for the standard setters to develop definitions that are sufficiently watertight to overcome the problem of off balance sheet finance. The fact that the value of the operating leasing industry has increased dramatically since SSAP 21 came into effect is entirely consistent with this conclusion. A study of a sample of over 200 companies by Goodacre and Beattie (1999) showed payments due within one year under operating leases to have increased from approximately £0.5 million in 1984 to over £9 million ten years later. As Whittred and Zimmer put it: 'If study of this topic does nothing else, it shows how difficult it is for regulation to obviate opportunistic behaviour by contracting parties' (*Financial Accounting*, p. 280). Possibly, the only effective solution – one being given serious consideration – is to require assets and liabilities relating to all lease arrangements to be reflected on the face of the balance sheet.

4.9 GOODWILL AND INTANGIBLE ASSETS

Over the years companies have experimented with a variety of methods to account for purchased goodwill. These include:

(a) permanent retention at cost in the balance sheet;

(b) reporting goodwill in the balance sheet as a permanent deduction from shareholders' equity, without actually writing the item off – the 'dangling debit';

(c) immediate write-off against reserves; and

(d) amortization over the asset's useful economic life through the profit and loss account.

The recent history of regulations relating to goodwill is a good example of efforts made by the ASB and its predecessor body, the ASC, to narrow areas of difference in accounting practice and of the difficulties that they have faced in achieving this objective.

The ASC issued SSAP 22 dealing with the subject of goodwill in 1984. It narrowed down the choice to two alternatives:

• immediate write-off against reserves – (c) above

• amortization over the asset's useful economic life – (d) above

The ASC therefore made some progress by reducing the available options from 4 to 2, but those that remained permissible could hardly have been more diverse. One method required goodwill to be recorded in the balance sheet and then written off through the profit and loss account so as to ensure that the reported profit figure reflected the benefit derived from the use of the asset. The other option bypassed entirely both the balance sheet and the profit and loss account. The latter option was favoured by the vast majority of companies. According to Joan Brown, Project Director of the ASB, however:

> *This method has increasingly been criticized for failing to hold acquirers accountable for amounts spent on goodwill; it does not require companies to charge any loss in value to the P&L account, and*

the rates of the return on acquisitions reported by the financial statements are inflated by the exclusion of goodwill from net assets. The additional problem with immediate elimination of goodwill is that it implies a reduction in equity. (Accountancy, August 1998, p. 84)

As is often the case, some company directors worked hard to get the best of both worlds. They favoured the immediate write-off option because of the beneficial effect on reported profit but, at the same time, preferred to avoid a reduction in shareholders' equity (net assets) and therefore the apparent financial strength of the undertaking. One solution was to classify the bulk of 'goodwill' as identifiable intangible assets, such as brands, to retain them in the balance sheet permanently at cost, and to write off only the residual balance against reserves.

There are potentially significant differences between goodwill and other intangible assets but there are also close similarities. Its is sometimes very difficult to distinguish one from the other, and it is for this reason that the successor of SSAP 22 – FRS 10 entitled 'Goodwill and intangible assets' – covers both categories of asset.

The objective of FRS 10 is to ensure that:

- capitalized goodwill and intangible assets are charged in the profit and loss account in the periods in which they are depleted; and

- sufficient information is disclosed in the financial statement to enable users to determine the impact of goodwill and intangible assets on the financial position and performance of the reporting entity.

For the purpose of recognizing intangible assets (including goodwill) in published financial statements (and then accounting for them in an appropriate manner), FRS 10 covers four separate categories that are in certain respects overlapping:

1. Intangible assets that are capable of being purchased separately. This category includes: licenses; quotas; patents; copyrights; franchises; trademarks; brands; publishing titles; patented drugs and engineering design patents.

2. Internally developed intangible fixed assets that have a readily ascertainable market value, that is a value which is established by reference to a market, where:

- the asset belongs to a homogenous population of assets that are equivalent in all material respects; and

- an active market, evidenced by frequent transactions, exists for that population of assets

Intangible assets that probably meet these stringent criteria include licences, franchises and quotas. The group does not include brands, publishing titles, patented drugs and engineering design patents that are considered to be one-offs that, by their nature, cannot be equivalent 'in all material respects' to a group of other assets

3. Intangible assets acquired as the result of the purchase of another business. To qualify for separate recognition, they must be identifiable and therefore separable and capable of being reliably measured.

4. Purchased goodwill. This is a nebulous concept and comprises 'the difference between the cost of an acquired entity and the aggregate of the fair values of its identifiable assets and liabilities'.

The calculation of the goodwill figure may be shown diagrammatically and demonstrated by means of an example.

	£
Price paid for the new business	X
Deduct: Sum of the fair values of the identifiable assets and liabilities, including intangible assets that can be reliably measures	X
Purchased goodwill	X̲

Example 4.13

Villeneuve Ltd acquired the assets and took responsibility for discharging some of the liabilities of Montaigu Ltd on 1 July 20X3 for £22,500,000.

The fair values of the tangible, identifiable intangible assets and the liabilities taken over were as follows:

	£000
Trade creditors	1,250
Stocks	3,200
Property, fixtures and fittings	9,000
Brand name	2,200
Franchise rights	750
Trade debtors	4,100

Required:
Compute the goodwill arising on the purchase of Montaigu Ltd.

Solution

	£000	£000
Price paid		22,500
Less:		
Trade creditors	−1,250	
Stocks	3,200	
Property, fixtures and fittings	9,000	
Brand name	2,200	
Franchise rights	750	
Trade debtors	4,100	
		18,000
Purchased goodwill		4,500

Goodwill is thus unique – a non-identifiable asset. The only way that its existence can be computed is 'by difference'. The nature of the asset is equally vague. It has been referred to as 'easy to describe but difficult to define' and 'no more than the expectation that the old customer will return to the old place'. It is what distinguishes an established and successful business from one recently set up and includes 'intangible' advantages such as management's ability, the expertise of the workforce, the reputation of the company's products and a successfully targeted customer base. A decline in any of these ingredients will affect the value of goodwill and be reflected in a fall in the market price; an example would be Marks and Spencer's alleged loss of traditional market base during the year 2000 linked with a deterioration in customer perception of the attractiveness of its product lines.

Goodwill is also unique in that it cannot be sold separately from the business as a whole. An arms' length sale of a business is the only occasion on which it is possible to compute a reliable market value, and it is for this reason that FRS 10 rules out the inclusion in company accounts of non-purchased goodwill, i.e. the amount that is alternatively referred to as internally generated goodwill or inherent goodwill.

4.9.1 Amortization of Intangible Assets and Goodwill

The general rule, applied also to other fixed assets, is that intangible assets and goodwill should be written off against profit over their useful economic life. FRS 10 makes the rebuttable presumption that useful economic life does not exceed 20 years. Assuming this to be the case, impairment reviews (see section 4.10, below) are required only:

- at the end of the first full financial year following acquisition; and

- in other periods when events or changes in circumstances indicate that the present carrying values may not be recoverable.

The reason for the review at the end of the first year is the natural uncertainty associated with the asset's value prompting a reconsideration of expectations held at the acquisition date.

The assumption that intangible assets have a life of no more than 20 years can be rebutted only where:

- the durability of the acquired business or intangible asset can be demonstrated to justify an estimated useful life exceeding 20 years – indeed, where goodwill and intangible assets are regarded as having indefinite useful economic lives, they need not be amortized at all; and

- the goodwill or intangible asset is capable of continued measurement so that annual impairment reviews are a feasible proposition.

If such circumstances are satisfied and amortization is to occur over a period in excess of 20 years, there exists again a significant 'sting in the tail', namely that annual impairment reviews must take place.

Example 4.14

The accounts of Villeneuve (see Example 4.13) for the calendar year 20X3 are in the course of preparation. You discover the following relating to certain of the assets acquired on 1 July 20X3:

- The franchise has three years to run

- The brand name is expected to have an indefinite useful life provided its value is supported by appropriate advertising expenditure and marketing activity.

- The goodwill is estimated to have a useful economic life of 18 years.

- The property includes land with a fair value on acquisition of £2 million. The buildings are estimated to have a useful economic life of 20 years and a residual value at the end of that period of £1 million.

Required:
(a) Calculations, for 20X3, of the depreciation charges to be debited to the profit and loss account and of the values at which each of the fixed assets acquired from Montaigu should be reported in the balance sheet of Villeneuve.

(b) A statement of requirements for impairment, if any, attaching to each of the fixed assets.

Note:
Villeneuve's relevant accounting policy is to charge a full year's depreciation/amortization in the year of acquisition and none in the year of disposal.

Solution

(a)

	Workings £000	Profit and Loss Account £000	Balance Sheet £000
Intangible fixed assets			
Goodwill	4,500/18	250	4,250
Brand name	2,200	–	2,200
Franchise rights	750/3	250	500
Tangible fixed assets			
Property, fixtures and fittings	9,000-[2,000+1,000]/20	300	8,700

(b)
- There should be an impairment review of each of the intangible assets at the end of the first full financial year; as the assets were acquired on 1 July 20X3, one should therefore be undertaken at the end of 20X4.

- Because the brands are assumed to have a useful life in excess of 20 years, there must be an annual impairment review.

- Any of the fixed assets will need to be the subject of an impairment review in any year that events or changes in circumstances indicate that the carrying amount may not be recoverable.

We have noted, above, that FRS 10 rules out the option available under its predecessor standard, SSAP 22, to write off goodwill immediately against reserves. In drafting the new standard, it was therefore necessary for the regulators to decide how to treat goodwill previously written off in this manner given the fact that it conflicted with the single, newly approved method. The basic alternatives were to leave it written off or to require its reinstatement. The new standard allows companies to choose between these two options. If the decision is made to reinstate goodwill, it should be brought back into the accounts at its original fair value less amortization or impairment attributable to previous periods by making a prior year adjustment. The remaining balance must then be amortized in the normal way.

Example 4.15

Assume that 20X3 is the first year in which Villeneuve applies the provisions of FRS 10. It is also discovered that goodwill with a fair value of £5,000,000 arose on the acquisition of a small local business on 1 January 20X1. In accordance with the provisions of SSAP 22 then in force, the goodwill was written off directly against reserves. It is now decided to adopt the option available under FRS 10 to reinstate goodwill in order to achieve consistency with the treatment now required to be adopted for the acquisition of Montaigu. It is estimated that the goodwill to be reinstated had a useful economic life of 10 years at the date of acquisition and no amendment to this initial estimate is required.

Required:
(a) The entries in the books of Villeneuve Ltd as at 1 January 20X3 to reinstate the goodwill arising on the 20X1 business acquisition; and

(b) The relevant entries in the final accounts of Villeneuve for 20X3.

Solution

		£
(a)	Entry	
	Credit: reserves at 1 January 20X3,	5,000,000
	Debit: goodwill at 1 January 20X3	5,000,000
	Debit: reserves at 1 January 20X3, 5,000,000/10x2	1,000,000
	Credit: amortization of goodwill at 1 January 20X3	1,000,000

			£
(b)	Final accounts for 20X3		
	Profit and loss account:	Amortization charge: 5,000,000/10	500,000
	Movement on reserves:	Prior year adjustment	4,000,000
	Balance sheet:	Goodwill at cost	5,000,000
		Less: amortization	<u>1,500,000</u>
			<u>3,500,00</u>

4.10. IMPAIRMENT OF FIXED ASSETS AND GOODWILL

There are now three FRSs on fixed assets – FRS 11 entitled 'Impairment of fixed assets and goodwill', the previously published FRS 10 on 'Goodwill and intangible assets' and the subsequently published FRS 15 entitled 'Tangible fixed assets'. The need for a standard on impairment was signalled by the prior publication of FRS 10 which, as we have seen, specifies a number of circumstances in which an impairment review is required. The concept of impairment is by no means new. There was a long-standing principle enshrined in the Companies Act 1985 requiring fixed assets to be written down if their carrying value exceeded their economic worth to the entity. However, prior to FRS 11, there was virtually no guidance on how to compute the recoverable amount and what to do about any identified deficiency. FRS 11 is, therefore, very much a 'how to do it' standard.

We have seen that there are requirements to review intangible assets and goodwill for impairment at the end of the first year of operations following their acquisition. Also, if it is decided to retain any fixed assets in the books permanently at cost, an annual impairment review must take place.

Apart from the above, fixed assets (tangible and intangible) have to be reviewed for impairment only when there is an indicator that carrying values may not be recoverable. In the normal course of events, you would not expect assets that are being depreciated in the normal way to become impaired. The most obvious circumstance in which an impairment review becomes necessary is where any part of a company's business operations begins to make a loss. Other circumstances which trigger the need for a review include:

- a significant fall in the asset's market value;

- physical damage to, or obsolescence of, a fixed asset;

- an adverse change in the company's competitive or regulatory environment, for example a new business opens up as a competitor;

- a significant reorganization of business operations;

- the loss of key employees;

- a significant increase in market interest rates; and

- a key employer in the locality where a company carries on business closes down.

The calculation and allocation of an impairment loss between assets is explained in the standard and consists of the following principal steps:

1. *Identify income generating units.* These are units that produce an identifiable income stream. Ideally, they consist of a single asset, but it is highly unlikely that the income stream of a particular business will be capable of allocation between each individual asset. It will therefore be necessary to identify the smallest possible group of assets that together generate an identifiable stream of cash flows.

    The standard gives the example of a restaurant chain which has a number of outlets across the country. The cash inflows of each restaurant can be individually monitored and sensible allocations of costs to each restaurant can be made. In these circumstances, each restaurant is an income-generating unit. However, any impairment of individual restaurants is unlikely to be material. A material impairment is likely to occur only where a number of restaurants are affected simultaneously by the same economic factors. It may therefore be appropriate to consider groupings of restaurants affected by common economic factors, for impairment purposes, rather than assess each individual restaurant.

2. *Compute cash flow estimates.* There are two elements. Firstly, up-to-date budgets and plans approved by management which should usually be for a period not exceeding 5 years. Secondly, cash flows thereafter, which should be based on the assumption of steady or declining (not increasing) growth rates, with the rate used not exceeding the long-term average of the country or countries in which the entity operates. The purpose of the limitation placed on assumptions concerning future growth rates is to help to ensure realistic, perhaps prudent, rather than over-optimistic forecasts being made.

3. *Compute discounted present value (DPV)* The relevant discount rate should be applied to the estimated cash flows for the income generating unit in order to establish DPV. The rate used should be an estimate of the rate the market would expect on an equally risky investment. The identification of such a rate is likely to be extremely difficult in practice but will be provided in examination questions.

4. *Compute recoverable amount* Where impairment has occurred, assets must be

written down from carrying value to their 'recoverable amount'. Recoverable amount is the higher of:

- the amount that could be achieved from sale (NRV); and

- DPV

The process required here is consistent with the content of the *Statement of Principles* discussed above, and its modified diagrammatic presentation as portrayed in Figure 4.3.

The above four steps are illustrated in Example 4.16.

Example 4.16

The accountants of Alencon plc have prepared the following information relating to the company's business operations which can be divided into two income generating units.

	IGU I	IGU II
	£000	£000
Cash flows:		
Year 1	800	2,000
Year 2	600	2,200
Year 3	900	2,700
Year 4	1,000	2,400
Year 5	1,100	1,500
Year 6	1,200	3,000

The discount rate appropriate to the activities of IGU I is 10% and that of IGU II 12%.

The net realizable value of the assets of IGU I is £5 million and those of IGU II £7 million.

Required:
(a) Compute the discounted present value of IGU I and IGU II.
(b) Compute the recoverable amount of IGU I and IGU II.

Note:
Discount factors for the present value of £1 are given in Appendix B.

Solution

(a)	IGU I	Discount factor 10%	DPV	IGU II	Discount factor 12%	DPV
Cash flows:	£000			£000		
Year 1	800	0.909	727.2	2,000	0.893	1,786.0
Year 2	600	0.826	495.6	2,200	0.797	1,753.4
Year 3	900	0.751	675.9	2,700	0.712	1,922.4
Year 4	1,000	0.683	683.0	2,400	0.636	1,526.4
Year 5	1,100	0.620	682.0	1,500	0.567	850.5
Year 6	1,200	0.564	676.8	3,000	0.507	1,521.0
			3,940.5			9,359.7

(b)		IGU I			IGU II
		£000			£000
DPV		3,940.5			9,359.7
NRV		5,000.0			7,000.0
Recoverable amount:					
higher of DPV/NRV	NRV	5,000.0		DPV	9,359.7

5. *Allocate impairment loss.* Where cash flows are computed on the basis of individual assets, the value of the asset is simply reduced by the amount of the impairment loss. Where, as is more likely, the exercise is based on an income-generating unit, it will be necessary to allocate the impairment loss first to those assets whose valuation is judged to be most subjective. The appropriate sequence for allocation is therefore:

1. Goodwill

2. Other intangible assets

3. Tangible assets on a pro rata or more appropriate basis

This process is illustrated in Example 4.17.

Example 4.17

The following information is provided relating to the carrying value of the assets comprising the income-generating units of Alencon (see example 4.16).

	IGU I	IGU II
	£000	£000
Goodwill	–	2,100
Patents	1,000	400
Tangible fixed assets	1,600	10,700
Stocks	2,200	2,300

Required:

(a)   Calculation of the impairment loss, if any, for IGU I and IGU II.

(b)   The allocation of the impairment loss, if any, between the assets of IGU I and/or IGU II.

Solution

	IGU I	Workings	IGU II	Revised values
	£000		£000	
Carrying value	4,800		15,500.0	
Recoverable amount	5,000		9,359.7	
Lower of carrying value and recoverable amount	4,800		9,359.7	
Impairment loss	0		6,140.3	
Allocated as follows:				
Goodwill			2,100.0	0
Patents			400.0	0
Tangible fixed assets		6,140.3 – 2,500 x (10,700/13,000)	2,996.2	7,703.8
Stocks		6,140.3 – 2,500 x (2,300/13,000)	644.1	1,655.9
			6,140.3	9,359.7

Where the exercise results in the use of discounted present value (IGU II above), the standard requires that, for a period of 5 years following the review, the cash flows actually achieved should be compared with the earlier estimates. This produces three possibilities

- actual cash flows are broadly in line with those estimated, in which case no further action is required

- cash flows turn out to be better than had been forecast, in which case it may be possible to recognize a complete or partial reversal of the impairment loss

- the actual cash flows are worse than expected, in which case it will be necessary to repeat the exercise in order to discover whether an additional impairment loss needs to be provided for.

Recognition of the loss in the profit and loss account or the statement of total recognised gains and losses must take place in accordance with the normal rules for downward revaluations discussed in section 4.5.2 above

4.11 FURTHER READING

Alexander, D. and Britton, A. (1999) *Financial Reporting*, fifth edition, London: International Thomson Business Press, Chapters 16 and 19.

Davies, Mike, Ron Paterson and Allister Wilson (1999), *Generally Accepted Accounting Practice in the United Kingdom*, sixth edition, Croydon: Butterworth Tolley, Chapters 10, 13, and 17-18.

Elliott, B. and Elliott, J. (2000) *Financial Accounting and Reporting*, fifth edition, Hemel Hempstead: Prentice Hall, Chapters 14-16.

Goodacre, A. and Beattie, V. (1999) 'Gearing up', *Accountancy*, June, pp. 86-87.

Lewis, Richard and David Pendrill (2000), *Advanced Financial Accounting*, sixth edition, Pitman, Chapters 4, 6 and 8.

Robins, P. (1999) 'FRS 15, tangible fixed assets', *ACCA Students' Newsletter*, September, pp. 78-81.

Robins, P. (2000) 'FRS 10, goodwill and intangible assets', *ACCA Students' Newsletter*, April, pp. 76-8.

4.12 QUESTIONS

Question 4.1

A property was purchased for £12,500,000 on 1 January 20X0. Annual depreciation of £300,000 was charged for 5 years from 20X0 to 20X4 inclusive. On 1 January 20X5, when the carrying value of the property was £11,000,000, the property was revalued to £12,000,000. The appropriate annual depreciation was reassessed at £330,000 and this was charged from 20X5 to 20X9 inclusive. On 1 January 20X-10, when the carrying value of the property was £10,375,000, the property was revalued again and the revalued amount was £8,500,000 on an existing-use basis. The revaluation deficit was caused by a general fall in property prices rather than by a consumption of economic benefits.

Required:
Calculate the amount of the revaluation deficit and explain its treatment in the accounts.

Question 4.2

Cooper Ltd is a manufacturing company which leased an item of machinery from Critical plc on 1 January 20X0. The following additional information is provided:

- The lease provided for an immediate rental payment of £1 million and three further annual rental payments of £1 million commencing 1 January 20X1.

- The machine has an estimated four-year life and a zero residual value at the end of that period.

- You discover that Critical plc also sells the machine for cash, £3,210,000, and that the interest rate implicit in the lease payments is 17%.

- The summarized balance sheet of Cooper Ltd on 1 January 20X0, immediately before the above transactions, is as follows.

Balance Sheet of Cooper Ltd at 1 January 20X0

	£000
Fixed assets at book value	900
Current assets, including cash of £1,300,00	3,000
	3,900
Less: Creditors payable within one year	1,600
	2,300
Less: Creditors payable in more than one year	
15% Debenture 20X-10	200
	2,100
Financed by:	
Share capital	1,600
Retained profit	500
	2,100

Required:
(a) Indicate the adjustments that must be made to the above balance sheet at 1 January 20X0, if any, assuming the transaction is accounted for as:

(i)   an operating lease
(ii) a finance lease

(b) Give all the relevant entries in the profit and loss account and balance sheet of Cooper Ltd.
     relating to the lease transaction for each of the years 20X0 – 20X3, assuming the transaction is
     accounted for as:
     (i)   an operating lease
     (ii) a finance lease

(c) Explain the purpose of the entries prepared under (a)(i) and (a)(ii), and comment on the
     possible economic consequences of these adjustments.

Note:
Calculations to nearest £000

Question 4.3

The following is the trial balance of Hengoed Ltd as at 31 December 20X1

	£000	£000
Properties (see note 1)	24,400	
Turnover		106,000
Cost of goods sold	75,100	
Administrative expenses	20,600	
Selling and distribution costs	3,300	
Net current assets	33,800	
Issued ordinary share capital		10,000
Revaluation reserve		5,400
Retained profit at 1 January 20X1		35,800
	157,200	157,200

The following additional information is provided.
1.   The balance on the properties account at 1 January 20X1 was made up as follows:

	Property A	Property B
	£000	£000
Cost or revalued amount	10,600	20,000
Accumulated depreciation	2,200	4,000

Property A is stated above at cost, but was revalued at £17 million on 1 January 20X1 when it was
estimated that the property had a remaining useful life of ten years and a zero residual value at the
end of that time. The directors have now decided to use the revalued figure for the purpose of the
20X1 accounts.

The credit balance on revaluation reserve relates to Property B which was revalued in the early
19X0s at £20 million. The property was sold on 31 December 20X1 for £25.4 million and a
cheque for that amount has been received. The transaction has been erroneously omitted from
the above trial balance.

2   The cost of goods sold includes a lease rental payment to Bargoed of £1,200,000 made on 1 January 20X1, in respect of plant and machinery that has been hired. The rental is the first of eight annual payments for the plant and machinery which is expected to have an eight-year life and, then, a zero residual value. The plant and machinery is known to sell for a cash price of £6,346,000, when new, and the interest rate implicit in the lease is 14%.

Required:
(a)   The profit and loss account for Hengoed Ltd for 20X1 and balance sheet at 31 December 20X1. The accounts should comply with standard accounting practice so far as the information permits.

(b)   A discussion of your accounting treatment of the two properties. The discussion should include consideration of the alternative possible treatment of the disposal ruled out by FRS 3 entitled 'Reporting Financial Performance'.

Notes:
Calculations to the nearest £000
Ignore taxation

Question 4.4

It has been stated that the Accounting Standards Board has the broad aim of incorporating current values into accounts in a more pervasive and systematic way.

Examine the evidence in favour of this proposition, drawing on the relevant content of the following publications issued by the Accounting Standards Board:

•   The Statement of Principles;

•   FRS 10, Goodwill and intangible assets;

•   FRS 11, Impairment of fixed assets and goodwill; and

•   FRS 15, Tangible fixed assets.   [20 marks]

Question 4.5

The use of 'off balance sheet finance' has been, arguably, the major problem area in financial reporting over the last two decades. The following extracts from UK GAAP, by Mike Davies, Ron Paterson and Allistair Wilson, give some indication of the nature and significance of this issue:

> *"SSAP 21 entitled 'Leases and Hire Purchase Contracts' broke new ground in UK financial reporting in two ways: first, it was the first accounting standard to apply the concept of substance over form. Through this, the requirement for companies to capitalize assets in their balance sheets (together with the corresponding obligations) in prescribed circumstances was introduced – irrespective of the fact that legal title to those assets vested in another party."*
>
> (5th edition, 1997, p.979)

> *"Off balance sheet finance can be difficult to define, and this poses the first problem in discussing the subject. The term implies that certain things belong on the balance sheet and that those which escape the net are deviations from this norm. But there are as yet no authoritative general principles which determine conclusively what should be on the balance sheet and when. The ASB is attempting to establish such principles in its Statement of Principles project and has used these as the basis of FRS5 – Reporting the substance of transactions – which directly addresses the issue of off balance sheet finance."*
>
> (5th edition, 1997, p, 923)

(These extracts have been reproduced with the kind permission of Macmillan Press.)

The problems posed by 'off balance sheet financing' have therefore been tackled through the issue of two statements by the ASB and its predecessor, the ASC. The concerns addressed by the former of these two pronouncements – SSAP21 – are reflected in how best to report the financial transactions of Carroll plc, outlined below, in the balance sheet at 1 January 1999 and in the accounting statements it subsequently prepares.

Balance Sheet of Carroll plc at 1 January 1999

	£000
Fixed assets	4,300
Current assets	3,100
Current liabilities	−1.200
Total assets less current liabilities	6,200
12% Debentures	2,000
	4,200
Shareholders' equity	4,200

Carroll plc entered into an arrangement with Financial Services plc to lease an item of plant for its entire expected useful life of four years commencing 1 January 1999. The lease contract provides for an initial payment of £1 million on 1 January 1999 and three further annual payments of the same amount on 1 January each year. The plant can be purchased for cash at a cost of £3,488,000 and the interest rate implicit in the lease is 10%. The company applies straight-line depreciation to all its fixed assets and assumes a zero residual value at the end of their useful life.

Required:
(a) Prepare revised balance sheets for Carroll plc as at 1 January 1999 that take account of the lease arrangement entered into with Financial Services plc on the separate assumptions that it should be accounted for as:
   (i) an operating lease;
   (ii) a finance lease.   [7 marks]

(b) Show how the lease arrangement should be reflected in the profit and loss account of Carroll plc for the year ended 31 December 1999 and the balance sheet at that date on the separate assumptions that it should be accounted for as:
   (i) an operating lease;
   (ii) a finance lease.   [9 marks]

(c) Compare and contrast the methods of accounting for leases illustrated by your calculations under (a) and (b), paying particular attention to the concept of substance over form and the effect on the gearing ratio.   [8 marks]

[Total – 24 marks]

5

REPORTING OTHER
ASSETS AND
LIABILITIES IN
COMPANY ACCOUNTS

Chapter 4 dealt with the treatment of fixed assets in company accounts. In Chapter 5, we consider the treatment in published accounts of the remaining assets and liabilities of a business. These are:

	Section
• Stock and Long-Term Contracts	5.1
• Research and Development Expenditure	5.2
• Taxation	5.3
• Capital Instruments	5.4
• Reporting the Substance of Transactions	5.5
• Provisions and Contingencies	5.6
• Post balance Sheet Events	5.7
• Investments	5.8
• Pension Costs	5.9

5.1 STOCK AND LONG-TERM CONTRACTS

The quantity of resources tied up in stock depends on factors such as delivery periods, the length of the production cycle, and production policy, i.e. whether the level of production is matched closely with sales, or whether output is maintained at a steady level so that stock is built up during quiet periods to meet demand in the busier periods ahead. Nevertheless, for most companies stock comprises a significant proportion of gross assets and, for this reason, the level of reported profit can vary a great deal depending on the valuation method used. For example, assume that, at the end of its first year in business, a company's accounts show gross assets of £2m, including closing stock of £600,000 and reported profits amount to £200,000. An alternative valuation method might result in a stock figure of £450,000. If the alternative is adopted, the values of stock and gross assets will be reduced respectively by 25% and 7.5%, while reported profit will fall by 75% to £50,000.

Both SSAP 9 and the Companies Act require companies to value stock at cost, except where this exceeds net realizable value (i.e. market price less all further costs to completion and less all costs to be incurred in marketing, selling and distributing the item), in which case the latter figure should be used. To ensure that full provision is made for foreseeable losses, SSAP9 requires the comparison between cost and net realizable value to be based on individual items of stock, with the proviso that groups of similar items may be compared where the comparison of individual items is impracticable. The 'lower of cost and net realizable value' rule is therefore consistent with the fundamental accounting concepts discussed in Chapter 2.3.2.

Example 5.1

The following information is provided in respect of a group of items of stock belonging to Banbury Ltd:

Item of Stock	Cost	Net Realizable Value (NRV)
A	500	580
B	300	370
C	250	330
D	760	600

Required:
Calculations of the total value of Banbury's stock, based on the lower of cost and net realizable value rule, assuming that cost is compared with net realizable value:

(a) on an individual item basis;

(b) on the group basis.

Solution

(a) Individual item basis:

Item of Stock	Cost	NRV	Lower of Cost and NRV Individual Item Basis
	£	£	£
A	500	580	500
B	300	370	300
C	250	330	250
D	760	600	600
			1,650

(b) Group basis:

Item of Stock	Cost	NRV	Lower of Cost and NRV Group Basis
	£	£	£
A+11+C+13	1,810	1,880	1,810

Comparing cost with the NRV of individual items results in a lower stock value (£1,650 as compared with £1,810) and therefore a lower profit figure. This is because the comparison of total figures for cost and NRV results in a foreseeable loss of £160 on item D (£760 cost- £600 NRV) being offset by total unrealized gains of £230 on items A-C (£1,280 NRV-£1,050 cost).

The principal situations in which NRV is likely to be below cost are where there has been:

- a major increase in costs with no compensating increase in selling price;

- a fall in selling price;

- physical deterioration of stocks;

- obsolescence of products;

- a decision, as part of a company's marketing strategy, to manufacture and sell particular products at a loss;

- errors in production or purchasing.

In practice, any of the above circumstances is unlikely to apply to more than a small proportion of the company's stock. For the remainder, NRV will exceed cost and can be ignored when valuing stock for inclusion in the accounts. However, there will still remain the problem of deciding how to compute cost. There are two basic areas of difficulty:

- whether to value stock on the marginal cost or the total cost basis (see section 5.1.1);

- how to identify purchases with issues to production and match finished goods with sales, i.e. a choice has to be made between, for instance, first in, first out and last in, first out (see section 5.1.2).

5.1.1 Marginal Cost or Total Cost

The main difference between these two methods is their treatment of fixed factory costs, and it is therefore a problem that is primarily confined to manufacturing companies. The marginal cost basis includes only the variable costs associated with producing a single extra unit of output, whereas the total (or absorption) cost basis also includes a proportion of fixed factory costs. The main arguments for and against the total cost basis, which are broadly the reverse of the arguments for and against the marginal cost basis, are as follows.

For total cost:
- Each unit manufactured benefits from the provision of facilities that result in fixed costs being incurred, and a proportion of their cost should therefore be included in the value of stock.

- The accruals concept requires costs to be matched with related revenues, and the total cost of stock unsold at the balance sheet date should therefore be carried forward and matched against revenue arising during the following accounting period.

Against total cost:
- Fixed costs are a function of time rather than production, and should not therefore be carried forward but should be charged against the revenue arising during the period when they are incurred.

- The valuation of stock and, therefore, the level of reported profit fluctuates depending on the level of production. This is because the quantity manufactured determines the proportion of fixed cost attributed to each item, e.g. a low level of output causes each unit to be charged with a high element of fixed cost.

- Fixed costs cannot be directly related to particular items of stock and are therefore apportioned on an arbitrary basis.

Both SSAP 9 and the Companies Act require companies to use the total cost basis for external reporting purposes. The statement defines total cost as those costs incurred 'in bringing the product or service to its present location and condition'. This normally means that the valuation should include a share of factory overheads, but not distribution costs or administrative expenses. The problem, implicit in the second argument against the use of total cost, listed above, is avoided by the requirement that the calculation of the overhead element should be based on the 'normal level of activity, taking one year with another'.

Example 5.2 tests students' understanding of the difference between the marginal (prime) cost and total cost bases of stock valuation. It should, as usual, be worked by students before examining the solution provided.

Example 5.2

At the beginning of 20X1 Deer Ltd was incorporated. The company manufactures a single product. At the end of the first year's operations the company's accountant prepared a draft profit and loss account which contained the following financial information:

PROFIT AND LOSS ACCOUNT OF DEER LTD FOR 20X1

	£	£
Sales (200,000 units)		600,000
Less: Prime cost of units manufactured during 20X1		
(500,000 units)	800,000	
Deduct closing stock	480,000	
Prime cost of goods sold	320,000	
Fixed Costs:		
Factory expenses	200,000	
General expenses	100,000	620,000
Net loss		20,000

Additional finance is required, and the directors are worried that the company's bank manager is unlikely to regard the financial facts shown above as a satisfactory basis for a further advance. The company's accountant made the following observation and suggestion:

The cause of the poor result for 20X1 was the decision to value closing stock on the prime cost basis. An acceptable alternative practice would involve charging factory expenses to the total number of units produced and carrying forward an appropriate proportion of those expenses as part of the closing stock value.

Required:

(a) A revised profit and loss account, for presentation to the company's bank, valuing closing stock on the total (absorption) cost basis suggested by the company's accountant.

(b) Assuming that, in 20X2, the company again produces 500,000 units but sells 700,000 units, calculate the expected profit using each of the two stock valuation bases. Assume also that, in 20X2, sales price per unit and costs incurred will be the same as for 20X1.

(c) Comment briefly on the accountant's suggestion and its likely effect on the bank manager's response to the request for additional finance.

Solution:

(a) *Profit and Loss Account for 20X1 – total cost basis*

	£000		£000
Sales			600
Less: Prime costs	800		
Factory expenses	200		
Total cost of manufacture	1,000		
Deduct closing stock	600	(W1)	
Cost of goods sold	400		
General expenses	100		
			500
Net profit			100

W1. The company produced 500,000 units but sold only 200,000 units, and so it had 300,000 units in stock. The total cost basis therefore results in a stock valuation of (£1,000,000 ÷ 500,000) x 300,000 = £600,000.

(b) *Forecast Profit and Loss Accounts for 20X2*

	Prime Cost			Total Cost		
	£000		£000	£000		£000
Sales			2,100			2,100
Less: Opening stock	480			600		
Prime costs	800			800		
Factory expenses	–			200		
	1,280			1,600		
Deduct closing stock	160	(W2)		200	(W2)	
	1,120			1,400		
Factory expenses	200			–		
General expenses	100			100		
			1,420			1,500
Net profit			680			600

W2. The opening stock is 300,000 units and 500,000 units are expected to be manufactured during 19X2. Assuming 700,000 units are sold, 100,000 units will remain in stock at the end of 20X2.

The closing stock valuations are therefore:

Prime cost basis: (£800,000 ÷ 500,000) x 100,000 = £160,000
Total cost basis: (£1,000,000 ÷ 500,000) x 100,000 = £200,000

(c) Total cost is an acceptable basis for valuing stock; indeed it is the method required for external reporting purposes by SSAP 9 and the Companies Act. Provided the resulting valuation does not exceed net realizable value, it should be used.

The use of different valuation bases does not, of course, alter the underlying financial facts, but it can affect the allocation of profit between consecutive accounting periods. Use of the total cost basis, which relates indirect manufacturing costs to output rather than time, produces higher profits than the marginal (prime) cost basis when production exceeds sales. Three-fifths of the fixed factory costs (£200,000 x 3/5 = £120,000) are added to the value of closing stock for the purpose of preparing the revised profit and loss account for 20X1, and this converts a reported loss of £20,000 into a reported profit of £100,000. The situation is reversed when sales exceed production (see forecast results for 20X2 above).

The company's bank manager no doubt will be aware of the effect of different accounting policies on reported profit and he should not be significantly influenced by a change of method which gives an improved appearance to the underlying facts. Nevertheless, use of the marginal cost approach, when output exceeds sales, unduly deflates profits where there is a ready market for the goods manufactured. In such circumstances, use of the total cost basis is fully justified.

5.1.2 FIFO or LIFO

The price at which goods are purchased normally increases during the year and, consequently, items in stock at the year end will have been purchased at a variety of different prices. In theory, the accruals concept requires the cost of items sold to be matched individually against their sales proceeds, but this is usually impracticable because of the large number of items bought and sold during an accounting period. To simplify the process, assumptions are made concerning the flow of goods through the firm. The main alternative assumptions are 'first in, first out' (FIFO), 'last in, first out' (LIFO) and 'weighted average cost' (AVCO). The effect of different cost flow assumptions on reported profit and the balance sheet value of stock is illustrated by comparing and contrasting FIFO and LIFO (AVCO produces results that fall somewhere between these two extremes).

FIFO: This assumes that the items that have been longest in stock are used first, and stock on hand represents the latest purchases or production. The effect is that, during a period of rising prices, cost of sales is reported at a low figure, reported profit is maximized and the balance sheet figure for stock represents most recent purchase prices.

LIFO: This assumes that the items purchased or produced most recently are used first, and the quantities of stock on hand represent earliest purchases or production. The result is that cost of sales is higher than under the FIFO assumption, and reported profit is correspondingly lower. In the balance sheet stocks are valued at a relatively low figure, representing prices ruling weeks, months or even years earlier.

Both FIFO and LIFO have their advocates. Some argue that FIFO is superior because it is more likely to approximate the actual flow of goods through the company. Supporters of LIFO argue that their method works better during a period of inflation, because it produces a more realistic measure of profit.

Example 5.3

Glenusk Ltd bought an item of stock for £100 on 1 January 20X1, and a second item for £103 on the morning of 10 January. On the afternoon of 10 January one of the items was sold for £110.

Required:
Using (a) FIFO and (b) LIFO for identifying purchases with sales, calculate the gross profit arising on the item of stocks sold and give the balance sheet value of the item remaining in stock at close of business on 10 January 20X1. Discuss the differences between the results of these calculations.

Solution

	(a) *FIFO*	(b) *LIFO*
Sales	110	110
Cost of goods sold	100	103
Gross profit	10	7
Balance sheet value of stocks	103	100

Between 1 January and 10 January the cost of Glenusk's stock increased from £100 to £103. It is therefore argued, in certain quarters, that £3 represents a gain arising from holding stock during a period of rising prices (see Chapter 2.2.2) and only the remaining £7 should be reported as normal profit arising from business operations. Looked at another way, in the absence of inflation the item would have sold for £107, but the customer had to pay £3 extra to compensate Glenusk for the higher purchase price which it must pay to replace the item sold. The drawback of LIFO is that stock is reported at a low figure in the balance sheet. This is not particularly noticeable in this example, but a company which uses LIFO for a number of years will report stock, in the balance sheet, at only a fraction of its current cost.

The Companies Act approves FIFO, LIFO and AVCO, whereas SSAP 9 rejects LIFO on the grounds that it fails to produce a balance sheet figure for stock that bears a reasonable relationship to actual cost. The conflict between these two regulations has not yet been resolved, but use of LIFO has not increased significantly since it was given statutory approval. This suggests that business agrees with SSAP 9's conclusion that LIFO is an inappropriate method of stock valuation. An additional statutory requirement, of particular relevance in those cases where LIFO is used, is for companies to disclose by way of note any material difference between the balance sheet value of stocks and their replacement cost.

5.1.3 Long-term Contracts

Companies in the manufacturing and construction industries sometimes undertake contracts that extend over a number of accounting periods. A strict application of the prudence concept would require such companies to defer recognition of profit until the contract is complete. This would produce unsatisfactory results, with reported profits fluctuating a great deal depending on how many jobs happened to be completed during a particular accounting period. An alternative practice, which is thought to provide a better measure of corporate performance, is to recognize profit as work proceeds.

The valuation and disclosure of information relating to long-term contracts is dealt with in SSAP 9. This states that profit should be recognized on uncompleted contracts, subject to the following:

- The contract must be far enough advanced for its outcome to be assessed with reasonable certainty before any profit may be identified and reported in the accounts. No guidance is provided to help to decide whether this condition is met, and each case must be considered on its merits. As a general rule, a contract that is less than 25% complete is unlikely to be sufficiently well advanced, and the information provided in examination questions will make it possible to judge whether the outcome can be assessed with reasonable certainty.

- The profit recognized (called attributable profit) should be related only to the portion of a long- term contract completed at the accounting date.

- Each long-term contract must be considered separately, and the expected outcome examined after allowing for future cost increases and any likely claims or penalties.

- In line with the concept of prudence, any losses predicted on individual contracts must be provided for in full.

Example 5.4

Longrun Ltd has entered into two contracts, each worth £400,000. At the balance sheet date, 31 December 19X2, when each contract is well advanced, it is estimated that total contract costs will amount to £250,000 on contract A and £450,000 on contract B.

Required:
Calculations of the overall profit or loss expected to arise on each contract, and your advice on how they should be treated in the accounts.

Solution

Profit (loss) calculations:

	Contract A	Contract B
	£000	£000
Total value of contract	400	400
Expected total cost	250	450
Overall profit (loss)	150	(50)

An overall profit is expected to arise on contract A and credit may be taken for the element attributable to work completed at 31 December 19X2. Full provision must be made for the expected loss on contract B.

The question which then arises is: how much profit should be recognized on contract A? Clearly not £150,000 because the contract is not yet complete. The answer is: the amount attributable to work completed at the balance sheet date. This may be found by comparing the value of work completed and invoiced to customers with the related costs. Let us assume that, for contract A, the value of completed work invoiced at 31 December 19X2 is £140,000 and the related costs are £95,000. In these circumstances the £140,000 and £95,000 are entered in the profit and loss account, with the result that the profit earned to date – attributable profit – of £45,000 is recognized in the accounts.

5.2 RESEARCH AND DEVELOPMENT EXPENDITURE

Companies incur research and development (R&D) expenditure with the aim of improving profits either by increasing the range or quality of the products in which they trade or by improving the efficiency of the processes which they use. The importance of accounting for R&D expenditure in a realiztic manner was brought dramatically to the attention of the business community by the failure of Rolls Royce Ltd. This company had been, for many years, the 'flagship' of British industry. It was at the forefront of technological research and had an enviable reputation for the quality of its highly expensive products, but it collapsed monumentally in 1971. The immediate cause of the collapse was the drain on the company's finances brought about by the RB211 project undertaken for the American company, Lockheed. Cost estimates on which the contract was based were far too low; by the time the receiver was appointed (1971), the forecast 'launch' cost of the engine was over twice the estimate, of £90m, advised to the government in autumn 1968.

Investigations showed that, during the 1960s, the company began to capitalize a proportion of R&D expenditure; previously the policy had been one of immediate write-off against revenue in the year the expenditure was incurred. The effect of the change was to enable the company to report profits and pay out higher dividends than would otherwise have been possible. The problem was that the management's optimistic view that R&D expenditure would be covered by the contract price, and should therefore be carried forward as an asset, proved totally unjustified. The contract was 'overspent' and R&D expenditure should have been written off as a loss. If this had been done, the published accounts would have provided users with a fairer measure of the company's financial position and alerted them earlier to the deteriorating financial condition. It is not beyond the bounds of possibility that such disclosure would have caused shareholders and creditors to pressure management into taking action that would have averted the forthcoming catastrophe.

The accounting treatment of R&D expenditure is now regulated by SSAP13. This recognizes that the difficulty of forecasting and quantifying future benefit varies depending on the exact nature of the R&D expenditure involved. Four separate categories are identified:

- Fixed assets used to provide facilities for R&D activities.

- Pure (or basic) research, i.e. original investigation undertaken in order to gain new scientific or technical knowledge and understanding. Basic research is not primarily directed towards any specific practical aim or application. For example, where a pharmaceutical company engages in research into the general nature of a headache.

- Applied research, i.e. original investigation undertaken in order to gain new scientific or technical knowledge and directed towards a specific practical aim or objective. For example, where the pharmaceutical company is attempting to discover a means of ameliorating the pain associated with a headache.

- Development, i.e. the use of scientific or technical knowledge in order to produce new or substantially improved materials, devices, products, processes, systems or services prior to the commencement of commercial production. For example, where the pharmaceutical company develops a pill to be marketed, based on its applied research.

SSAP13 requires expenditure on fixed assets to be capitalized and written off over the assets' expected useful life in the normal way. Pure and applied research expenditures should be written off immediately, while development expenditure may be capitalized where certain stringent conditions are fulfilled. These conditions require management to produce evidence which shows that the development expenditure relates to a clearly defined project that will result in the company providing a new or improved product or service which it can reasonably expect to market at a profit. In such circumstances, development expenditure may be carried forward and written off against revenue over the periods benefiting from the sale of the product. The Companies Act gives legal support to the main provisions contained in SSAP13.

SSAP13 is a compromise between the more extreme proposals that all R&D expenditure should either be written off immediately or accounted for as an asset to the extent that its ultimate recovery is reasonably assured. The strong argument for immediate write-off is that it avoids the need to exercise subjective judgement and, therefore, eliminates the risk of profit overstatement of the type which occurred at Rolls Royce. It is further pointed out that the approach gives high priority to the fundamental accounting concept of prudence in a valuation area fraught with uncertainty. Opponents of immediate write-off claim that it contravenes one of the other fundamental accounting concepts, the 'accruals' concept, which requires costs to be matched with related benefits. It is also claimed that an unduly prudent approach, which excludes a valuable asset from the balance sheet and understates current profits, is likely to be highly misleading. It is therefore argued that, where R&D expenditure is expected to produce future revenues, it should be carried forward as an asset and amortized over the period of expected benefit.

The provisions of SSAP13 are inclined towards treating R&D expenditure as an expense rather than an asset, i.e. the prudence concept is given precedence over the accruals concept. The underlying assumption seems to be that the potential hazards from understating profits and balance sheet values are less than those associated with overstatement. The Statement has proved acceptable to the business community, and its fairly stringent provisions have meant that capitalization occurs only in a relatively small number of cases.

Example 5.5

The following expenses were incurred by the research and development department of New Ideas Ltd during 20X6:

(i)   Purchase of a machine for testing new products developed by the department: £16,000. The machine was purchased on 1 January 20X6 and is expected to last five years and then be valueless.

(ii) Research expenditure incurred in an endeavour to discover new uses for materials available to the company in plentiful supply: £13,000. No uses have yet been discovered, but the department's manager hopes that progress will be made in due course.

(iii) Expenditure on successfully developing a new compound to replace raw materials which are expected to be in short supply over next three years: £21,000. The materials are incorporated in a highly profitable product line.

Required:
Explain how each of the above items should be treated in the accounts for the year to 31 December 20X6.

Solution

(i)   The fixed assets are used to provide facilities for R&D expenditure and may be written off over their expected useful life. The depreciation charge is £3,200 (£16,000 ÷ 5) and the balance of £12,800 is carried forward as an asset.

(ii) Research expenditure must be written off against revenue arising during 20X6.

(iii) The development expenditure appears to be recoverable and may be either written off or reported as an intangible asset in the balance sheet at 31 December 20X6. In the latter case, the expenditure should be amortized over the period of benefit, three years, at the rate of £7,000 per annum.

5.3 TAXATION

5.3.1 Corporation Tax

The rates of corporation tax are announced in the budget each year and are the subject of almost continuous amendment on that occasion. For the financial year 2000 (commencing 1 April 2000) corporation tax was levied at 20% (the small companies rate) on taxable profits up to £300,000 and 30% on profits of £1,500,000 or above. A sliding scale at an effective rate of 32.5% operated where profits were in the range £300,000 to £1,500,000.

Some illustrative calculations of tax liability are as follows:

Taxable profit	Calculation of tax payable	Tax payable
£250,000	£250,000 x 20%	£50,000
£1,000,000	£300,000 x 20%	£60,000
	£700,000 x 32.5%	£227,500
		£287,000
£4,000,000	£4,000,000 x 30%	£1,200,000

Companies are required to disclose the amount of the charge in the profit and loss account. Any overprovision or underprovision in respect of the previous year must be adjusted against the charge for the current year. Corporation tax is payable nine months after the end of the accounting period to which it relates and should therefore be reported as a current liability in the balance sheet.

Example 5.6

The following information is provided for Somerton plc which makes up its accounts on the calendar year basis.

	£000
Profit before taxation for 1998	17,000
Profit before taxation for 1999	11,000
Profit before taxation for 2000	23,000
Provision for taxation for 1998	5,720
Provision for taxation for 1999	3,710
Provision for taxation for 2000	7,160
Tax paid for 1998	5,500
Tax paid for 1999	4,020
Tax paid for 2000	7,000

Required
The relevant entries in the profit and loss account and balance sheet of Somerton plc for 1999 and 2000.

Solution

Profit and loss account		1999		2000
	£000	£000	£000	£000
Profit before taxation		11,000		23,000
Corporation tax charge	3,710		7,160	
-Over/under provision previous year	−220	3,490	310	7,470
		7,510		15,530
Balance sheet				
Creditors due within one year:				
Corporation tax		3,710		7,160

5.3.2 Deferred Taxation

An important point for students to grasp is that the profit figure on which tax is paid (taxable profit) is rarely the same as the figure for profit reported in a company's accounts (reported profit). This is because there are significant differences between the procedures followed when calculating each of these profit figures. These differences fall into two basic categories:

(a) *Permanent differences.* Examples of transactions that give rise to permanent differences between taxable profit and reported profit are tax-free income, such as some government grants, and business expenditure disallowed for tax purposes, such as charitable and political donations and most entertainment expenditure.

(b) *Timing differences.* These arise when items of income and expenditure are taken into account in different accounting periods for the purpose of computing reported profit and taxable profit. These items therefore cause differences between the two profit figures which cancel out over time. Examples of timing differences are:

- Interest receivable and payable which is included in the accounts on an accruals basis but taxed on a cash basis.

- General provisions for bad debts, which are not allowed for tax until they become specific.

- Expenditure on fixed assets, which results in depreciation being charged in the accounts whereas uniform capital allowances are granted for tax purposes, e.g. a tax writing down allowance (WDA) of 25% per annum, reducing balance basis, is given on all eligible plant and machinery.

Deductions from taxable profits in excess of the amount charged in the profit and loss account give rise to 'originating' timing differences, whereas the opposite circumstances give rise to 'reversing' timing differences. The effect of timing differences on reported profit after tax is illustrated in Example 5.7.

Example 5.7

Bulmore Ltd was formed on I January 19X1 and purchased plant costing £1,920,000 on that date. The plant was expected to have a three-year life and be worth £810,000 at the end of that period. Annual profits before tax were £1,200,000 for the period 19X1 – 19X3 and the company's policy is to depreciate plant on the straight-line basis. The tax writing down allowance is 25% per annum, reducing balance.

Required:

(a) Calculate the timing difference for each of the years 19X1-X3.

(b) Calculate the corporation tax charge for each of the years 19X1-X3.

(c) Prepare profit and loss appropriation accounts for each of the years 19X1-X3 so far as the information permits.

Note:
Assume a corporation tax rate of 33% for illustrative purposes.

Solution

(a)

	19X1	19X2	19X3
	£000	£000	£000
Writing down allowance (WI)	480	360	270
Less: Depreciation (W2)	370	370	370
Originating (reversing) timing difference	110	(10)	(100)

W1		£000
Cost 19X1		1,920
Tax WDA for 19X1 (25%)		480
Tax written down value at 31 Dec. 19X1		1,440
Tax WDA for 19X2 (25%)		360
Tax written down value at 31 Dec. 19X2		1,080
Tax WDA for 19X3 (25%)		270
Tax written down value at 31 Dec. 19X3		810
W2 £1,920,000 (cost) – £810,000 (residual value) ÷ 3 =		370,000

(b) Assuming there are no other differences between reported and taxable profit, corporation tax payable is calculated as follows:

	19X1	19X2	19X3
	£000	£000	£000
Reported profit before tax	1,200	1,200	1,200
Less: Originating timing difference	110		
Add: Reversing timing difference	___	10	100
Taxable profit	1,090	1,210	1,300
Tax at 33%	359.7	399.3	429

(c)

	19X1	19X2	19X3
	£000	£000	£000
Profit before tax	1,200.0	1,200.0	1,200.0
Less: Corporation tax	359.7	399.3	429.0
Profit after tax	840.3	800.7	771.0

Profits after tax are used as a basis for assessing corporate performance and, for this reason, timing differences can result in wrong conclusions being reached by users of accounting reports. An examination of Bulmore's after-tax profits suggests that the company was more profitable in 19X1 than in the following two years. This was not the case, and the only reason why Bulmore appears more profitable, in 19X1, is because the system of capital allowances results in a much smaller tax charge in that year.

The deferred tax account (DTA) is used as a device for neutralizing the effect of timing differences on reported profits. The procedure is to make transfers, equal to the amount of tax 'saved', from profit to the credit of the DTA when there are originating timing differences. When the differences reverse, an appropriate transfer is made from the DTA to the credit of the profit and loss account.

Example 5.8

Using the information provided in Example 5.7:

(a) Calculate the annual transfers to (from) the DTA for 19X1-X3.

(b) Prepare revised profit and loss appropriate accounts for 19X1-X3.

(c) Give the balances on the DTA reported in balance sheets prepared at 31 December 19X1-X3.

Solution

(a)

	19X1	19X2	19X3
	£000	£000	£000
Originating (reversing) timing difference	−110	(10)	(100)
Transfer to (from) DTA, 33% of originating (reversing) timing difference	36.3	(3.3)	(33)

(b) *Profit and Loss Account*

	19X1		19X2		19X3	
	£000	£000	£000	£000	£000	£000
Profit before tax		1,200		1,200		1,200
Less: Corporation tax:						
Charge for the year	359.7		399.3		429	
Transfer to (from) DTA	36.3		(3.3)		(33)	
		396		396		396
Profit after tax		804		804		804

(c) *Balance Sheet Extract*

Provision for deferred taxation	36.3	33	−

The effect of using DTA is that the total corporation tax charge each year is 33% of the pre-tax profit, while profit after tax is steady at £804,000. The DTA shows a credit balance of £36,300 in 19X1, and this amount is sometimes described as an interest-free loan from the government. The loan arises because tax paid for 19X1 was £359,700 instead of £396,000, due to the existence of capital allowances, and it is repaid by annual instalments of £3,300 and £33,000. It should be noted, however, that transfers between the profit and loss account and the DTA are merely book entries and do not affect the amount of tax paid, which is £359,700 for 19X1, £399,300 for 19X2 and £429,000 for 19X3, irrespective of whether the adjustments are made. Nor does the creation and utilization of a DTA affect the total profit reported over the three-year period, although it does affect the amount reported in individual years:

	19X1 £000	19X2 £000	19X3 £000	Total £000
Reported profit after tax:				
Without a DTA (Example 5.7)	840.3	800.7	771.0	2,412
With a DTA (Example 5.8)	804.0	804.0	804.0	2,412

Originating timing differences usually produce a deferral of tax but, in certain circumstances, a prepayment of tax will result – this is called accelerated taxation. For example, a company may take the view that, due to the rapid rate of technological advance, its computing facility should be fully depreciated over, say, a two-year period for the purpose of the accounts, i.e. depreciation of 50% per annum is charged on the straight-line basis. In this case the tax writing down allowance is much lower, i.e. 25% on the reducing-balance basis, and the payment of tax is accelerated by the existence of a system of capital allowances. Another circumstance in which a prepayment of tax arises is where the interest paid during the year (and allowed for tax) is lower than the interest charged, on the accruals basis, in the profit and loss account.

5.4 CAPITAL INSTRUMENTS

Capital instruments are defined in FRS 4 as: 'All instruments that are issued by reporting entities as a means of raising finance, including shares, debentures, loans and debt instruments, options and warrants, that give the holder the right to subscribe for or obtain capital instruments.' (para. 2)

The traditionally well-established distinction between equity shares and debt is clear cut. The equity shareholders are the owners of the company and dividends due to them are reported as an appropriation of profit. Debt capital is an external liability with associated finance costs deducted in arriving at the profit for the year. The numerical relationship between debt and equity is a measure of a company's gearing. Historically, the only real complication has been the appropriate location in the accounts of preference shares and related dividends. Given the fact that preference shares are usually redeemable and that preference dividends are payable provided adequate profits exist, such capital instruments have always appeared to possess rather more of the characteristics of debt capital than equity capital.

The distinction between debt and equity became significantly blurred during the 1980s as the result of the increasing number and variety of capital instruments that were devised during this decade. Many of these 'hybrid' forms of finance contained both debt and equity characteristics. In the absence of regulatory requirements, there was considerable variation in their treatment between companies and, as a result, a lack of comparability.

The principal objective of FRS 4 entitled 'Capital instruments' is therefore to provide criteria for determining whether a particular security is debt or equity and how it should be treated in the accounts. An achievement of a proper classification will:

- result in more reliable measures of a company's gearing – one of the reasons for the development of new forms of capital instrument was to permit securities, which were in substance debt, to be classified as equity and therefore improve apparent gearing.

- ensure that financing charges are properly classified either above or below the line and, therefore, produce a more reliable measure of profit and, where based on profit, more meaningful accounting ratios.

Central to FRS 4 is the identification of a capital instrument that needs to be classified as a liability. Here the test to be applied is consistent with the definition of a liability contained in the *Statement of Principles* (Chapter 4, para. 24): 'Capital instruments should be classified as liabilities if they contain an obligation to transfer economic benefits'. Any capital instrument that fails to meet this criterion must be reported as part of the shareholders' funds.

The finance costs associated with such liabilities should naturally be charged in the profit and loss account above the line.

Where the nominal value of debt capital is the same as the issue proceeds and the interest rate remains constant throughout the life of the debt, the determination of the amount to appear in the balance sheet and the charge to be debited to the profit and loss account is entirely straightforward. Complications arise where these conditions are not fulfilled, as in the following circumstances:

- The issue proceeds are less than nominal value due to the issue having being made at a discount and/or because there are material issue costs which, in accordance with required practice, must be deducted from issue proceeds. (see Example 5.9)

- Where interest is payable in some years but not in others.

- Where interest is payable at different rates in different years. (see Example 5.10)

The difference between the net issue proceeds and the amount payable to the supplier of debt finance represents the total interest cost which must be allocated between years in order to achieve the two following objectives:

- Interest must be charged at a constant rate based on the carrying amount. That is, the actuarial method used in Chapter 4 for allocating the interest charged in lease arrangements must be applied.

- At the debt redemption date, the carrying amount must be equal to the amount payable at that time.

In the case of non-equity shares, the principles relating to debt capital apply with the only difference being that the dividends paid and any adjustment required to ensure that the financial charge represents a constant return on the amount of finance raised should be reported as appropriations of profits.

Example 5.9

On 1 January 20X0, Bergerac plc issues a debt instrument for £475 million which is repayable at its nominal value of £500 million at the end of four years. Interest is payable at 8% per annum on nominal value and the costs incurred in issuing the securities total £30 million. The effective rate of interest – annual payment plus amortization of discount on the issue price – is 11.59%.

Required:
Calculate for each of the years 20X0-X3:

(a) the annual finance charge to be debited to the profit and loss account

(b) the carrying value of the liability in the balance sheet

Note:
Calculations to the nearest £000.

Solution

Year	Interest paid, 8%	Interest charge in the P&L account, 11.59%	Amortization of discount and issue costs	Carrying value, balance sheet
	£000	£000	£000	£000
				445.0
20X0	40.0	51.6	11.6	456.6
20X1	40.0	52.9	12.9	469.5
20X2	40.0	54.4	14.4	483.9
20X3	40.0	56.1	16.1	500.0

Example 5.10

On 1 January 20X0, Castlenaud plc issues non-equity shares for £50 million which are redeemable for the same amount at the end of ten years. Dividends are payable of £4 million per annum for the first three years, £5 million for the next three years and £6.5 million for the remaining four years. The actuarial rate of return over the issue period is 10.06%.

Required:
Calculate for each of the years 20X0-20X9:

(a) the annual amount to be debited to the profit and loss account appropriation account

(b) the carrying value of the non-equity shares in the balance sheet

Note:
Calculations to the nearest £000.

Solution

Year	Dividend paid	(a) Dividend debited to profit and loss appropriation account, 10.06%	Adjustment to carrying value	(b) Carrying value, balance sheet
	£000	£000	£000	£000
				50.0
20X0	4.0	5.0	1.0	51.0
20X1	4.0	5.1	1.1	52.1
20X2	4.0	5.2	1.2	53.3
20X3	5.0	5.4	0.4	53.7
20X4	5.0	5.4	0.4	54.1
20X5	5.0	5.5	0.5	54.6
20X6	6.5	5.5	−1.0	53.6
20X7	6.5	5.4	−1.1	52.5
20X8	6.5	5.3	−1.2	51.3
20X9	6.5	5.2	−1.3	50.0

5.5 REPORTING THE SUBSTANCE OF TRANSACTIONS

Most people regard the purpose of financial reporting as being to provide user groups with neutral and objective measurements of business performance. Someone reading the information contained in published accounts would, in such circumstances, expect to be fairly and accurately informed of corporate performance during the period under review. The process of communication may be shown diagrammatically:

A   B   C

economic activity ⟶ accounting measurement ⟶ user perception

In practice, financial reporting is not a neutral and unproblematic process. The interests and objectives of the suppliers of accounting information – the directors of a limited company, for example – may well not coincide with those of external stakeholders such as shareholders and lenders. In such circumstances, the directors may manipulate either the way in which the economic activity is legally structured (A) or the way it is measured (B) in order to influence user perception (C) through, for example, publication of an artificially high earnings figure or low measure of gearing.

More specifically, such manipulations – 'creative accounting' as it is often described – may be defined as:

1. The process of manipulating accounting figures so as to exploit choices available, within existing accounting regulations and generally accepted accounting procedures, in relation to measurement and disclosure practices.

2. The process of structuring a transaction in such a way that, if reported in accordance with its legal form, the apparent position differs from the underlying economic reality.

In either case, the aim is to transform financial statements from what they should be into what suppliers of such information would prefer to see reported.

Manipulation type 1 involves exploiting choices available concerning depreciation methods, techniques of stock valuation and ways of accounting for development expenditure.

Manipulation type 2, dealt with here, covers the potential conflict between economic substance and legal form as the appropriate basis for financial reporting.

In most cases, it is a straightforward matter to report the economic substance of transactions in a company's accounts because it coincides also with the legal form of the transaction.

Company A purchases stock on credit from an unrelated company, Company B. Company A will enter (recognize) the stock in its balance sheet as an asset – stock-in-trade – and also as a liability – the amount due to Company B. Company A will remove (derecognize) the asset when it is sold to another unrelated company (say Company C) and instead recognize in its balance sheet the cash received from Company C or the debt due from Company C.

The position has become clouded as the result of the development of numerous artificial transactions intended to make the financial position of an entity look better than it actually is. As noted in Chapter 4, the problem became evident in the 1980s with the development of what became known as 'off balance sheet financing'. During that period, a number of complex arrangements were developed that, if accounted for in accordance with their strict legal form, resulted in accounts that did not report the commercial effects of the arrangement. These developments raised fundamental questions about the nature of assets and liabilities and whether and when they should be included in the accounts. And although the most widely recognized effect of such arrangements is the omission of liabilities from the balance sheet, it must be remembered that such schemes also involve the omission from the balance sheet of the assets 'acquired' with off balance sheet finance with the result that both the resources of the entity and its financing are understated. The most common method of off balance sheet financing was the finance lease whose treatment, as we have seen in Chapter 4, was tacked by the introduction of SSAP 21 entitled 'Accounting for leases and hire purchase contracts'.

The transactions dealt with by FRS 5, entitled 'Reporting the Substance of Transactions', are often extremely complex but the underlying principle to be kept in mind when examining these transactions is their purpose. It is necessary to decide whether the reporting entity has created new assets or liabilities as the result of the transaction, or whether it has changed any of its existing assets or liabilities. It is therefore necessary to look at the relationship between the entities involved in a transaction and consider what is likely to have been the object of the arrangement. If first examination of the details of the transaction suggest that its purpose is something other than the commonsense conclusion, the likelihood is that one needs to dig more deeply in order to discover features of the arrangement that would produce the commonsense conclusion.

The nature of assets and liabilities, as defined by FRS 5, is entirely consistent with the *Statement of Principles*:

* Assets are rights or other access to future economic benefits controlled by an entity as a result of past transactions or events.

* Liabilities are an entity's obligations to transfer economic benefits as the result of past transactions or events.

Once identified, an asset or liability should be recognized (i.e. included) in the balance sheet provided:

* There is sufficient evidence that an asset or liability exists; and

* The asset or liability can be measured at a monetary amount with sufficient reliability.

Consistent with the earlier discussions on leasing, the concept of 'risks and rewards' is significant in determining which entity possesses an asset and which has incurred a liability. SSAP 21 dealt with the specific example of leasing and, although it countered activities in that area with some success, business persons subsequently exploited a myriad of alternative arrangements capable of achieving the objective of off balance sheet finance. FRS 5 therefore follows a different approach in attempting to lay down general principles for dealing with artificial transactions. Thus, there arises the question of the relationship between FRS 5 and other standards such as SSAP 21. The general principle is that, whenever a transaction is covered by more than one rule, the more specific rule should be regarded as more authoritative. We shall see that this may not work all that well in relation to SSAP 21.

FRS 5 (para. 47) sets out three broad areas that require consideration in order to decide where the risks and rewards reside in relation to what might be an extremely complex contractual arrangement.

1. The separation of legal title to an item from the rights or other access to the principal future economic benefits associated with it. Also, exposure to the principal risks inherent in those benefits.

2. The linking of a transaction with others in such a way that the commercial effect can be understood only by considering the series of transactions as a whole.

3. The inclusion of options or conditions on terms that makes it highly likely that the option will be exercised or the conditions fulfilled.

FRS 5 therefore sets out general principles, but it also deals specifically with quasi-subsidiaries and contains 'application notes' that explore the issues surrounding six specific categories of complex transaction and provides advice concerning their appropriate treatment. The six categories are: sale and repurchase agreements; consignment stock; factoring of debts; securitized assets; loan transfers and private finance initiatives.

Each of the above three 'broad areas' can, of course, be incorporated into arrangements concerning quasi-subsidiaries or those falling into any of the six categories covered by the application notes. The greater the extent to which the three provisions are contained in a particular arrangement, the more complex the scheme becomes and the more difficult it is, sometimes, to identify the substance of the transaction. The significance of the three 'broad areas' is illustrated, below, by reference to sale and repurchase agreements, quasi-subsidiaries and consignment stock.

5.5.1 Sale and Repurchase Agreements

The essential feature of a sale and repurchase agreement is that the company that purports to have sold the asset in question has not relinquished all the risks and rewards associated with that asset in a manner which one would expect in the case of a normal sale.

Example 5.11

A whiskey blending company contracts to sell part of its stock of whiskey to a bank for £10 million on 1 January 20X1. The agreement makes provision for the whiskey company to buy back the whiskey two years later for £12.1 million. The whiskey remains located at the whiskey blending company's premises.

The market rate of interest for an advance to a whisky blending company is known to be 10%.

Required:
Explain the substance of this transaction and how it should be accounted for in the books and accounts of the whiskey company.

Solution

An examination of the purpose of this transaction reveals it to be a financing arrangement rather than a normal sale. The whiskey company has transferred no risks and rewards of ownership to the bank and has merely borrowed money on the security of an appreciating asset.

The stock should remain in the balance sheet of the whisky blending company, at the date of the initial advance (1 January 20X1) at £10 million, with the cash received from the bank shown as a liability. In the accounts for 20X1, there should appear in the profit and loss account a finance charge of £1 million, representing 10% of the amount of the effective advance. The amount of the 'loan' will be shown in the balance sheet at £11 million – £10 million initial advance and £1 million interest accrued and unpaid.

For 20X2, the finance charge should be £1.1 million; the original advance was £10 million and the interest for 20X1 of £1 million has not yet been paid and so the total advance for the duration of 20X2 is £11 million (therefore, £11 million x 10% = £1.1 million interest). The recorded value of the advance is increased to £12.1 million and should be deleted from the balance sheet when repayment is made on 1 January 20X3.

Had the transaction instead been accounted for as a normal sale, stock would have been reduced by £10 million and cash would have been increased by £10 million in the whisky blending company's balance sheet. In such a case the financing arrangement would remain off balance sheet and the assets of the company would also be understated.

This is a straightforward financing arrangement but additional provisions may be included which make it less easy to determine the substance of the transaction. Examples:

- The nature of the asset – it is perhaps unlikely that a bank would want to retain ownership of a stock of whisky but the position might be different, and the appropriate accounting treatment would then be different, in the case of property.

- The nature of the repurchase provision – is there an unconditional commitment by both parties or does either or both possess options concerning repurchase arrangements?

- The initial sale price and the repurchase price – do these look like artificial prices designed to operationalize a financing arrangement or are they the actual market prices at one or both dates? If the figures used at each date are market prices, the arrangement begins to look more like a normal sale in which risks and rewards are transferred, particularly if either or both parties enjoy appropriate options, e.g. the 'purchaser' has the option to retain the asset rather than resell it to the initial vendor.

- The location of the asset and the right of the seller to use the asset while it is owned by the buyer. Where the asset remains on the vendor's premises or the vendor retains a right of access to the asset, the transaction would appear not to possess the characteristics of a normal sale.

5.5.2 Quasi-Subsidiaries

For much of the first half of the 20th century it was possible for a holding company to conceal the extent of its gearing by operating through subsidiary companies which raised loan finance. The Companies Act 1948 removed this possibility by obliging holding companies, in most cases, to publish consolidated accounts that combine the results of the subsidiaries with those of the holding company. By the 1980s, managements had devised the 'quasi-subsidiary' to achieve the same results as those produced by the formation of subsidiary companies a half a century earlier.

The quasi-subsidiary of a reporting entity is a company, trust, partnership or other vehicle that, though not fulfilling the definition of a subsidiary, is directly or indirectly controlled by the reporting entity and gives rise to benefits for that entity that are in substance no different from those that would arise were the vehicle a subsidiary. (FRS 5, para. 7)

It is therefore necessary to consider the full details of the arrangements in order to penetrate the substance of a series of transactions.

Example 5.12

Brive Ltd, the owner of a large chain of restaurants, sells ten of them to Limoges Ltd which has been established as the subsidiary of a finance institution, Finance plc. Limoges receives its finance in the form of loans at the normal market rate of interest from Finance plc. Brive and Limoges enter into a management agreement whereby Brive undertakes full responsibility for managing the restaurants. The remuneration for this service, in the form of a management charge, is set at a level that absorbs all the profits of Limoges after first paying interest on the loan finance. There is also an arrangement between Brive and Limoges that, if the latter disposes of any of the restaurants, the management charge for that year is adjusted by the amount of the gain or the loss.

Required:

(a) Explain the substance of the arrangement between Brive, Limoges and Finance Plc.

(b) State how the affairs of Limoges should be treated by Brive when preparing its annual accounts.

Solution

(a) Finance plc is the legal owner of Limoges which in turn owns the ten restaurants, but these are mere technicalities. The substance of the transaction is that Brive continues to enjoy all the risks and rewards of owning the restaurants. Finance plc finances a proportion of Brive's total business operations and is remunerated for this service at the market rate of interest.

(b) The assets and liabilities of Limoges should be combined with those of Brive for consolidation purposes so that the group balance sheet will show the restaurants as an asset and the loans from Finance plc as a liability.

5.5.3 Consignment Stock

The transfer of stocks on a consignment basis is common in certain trades, particularly motor vehicle dealerships. The essence of consignment stock is that the goods are held by one party (the dealer) but owned by another party (the manufacturer) on terms that give the dealer the right to sell the stock in the normal course of its business or, at its option, to return the vehicles unsold to the legal owner.

Such as arrangement has a number of commercial advantages for both parties. For example, the dealer is able to hold a wider range of stocks than might otherwise be practicable while the manufacturer can avoid a build up of stock on its premises.

Both parties benefit from greater sales potential as the result of the arrangement. The kind of factors to be taken into account in determining the substance of the transaction – that is, whether or not the consignment stock should be treated as an asset of the manufacturer or the dealer – is set out in a table to the application notes contained in FRS 5 and is reproduced below.

Indications that the stock is not an asset of the dealer at delivery	*Indications that the stock is an asset of the dealer at delivery*
Manufacturer can require the dealer to return stock (or transfer stock to another dealer) without compensation, or	Manufacturer cannot require dealer to return or transfer stock, or
Penalty paid by the dealer to prevent returns/ transfers of stock at the manufacturer's request.	Financial incentives given to persuade dealer to transfer stock at manufacturer's request.
Dealer has unfettered right to return stock to the manufacturer without penalty and actually exercises the right in practice.	Dealer has no right to return stock or is commercially compelled not to exercise its right of return.
Manufacturer bears obsolescence risk, eg:	Dealer bears obsolescence risk, e.g.
– obsolete stock is returned to the manufacturer without penalty; or	– penalty charged if dealer returns stock to the manufacturer; or
– financial incentives given by manufacturers to prevent stock being returned to it (e.g. on a model change or if it becomes obsolete).	– obsolete stock cannot be returned to manufacture and no compensation is paid by manufacturer for losses due to obsolescence.
Stock transfer price charged by manufacturer is based on manufacturer's list price at date of transfer of legal title.	Stock transfer price charged by manufacturer is based on manufacturer's list price at date of delivery.
Manufacturer bears slow movement risk, e.g.	Dealer bears slow movement risk. e.g.
– transfer price set independently of time for which dealer holds stock, and there is no deposit.	– dealer is effectively charged interest as transfer price or other payments to manufacturer vary with time for which dealer holds stock; or
	– dealer makes substantial interest-free deposit that varies with the levels of stock held.

To provide guidance for accountants and other business persons, the application notes contain similar tables for each of the other five types of transaction covered.

5.6 PROVISIONS AND CONTINGENCIES

It will be useful to start this section with two definitions:

- Liabilities are obligations of an entity to transfer economic benefits as a result of past transactions or events;

- A provision is a liability of uncertain timing or uncertain amount .

We can see that provisions, by their nature, are uncertain and, therefore, provide scope for the exercise of subjective judgement. Provisions arise in a wide range of circumstances and cover such matters as restructuring, repairs and maintenance, warranties, decommissioning costs and operating losses.

To portray as fairly as possible the financial position of an entity, it is therefore important that a provision should be recognized whenever a relevant liability exists. It is equally important for a provision to be made only when such a liability exists. It follows that the intention to incur expenditure does not, in itself, result in a liability.

The new guidelines contrast with past practice when the mere intention to incur expenditure often triggered the inclusion of a provision in the accounts. Once the provision was made, an equivalent amount of subsequent expenditure bypassed the profit and loss account, being charged directly against the provision. The original provision would have been made against profit, of course, but usually in circumstances when its negative effect on performance assessment was perceived to be minimized. Examples:

- The original provision is described as an exceptional item and explained away by management as not really germane to any assessment of performance. An extremely large and wide-ranging provision, that appeared in the accounts of British Gas plc for 1993, fell into this category. It was described as 'An *exceptional* charge of £1,650 million for the major restructuring of the UK Gas Business' (emphasis added).

- A company suffers a significant loss during the year and management is aware of the fact that public perception of performance will be unfavourable. Depending upon the precise circumstances, it may therefore be considered desirable to make generous provisions against some kind of future expenditure on the grounds that the public's perception of this year's results will not materially worsen and next years profits will be inflated, thereby helping to reinforce the market's conclusion that that earlier problems have been resolved.

- At the time of acquiring a new subsidiary, there could be an incentive to deflate the profits of the acquired company for the period immediately prior to acquisition. This could be done by making overgenerous provisions for future losses and/or the cost of rationalizing and restructuring the new entity in order to better match the overall requirements of the group. The artificially deflated profit figures are then 'blamed' on previous management and the apparent performance of the new management team is significantly enhanced as the result of charging a proportion of future costs against the provisions rather than revenue.

FRS 12 entitled 'Provisions, contingent liabilities and contingent assets' was issued in 1998 to address these problems. According to Margaret Cassidy and Ken Wild of Deloitte & Touche, the new standard met with 'a mixed reception of bouquets and brickbats'.

> *FRS 12's unspoken aim was to eliminate abuses of provisioning that had been taking place over a number of years ... the bouquets therefore came from the accounting profession and those companies that had not indulged in such dubious practices. The brickbats, understandably, came from those companies whose devious plans had been scuppered, but also from a number of 'innocent' companies that found themselves unable to provide for certain things that had been taken for granted in the past. (Accountancy, September 1999, p. 84).*

The reference to 'innocent companies' reflects the fact that the new standard attempts to alter one of the notions drummed into accountants throughout their training, namely the concept of prudence which requires:

- provision to be made for all foreseeable losses as soon as there is a significant possibility that they will occur; and

- accountants to err on the 'safe side' when fixing their amount.

In the new world of FRS 12, the objective is to encourage business persons and accountants to take a realistic approach rather than a pessimistic approach when measuring provisions and liabilities for inclusion in the accounts.

Returning to the definition of a liability contained in FRS 12 and given at the start of this section, it will be noted that the wording is entirely consistent with both FRS 5 and the *Statement of Principles*. The standard therefore plays an important part in developing a system of financial reporting consistent with the conceptual framework, whereby only items that qualify as assets, liabilities or equity should be recognized in an entity's financial report. We can see that a provision is less certain than a liability – either the precise amount and/or its timing is uncertain – and the aim of FRS 12 is to ensure that the provision should be recognized in the accounts only when there exists, to all intents and purposes, a liability.

A provision must therefore be made only where the following conditions are satisfied:

- It is probable that a transfer of economic benefit will be required to settle the obligation. Transfer is regarded as probable if the event is more likely to occur than not to occur.

- There exists an obligating event. An obligating event is deemed to exist only where there is either a contractual obligation or a constructive obligation. The latter results from an entity's actions where:

  – by an established pattern of past practice, published policies or a sufficiently specific current statement, the entity has indicated to other parties that it will accept certain responsibilities; and

  – as a result, the entity has created a valid expectation on the part of those other parties that it will discharge those responsibilities.

In other words, an obligating event results in an entity having no realistic alternative to settling that obligation – there is effectively a liability. If expenditure, although appearing prudent, is avoidable, it must not be provided for in the accounts although it probably should be referred to in the narrative in order to ensure that users are properly informed of the company's intentions. A good example of this concerned the so-called 'millennium bug'. Back in the mid-1990s, a company might have considered it sensible to incur expenditure in order to ensure that their software would be year 2000 compliant. They were not entitled to make a provision for such expenditure in the accounts, however, as they had no legal or constructive obligation to incur such expenditure. Of course, having actually incurred such expenditure, they would be entitled to treat it as a cost and any amount owing and unpaid as a liability.

• It must be possible to make a reliable estimate of the amount of the obligation.

The decision tree (Figure 5.1), taken from Appendix II of FRS 12, can be used in order to decide whether to provide for a contingent liability, disclose a contingent liability or do nothing. It summarizes the main requirements of the FRS. It does not form part of the FRS and should be read in the context of the full text.

The following table summarizes the treatment of contingencies under FRS 12:

Likelihood of outcome	Accounting treatment: contingent liability	Accounting treatment: contingent asset
1 Virtually certain (say, >95% probable)	Not a contingent liability but an effective liability, therefore provide	Not a contingent asset but an effective asset, therefore recognize
2 Probable (say, 50-95% probable)	Not a contingent liability but a likely liability, therefore provide	Disclose
3 Possible but not probable (say, >5% probable)	Disclosure	No disclosure permitted
4 Remote (say, <5% probable)	No disclosure required	No disclosure permitted

We can see asymmetry of treatment for categories 2 and 3. In these cases the degree of accounting visibility given to the event is less in the case of a contingent liability than in the case of a contingent asset. This is an example of the continuing application of the prudence concept in accounting despite the ASB's endeavours to enforce realism rather than conservatism as the appropriate basis for financial reports.

The standard makes it clear that, where the time value of money is a material factor (i. e., there is a significant time lag between the date of the accounts and the date on which the liability will be incurred), the amount of any provision should be the present value of the expenditure expected to be required to settle the obligation.

We consider below a number of situations that give rise to the possible need for provisions to be made.

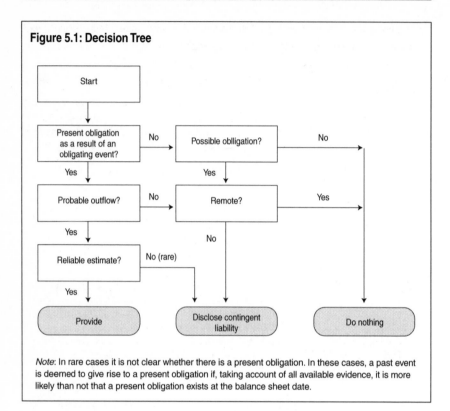

Figure 5.1: Decision Tree

Note: In rare cases it is not clear whether there is a present obligation. In these cases, a past event is deemed to give rise to a present obligation if, taking account of all available evidence, it is more likely than not that a present obligation exists at the balance sheet date.

5.6.1 Restructuring

The cost of restructuring may be provided for only when an entity has an obligation to carry out such work. The obligation to restructure is usually constructive and arises when there is a detailed formal plan for restructuring to take place, identifying:

- The business or part of the business concerned

- The principal locations affected

- The location, function, and approximate number of employees who will be compensated for terminating their services

- The expenditure to be undertaken

- When the plan will be implemented

The entity must also have raised a valid expectation among those affected that it will carry out the restructuring either by actually starting to implement that plan or by announcing its main features to affected personnel.

Example 5.13

The directors Poiters Ltd announced the decision to restructure one of its divisions on 30 June 20X0. The main changes were to occur at its Denham factory resulting in the redesign of its production line at a cost of £2 million and redundancy costs due to reduced staffing requirements of £1.6 million. The plan is expected to be implemented by 31 March 20X1 and agreement from relevant unions and employees has been obtained. The company makes up its accounts on the calendar year basis.

Note:
Ignore the time value of money

Required:
An explanation of whether any provision for restructuring should be recognized in the accounts for 20X0.

Solution

The information provided suggests that a provision for exceptional restructuring costs of £3.6 million would be made in the accounts for 20X0. At that date there is a constructive obligation to incur expenditure which results in a highly probable cash outflow that appears to be reliably estimated at £3.6 million.

The fact that there has been a public announcement and that the restructuring has been discussed with relevant parties suggests that events have gone beyond the directors power of recall, and have together produced the expectation that it will be put into effect without significant delay or alteration.

Prior to FRS 12, it was sometimes the case that provision would be made prematurely, perhaps at the time when the board had made a decision indicating that a liability would be incurred but little or nothing had been done to implement that decision. The introduction of FRS 12 found De La Rue plc in such a position. The company was therefore required to make a prior year adjustment in its 1997-8 accounts stating that a charge made for reorganization costs of £14.8 million in the 1996-7 accounts had now been reversed and recharged in the accounts for the following year.

5.6.2 Repairs and Maintenance
Pre-FRS 12, it was the practice of some companies to equalize repair and maintenance costs relating to large assets by making regular annual provisions against which actual expenditure could be charged as and when it was incurred. Such provisions – e.g. for the relining of a furnace every five years or for overhauling an

aircraft every three years – may not now be the subject of provisions on the grounds that there is no obligation to incur the expenditure resulting from past events.

> *There are no grounds for recognizing a provision for future repairs and maintenance expenditures because these relate to the future operation of the business, the restoration of service potential, and are therefore either to be capitalized as assets or written off as operating expenses when incurred.* (FRS 12, appendix VII, para. 38)

5.6.3 Warranties

Warranty provisions are admissible on the grounds that the event giving rise to the legal obligation is the past sale of the product on which the warranty is given.

Example 5.14

Penne Ltd sells goods with a warranty under which customers are covered for the cost of repairing any manufacturing defect that becomes apparent within the first twelve months after purchase. The following further information is provided at 31 December 20X2:

- If minor defects were detected in all products sold, repair costs of £1 million would result.

- If major defects were detected in all products sold, repair costs of £4 million would result.

Penne's past experience and future expectations indicate that, for the coming year, 75% of the goods sold will have no defects, 20% of the goods sold will have minor defects and 5% of the goods sold will have major defects.

It is estimated that the costs will be incurred exactly 12 months after the balance sheet date.

The relevant discount rate is 10%.

Required:
(a) Compute the amount of the provision to be made in the accounts for 20X2.

(b) Explain how the warranty costs will be accounted for in 20X3 assuming the expectations are exactly fulfilled.

Solution

(a) Cash value of provision: (75% of nil) + (20% of £1 million)
                                                  + (5% of £4 million)   =   £400,000

       Present value of warranty   £400,000 x 100 ÷ 110   =   £363,636
       costs to be charged against
       profit and credited
       to provision account:

(b) Interest charge debited to   £363,636 x 10%   =   £36,364
       profit and loss account and
       credited to provision:

       The amount of the payment on 31 December 20X3, £400,000, will exactly match the provision built up in the books.

5.6.4 Decommissioning Costs

These are the costs that arise when, for example, an oil rig or a nuclear power station has to be dismantled at the end of its useful economic life. Previous practice concerning decommissioning costs was to build up provisions over the life of the asset. In contrast, FRS 12 requires that the liability should be recognized in the accounts as soon as the obligation exists which, to a substantial extent, may well be at the commencement of operations. For example, the standard refers to the situation where approximately 90% of the damage done by an oil rig usually occurs during construction and just 10% when extracting the oil.

Example 5.15

Puy Ltd constructs an oil rig in the North Sea on 1 January 20X1. It is estimated that total decommissioning costs will be £300 million and the obligation to incur 90% of these costs has arisen during the construction of the rig and the remainder will accrue on an equal annual basis. Decommissioning is expected to take place at the end of 20X6.

Required:
An explanation of how the decommissioning costs should be treated in the accounts of Puy Ltd.

Note:
Ignore the time value of money

Solution

A provision of £270 million should be made in the accounts of 20X0. Given the fact that such expenditure is expected to produce future economic benefits, the amount of £270 million should be capitalized as an asset in the balance sheet and written off, in accordance with the accruals concept, at the rate of £45 million per annum, over the 6 years that the oil rig is expected to operate.

The additional decommissioning costs of £5 million arising each year as a result of working the rig will also have to be accounted for and charged against revenue, giving a combined charge for each year of £50 million.

| | Balance sheet | | Profit and loss account | |
| | £ million | £ million | £ million | £ million |
	Asset	Provision	Initial costs	Annual costs
1 January, 20X1	270	270		
31 December, 20X1	225	275	45	5
31 December, 20X2	180	280	45	5
31 December, 20X3	135	285	45	5
31 December, 20X4	90	290	45	5
31 December, 20X5	45	295	45	5
31 December, 20X6	0	300	45	5

On 31 December 20X6 the payment on decommissioning of £300 million will be matched with the provision.

The amounts involved are of course sufficiently material to require, in practice, the forecast outflows to be discounted to present value. In such circumstances, the interest accruing over the life of the rig will gradually 'unwind' and needs also to be charged in the profit and loss account.

Overall, the affect on reported profits of the new rules is not likely to be significantly different from under previous practice, assuming broadly annual provisions would have been made for estimated decommissioning costs. However, with or without the time value of money, the balance sheet will look very different. There will be an initial capitalization (ignoring time value of money) of £270 million (or £144.5 million taking account of the time value of money) and a provision of an equivalent amount.

With or without the time value of money the balance sheet will look very different. There will be an initial capitalization, ignoring the time value of money, of £270 million, or £144.5 million taking account of the time value of money.

5.6.5 Operating Losses
FRS 12 makes it absolutely clear that 'provisions should not be recognized for future

operating losses' (para. 68). Instead, such costs should be reported as they arise in the same way as future profits. It would seem that the standard is here referring to losses of the business as a whole because it is quite clear that provision must be made for future losses in a range of circumstances under existing standard accounting practice, including

- FRS 3. Provision must be made for the future operating losses of operations that are committed to be sold or terminated.

- SSAP 9. Stocks must be written down to net realizable value where this is below cost with the effect that the loss is recognized now rather than in a future trading period.

- FRS 10 and FRS 11. One of the triggers that gives rise to the need for an impairment review is the expectation of future operating losses.

5.7 POST BALANCE SHEET EVENTS

SSAP 17 entitled 'Accounting for Post Balance Sheet Events' gives the accounting treatment for significant events which occur between the balance sheet date and when the accounts are published. The aim is to ensure that published information is as up-to-date as possible. The Statement distinguished between adjusting and non-adjusting events.

Adjusting events cover information that subsequently becomes available concerning conditions existing at the balance sheet date. Examples are: the news that a debtor has become insolvent; and a valuation of a company's freehold offices which indicates a permanent reduction in value below the balance sheet figure. Adjusting events also include transactions which, because of statutory or conventional requirements, must be reflected in the accounts, e.g. 'dividends payable and receivable'. The appropriate accounting treatment of an adjusting event is to revise the financial statements to take account of the new facts.

Non-adjusting events concern new information that does not relate to the conditions existing at the balance sheet date. Examples are subsequent mergers, labour disputes and a share issue. No adjustment of the accounts is required, but the event should be disclosed by way of a note where relevant to a proper appreciation of a company's financial position. Where a transaction is entered into, primarily to alter the appearance of the company's balance sheet, and is subsequently reversed, it must also be accounted for as a non-adjusting event. Such transactions are normally referred to as 'window dressing'. An example is a loan swap between two companies, immediately before their balance sheet dates, to improve their respective short-term liquidity positions.

Certain serious post balance sheet events, although within the non-adjusting definition, cast doubt on whether it is appropriate to use the going concern concept when preparing the accounts. Such 'disasters' must be accounted for as adjusting events.

Example 5.16

Tendon Ltd is a travel agency which arranges holidays to Scandinavia, America and New Zealand. It makes up its accounts on the calendar year basis and publishes them in April following the year end. The following information is provided:

1. A company in which Tendon has invested paid a dividend of £10,000, in respect of the year ended 31 December 20X1, on 5 January 20X2.

2. The New Zealand activities were shut down on 6 March 20X2 giving rise to closure costs of £65,000.

3. In December 20X1 the company received a damages claim for breach of contract of £50,000. In the director's view, the claim is without foundation, and the company's legal advisers agree with this assessment.

4. The company has an arrangement with hotels in Scandinavia whereby, if holidaymakers sent by Tendon fail to spend a certain sum at the bar, Tendon reimburses the shortfall. No claims have yet been received for the 20X1 season but, in past years, payments in the region of £17,500 have been made in March in respect of the previous summer holiday season.

Required:
State how the above items should be dealt with, if at all, in Tendon's financial accounts for 20X1. You should briefly explain your treatment. Answers should take account of the requirements of SSAP17 and FRS12.

Notes:
All events are material. Ignore taxation.

Solution

1. This is an adjusting post balance sheet event. The dividend should be credited to the profit and loss account and treated as a current asset in the balance sheet.

2. This is a non-adjusting post balance sheet event. Details should be given by way of a note.

3. This is a contingent loss and so details need be given only in a note to the accounts.

4. This is a contingent loss. Provision should be made as past experience suggests that the loss is not remote. £17,500 should be charged against profit and included as a current liability.

5.8 INVESTMENTS

Depending upon their precise nature, the Companies Act 1985 requires investments to be shown in the balance sheet as either fixed assets or current assets. The broad distinction is based on the normal rule that a fixed asset is one that is intended for use on a continuing basis as part of the company's activities, whereas a current asset is held on a temporary basis for conversion into cash.

A fixed asset investment will be shown in a company's legal entity-based accounts (most will disappear on the preparation of consolidated accounts for a group) at purchase price including any expenses incidental to acquisition. Under the 'alternative accounting rules' approved by the Companies Act, fixed-asset investments may instead be carried at their market value at the date of their last valuation or at a directors' valuation.

Current asset investments may also be shown at acquisition cost although there is the further requirement that they must be written down to net realizable value where this is a lower figure. Such write-down should be reversed if the reasons for it having initially being made cease to apply. Where the alternative accounting rules are adopted, a current asset investment will be restated at current cost.

Where fixed or current asset investments are revalued, any revaluation surplus must be credited to revaluation reserve. Any revaluation deficit must also be taken to revaluation reserve to the extent it reverses a previous revaluation surplus in respect of the same investment; otherwise, the revaluation deficit must be charged to the profit and loss account. Income arising from such investments is recognized only to the extent that it is receivable as dividends, although some companies take the even more prudent approach of recognizing such dividends only when actually received in cash.

5.9 PENSION COSTS

The provision of a pension is part of the remuneration package of many employees. Pension costs form a significant proportion of payroll costs and give rise to problems of estimation and allocation between accounting periods. FRS 17 entitled 'Retirement benefits', which deals with occupational pension schemes, is designed to ensure that standard accounting practice exists concerning the recognition of such costs in the published financial statements of employer companies. The standard deals with occupational pension schemes set up by the employer. These may be:

- non-contributory – that is, contributions made only by the employer.

- contributory – that is, contributions made by both employer and employees

FRS 17 does not deal with state earnings related pensions schemes (SERPS) or personal pension plans.

Occupational pension schemes may be unfunded or funded. For the former, the pension payments are simply met from the company's financial resources on a 'pay-as-you-go' basis. This is clearly the more risky arrangement as far as the employee is concerned – the money may simply not be there when it is needed! For a funded scheme, the resources are separately invested in assets expected to yield income and/or capital gains and thus increase the value of the fund. Such fund is administered by a group of trustees, which includes employee representatives, and it may be located in a separate pension company set up as a subsidiary of the employer company. There are two broad types of funded schemes: the defined contribution scheme and the defined benefit scheme.

5.9.1 Defined contribution scheme

The liability of the contributor(s) (possibly only the employer but probably also the employee) under this scheme is defined and the amount payable to the pensioners depends on the level to which the fund has accumulated. That is, the contributions are fixed and the level of the pension is variable.

The operation of the scheme gives rise to no particular accounting problems. If the amount paid into the scheme in any year is more or less than the amount contractually payable, the relevant amount will have to be prepaid or accrued in the normal way. The disclosure requirements of FRS 17 are: nature of scheme – defined contribution scheme – to be stated; charge for period; and contributions outstanding or prepaid at accounting date

Example of disclosure – defined contribution scheme:

The company operates a defined contribution pension scheme. The assets of the scheme are held separately from those of the company in an independently administered fund. The pension cost charge represents contributions payable by the company to the fund and amounted to £600,000 (20X0, £520,000). Contributions totalling £30,000 (20X0, £27,000) were payable to the fund at the year end and are included in creditors.

5.9.2 Defined benefit scheme

Under defined benefit schemes, the amount paid in by the employee is pre-determined (usually as a percentage of salary) as is the pension payable. The amount payable by the employer is the variable and, in order to fix its amount, actuaries must calculate the costs to be incurred in providing pensions over, possibly, a long future time period. This exercise will naturally require the estimation of a number of variables that include:

- number of employees in the scheme at various dates; their age distribution; retirement age; life expectancy; labour turnover; future salaries; marital position; and defined benefits.

The estimated liabilities, once computed, must be discounted at the current rate of return on a high quality corporate bond in order to discover the current value of the amount to be contributed during future accounting periods. The assumption underlying use of a high quality corporate bond rate is that the company should be able to invest pension funds in a realistic range of securities to produce a return of at least that amount.

Illustration

Dausse Ltd has a single employee, Jean aged 51. Jean's present salary is £40,000 and is expected to increase at the rate of 8% per annum. Jean is due to retire at 65 and life expectancy thereafter, for the category of individual that includes Jean, is 15 years.

Under the company's pension scheme, Jean's pension is fixed at one-half of his final salary. The annual pension contribution is to be paid into the scheme at the end of each year and the current rate of return on a high quality corporate bond is 6% per annum.

The actuarial calculation would proceed as follows:

- Present salary   £40,000

- Assumed salary increase   8% per annum

- Calculated salary on retirement (£40,000 compounded at 8% per annum for 14 years)   £117,487

- Pension – one-half of final salary   £58,743

- Required capital value of fund at age 65 to enable a pension of £58,743 to be paid for 15 years assuming a 6% return earned during that period on the capital value   £619,550

- Required annual contribution assuming a 6% return on money contributed to fund up to age of 65   40%

The accounting treatment of pension costs is dictated by FRS 17 which requires that 'the operating costs of providing retirement benefits to employees are recognised in the accounting period(s) in which the benefits are earned by the employees, and the related finance costs and any other changes in value of the assets and liabilities are recognised in the accounting periods in which they arise'.

A typical occupational pension scheme enables employees to earn one sixtieth of their salary for each year worked with a maximum pension of two-thirds (forty-sixtieths) of final salary (i.e. Dausse Ltd operates a very generous scheme). The pension may or may not then be inflation-proofed by reference to movements in, say, the retail prices index. The length of time involved, at the outset, in the operation of such schemes results in the need for a great deal of actuarial work in order to fix the amount to be paid by employers, with such amounts necessarily the subject of periodic revision.

The annual cost of the pension scheme, in the case of Dausse Ltd, was initially established at 40% based on assumptions made in relation to the various matters identified above. This amount, having been established, is charged *to the profit and loss account* each year, subject only to adjustment for payments in advance or arrears.

Revision of pension contributions Defined benefit schemes, following their creation, must be the subject of periodic actuarial assessments to confirm whether the pension fund, as initially established, remains likely to generate sufficient cash to meet pension obligations. Full actuarial valuations by a professionally qualified actuary should be obtained at intervals not exceeding three years. In addition, the actuary should review the most recent actuarial valuation at the balance sheet date and update it to reflect current conditions, e.g. the assumption made concerning the discount rate to be used in the actuarial process may need to be reviewed.

At the time of the three-yearly re-assessment, variations in contributions may be required because of any of the following:

1. Experience surpluses and deficits. The actuarial assumptions made when the regular cost was previously established have not been borne out by subsequent experience, e.g. employee turnover has been at a different rate than expected.

2. Changes in actuarial assumptions, e.g. concerning the future rate of increase in salaries. The difference between this type of assumption and that referred to under 1 is that changes in actuarial assumptions relate to the future rather than the past.

3. Retroactive changes in the benefits or conditions of membership, e.g. it may be decided to extend the scheme to an additional category of employee previously excluded.

4. Increases in the level of pensions being paid or to be paid.

For the purpose of the actuarial exercise, pension fund assets are valued at market prices.

The actuarial assessment may well result in the need to revise the amount of the regular contribution as well as giving rise to the identification of a surplus or deficit within the pension fund. All actuarial surpluses and deficits must be recognised in the statement of total recognised gains and losses (STRGL). Any deficit will need to be funded and, if not advanced immediately, will give rise to an accrual that must be recognised in the accounts.

Example 5.17

Lauzerte Ltd operates a non-contributory defined benefit scheme. The fund was established in 20X0. The annual pensionable salary bill amounts to £1,200,000 and the required contribution rate is put at 15% of the salary bill by actuaries engaged by the company. The first three-yearly actuarial valuation is made during 20X3 and, at that stage, it is discovered that:

- The annual cost should be increased to 17%.

- There was an actuarial deficit of £156,000 due to a lower rate of employee turnover than originally anticipated. The amount of the deficit is to be made good by a transfer to the pension fund in 20X4.

The average remaining service life of members of the scheme is 12 years

Required:
The entries in the profit and loss account, statement of total recognised gains and losses and balance sheet of Lauzerte Ltd for 20X3 so far as the information provided permits.

Solution

	£000
Profit and Loss Account for 20X3	
Regular charge, £1,200,000 x 17%	204
Statement of Total Recognised Gains and Losses	
Experience deficit	156
Balance Sheet at 31 December 20X3	
Current liability	
Owing to pension fund	156

Where the result of the actuarial exercise is to show a surplus on the pension fund, there are a number of possible uses:

- Reduce future employer and/or employee contributions – at the extreme, there can be a pension contribution free holiday for employers and/or employees.

- Employee to receive refunds, with a disadvantage of this option being unfavourable tax implications – contributions are allowable for tax and so refunds are subject to tax.

- Benefits payable to members could be increased

The most popular course is to reduce/eliminate employers' contributions – i.e. to take a 'pension holiday'.

5.10 FURTHER READING

Alexander, D. and Britton, A. (1999) *Financial Reporting*, fifth edition, London: International Thomson Business Press, Chapters 17, 18 and 20-23.

Davies, Mike, Ron Paterson and Allister Wilson (1999), *UK GAAP*, sixth edition, Croydon: Butterworth Tolley, Chapters 11, 12, 14-16, 20-1 and 25.

Elliott, B. and Elliott, J. (2000) *Financial Accounting and Reporting*, fifth edition, Hemel Hempstead: Prentice Hall, Chapters 12-13, and 16-18.

Lewis, Richard and David Pendrill (2000), *Advanced Financial Accounting*, sixth edition, Pitman, Chapters 4-7.

Simon, J. (1998) 'Why do companies use creative accounting?', *ACCA Students' Newsletter*, May, pp. 42-4.

5.11 QUESTIONS

Question 5.1

French Ltd makes up its accounts to 30 September. The accounts for the year to 30 September 1994 are being prepared at present.

1. The following information is provided in respect of three entirely different items of stock belonging to French Ltd as at 30 September 1994:

Stock Item	Cost	Net realizable value
A	3,600	3,900
B	2,500	2,800
C	7,100	5,000
	13,200	11,700

2. French Ltd has a stock of Product D which has been assembled at a total cost of £50,000. The cost of each unit of Product D is £50 and the selling price at 30 September 1994 was £60. The company pays a distribution firm £2 for each unit delivered to a customer.

3. Assume the same costs as given under item 2 above. On 10 October 1994 the market for Product D collapsed. It is expected that the company will be able to sell each unit in stock to customers for £40.

4. French Ltd manufactures 'cambers' and incurred the following costs during the year to 30 September 1994:

	£
Materials costs	10,000
Direct labour costs	8,000
Factory overheads	20,000
Administrative overheads	8,500

The company planned to manufacture 800 cambers during the year to 30 September 1994 – the normal level of production. Due to unexpected stoppages, only 500 units were produced, of which 400 were sold and 100 remained in stock at the end of the year. There was no opening stock on 1 October 1993.

Required:
(a) Outline the basic rules governing the valuation of stock.

(b) Taking each of the above items of information (1-4) separately:　　　　　　　　　　[6]

    (i)   Calculate the amount of the stock value to be included in the accounts.

    (ii) Outline the accounting principles underlying each of the calculations, and explain how they affect your answers.　　　　　　　　　　[14]

[Total – 20 marks]

Question 5.2

Abbott Ltd was established on 1 January 1997, and its draft accounts at the end of its first year of trading were as follows:

Profits and Loss Account for the year to 31 December 1997

	£000	£000
Sales		15,330
Cost of goods sold		8,000
Gross profit		7,330
Depreciation	1,000	
Research expenditure	1,050	
Other expenses	4,000	
		6,050
Net profit		1,280

Balance Sheet at 31 December 1997

	£000	£000
Assets		
Plant and equipment at cost		5,000
Less: accumulated depreciation		1,000
		4,000
Development expenditure		600
Stock	900	
Debtors	1,250	
Cash	25	
	2,175	
Creditors	995	
		1,180
		5,780
Financed by		
Ordinary shares of £1 each		4,500
Profit and loss account		1,280
		5,780

The above accounts have been prepared on the expectation that the plant and equipment will have a useful economic life of five years and zero residual value. The development expenditure relates to a new product which is to be launched in early 1998.

Required:
(a) Prepare **three** revised profit and loss accounts and balance sheets of Abbott Ltd for the year 1997 incorporating, separately, each of the following three adjustments:

   (i) The plant and equipment is to be depreciated using the reducing-balance method at an annual rate of 30% and the development expenditure is to be capitalized.

   (ii) The development expenditure is to be written off as it is incurred and the plant and equipment is to be depreciated using the straight-line basis.

(iii) The plant and equipment is to be depreciated using the reducing-balance method at an annual rate of 30% and the development expenditure is to be written off as it is incurred.

The accounts should be presented in columnar format. [10 marks]

(b) Separate calculations (four in all) to one decimal place, of the rate of return earned for the shareholders of Abbott Ltd, in respect of the year ending 31 December 1997, based on the accounts given in the question above and those prepared by yourselves in answer to requirement (a). [4 marks]

(c) (i) Explain briefly the meaning of the accounting concepts of accruals and prudence.

(ii) Identify their relevance for the accounting treatment of research and development expenditure.

(iii) Indicate the extent to which SSAP 13, entitled 'Accounting for Research and Development', gives practical recognition to these two concepts. [6 marks]
[Total – 20 marks]

Question 5.3

Florence plc issued a £200 million debenture at a discounted price of £90 million on 1 January 2000. The debenture is repayable at par on 31 December 2009 with annual interest of 3% payable on the par value. The interest rate inherent in these finance arrangements is 13.23%. Florence makes up its accounts on the calendar year basis.

Required:
(a) FRS 4 entitled 'Capital instruments' was issued by the Accounting Standards Board in December 1993.

Define capital instruments in accordance with the provisions of FRS 4. [4 marks]

(b) Examine the distinction between debt and share capital and discuss how these items and the payments that they give rise to should be reported in the profit and loss account and the balance sheet. [10 marks]

(c) Show the finance charge to be debited to the profit and loss account of Florence plc and the debenture loan liability to be reported in the balance sheet for each of the years 2000-2009. [6 marks]

Notes:
Calculations to nearest £000
Ignore issue costs of debentures

[Total – 20 marks]

Question 5.4

Glazier Ltd was incorporated on 1 October 19X9 and the published accounts for the year to 30 September 19X9 are in the course of preparation. The recently appointed accountant of Glazier, who is a friend of yours, asks your advice on the appropriate accounting treatment of the items detailed below:

(1) Freehold premises were acquired on 1 October 19X9 for £200,000, including land valued at £10,000. Solicitors' fees and other incidental costs associated with the purchase amounted to a further £8,000. The useful life of the building is estimated at 25 years and it will then possess a zero residual value. The land is not expected to decline in value over this period.

(2) The goodwill and other business assets of a small local business were acquired for £60,000 on 1 April 19X9. The tangible and identifiable intangible assets were considered to be worth £48,000 at that date. It is estimated that the goodwill has a useful economic life of six years.

(3) The company purchased, from a German supplier, a specialized item of plant which was installed on 1 July 19X9. The total price paid was £30,000. It is estimated that the item will last for three years and then possess a zero residual value. It is further estimated that this machine will be used for 1,500 hours in its first year of operation and 750 hours in each of the remaining years.

(4) The plant, referred to under (3), was acquired to manufacture a new product developed by the company. Development costs totalled £6,000, and there is no doubt that the new product, which was first sold on 1 October 19X9, will prove highly profitable.

(5) Purchases of raw material 3ZN amounted to £75,000 during the current year. The following information has been assembled relating to the stock of 3ZN on hand at 30 September 19X9.

Cost: first in, first out	£12,000
weight average	£11,200
replacement	£14,000
Net realizable value	£25,000

(6) The company also trades in an item designated BL5. Purchases during the year cost £50,000, net of trade discount. The stock of this item, at 30 September 19X9, was purchased at a retail price of £7,500, on which the company is entitled to a trade discount of 33⅓%. The net realizable value of this stock is estimated at £6,800 at the year end.

(7) The debtors ledger shows a total balance outstanding at 30 September 19X9 of £86,200. Debts known to be bad amount to £800 and the directors feel that another customer, who has gone into liquidation owing £1,600, will eventually pay a dividend of only 25p in the £. A general bad debt provision of 2% should be made in respect of the remaining debtor balances.

Required.
For each of the items (1)-(7) calculate: (a) the amount to be charged against revenue in the profit and loss account; and (b) the balance, if any, which should be carried forward in the balance sheet. You should explain your treatment in each case.

The calculations should be made in accordance with best accounting practice and relevant Standard Accounting Practice. Where more than one accounting treatment is permissible, you should specify the alternatives and state which one results in the lower profit being reported for the year to 30 September 19X9.

[30]

Question 5.5

The following draft accounts have been prepared in respect of Abbott plc for the year to 30 September 2000,

Profit and Loss Account for the year ending 30 September 2000

	Notes	£000	£000
Turnover			50,600
Cost of goods sold		29,000	
Rental	1	2,400	
Provision for closure	2	5,130	
Administration, selling and distribution expenses		8,511	45,041
Net profit			5,559
Dividend from Millerson	3		200
Retained profit for the year			5,759
Retained profit at I October 1999			3,040
			8,799
Goodwill written off	4		1,100
Retained profit at 30 September 2000			7,699

Balance sheet at 30 September 2000

	Notes	£000	£000
Tangible fixed assets			
Freehold property at revaluation	5		15,000
Plant at cost		9,000	
Less: Accumulated depreciation		6,200	2,800
			17,800
Research and development expenditure	6		1,720
Net current assets			5,179
			24,699
Share capital and reserves			
Ordinary share capital (£1 ordinary shares)			10,000
Revaluation reserve	5		7,000
Retained profit			7,699
			24,699

The following further information is provided in respect of the items indicated by Notes 1-6 above.

Notes:
1. This payment was made on 1 April 2000 and is the first of eight annual instalments due for plant and machinery acquired under a leasing contract on 1 April 2000. The plant and machinery is expected to have an eight-year life and, then, a zero residual value. The plant and machinery is known to sell for a cash price of £12,700,000, when new, and the interest rate implicit in the lease is 14%.

2. On 2 September 2000 the directors made the decision to close down a loss-making division with effect from 31 March 2001. The figure contained in the accounts is the provision for expected losses between 1 October 2000 and 31 March 2001 together with the estimated costs associated

with the closure. At 30 September 2000, the balance sheet date, the closure decision remained confidential.

3. Abbott acquired 25% of the ordinary share capital of Millerson Ltd on 1 October 1999 and, through representation on the board of directors, is able to exercise a significant influence over the financial and operating policies of that company. The 'Share capital and reserves' section of the balance sheet of Millerson at the acquisition date contained the following information:

Share capital and reserves	*£000*
Ordinary share capital	16,000
Retained profit	12,800

The profit made by Millerson in the year to 30 September 2000 amounted to £1,400,000. The purchase consideration was £9,000,000 and was satisfied by the issue of 3 million ordinary shares of £1 each in Abbott. No entry has been made in the above accounts of Abbott in respect of the acquisition.

4. This represents the goodwill arising on the acquisition of the tangible and intangible assets of a local business, Delamont, on 1 October 1999.

5. The company's freehold property was professionally revalued on 30 September 2000 at £15 million. Book value at that date, after deducting a depreciation charge of £200,000 for the year, amounted to £8 million.

6. The balance is made up of the following:
    i   Development expenditure brought forward on 1 October 1999 of £1,350,000. This was incurred to develop a new and highly profitable product, which came on to the market on 1 October 1999 and is expected to be discontinued on 30 September 2008.

    ii Applied research expenditure of £370,000 incurred during the year to 30 September 2000 in the endeavour to invent a new design for one of Abbott's leading products. The directors are convinced that this will result in the creation of an improved design in due course.

Required:
(a) Define, with examples, the term 'creative accounting,' and discuss the incentives for directors to engage in this practice when preparing accounts for publication.   [10 marks]

(b) Critically examine the accounting issues raised by the proposed treatment of assets and liabilities detailed in Notes 1-6 above. Identify and explain any amendments to the accounts necessary to comply with UK standard accounting practice.   [20 marks]

(c) Prepare the accounts of Abbott plc for the year ended 30 September 2000 revised, as appropriate, to comply with UK standard accounting practice.   [10 marks]

Notes:
(1) Make and state any assumptions that you consider appropriate.
(2) Ignore taxation.
(3) Calculations to the nearest £000.
(4) Assume all figures to be material.   [Total – 40 marks]

6

GROUP ACCOUNTS

6.1 INTRODUCTION

There was a substantial increase in the average size of the business unit during the last century which started with many industries still characterised by the 'one-man business'. Today the sole trader remains an important feature of business life but, in many industries, the large-scale corporation is now dominant. This development has occurred as the result of both internal and external growth. Internal expansion involves the development of the existing company's business, whereas external growth involves combining together the activities of two or more separate entities in order to achieve particular business objectives. For instance, a company may wish to safeguard its source of essential raw materials, which are in scarce supply, or guarantee wholesale and retail outlets for the products which it manufactures. The economic term used to describe the process whereby companies expand backwards or forwards along the chain of production and distribution is vertical integration. In contrast, horizontal integration occurs when companies, at the same stage in the chain, join together; this strategy may be adopted in order to reduce competition, and perhaps also to reap some of the benefits commonly associated with large-scale production. Diversification occurs when companies expand into unrelated fields for such reasons as risk-spreading or to utilize available funds when there is no room for further expansion in their present line of business. Obviously a company may, at different times, or even at the same time, expand in all three directions.

6.2 COMBINATIONS BASED ON ASSETS OR SHARES

The combination of two or more businesses may be based on the purchase of assets or shares.

Combinations Based on the Purchase of Assets These occur where one company, company A, acquires the assets of another company, company B, and ownership of B's assets is transferred to A. B then goes into liquidation and A carries on the combined activities formerly undertaken by two companies. Alternatively, company C may be formed to acquire the assets of both A and B. Companies A and B may then be wound up and a single legal entity, company C, emerges to carry on the activities previously undertaken by the two companies. In both cases it is necessary to value the assets transferred for inclusion in the acquiring company's books. Once this has been done, however, the assets are accounted for in the normal way and the reporting problems that arise when the combination is based on shares are avoided.

Combinations Based on the Purchase of Shares This is achieved by one company acquiring enough shares of another to give it control, e.g. company A acquires the entire share capital of company B. Readers should note that agreement is reached between company A and the shareholders of company B; the transaction does not affect company B directly and it remains in existence as a separate legal entity. A combination based on shares may, alternatively, involve the formation of a new company, company C, to acquire the shares of A and B. Again, companies A and B remain in existence as separate legal entities. The reasons for basing a combination on an acquisition of shares rather than assets are as follows:

- Economy. It is not necessary to purchase all the target company's shares, merely enough to ensure effective control over its activities.

- Continuity. Where the acquired company maintains a separate identity, its goodwill is more likely to survive unimpaired.

- Decentralization of both managerial and decision-making processes is facilitated where companies retain their own identity.

6.3 THE GROUP

Combinations based on shares give rise to a group of companies within which the company which purchases the shares is called the 'parent' company (formerly referred to as the 'holding company') and the company whose shares are acquired is called the 'subsidiary' company.

Example 6.1

PC Ltd purchased the entire share capital of SC Ltd. The relationship between the two companies can be shown diagrammatically as follows:

PC Ltd
↓
100%
↓
SC Ltd

The arrow indicates that PC is the parent company and SC is the subsidiary, while the percentage superimposed on the arrow indicates the extent of the shareholding. Together PC and SC comprise a group of companies.

The external reporting requirements imposed by the Companies Acts, up until 1948, applied only to separate legal entities. In Example 6.1, for instance, PC and SC each had to publish separate accounts, but these accounts were confined to the transactions directly affecting them as separate legal entities. The accounts published by PC therefore included cash actually received from SC in the form of dividends, but any profits earned and retained by the subsidiary were not reported by the parent company. This provided management with enormous scope for publishing misleading financial information if it was inclined to do so. For instance, when the parent company's profits were low, management was often able to conceal this fact by making large undisclosed transfers of dividends from profitable subsidiaries. In different circumstances, management allowed subsidiaries to retain all their profits, and even made generous provisions for actual or potential losses of subsidiaries to depress a highly favourable profit figure which might otherwise have become the basis for unwelcome wage demands or dividend claims. Admittedly, these are extreme examples, but they indicate the scope for potential abuse where accounting reports are confined to the legal entity.

Where abuses occurred, the parent company's accounts were of little use either for assessment purposes or as a basis for resource allocation decisions. The legislature's response was to require parent companies to supplement their legal entity-based accounts with financial statements based on the affairs of the entire economic entity. Referring back to Example 6.1, both PC and SC are separate legal entities which continue to publish legal entity-based accounts but, in addition, PC is required to publish group accounts dealing with the affairs of the economic entity formed by SC and itself.

6.3.1 Group Accounting Regulations

The main reporting obligations imposed on the directors of parent companies are today contained in the Companies Act 1985, FRS2 entitled 'Accounting for Subsidiary Undertakings', and FRS6 entitled 'Acquisitions and Mergers'. To establish whether the relevant provisions apply, it is first necessary to discover whether two or more companies are to be treated as a group for accounting purposes. The basic rule is that a parent company/subsidiary company relationship exists where the first company owns a majority of the voting share capital of the latter company, and is therefore able to control the conduct of its affairs. In a simple and straightforward world this would be enough, but the business world is neither simple nor straightforward. Various schemes have been devised with the objective of conducting a part of a company's business operations through another organization which, although in law, is not a subsidiary, in reality is a subsidiary. It has therefore become necessary to define the parent/subsidiary relationship more closely in order to prevent these abuses. The details are now set out in FRS2, paragraph 14. They include (in addition to the majority shareholding referred to above) the situation:

- where one company (the parent) holds some shares in another company (the subsidiary) and has the right to appoint or remove directors holding a majority of the voting rights at board meetings.

- where one company (the parent) has the right to exercise a dominant influence over another company (the subsidiary) by virtue of a contractual arrangement which may be contained in the subsidiary's memorandum or articles of association. By 'dominant influence' is meant the right to give directions with respect to the operating and financial policies of the subsidiary.

Often two or more of the above tests produce the same result. For example, it is usually necessary to acquire more than half the voting shares in order to control the composition of the board of directors.

Example 6.2

PC Ltd purchased 102,000 ordinary shares in SC Ltd on 1 January 20X1. The issued share capital of SC consists of 200,000 ordinary shares of £1 each, which carry equal voting rights.

PC is therefore the parent company of SC, as from 1 January 20X1, on two bases:

1. It holds more than half the voting power, and is therefore able to control the composition of the board of directors.

2. It owns more than half the equity share capital, and the relationship between the two companies can be presented as follows:

In certain circumstances, a parent company/subsidiary company relationship may exist applying one test but not the other.

Example 6.3

PC Ltd purchased 50,000 A ordinary shares in SC Ltd on I January 20X1. The issued share capital of SC consists of 75,000 A ordinary shares and 125,000 B ordinary shares. Category A shares are voting shares and category B non-voting.

*   PC is a holding company because it owns a majority of the voting shares and is therefore able to control the composition of the board of directors.

*   PC is not a holding company because it owns only 25% of the equity shares.

One of the tests is satisfied and so PC is the holding company of SC.

In the remainder of this chapter, it is assumed that all equity shares carry equal voting rights and there are no special contractual arrangements, so that a parent company/subsidiary company relationship exists only where a majority of the equity shares are held.

Group accounts can, in theory, take a variety of different forms, but the Companies Acts stipulate that they should normally consist of a consolidated balance sheet dealing with the combined state of affairs of the parent company and its subsidiaries, as if they were a single entity, and a consolidated profit and loss account dealing with the combined profits and losses of the group. Steps should be taken to ensure that, as far as possible, uniform accounting policies are employed when preparing the accounts of companies which are to be consolidated. When this is impracticable, however, details should be given of the different accounting policies used, their financial effect, and the reasons for the divergent treatment.

The accounting procedures to be followed when preparing a consolidated balance sheet differ depending upon the form which the combination takes: where one company acquires another, the acquisition basis is used and the rules set out in FRS2 are followed (see section 6.4); where two companies merge together, the merger basis may be used, in which case the rules set out in FRS6 are followed (see section 6.5).

6.4 CONSOLIDATION: ACQUISITION METHOD

The concept underlying the preparation of consolidated accounts is extremely simple. The objective is to provide the shareholders of the parent company with full information concerning the activities of the entire economic unit in which they have invested, and this is achieved by combining all of the assets and liabilities of the parent company and its subsidiary into a single balance sheet so as to disclose the overall financial position of the group.

The effect of a share purchase on the balance sheets of the separate legal entities is considered first. We then turn our attention to the preparation of the consolidated balance sheet.

6.4.1 Parent Company's Balance Sheet: Acquisition Method

A parent company may acquire the shares of a subsidiary either for cash, or in exchange for its own shares or loan stock. Readers should note that where consideration is entirely in the form of cash, former shareholders of the subsidiary no longer retain any financial involvement with the group. At the other extreme, where consideration is entirely in the form of shares, the former shareholders of the subsidiary combine with the shareholders of the parent company and have a joint interest in the activities of the group.

In the parent company's balance sheet, the investment in the subsidiary is shown at the 'fair value' of the purchase consideration. Where the purchase consideration is entirely in the form of cash, the investment is valued at the amount of cash paid. Where part of the consideration is shares or loan stock issued by the parent company, these securities are included at market price to arrive at the value of the investment.

Example 6.4

The summarized balance sheets of PC Ltd and SC Ltd at 31 December 20X1 are as follows:

Balance Sheet at 31 December 20X1

	PC Ltd	SC Ltd
	£	£
Fixed assets at book value	36,000	27,000
Current assets: Stocks	20,000	7,000
Debtors	18,000	8,000
Bank	37,000	1,000
	111,000	43,000
Financed by:		
Share capital (£1 ordinary shares)	60,000	25,000
Retained profits	36,000	10,000
	96,000	35,000
Liabilities	15,000	8,000
	111,000	43,000

PC Ltd purchased the entire share capital of SC Ltd for £35,000 on 31 December 20X1.

Required:
Revised balance sheets for PC Ltd on the following alternative assumptions:

(a) The purchase consideration is paid entirely in cash.

(b) The purchase consideration consists of two elements: cash of £20,000; 10,000 shares in PC Ltd valued at £1.50 each.

Solution

Revised Balance Sheets of PC Ltd at 31 December 20X1

	(a)	(b)
	£	£
Fixed assets at book value	36,000	36,000
Investment in SC Ltd	35,000	35,000
Current assets: Stocks	20,000	20,000
Debtors	18,000	18,000
Bank	2,000	17,000
	111,000	126,000
Financed by:		
Share capital (£1 ordinary shares)	60,000	70,000
Share premium account	–	5,000
Reserves	36,000	36,000
	96,000	111,000
Liabilities	15,000	15,000
	111,000	126,000

The investment in SC Ltd is shown in each case at the fair value of the purchase consideration, namely £35,000. Under (a) the only change is a redistribution of PC Ltd's assets; £35,000 is transferred from 'Bank' to 'Investment in SC Ltd'. Under (b), 'Bank' is reduced by £20,000; the remainder of the consideration is shares valued at £15,000. This gives rise to an increase in 'Share capital' of £10,000 and a balance on 'Share premium account' of £5,000. The balance sheet of SC Ltd remains unchanged in either case; the transaction is with the shareholders of SC Ltd and no resources transfer into or out of the subsidiary company as a result of the share purchase.

6.4.2 Consolidated Balance Sheet: Acquisition Method

The reason for producing consolidated accounts is that the group of companies is in substance, though not in law, a single undertaking. It therefore follows that the essence of consolidation procedures is the cancellation of inter-company balances and the aggregation of those balances that remain. Following the acquisition, PC Ltd's revised balance sheet contains an asset entitled 'Investment in SC Ltd, £35,000', whereas SC Ltd's balance sheet shows a similar amount 'owing' to its shareholders, namely PC Ltd. When preparing a consolidated balance sheet, these inter-company balances cancel out and the remaining assets and liabilities are combined to produce total figures for the group.

Example 6.5

Prepare the consolidated balance sheet of PC Ltd and its subsidiary using the information given in Example 6.4 and assuming that the purchase consideration is entirely in the form of cash.

Solution

Consolidated Balance Sheet of PC Ltd and Subsidiary

	PC	Workings: SC	
	£	£	£
Fixed assets at book value	36,000	+ 27,000	63,000
Investment in SC Ltd	~~35,000~~*		
Current assets: Stocks	20,000	+ 7,000	27,000
Debtors	18,000	+ 8,000	26,000
Bank	2,000	+ 1,000	3,000
	111,000	43,000	119,000
Financed by:			
Share capital	60,000	~~35,000~~	60,000
Reserves	36,000	~~10,000~~	36,000
	96,000	~~35,000~~	96,000
Liabilities	15,000	8,000	23,000
	111,000	43,000	119,000

*These inter-company balances are crossed out because they cancel on consolidation.

Example 6.5 illustrates the essence of consolidation procedures, but it is an over-simplification. It is very unlikely for the price paid on acquisition to exactly equal the figure for shareholders' equity in the subsidiary company's balance sheet. Furthermore, a period of time usually elapses between the date when the shares are acquired and the consolidation date. Finally the investing company may well take the opportunity, which this form of business combination permits, to achieve control while purchasing less than the entire share capital. Consequently the preparation of consolidated accounts, under the acquisition method, involves the following three principal calculations:

- goodwill;

- post-acquisition profits;

- minority interest.

The calculation of these balances is now examined.

6.4.3 Goodwill

Often the price paid significantly exceeds the 'book' value of the net assets of the subsidiary acquired. Part of this surplus is attributable to the favourable trading connections, or goodwill, built up by the subsidiary company over the years; the residual difference is a consequence of the fact that there exists a disparity between the book value and the current or fair value of the assets at the takeover date. It is for this reason that FRS2 requires management to:

- restate the subsidiary company's assets at their fair value;

  and

- compute goodwill as the difference between the price paid by the parent company and the fair value of the net tangible and identifiable intangible assets belonging to the subsidiary company at the date of acquisition.

Fair values are intended to reflect conditions at the time of acquisition. They need not be written into the books of the subsidiary company and used for the purpose of its legal entity-based accounts, but they must be used for consolidation purposes. FRS7 'Fair Values in Acquisition Accounting' gives rules for establishing fair values. it defines fair value as the amount exchanged in an arm's length transaction between informed and willing parties, other than in a forced or liquidation sale.

FRS7 also deals with the valuations of acquired liabilities and specifically excludes provisions for future losses or reorganization costs expected to be incurred as a result of the acquisition because they are not liabilities of the acquired company at the time of acquisition.

The accounting treatment of goodwill is dealt with by FRS10 'Goodwill and Intangible Assets'. The requirement is that goodwill should be capitalized and amortized through the profit and loss account over its useful life. A maximum life of 20 years is assumed by the standard, although directors can argue for a life in excess of this.

Example 6.6

The summarized balance sheets of A Ltd and B Ltd at 31 December 20X1 are as follows:

	A Ltd £	B Ltd £
Fixed assets at book value	60,000	46,000
Investment in B Ltd	75,000	
Current assets: Stocks	32,000	13,000
Debtors	27,000	17,000
Bank	1,000	2,000
	195,000	78,000
Financed by:		
Share capital (£1 ordinary shares)	100,000	50,000
Retained profits	70,000	12,000
	170,000	62,000
Liabilities	25,000	16,000
	195,000	78,000

A Ltd purchased the entire share capital of B Ltd on 31 December 20X1. The fixed assets of B Ltd are considered to possess a fair value of £54,000, but there are no material differences between the book values and fair values of the remaining assets.

Required:
(a) Calculate the goodwill arising on consolidation.

(b) Prepare the consolidated balance sheet of A Ltd and its subsidiary at 31 December 20X1.

Note:
Ignore depreciation and amortization of goodwill.

Solution

(a) Calculation of goodwill arising on consolidation (net asset approach):

	£	£
Price paid		75,000
Less: Value of business acquired:		
Fixed assets (fair value)	54,000	
Stock	13,000	
Debtors	17,000	
Bank	2,000	
Liabilities	(16,000)	
		70,000
Goodwill		5,000

Note:

It is generally necessary to calculate the 'value of business acquired' using the equity components rather than the net asset approach. The result is the same, but the former procedure is followed because, in most group accounting questions, a period of time will have elapsed between the dates of takeover and consolidation. Consequently the figures for assets and liabilities at the date of takeover are unlikely to be provided, but sufficient information will be given to enable examinees to build up the shareholders' equity interest at that date. The calculation of goodwill applying the shareholders' equity approach to the information given in Example 6.6 is as follows:

Calculation of goodwill arising on consolidation (shareholders' equity approach):

	£	£
Price paid		75,000
Less: Value of business acquired:		
Share capital	50,000	
Revaluation surplus	8,000*	
Retained profits	12,000	
		70,000
Goodwill		5,000

*£54,000 (fair value of B's fixed assets) − £46,000 (book value).

(b) *Consolidated Balance Sheet of A Ltd at 31 December 20X1*

	£
Goodwill arising on consolidation	5,000 *
Fixed assets	114,000 **
Current assets: Stocks	45,000
Debtors	44,000
Bank	3,000
	211,000

Financed by:

Share capital (£1 ordinary shares)	100,000
Retained profits	70,000
	170,000
Liabilities	41,000
	211,000

*Goodwill will be accounted for in compliance with FRS10.
**Includes the fixed assets of B Ltd at their fair value.

The consolidated profit figure consists only of the retained profits of the parent company and includes no part of the retained profits of the subsidiary at the takeover date. This is because profits earned prior to the date of acquisition (preacquisition profits) accrue to the former shareholders of B Ltd, and are paid for in the purchase price. They are therefore not available for distribution to the shareholders of A Ltd, and are instead treated as part of the capitalized value of the business at the takeover date. This is clearly demonstrated in the calculation of goodwill which uses the shareholders' equity approach. The retained profits and revaluation surplus, which is also preacquisition, are added to share capital to produce a figure of £70,000 for shareholders' equity. This is offset against the price paid, £75,000, and results in a balance of £5,000 which is described as 'goodwill arising on consolidation' in the consolidated balance sheet. Profits earned after the date of acquisition accrue to the parent company's shareholders, and their accounting treatment is examined in the next section of this chapter.

Sometimes the price paid by the parent company is less than the book value of the company acquired. In such circumstances, it is quite likely that a downward revision of asset values will be needed. Where a credit balance remains, even after any necessary adjustments to book value have been made, it is reported as a 'non-distributable capital reserve' or 'negative goodwill' in the consolidated balance sheet.

6.4.4 Post-Acquisition Profits

A period of time usually elapses between the acquisition of a controlling interest and the date of the consolidated accounts. The subsidiary company may have generated profits during the interim period. These profits accrue to the shareholders of the parent company and, when transferred, are available for distribution. Their accounting treatment is dealt with in the following examples.

Example 6.7

The same information as for Example 6.6, except that a share acquisition date of 31 December 20X0 is assumed, at which time the retained profits of B Ltd amounted to £9,500.

Required:
(a) Calculate (i) goodwill, and (ii) post-acquisition profits of B Ltd.

(b) Prepare the consolidated balance sheet of the group at 31 December 20X1.

Notes:
Goodwill arising on consolidation should be amortized over an estimated useful economic life of five years. Ignore depreciation of other fixed assets.

Solution

(a) *Calculations*:

	£	£
(i) Goodwill:		
Price paid		75,000
Less: Value of business acquired		
Share capital	50,000	
Revaluation surplus	8,000	
Retained profits	9,500	67,500
		7,500
(ii) Post-acquisition profits of B:		
Retained profits at 31 December 20X1		12,000
Less: Retained profits at 31 December 20X0		9,500
		2,500

The retained profit of the group therefore consists of the retained profit of A Ltd, £70,000, plus the post-acquisition profit of B Ltd, £2,500, minus goodwill amortized, £1,500 (£7,500 ÷ 5) = £71,000.

(b) *Consolidated Balance Sheet of A Ltd and Subsidiary at 31 December 20X1*

	£
Goodwill arising on consolidation (7,500-1,500)	6,000
Fixed assets at book value	114,000
Current assets: Stocks	45,000
Debtors	44,000
Bank	3,000
	212,000
Financed by:	
Share capital (£1 shares)	100,000
Retained profits	71,000
	171,000
Liabilities	41,000
	212,000

There are three further matters that require emphasis concerning the calculation of reported profits for inclusion in the consolidated balance sheet:

- Losses suffered by a subsidiary company since the acquisition date are attributable to the shareholders of the parent company in the same way as profit earned. Post-acquisition losses must therefore be deducted from the parent company's balance of retained profits to compute the reported profit of the group.

- We have seen that a subsidiary company's fixed assets must be stated at fair value in the consolidated accounts. Where the subsidiary chooses to retain fixed assets at historical cost, for the purpose of its own accounts, a consolidation adjustment must be made equal to the difference between the historical cost-based depreciation charge, already made, and an appropriate charge based on the revalued amount (see Example 6.12 below).

- To the extent that post-acquisition profits earned by a subsidiary are transferred to the parent company by way of dividends, the amount to be aggregated when consolidation takes place is correspondingly reduced. For instance, in Example 6.7 assume B Ltd had paid an interim dividend of £800 during July 20X1. A Ltd's retained profits increase to £70,800, the retained profit of B Ltd falls to £11,200, and the post-acquisition retained profits of B Ltd become £1,700 (£11,200 – £9,500). The consolidated balance of reported profit remains unchanged, however, at £71,000 (£70,800 + £1,700 – £1,500, goodwill amortized).

6.4.5 Minority Interest

In many cases the parent company may either choose, in the interests of economy, or be forced to accept in view of the obstinacy of certain shareholders, a controlling interest of less than 100%. In these circumstances, the investment confers an interest in the subsidiary company's net assets based on the proportion which the number of equity shares acquired bears to the total number of equity shares then in issue. This must be taken into account when preparing the consolidated balance sheet. The appropriate procedure is to include the full amount of the subsidiary's assets and liabilities in the consolidated balance sheet, with the proportion financed by outside investors represented by a credit balance described as 'Minority interest'. This is shown as a separate item, normally immediately following shareholders' equity. The minority interest consists of an appropriate proportion of the share capital plus reserves and any other credit balances which accrue to the equity shareholders at the consolidation date.

Example 6.8

The summarized balance sheets of C Ltd and D Ltd at 31 December 20X1 are as follows:

	C Ltd £		D Ltd £
Fixed assets at book value	94,000		58,000
Investment in D Ltd	90,000		–
Current assets: Stocks	103,000		52,000
Debtors	79,000		25,000
Bank Balance (South Bank)	35,000		–
	401,000		135,000

	£	£	£	£
Financed by:				
Share capital (£1 ordinary shares)		200,000		80,000
Retained profits at 1 January 20X1	77,000		7,000	
Add: Profit for 20X1	18,000		6,000	
		95,000		13,000
		295,000		93,000
Current liabilities: Trade creditors		106,000		25,000
Bank overdraft (North Bank)		–		17,000
		401,000		135,000

Further information:

1. The investment in D Ltd consists of 60,000 ordinary shares purchased on 1 January 20X1.

2. It may be assumed that there are no significant differences between the book value and fair value of D Ltd's assets.

3. The company's policy is to write off goodwill arising on consolidation over 10 years.

Required:
(a) Calculate (i) goodwill, (ii) retained profits of the group, (iii) minority interest.

(b) Prepare the consolidated balance sheet at 31 December 19X1.

Solution

When answering a question involving the preparation of consolidated accounts, the starting point is to determine the exact relationship between the members of the group. The relationship is best presented in the form of a diagram.

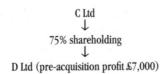

C Ltd
↓
75% shareholding
↓
D Ltd (pre-acquisition profit £7,000)

(a) *Calculations:*   £   £
    (i) Goodwill:

Price paid		90,000
Less: Value of business acquired		
Share capital	80,000	
Revaluation surplus	7,000	
	87,000	
Proportion of shares acquired 75% x	87,000	65,250
		24,750
(ii) Retained profits: C Ltd	95,000	
D Ltd 6,000 (post acquisition		
profit) x 75%	4,500	
	99,500	
Less: Goodwill written off (24,750/10)	2,475	
	97,025	
(iii) Minority interest:		
Total equity of D Ltd at the consolidation date:		
Share capital	80,000	
Retained profits	13,000	
	93,000	
Proportion attributable to minority shareholders,		
25% x 93,000	23,250	

Note:

The figures for goodwill, post-acquisition profit and minority interest may alternatively be calculated by constructing a table (see below) in the following manner:

1. The subsidiary's balance of total equity (including any revaluation reserve and consequential depreciation adjustment) is distributed between the parent company, distinguishing between the positions 'at' and 'since' acquisition, and the minority interest.

2. Goodwill is calculated by comparing the value of the subsidiary 'at acquisition' with the price paid.

3. The parent company's retained profits are added to the subsidiary's profits arising 'since acquisition' to arrive at group retained profits.

4. Goodwill is amortized or written off, as appropriate.

5. The balances for goodwill, if any, reported profit and minority interest are transferred to the consolidated balance sheet.

D Ltd	Total Equity £	At Acquisition £	C Ltd 75% Since Acquisition £	Minority Interest 25% £
Share capital	80,000	60,000		20,000
Retained profits: At acquisition	7,000	5,250		1,750
Since acquisition	6,000	—	4,500	1,500
	93,000	65,250	4,500	23,250
Price paid		90,000		
Goodwill on acquisition		24,750		
Retained profits, C Ltd			95,000	
Goodwill written off		(2,475)	(2,475)	
Balance of goodwill and Group retained profits		22,275	97,025	

An advantage of the above presentation is that it is easy to check whether total equity has been fully allocated for the purpose of calculating goodwill, retained profits and minority interest. Also, provided the additions and cross-casts are checked, the possibility of arithmetical error is reduced.

(b) *Consolidated Balance Sheet of C Ltd and Subsidiary*

	£
Goodwill	22,275
Fixed assets at book value	152,000
Current assets: Stocks	155,000
Debtors	104,000
Bank balance	35,000 (WI)
	468,275
Financed by:	
Share capital	200,000
Retained profits	97,025
	297,025
Minority interest	23,250
Current Liabilities: Trade creditors	131,000
Bank overdraft	17,000 (WI)
	468,275

WI The bank overdraft and bank balance are at different banks. Best accounting practice therefore requires these items to be shown separately and not offset against one another; if they were offset current assets and current liabilities would both be understated.

A further illustration of consolidation procedures, incorporating the matters considered so far and involving two subsidiaries, is given in Example 6.9. You are recommended to work the question before referring to the solution.

Example 6.9

The summarized balance sheets of Clubs Ltd and its subsidiary companies Diamonds Ltd and Hearts Ltd at 31 December 20X1 were as follows:

	Clubs Ltd £	Diamonds Ltd £	Hearts Ltd £
Fixed assets at book value	59,000	299,500	129,700
80,000 shares in Diamonds Ltd	126,000		
30,000 shares in Hearts Ltd	44,000		
Current assets	79,000	62,500	29,500
	308,000	362,000	159,200
Financed by:			
Share capital (£1 shares)	200,000	80,000	40,000
Profit and loss account at			
31 December 20X0	36,000	33,200	7,200
Profit (Loss) for 20X1	7,000	11,400	(13,600)
15% Debentures	–	200,000	50,000
Current liabilities	65,000	37,400	75,600
	308,000	362,000	159,200

Clubs Ltd acquired the shares in both subsidiaries on 31 December 20X0. Neither subsidiary paid a dividend in respect of 20X0 and none are proposed for 20X1.

Required:
The consolidated balance sheet for the group at 31 December 20X1, presented in vertical format to disclose the balance for working capital.

Notes:
Ignore taxation.

Assume no differences between the book values and fair values of the assets and liabilities of Diamonds Ltd and Hearts Ltd.

Goodwill arising on consolidation should be amortized over an estimated useful life of four years.

Interest on debentures has been charged in arriving at the profit (loss) for the year.

Solution

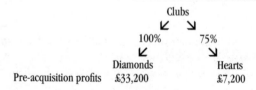

Calculations:

	Total Equity £	At Acquisition £	Since Acquisition £	Minority Interest £
Diamonds				
Share capital	80,000	80,000		
Profit and loss account:				
At acquisition	33,200	33,200		
Since acquisition	11,400		11,400	
	124,600	113,200	11,400	
Hearts				
Share capital	40,000	30,000		10,000
Profit and loss account:				
At acquisition	7,200	5,400		1,800
Since acquisition	(13,600)		(10,200)	(3,400)
	33,600	35,400	(10,200)	8,400
Totals (Diamonds and Hearts)	158,200	148,600	1,200	8,400
Total price paid				
(£126,000 + £44,000)		170,000		
Goodwill on acquisition		21,400		
Profit and loss account, Clubs Ltd.			43,000	
Goodwill amortized (21,400 ÷ 4)		(5,350)	(5,350)	
Balances of goodwill and profit		16,050	38,850	

Consolidated Balance Sheet of Clubs Ltd and subsidiaries at 31 December 20X1

	£	£
Goodwill		16,050
Fixed assets at book value		488,200
Current assets	171,000	
Less: Current liabilities	178,000	
Working capital		(7,000)
Total assets less current liabilities		497,250
Less: 15% Debentures		250,000
		247,250
Financed by.		
Share capital (£1 shares)		200,000
Profit and loss account		38,850
		238,850
Minority interest		8,400
		247,250

6.5 CONSOLIDATION: MERGER METHOD

The merger method of preparing consolidated accounts is dealt with by FRS6, entitled 'Acquisitions and Mergers', and is given statutory backing by the Companies Act 1989. The method is considered appropriate where two companies combine their activities on the basis of a share-for-share exchange, so that the two groups of shareholders retain a joint interest in the affairs of both companies, i.e. there is a genuine pooling of interests to form a new entity in which neither party is dominant. The legal requirements are:

- At least 90% of the equity shares must be acquired by the bidding company.

- The acquisition must take place by share exchange.

- The fair value of anything given in exchange for the shares, other than the bidder's own shares, must not exceed 10% of the nominal value of the equity shares issued.

FRS6 spells out the criteria to be used to identify when a genuine merger has taken place:

- Neither set of directors must identify either of the companies as an acquirer.

- The management structure of the merged entity must be established by consensus.

- Neither of the companies must be able to dominate the relationship by being substantially larger than the other. In practice, one company would be deemed to dominate the other if it is more than 50% larger than the other as measured by its equity portion of the combined companies.

The purpose of the above rules is to discover whether or not the transaction is a merger with a strictly limited amount of resources leaving the group and neither party is dominant. Where all of these criteria are satisfied, merger accounting must be used; if they are not met, companies must use the acquisition method.

6.5.1 Parent Company's Balance Sheet: Merger Method
In the parent company's accounts, an investment in a subsidiary is shown at the nominal value of shares issued in exchange.

Example 6.10

The summarized balance sheets of X Ltd and Y Ltd, on 31 December 20X6 are as follows:

	X Ltd £	Y Ltd £
Net assets	63,000	85,000
Financed by:		
Ordinary share capital (£1 shares)	50,000	60,000
Reserves (all distributable)	13,000	25,000
	63,000	85,000

X Ltd issued 45,000 ordinary shares in exchange for the entire share capital of Y Ltd on 31 December 20X6.

Required:
The revised balance sheet for X Ltd assuming the company plans to account for the combination on the merger basis.

Solution

Revised Balance Sheet of X Ltd at 31 December 20X6

	£
Investment in Y Ltd	45,000
Other net assets	63,000
	108,000
Financed by:	
Ordinary share capital (£50,000 + £45,000)	95,000
Reserves	13,000
	108,000

Any part of the total consideration, paid in a form other than shares, is reported at its fair value. For example, cash consideration is included at the amount paid and loan stock at market price.

6.5.2 Consolidated Balance Sheet: Merger Method

The artificial assumption underlying the preparation of consolidated accounts, on the merger basis, is that the combining companies have always been members of the same group. The justification for the assumption is the continuity of ownership. The accounting effect of the assumption is that the preparation of consolidated accounts is a relatively straightforward matter. The procedure is as follows:

- The assets are combined at their existing book values, historical cost or revalued amount. Re-statement at fair value is not required.

- The entire distributable profits of the subsidiary are combined with those of the parent company, i.e. no distinction is made between pre- and post-acquisition profit. It therefore follows that the subsidiary's profits or losses for the entire merger period are included in the reported profits of the group for the year in which the merger takes place.

- The difference, if any, between the value at which the investment is carried in the parent company's books – the 'Carrying value' – and the nominal value of the shares acquired is accounted for as follows:

  (a) Where the carrying value of the investment is less than the nominal value of the shares acquired, the difference (credit balance) is treated as a non-distributable 'merger' reserve arising on consolidation.

  (b) Where the carrying value of the investment exceeds the nominal value of the shares transferred, the difference (debit balance) is treated as a capitalization of reserves which are reduced by an equivalent amount.

- The calculation of the minority interest, if any, is the same as under the acquisition method.

Example 6.11

The balance sheets of A Ltd and B Ltd, on 31 December 20X4, are as follows:

	A Ltd	B Ltd
	£	£
Net assets at book value	28,000	25,500
Financed by:		
Ordinary share capital (£1 shares)	20,000	18,000
Reserves (all distributable)	8,000	7,500
	28,000	25,500

Required:

The consolidated balance sheet for A Ltd and its subsidiary, on the merger basis, under the following alternative assumptions.

(a) On 31 December 20X4, A Ltd issues 15,000 ordinary shares in exchange for the entire share capital of B Ltd.

(b) On 31 December 20X4, A Ltd issues 24,000 ordinary shares in exchange for the entire share capital of B Ltd.

Solution

Consolidated Balance Sheet of A Ltd and its subsidiary

	(a)	(b)
Net assets (£28,000 + £25,500)	53,500	53,500
Financed by		
Ordinary share capital (£1 shares)	35,000	44,000
Merger reserve	(WI) 3,000	
Distributable reserves	15,500	(W2) 9,500
	53,500	53,500

	(a)	(b)
WI Carrying value of investment:		
Nominal value of shares issued	15,000	24,000
Less: Nominal value of shares acquired	18,000	18,000
Credit balance – merger reserve	3,000	
Debit balance – deducted from reserves		6,000

6.6 THE MERGER AND ACQUISITION METHODS COMPARED

Users and preparers of consolidated accounts based on the merger method must be aware of the differences underlying them when compared with the use of acquisition accounting.

- The preparation of consolidated accounts is a less complex process.

- Reported profits for the year in which the combination occurs are higher under the merger method because profits earned by the subsidiary for the entire year are included (conversely where there are losses). Under the acquisition method, only profits earned since the acquisition date are reported, e.g. if the shares are purchased three-quarters of the way through the year, only the profits arising during the last three months are reported.

- Accumulated distributable profits are carried forward to the postmerger period and so can be paid out as dividends. Under the acquisition method, distributable profits are 'frozen' at the date of takeover and are no longer available for distribution.

- The merger method avoids the obligation to restate assets at fair value which, under the acquisition method, usually leads to a higher depreciation charge and lower profits.

- The merger method includes the assets of the target company in the group results at historical cost whereas, under the acquisition method, they must be restated at more realistic fair values. Against this it should be pointed out that, for material mergers, the parent company is required to disclose the fair value of the consideration given by way of a note.

- The merger method ignores the existence of goodwill.

The merger method is not without its critics who point out that it enables companies to acquire instant earnings and, perhaps, publish accounts which mislead users regarding corporate progress. This means that directors, anticipating that reported profits and the stock market indicator of earnings per share are likely to fall, seek target companies with high forecast profits to bolster the reported results of the group. FRS 6 (like FRS2) does, however, together with FRS3 contain a requirement that companies should disclose sufficient information about new subsidiaries to enable shareholders to appreciate the effect of the takeover on reported results.

The relative effect on reported profit and balance sheet values, of accounting for business combinations on the acquisition basis and the merger basis, is illustrated in Example 6.12.

Example 6.12

The summarized balance sheets of P Ltd and Q Ltd at 31 December 20X9 are as follows:

	P Ltd £	Q Ltd £
Net assets at book value	140,000	150,000
Financed by:		
Ordinary share capital (£1 shares)	60,000	40,000
Retained profits	80,000	110,000
	140,000	150,000

The following additional information is provided:

1. P acquired the entire share capital of Q on 1 January 20X9 and issued 50,000 shares valued at £4 each in exchange.

2. The retained profits of Q at 1 January 20X9 amounted to £45,000.

3. The fair value of the net assets of Q at that date was £110,000 and the book value £85,000.

On the basis of this fair value, a depreciation charge of £24,000 is required for 20X9 rather than the charge of £20,000 actually made.

4. The share exchange has not been recorded in the books of P Ltd and its accounting effect does not appear in the above balance sheet.

5. Any goodwill arising on consolidation is to be written off over 3 years.

Required:
(a) The balance sheet of P Ltd, at 31 December 19X9, incorporating the effect of the share exchange assuming the transaction is accounted for on:
 (i) the acquisition basis;
 (ii) the merger basis.

(b) The consolidated balance sheet of P Ltd and its subsidiary, at 31 December 20X9, on:
 (i) the acquisition basis;
 (ii) the merger basis.

Solution

(a) *Balance Sheet of P Ltd*

	Acquisition Method £000	Merger Method £000
Investment in Q Ltd: at market value	200 (WI)	–
at nominal value	–	50
Other net assets	140	140
	340	190
Financed by:		
Ordinary share capital (£60,000+£50,000)	110	110
Share premium account	150 (WI)	–
Retained profit	80	80
	340	190
WI Market value of shares issued	200,000	
Less: Nominal value of shares issued	50,000	
Share premium account	150,000	

(b) *Consolidated Balance Sheet*

	Acquisition Method £000	Merger Method £000
Goodwill	60 (W2)	–
Other net assets	311 (W3)	290
	371	290
Financed by:		
Ordinary share capital	110	110
Share premium account	150	–
Retained profit	111 (W2)	180 (W4)
	371	290

W2	Total Equity £000	At Acquisition £000	Since Acquisition £000
Share capital	40	40	
Revaluation reserve			
(£110,000-£85,000)	25	25	
Profit: At acquisition	45	45	
Since acquisition	65		65
Additional depreciation	(4)		(4)
	171	110	61
Less: Purchase price		200	
Goodwill on acquisition		90	
Profit of P			80
Goodwill amortized £90,000 x IA	(30)	(30)	
Balances of goodwill and profit		60	111

W3   Net assets of P, £140,000, plus net assets of Q at fair value, £171,000 (£150,000 + £25,000 – £4,000).

W4   Retained profits of P and Q, £190,000, less amount capitalized due to carrying value of investment (£50,000) exceeding nominal value of shares acquired (£40,000) by £10,000.

Inter-Company Unrealized Profits The accounting convention, that a 'transfer at arm's length' must occur before profit is recognized must be applied on a group basis when preparing consolidated accounts. Intra-group transfers of stock are quite common, particularly where the share purchase has resulted in an element of vertical integration designed to safeguard either sources of raw materials or consumer outlets. These transfers are normally made at a figure that approximates to market price, both to enable the performance of individual companies to be fairly assessed and to avoid unnecessary complications where minority shareholdings exist. Provided that the recipient company has resold the item transferred, either in its original form or incorporated in a different product, it is perfectly legitimate to recognize both elements of profit in the consolidated account, i.e. the profit arising on the intra-group transfer and the profit arising on the sale of the product to an external party. Where, however, the item transferred remains unsold by the transferee company at the end of the accounting period, consolidation adjustments must be made to reduce the value of the stock to a figure which represents its original cost to the group and to eliminate the unrealized profit.

Dividends Paid out of Pre-Acquisition Profits A controlling interest may be acquired after a new subsidiary has proposed a dividend payment but before it has been paid. The source of the dividend is therefore profits earned by the subsidiary before the combination took place. It is treated differently under the two methods. Under the acquisition method the investment is recorded at its fair value, which includes the value of the dividend proposed but not yet paid. When the cash transfer is made, it represents a partial return of the capital cost and must be accounted for as a reduction in the value of the investment. Under the merger method the dividend is a distributable profit as far as the parent company is concerned and may be credited to the parent company's profit and loss account. This is entirely consistent with the merger method's assumption that the two companies have always been members of the same group.

6.7 INTERPRETING CONSOLIDATED BALANCE SHEETS

The opening paragraph of section 6.4 draws attention to the fact that the basic objective of consolidated accounts is to provide the shareholders of the parent company with full information concerning the activities of the entire economic unit in which they have invested. We have examined the various procedures followed when preparing a consolidated balance sheet, and it is now possible to consider more fully what is meant by this statement. The parent company's legal entity-based accounts deal with the results of a single organization, whereas group accounts set out the combined results of at least two, and perhaps a much larger number of legally separate businesses. Therefore, it is not surprising that there are often significant differences between the two sets of accounts. Some important differences may well be clearly visible from a simple comparison of the totals appearing in the balance sheets. For instance, the parent company's balance sheet may contain a large overdraft, whereas the consolidated balance sheet shows a healthy cash surplus, indicating that the subsidiaries are in possession of substantial amounts of cash. A more searching comparison can be made of the information contained in economic entity and legal entity based accounts by using techniques such as ratio analysis (Chapter 9) and cash flow analysis (Chapter 10).

For illustrative purposes, a comparison is made below of the information contained in Clubs Ltd's own balance sheet (Example 6.9) and the balance sheet of the group. The main points of interest are as follows:

1. Revenue reserves: Clubs Ltd   £43,000

         Group   £38,850

This shows that the two subsidiaries are not improving the overall profitability of the group; the post-acquisition profits of Diamonds Ltd are cancelled out by the post-acquisition losses of Hearts Ltd.

2. Fixed assets: Clubs Ltd   £59,000

         Group   £488,200

This shows that most of the group's fixed assets are owned by the subsidiary companies, and this information would be of particular interest to prospective creditors of the parent company who might be keen to ensure that their advance is adequately secured. One option open to them would be to require subsidiaries to guarantee repayment of the loan.

3. Solvency:

    Working capital ratio: Clubs Ltd 1.2:1

             Group 0.96:1

The working capital position of Clubs Ltd is significantly higher than that of the group as a whole. This would suggest that there are underlying financial difficulties which are not evident in Clubs Ltd's own balance sheet. An examination of the subsidiary companies' balance sheets shows that the problem is at Hearts Ltd where current liabilities significantly exceed current assets.

4. Gearing:

    Debt/equity ratio: Clubs Ltd   Zero (no loans)

          Group   105%

Inter-company shareholdings cancel out on consolidation, whereas the debentures, all held outside the group, must be aggregated. Consequently, the consolidated statement reveals a much higher level of gearing than is evident from an examination of the individual balance sheet of Clubs Ltd and the other companies within the group. The group pays annual interest to debenture holders totalling £37,500 (£250,000 x 15%). Annual profit figures are not given but the interest charge is almost equal to the total retained profits and this would suggest that the group will find it difficult to meet its interest charges unless trading results improve.

Conclusion
The group accounts point to the existence of significant financial difficulties which are not evident from Clubs Ltd's own balance sheet.

6.8 ASSOCIATES AND JOINT VENTURES
During the 1960s companies increasingly conducted part of their activities through other companies in which a less than 50% equity interest was acquired, and which, consequently, escaped the group accounting provisions of the Companies Act 1948 (now incorporated in the 1985 Act). Effective control was exercised, however, either through the existence of some form of partnership agreement or because of a wide dispersion of shares. Consequently, the directors of the investing company were able to influence both the commercial and financial policies of the company in which shares were held. The growing demand for fuller disclosure was therefore fully justified:

- To remove obvious opportunities for the managers of investing companies to manipulate their reported results. For instance, by building up undisclosed profits in the accounts of the investee company, which could, when required, be transferred to the investing company in the form of a dividend.

- To provide more meaningful performance data concerning the activities of the entire economic unit over which some influence was exercised. In this context, the growing popularity of the price:earnings ratio emphasized the increasing significance attached to reported earnings as a performance indicator. It was therefore important to take steps to ensure that the investing companies' published earnings fairly represented their actual performance.

The matter was referred to the Accounting Standards Committee, as it then was, which concluded that, where management assumes a measure of direct responsibility for the performance of its investment, by actively participating in the commercial and policy-making decisions of an associated company, it must present a full account to its members. Accordingly, it was decided that group accounts, prepared in accordance with the Companies Act, should be extended to incorporate additional information concerning the activities of these associated companies. This decision obliged the committee to draft requirements covering two matters:

- a precise definition of the associated companies in relation to which further disclosures are required;

- the additional information to be published.

The requirements were contained in SSAP1, entitled 'Accounting for the Results of Associated Companies'. This standard was superseded in 1997 by the Accounting Standard Board's publication of FRS 9, entitled 'Accounting for Associates and Joint Ventures'. The ASB in this standard provides a definition of 'Associated Company' and 'Joint Venture' and specifies the accounting treatment to be applied to each. These are now examined below.

6.8.1 Definition of an Associated Company
FRS 9 defines an Associated Company as:

> *An entity (other than a subsidiary) in which another entity (the investor) has a participating interest and over whose operating and financial policies the investor exercises significant influence.*

Participation in the financial and operating policies of the associate need not necessarily amount to control of those policies. Representation on the board of directors is one indication of such participation but it is not conclusive proof.

6.8.2 Equity Accounting for the Results of Associated Companies
It is not appropriate to apply traditional consolidation procedures to associated companies because the investing company has only a minority interest in their affairs. The modified consolidation procedures used instead are commonly described as 'equity accounting'.

The following two calculations must be made:

1. The price paid is allocated between:

(i) The investing company's share of the net assets, other than goodwill, of the associated company at the acquisition date. For this purpose net assets should be restated at their fair value.

(ii) The investing company's share of any goodwill appearing in the balance sheet of the associated company at the acquisition date.

(iii) The premium paid (or discount arising) on the acquisition of the interest in the associated company. This calculation is analogous to the calculation of goodwill or capital reserve arising on the consolidation of a subsidiary company.

Example 6.13

On 31 December 20X1 Investment plc purchased 25% of the equity share capital of Associated plc for £1,000,000. The balance sheet of Associated plc at the acquisition date included net assets, other than goodwill, restated at a fair value of £2,800,000. Goodwill amounted to £800,000. Investment plc is able to exert a significant influence over the affairs of Associated plc.

Required:
Allocate the price paid for the shares in Associated plc between: (i) net assets other than goodwill, (ii) goodwill, and (iii) premium paid on acquisition.

Solution

	£	£
Price paid for shares		1,000,000
Allocate as follows:		
(i) Share of net assets, 25% x £2,800,000	700,000	
(ii) Share of goodwill, 25% of £800,000	200,000	
		900,000
(iii) Premium paid on acquisition		100,000

The above allocation may be disclosed either on the face of the balance sheet or by way of note.

2. The investing company's share of the undistributed post-tax profits less losses of associated companies must be computed. This amount is then brought into the investing company's balance sheet as an addition to retained profits (credit) and to the value of the investment in the associated company (debit). Refer back to

Example 6.13, and assume that, in 20X2, Associated plc earns a profit of £300,000, of which £140,000 is paid out as a dividend during the year (ignore taxation). Investment plc receives £35,000 (£140,000 x 25%) during the year, which is credited to dividend received and debited to cash. At the year end Investment plc's share of the post-acquisition retained profit is £40,000 (£160,000 x 25%), and this amount is credited to reserves and debited to the book value of the investment in the associated company which becomes £1,040,000 (£1,000,000 + £40,000).

Example 6.14

The results of J plc and its subsidiaries have already been consolidated. The results of K plc, an associated company, must now be incorporated by applying the instructions contained in FRS 9. The following information is provided.

Summarized Balance Sheets at 31 December 20X5

	J plc (group)		K plc	
	£m	£m	£m	£m
Fixed assets at cost less depreciation		54		178
Investment in K plc at cost		80		
Current assets	95		364	
Less: Current liabilities	55		192	
Net current assets		40		172
		174		350
Financed by:		£m		£m
Share capital (£1 ordinary shares)		137		170
Reserves		21		180
		158		350
Minority interest		16		–
		174		350

J plc acquired 25% of the share capital of K plc on 31 December 20X3, at which date the reserves of K plc stood at £40,000,000. At 31 December 20X3, the balance sheet of K plc contained no figure for goodwill and the net assets were estimated to possess a fair value of £260,000,000.

Goodwill has an estimated life of 5 years.

Required:
The consolidated balance sheet of the group as at 31 December 20X5, incorporating the results of its associated company K plc.

Note:
Ignore advance corporation tax.

Solution

Consolidated Balance Sheet as at 31 December 20X5

	£m	£m	
Fixed assets at cost less depreciation		54	
Investment in associated company		109	(WI)
Current assets	95		
Less: Current liabilities	55		
Net current assets		40	
		203	

	£m
Financed by:	
Share capital (£1 ordinary shares)	137
Reserves [21+35 (W2) – 6 (W3)]	50
	187
Minority interest	16
	203

W1	Investment in K plc:	£m	
	Group share of net assets:		
	Fair value at takeover date	65	
	Share of post-acquisition undistributed profit	35	(W2)
		100	
	Premium on acquisition	9	(W3)
		109	

W2	J plc's share of the post acquisition retained profits of K plc:	£
	Reserves at 31 December 20X5	180
	Less: Reserves at date of acquisition	40
	Post-acquisition retained profits	140
	Attributable to J plc, £140m 25%	35

W3	Allocation of purchase price:	£
	Price paid for shares	80
	Less: Share of net assets, £260m x 25%	65
	Premium paid on acquisition	15
	Less: Amortization for 2 years (15/5) x 2	6
		9

6.8.3. Definition of a Joint Venture

FRS 9 defines a Joint Venture as:

An entity in which the reporting entity holds an interest on a long-term basis and is jointly controlled by the reporting entity and one or more other venturers under a contractual arrangement

6.8.4 Gross Equity Accounting for Joint Ventures

To comply with FRS 9, joint ventures must be accounted for in the accounts of the investing company using the 'gross equity' method. The techniques are largely the same as those applied to associated companies, but additional disclosure is required to show the investor's:

- Share of the joint venture turnover in the profit and loss account. This requirement is met by adopting the following presentation:

	£	£
Turnover:		
Group and its share of joint ventures	X	
Less: Share of joint ventures	X	
Group turnover		X

- Share of gross assets and liabilities in the balance sheet.

Example 6.15

Take the information provided in Example 6.14 and assume that the revaluation at the date of acquiring the shares amounted to £50,000,000, all related to fixed assets and required no additional depreciation.

Require:
Prepare the consolidated balance sheet of the group as at 31 December 20X5 incorporating the results of K plc as a joint venture.

Solution

	£m	£m
Fixed assets at cost less depreciation		
Group	54	
Joint venture ([178 + 50] x 25%)	57	
		111
Goodwill on joint venture		9
Current assets		
Group	95	
Joint venture (364 x 25%)	91	
	186	
Current liabilities		
Group	55	
Joint venture (192 x 25%)	48	
	103	
Working capital		83
		203
Financed by		
Share capital (£1 ordinary shares)		137
Reserves		50
		187
Minority interest		16
		203

6.9 LIMITATIONS OF GROUP ACCOUNTS

The problem of deciding which companies are to be treated as members of the group, for the purposes of preparing consolidated accounts (the form which group accounts commonly take), has proved difficult, but the regulations contained in FRS 2, FRS 6 and FRS 9 are more stringent than those previously operated.

Certain other difficulties, associated with consolidated accounts, arise directly from the obligation to aggregate the assets and liabilities as well as the profits and losses of subsidiaries. Whereas a particular company will normally take steps to ensure that common accounting policies are adopted throughout the firm, such uniformity is less likely to exist throughout a group of companies. Where the group includes overseas subsidiaries, which have to comply with local legal requirements for disclosure or taxation purposes, the diversity of accounting policies is likely to increase. These aggregation problems are compounded where group companies undertake a wide range of commercial functions, and some doubt must be cast on the utility of positional statements which consist of a collection of diverse assets and the summation of capital structures which are appropriate for a wide range of different types of company.

A further problem, of increasing importance in recent years, is the large quantities of assets belonging to overseas subsidiaries located in economically and/or politically sensitive areas. In these circumstances it may be necessary to omit certain subsidiaries from consolidation, and instead give the information specified in FRS 2 (paras. 27-28), which is often the same as the disclosures required for associated companies, i.e. subsidiaries are accounted for on the equity basis.

The present system of group accounts has developed gradually over the last 90 years (many companies voluntarily published group accounts prior to the introduction of a legal requirement in 1948), and there is widespread support for the view that the reporting accountant has dealt in an effective manner with most of the difficulties which have been encountered. The result is the publication of useful information concerning the progress and financial position of parent companies, their subsidiaries and their investments. The limitations of group accounts must not, however, be forgotten. Economic entity-based accounting information is prepared primarily for the parent company's shareholders. Bankers and creditors of constituent companies, examining a set of consolidated accounts, must remember that, in the absence of cross-guarantees within the group, the fund against which they may proceed in law for repayment of their debt is restricted to the assets of the particular company with which a contractual relationship exists. At the same time, the parent company's bank may quite properly regard group accounts as a useful means of finding out about the nature and value of assets underlying investments in subsidiaries.

6.10 FURTHER READING

Lewis, R. and Pendrill, D. (2000), *Advanced Financial Accounting*, sixth edition, Pitman, Chapter 9.

Peerless, S. 'Accounting for Business Marriages', *Accountancy Magazine*, October 1994, p. 100

Phipps E. and Sharp, 1. 'FRS6 and FRS7: The Troublesome Twins', *Accountancy Magazine*, September 1996, pp. 86-87

Saksida, M. 'Fair Values in Acquisition Accounting', *Accountancy Magazine*, October 1997, pp. 84-85

Wild, K. and Everitt, H. 'Financial Reporting: FRSs 6 and 7. Are the New Standards Working?' *Accountancy Magazine*, November 1995, pp. 136-137

Powling, H. and Riglesford, K. 'The First Season of Goodwill', *Accountancy*, August 1999, pp. 84- 5

6.11 QUESTIONS

Question 6.1

The following balances relate to Park Ltd and Gate Ltd at 31 December 20X4.

	Park Ltd £	Gate Ltd £
Issued share capital (£1 ordinary shares)	200,000	80,000
Retained profits at 31 December 20X3	45,100	37,500
Profit for 20X4	17,600	28,500
Unsecured loan repayable 20X8	–	30,000
Current liabilities	53,700	26,000
	316,400	202,000
Freehold property, net of depreciation	–	99,000
Other fixed assets, net of depreciation	182,300	35,000
48,000 shares in Gate Ltd at cost	72,000	–
Current assets	62,100	68,000
	316,400	202,000

Park Ltd acquired its shares in Gate Ltd on 31 December 20X3.

The board of directors of Park Ltd require £400,000 to finance a new project and have approached the bank to borrow this amount.

Goodwill is to be amortized over 10 years.

Required:
(a) The consolidated balance sheet of the group at 31 December 20X4 presented in good style so far as the information permits. [16]

(b) Briefly advise the bank on security for the requested advance, based on the accounts of the companies. [4]

Note:
Ignore taxation.

Use acquisition basis for consolidation purposes. [Total marks – 20]

Question 6.2

The following are the summarized balance sheets of Queensbury Ltd and Wyke Ltd as at 31 March 20X3:

SUMMARIZED BALANCE SHEETS

	Queensbury Ltd		*Wyke Ltd*	
	£000	*£000*	*£000*	*£000*
Fixed assets at cost		800		480
Less: Accumulated depreciation		230		240
		570		240
Investment in Wyke Ltd		824		–
Net current assets		126		610
		1,520		850
Share capital (£1 ordinary shares)		1,000		600
Retained profit at 31 March 1991	320		70	
Profit 1991/2	125		80	
Profit 1992/93	75	520	100	250
		1,520		850

Queensbury Ltd purchased 450,000 shares in Wyke Ltd on 31 March 20X1. At that date the fixed assets of Wyke Ltd possessed a book value of £400,000 (cost £480,000 less depreciation £80,000), a fair value of £600,000, an estimated remaining useful economic life of five years and an expected residual value of zero.

Goodwill is assumed to have a useful economic life of two years.

Required:
(a) The consolidated balance sheet of Queensbury Ltd and its subsidiary Wyke Ltd as at 31 March 20X3. The consolidated balance sheet should be presented, as far as possible, in the above format. [16]

(b) An explanation of how the treatment of the investment in Wyke Ltd would have differed if Queensbury Ltd had instead purchased:
(i) 240,000 shares;
(ii) 60,000 shares.
Where possible, support your explanations with numerical calculations. [4]

Note:
Ignore taxation [Total marks – 20]

Question 6.3

On 1 January 1999, Howitt Ltd acquired the entire share capital of Garrett Ltd. The arrangement involved the shareholders of Garrett Ltd receiving one ordinary share in Howitt for every two shares presently held. The shares of Howitt Ltd were considered to be worth £4 each on I January 1999. The draft balance sheets of the two companies at 31 December 1999 were:

Draft Balance Sheets at 31 December 1999

	Howitt Ltd	Garrett Ltd
	£000	£ 000
Fixed assets at cost less depreciation	2,500	2,000
Working capital	1,100	1,000
	3,600	3,000
Ordinary shares of £1 each	2,000	1,600
Retained profit at 1 January 1999	1,200	800
Profit for 1999	400	600
	3,600	3,000

• No entry has been made in the above balance sheet of Howitt Ltd to record the issue of shares relating to the acquisition of Garrett Ltd.

• At 1 January 1999, the fair value of Garrett's fixed assets was £2,600,000 compared with a book value of £2,300,000. The use of fair value for the purpose of the accounts would lead to an additional depreciation charge for 1999 of £40,000.

• It is Howitt's policy to capitalize goodwill and write it off over its useful economic life, which is estimated to be four years.

• No dividends were paid and none are proposed by either company for 1999.

Required:
(a) Prepare the consolidated balance sheet of Howitt Ltd and its subsidiary company, Garrett Ltd, at 31 December 1999 using:

   (i)   The acquisition method of consolidation.

   (ii) The merger method of consolidation.   [10 marks]

The accounts should comply with relevant standard accounting practice.

(b) Examine the advantages of the merger method of consolidation, and explain the logic underlying the use of this method to consolidate the accounts of a group of companies.   [10 marks]

[Total marks – 20]

Question 6.4

The summarized balance sheets of Hagg Ltd, Oaken Ltd and Greave Ltd at 31 March 20X2 contained the following information:

BALANCE SHEET AS AT 31 MARCH 20X2

	Hagg Ltd £000	Oaken Ltd £000	Greave Ltd £000
Fixed assets at book value	2,600	2,100	1,300
Investments in subsidiaries	1,300	–	–
Net current assets	1,680	930	1,370
Total assets less current liabilities	5,580	3,030	2,670
Less: 16% debenture stock	500	2,000	1,500
	5,080	1,030	1,170
Capital and reserves			
Ordinary share capital (£1 shares)	3,300	500	1,000
Retained profit at 31 March 1991	1,360	320	140
Profit for year to 31 March 1992	420	210	30
	5,080	1,030	1,170

The three companies trade in complementary products and their directors arranged a merger of their activities on 31 March 20X1. The terms of the merger were as follows:

1. Hagg Ltd issued 500,000 £1 ordinary shares in exchange for the entire share capital of Oaken Ltd.

2. Hagg Ltd issued 800,000 £1 ordinary shares in exchange for the entire share capital of Greave Ltd.

   The terms are such that the combined company is not dominated by the management of any one of the merged companies, and so the presumption about dominance through size does not apply.

Required:
(a) The consolidated balance sheet of Hagg Ltd and its subsidiaries as at 31 March 20X2. Use the merger method of consolidation as prescribed by FRS 6. [8]

(b) Compare the financial position shown in the above balance sheet of Hagg Ltd with that appearing in the consolidated balance sheet prepared under (a). Your comparison should include calculations of the debt:equity ratio and interest cover. [8]

(c) Indicate TWO ways in which the financial position disclosed in the consolidated balance sheet might be affected by the use, instead, of the acquisition method of consolidation as prescribed by FRS 2. [4]

[Total marks – 20]

Question 6.5

The summarized balance sheets of Dingle Ltd, Eagle Ltd and Fender Ltd are as follows:

BALANCE SHEETS AS AT 31 DECEMBER 20X8

	Dingle £000	Eagle £000	Fender £000
Fixed assets	100	260	720
Current assets	85	170	555
	185	430	1,275
Ordinary Share capital (£1 shares)	80	200	500
Retained profit 1 Jan. 20X8	70	100	360
Profit for 20X8	20	80	200
Proposed dividend	—	(60)	(150)
	170	320	910
Trade creditors	15	50	215
Proposed dividend	—	60	150
	185	430	1,275

Grimshaw Ltd made the following investments on 1 January 20X8:

Company	Shares acquired	Price paid
Dingle	64,000	£178,000
Eagle	80,000	£151,000
Fender	50,000	£116,000

Required:
Calculate separately for each company the amounts (if any) to be included in the group accounts of Grimshaw Ltd in respect of each of the following items:

(i)   share of profit reported for 20X8;

(ii) goodwill/premium paid on acquisition;

(iii) minority interest at 31 December 20X8.

You should explain, briefly, the principles followed when making your calculations.

The result of your calculations under (i)-(iii) should be presented in the following format:

	Dingle £000	Eagle £000	Fender £000
Share of profit			
Goodwill/premium on acquisition			
Minority interest			

[20]

Note:
There were no significant differences, on 1 January 20X8, between the book values and market values of the assets of any of the companies.

Question 6.6

The summarized profit and loss accounts and balance sheets of Pleat ple and Sexton plc for 1998 contained the following information:

Profit and Loss Accounts for 1998

	Pleat plc	Sexton plc
	£m	£m
Operating profit less interest charges*	120	100
Reorganization cost	=	35
	120	65

*After charging depreciation of £126m by Pleat and £90m by Sexton.

Balance Sheets at 31 December 1998

	Pleat plc	Sexton plc
Net assets	£m	£m
Tangible fixed assets at cost	2,205	900
Less: Accumulated depreciation	1,063	450
	1,142	450
Stocks	571	317
Net monetary assets	213	266
Total assets less current liabilities	1,926	1,033
Share capital and reserves		
Ordinary share capital (£1 shares)	1,461	800
Retained profit at 1 January 1998	345	168
Retained profit for 1998	120	65
	1,926	1,033

Pleat plc acquired the entire share capital of Sexton plc on 1 January 1998 for £1,500m. The purchase consideration was satisfied by the issue of the following securities of Pleat plc:

	£m
Ordinary shares of £1 each	300
10% Debenture stock 2010/20	1,000

The financial effect of this arrangement is not reflected in the above accounts of Pleat plc other than the fact that interest due for the year on the debenture stock was paid on 31 December 1998.

The following further information is provided relating to the assets of Sexton plc at 1 January 1998 and the plans of the directors of Pleat plc at that date:

- *Tangible fixed assets.* These possessed a fair value of £810m. No amendment was required to the estimated useful life or residual value of these assets which were originally expected to last for ten years and were four years old on 1 January 1998. There were no acquisitions or disposals during 1998.

- *Stocks.* These possessed a book value of £306m and an estimated fair value of £322m.

- *Brands*. Sexton plc had developed a brand name over the years which was not reflected in its balance sheet at 1 January 1998 but had been reliably valued by an expert valuer at £126m at that date.

- *Reorganization costs*. The directors of Pleat plc planned to spend £35m in order to incorporate successfully the business of Sexton plc with that of the parent company.

- *Goodwill*. Any goodwill arising on the acquisition of the shares in Sexton plc is estimated to possess a useful economic life of 6 years. [20 marks]

Required:
(a) The consolidated balance sheet of Pleat ple and its subsidiary Sexton plc as at 31 December 1998 using acquisition accounting and complying, so far as the information permits, with relevant standard accounting practice.

(b) A full explanation and discussion of the changes that have been made by the Accounting Standards Board in recent years so far as they impact on the accounting treatment of any three of the following items:
  - Tangible fixed assets
  - Stocks
  - Brands
  - Reorganization costs
  - Goodwill [15 marks]

(c) Identify the most important differences between the consolidated balance sheet that you have prepared and the statement which would have been appropriate had the entire purchase consideration consisted of 900 million ordinary shares of £1 each in Pleat plc. Explain why these differences are significant. [5 marks]

Notes
Ignore taxation.
Make and state any assumptions you consider necessary. [Total marks – 40]

7

CAPITAL REDUCTION, REORGANIZATION AND RECONSTRUCTION

7.1 INTRODUCTION

A company should have a balanced capital structure when it is established, that is, its assets should be funded by the appropriate types of finance. Long-term sources, such as equity capital and debentures, should cover the investment in fixed assets with sufficient excess to make a significant contribution towards the funding of current assets. If the often quoted ideal working capital ratio of 2:1 is desired, then half the value of current assets should be financed by long-term capital, and the remainder financed by short-term sources, such as creditors. Within long-term sources of funds a satisfactory relationship should be created between the various types available, the optimum structure depending on such factors as the nature of the trade undertaken and the likely stability of profits.

Once a company starts to trade, the financial structure established at the outset is affected by the results of trading and the passage of time. The initial equity investment is increased by the amount of profit earned and retained in the business, and is reduced by losses. As time passes, the repayment date for long-term loans gets closer and, near to the very end of their term, such sources must be classified as current liabilities. The rate at which debtors pay and creditors are paid affects the balance between current assets and liabilities, as do credit purchases of additional stock required to expand a successful company. In the longer term, success may encourage the acquisition of extra production capacity which must be funded by an appropriate type of finance if the capital structure of the business is to remain balanced.

The financial position of a business is subject to continuous change, unless the company is dormant and does not trade. Flows of resources take place with trading, and these have an impact on the enterprise which can be beneficial or detrimental. The result is that the business may be either a success or failure. A very successful business, in this context, is one that manages to expand; while survival, with an adequate level of return but no expansion, is regarded as a satisfactory performance. If a company goes into liquidation, or has to be reconstructed, it is a failure. There are certain courses of action that may be followed as a result of the success or failure of a business; it is the purpose of this chapter to examine these alternatives and the accounting entries which are needed to reflect them. References to legislation, unless otherwise stated, are to the Companies Act 1985.

7.2 BONUS ISSUES

Bonus issues of shares are also referred to as 'Scrip Issues' or 'Capitalization Issues'. To make such an issue, a company allots fully paid shares to its existing members and capitalizes the corresponding value from its reserves, including any credit balance on its profit and loss account; the company does not receive any consideration for the issue. Every shareholder receives bonus shares in proportion to their existing stake in the company; for instance, the holder of 10% of the equity shares would receive 10% of any bonus issue. A company must have adequate reserves to make a bonus issue, and these will be possessed by a successful company that has retained a significant portion of its profits. A bonus issue may alternatively be made from any balance to the credit of a Share Premium Account or Capital Redemption Reserve. (The Capital Redemption Reserve is examined in 7.4.)

A company can make a bonus issue if authorized by its Articles of Association, which usually contain a requirement for a general meeting to approve the director's recommendation for bonus issue before it may be made. A further consideration is that there must, of course, be sufficient authorized, but unissued, capital to enable the issue to take place.

Example 7.1 – Making a Bonus Issue

The Good Company Ltd has traded successfully for a number of years and has ploughed profits back into the company. Its authorized share capital consists of four million shares of £1 each and its balance sheet at 31 December 20X1 is:

	£000
Fixed Assets	960
Working Capital	350
	1,310
Issued Share Capital:	
Ordinary Shares of £1 each	200
Share Premium	200
Profit and Loss Account	910
	1,310

It is decided to make a bonus issue of shares, four bonus shares being given for each share currently held. The issue is to utilize the balance on the share premium account, with the remainder taken from the profit and loss account.

Required:
The balance sheet of the Good Company Lid as it will appear after the bonus issue.

Solution

Good Company Ltd Balance Sheet 31 December 20X1

	£000
Fixed Assets	960
Working Capital	350
	1,310
Issued Share Capital:	
Ordinary Shares of £1 each	1,000
Profit and Loss Account	310
	1,310

It can be seen that the bonus issue has not brought any new resources to the company; the only effect is an alteration in the composition of the company's equity, the total of which remains unchanged at £1,310,000. There is also no effect on the relative interest of each member in the company: prior to the issue a holder of 40,000 shares owned 20% of the company with a book value of 20% x £1,310,000 = £262,000; after the issue the holding has risen to 200,000 shares, which is still 20% of the issued shares and has the same book value.

If the directors do not wish to increase the amount of profit distributed, they must take steps to reduce proportionally the dividend per share. For example, to maintain a constant total cash distribution, after a 3 for 1 bonus issue, a company would have to reduce the dividend per share to one quarter of its former amount. However, because each shareholder after the issue has four times as many shares as previously, each receives an unchanged dividend in cash terms. The increase in the number of shares in issue does not affect the value of the company, as is shown by the case of a public limited company with quoted shares, where the market price per share should fall proportionally to compensate for the increased number of shares on the market.

Example 7.2 – The Effects of a Bonus Issue

Traction plc is a listed company and has an issued share capital of 10 million ordinary shares with a nominal value of £1 each. The market value of each share is £6. You are required to illustrate the expected effect of a 2 for 1 bonus issue and a cut in the dividend per share from 12 pence to 4 pence on:

(a) the market value of one share;

(b) the market value of the entire company and the dividend it pays;

(c) the market value of a holding of 5,000 shares and the dividend received by the shareholder.

Solution

(a) Where one share is held before the bonus issue, three are held after it. The value of the single share was £6, and the total value of the three shares into which it is converted is £6. Therefore, the value of a single share after the bonus issue is £2.

(b)

	Value	Dividend Paid
Before bonus issue	10m x £6 = £60m	10m x £.12 = £1.2m
After bonus issue	30m x £2 = £60m	30m x £.04 = £1.2m

The gratuitous issue of an extra 20 million shares reduces the share price proportionally, and the total value of the company and cash dividend remain unchanged.

(c)

	Value	Dividend Received
Before bonus issue	5,000 x £6 = £30,000	5,000 x £.12 = £600
After bonus issue	15,000 x £2 = £30,000	15,000 x £.04 = £600

Again, the total value of the shares and the dividend received remain unchanged.

It is therefore clear that the effect of a bonus issue is simply to increase the number of shares a company has in issue. This raises the question: 'Why would a company wish to make such an issue?' Possible reasons are:

- Theoretically, the balance on the profit and loss account is distributable as cash dividends; in practice this course may not be open to the company because the funds have been permanently invested in the substance of the business. For instance, in Example 7.1, the Good Company Ltd could not distribute the balance on its profit and loss account without liquidating a substantial portion of its fixed assets. A bonus issue recognizes the company's inability to distribute retained profits and brings the balance sheet into line with this reality.

- The creation of an enlarged permanent equity capital base makes the company more attractive to potential investors and creditors, because the level of gearing cannot be increased by the withdrawal of profit that has been capitalized.

- A bonus issue is sometimes taken as an indication of the fact that the directors intend to increase the overall level of dividend. If the investors believe this will happen, the shares become more attractive, and the price will fall less than would be expected otherwise. In Example 7.2, the share price might finish up above £2.

- The larger number of shares in circulation should help create a more active market because holdings are made more easily divisible.

- A listed company that has a high and unwieldy share price may make a bonus issue to create a lower price per share. This is useful where, for example, a company acquires other companies by share exchanges and wishes to make the value of each of its own shares closer to that of likely acquisitions.

- A successful company with substantial accumulated profits may receive favourable publicity from its capitalization. The bonus issue draws attention to the success that has created the profits to enable the issue to take place.

- The reduction in the dividend per share may help to avoid any unfavourable publicity attached to the declaration of apparently high rates of dividend.

7.3 CAPITAL REDUCTION

Section 135 of the Act allows a company to reduce its share capital in any way it considers appropriate. The ability given in the Act is therefore a general one, but specific instances are also stated:

(a) Share capital that is lost or unrepresented by available assets may be cancelled (Example 7.3 below).

(b) Share capital in excess of the needs of the company may be repaid (Example 7.4 below).

(c) A company may extinguish or reduce the liability on any of its shares in respect of share capital not paid up.

In each of these cases, the right to reduce can be exercised only if certain conditions are met:

• The company must be authorized to reduce its share capital by its Articles of Association.

• The reduction must be agreed by a special resolution of the members, that is, a resolution passed by a majority of at least 75%.

• The reduction must be confirmed by the court. This requirement is particularly important in relation to (b) and (c) above. The repayment of capital (b) actually reduces the assets of the company, while the reduction or cancellation of liability on unpaid share capital (c) reduces the funds on which a company can call if required. A creditor of a company, which decides to reduce its capital, such as a bank with which the company has an overdraft, may consider that its likelihood of repayment is jeopardized by the reduction. Such a creditor may object to the court, which can direct either that payment of the debt is secured or that an agreed amount is set aside to meet it.

The cancellation of share capital unrepresented by available assets, and the repayment of share capital to members, are each likely to have a substantial effect on the content of the balance sheet. They are considered further below.

When a company has either been trading unprofitably for a number of years or suffers abnormally large losses in a single year, it may show a large debit balance on its profit and loss account. Despite these losses, which have eroded capital, a company may still be viable and able to earn profits in the future. In these circumstances it is reasonable to recognize that some of the capital has been lost and to reduce its value accordingly. A further reason for engaging in capital reduction is that the Companies

Act prohibits the distribution of current profits before past losses have been made good, but allows past losses to be removed from the calculation of distributable profits if they are written off in a capital reduction. Thus, a capital reduction scheme enables dividends to be paid from current profits despite the fact that losses have been made in the past. Also, a reduction scheme that removes a debit balance on the profit and loss account makes the company more attractive to prospective investors and sources of credit.

Example 7.3 – Capital Reduction, past losses

Getting Better Ltd is an old established company which, after trading profitably for a number of years, incurred substantial losses. Its balance sheet at 31 December 20X1 is:

	£000
Fixed Assets	520
Working Capital	230
	750
Ordinary Shares of £1 each	1,000
Profit and Loss Account	(250)
	750

The company has rationalized its methods of production and distribution and has returned to profitability. It wishes to raise additional equity capital, and, as a preliminary step, decides to reduce its share capital to eliminate the debit balance on the profit and loss account by cancelling one out of every four ordinary shares.

Required:
Prepare the company's balance sheet, after the capital reduction has taken place.

Solution

Getting Better Ltd Balance Sheet 31 December 20X1 after Capital Reduction

	£000
Fixed Assets	520
Working Capital	230
	750
Ordinary Shares of £1 each	750

In this example the existing shareholders retain three shares out of every four shares previously held. Alternatively, the company could keep one million shares in issue and reduce the nominal value of each share to 75 pence.

A company may find that it has assets in excess of its requirements, for instance it may dispose of a substantial part of its assets but not wish to re-invest the cash received. The scale of the undertaking's activities is reduced, with the result that its share capital is now too large for its new, smaller, level of operations. It may be decided that it is appropriate to reduce the size of the company's share capital by repaying to the shareholders the amount in excess of requirements.

Example 7.4 – Capital Reduction, surplus cash

Smaller Ltd has sold to a competitor for cash a substantial number of its retail outlets. The bulk of the company's shares are owned by the directors, the balance being held by members of their families. The company's balance sheet after the sale on 31 December 20X1 is:

	£000
Fixed Assets	200
Working Capital Requirements	150
Surplus Cash	750
	1,100
Ordinary Shares of £1 each	1,000
Profit and Loss Account	100
	1,100

The directors are nearing retirement age and, because they have no successors. decide to run the company at its reduced size and return the surplus assets to the shareholders. The reduction of capital is to be achieved by reducing the nominal value of each share to 25 pence and repaying 75 pence per share to the shareholders.

Required.
Prepare the company's balance sheet after the capital reduction has been carried out.

Solution

Smaller Ltd Balance Sheet 31 December 20X1 after Capital Reduction

	£000
Fixed Assets	200
Working Capital	150
	350
Ordinary Shares of 25 pence each	250
Profit and Loss Account	100
	350

7.4 REDEEMABLE SHARES AND THE PURCHASE BY A COMPANY OF ITS OWN SHARES

The Companies Act contains provisions that allow companies to issue redeemable shares of all types and to purchase their own shares. For the purpose of this book, we shall cover only the main provisions and simple examples; the complications that arise when the original issue of shares was made at a premium are excluded. In sections 7.4.1 to 7.4.3 we consider the position where a public limited company redeems some of its shares; the rules for a company purchasing its own shares are largely the same and are dealt with in 7.4.4. In all cases the company must have the appropriate power in its Articles.

7.4.1 The Legal Provisions

The intention of the Act is that the permanent capital of a company which redeems some of its shares should be maintained in value and not diminished as a result of the redemption. A company's permanent capital consists of its issued share capital plus any reserves that are not distributable by way of dividends; for example, a revaluation reserve is part of permanent capital, whereas the balance on the profit and loss account is not. To achieve this objective, the Act contains detailed instructions to be applied when shares are redeemed. These rules, in so far as they are within the syllabus, are:

- The shares must be fully paid.

- Companies must not convert shares into creditors; the terms of redemption must provide for payment on redemption.

- Redeemable shares may be redeemed only out of distributable profits of the company or out of the proceeds of a fresh issue of shares made for the purpose of the redemption.

- Any premium payable on redemption must be provided out of distributable profits.

- A transfer to a 'Capital Redemption Reserve' must be made:

   (i) Where the redemption is made entirely out of profits, a sum equal to the nominal value of the shares redeemed must be transferred from profit to the capital redemption reserve.

(ii) Where the redemption is made wholly or partly out of a new issue, the sum to be transferred from profit to the capital redemption reserve is the amount, if any, by which the nominal value of the shares redeemed exceeds the proceeds of the new issue.

- Redeemed shares must be treated as cancelled.

7.4.2 Redemption Met Entirely out of Distributable Profits

When the redemption is met entirely out of distributable profits, the nominal value of the permanent capital repaid on redemption is replaced by an equivalent transfer from distributable profits to the non-distributable capital redemption reserve. Any premium payable on redemption must be met from distributable reserves.

Example 7.5

The following extracts are taken from the balance sheet of Redeemer plc at 31 December 20X6:

	£000
Ordinary shares of £1 each	600
Redeemable shares of £1 each	100
Share premium account	400
Permanent capital	1,100
Distributable profits	300
Net assets (including cash)	1,400

The company intends to redeem the 100,000 redeemable shares, making no new issue.

Required:
Prepare balance sheet extracts, in the same format as above, to show the effect of the redemption in each of the following cases:

(a) The shares were issued and redeemed at par.

(b) The shares were issued at par and are redeemed at £1.10 per share, i.e. at a premium of 10p per share.

Solution

Revised Balance Sheet Extracts

	Case a £000	Case b £000
Ordinary shares of £1 each	600	600
Share premium account	400	400
Capital redemption reserve	100	100
Permanent capital	1,100	1,100
Distributable profits	200	190
Net assets (including cash)	1,300	1,290

Workings

	£000	£000
Transfer to capital redemption reserve (nominal value of capital redeemed)	100	100
Premium on redemption	–	10
Reduction in distributable profit (amount paid on redemption)	100	110

Note that in both cases the redemption is met out of distributable profits and the amount by which the company's issued capital is diminished is transferred to the capital redemption reserve. The permanent capital is thereby maintained intact at £1,100,000 as the result of applying the relevant provisions of the Act.

7.4.3 Shares Redeemed Wholly or Partly out of the Proceeds of a New Issue

A fresh issue of shares may be made to help to finance a redemption. In this case the procedure applied to maintain the value of permanent capital is slightly more complex than when no such issue is made. The transfer from distributable profit to the Capital Redemption Reserve needs be sufficient only to replace that part of the permanent capital redeemed that is not covered by the new permanent capital introduced.

Example 7.6

The following extracts are taken from the balance sheet of Redeemer plc at 31 December 20X6:

	£000
Ordinary shares of £1 each	600
Redeemable shares of £1 each	100
Share premium account	400
Permanent capital	1,100
Distributable profits	300
Net assets (including cash)	1,400

The company intends to redeem the 100,000 redeemable shares at a premium of 20p per share.

Required:
Prepare balance sheet extracts, in the same format as above, to show the effect of the redemption in each of the following cases:

	Case a	Case b
	£000	£000
Redeemable shares issued at:		
Nominal value	100	100
Premium	–	–
Fresh issue to help finance redemption:		
Nominal value	50	50
Premium	–	25

Solution

Revised Balance Sheet Extracts

	Case a £000	Case b £000
Ordinary shares of £1 each	650	650
Share premium account	400	425
Capital redemption reserve	50	25
Permanent capital	1,100	1,100
Distributable profits	230	255
Net assets (including cash)	1,330	1,355

Note that the permanent capital is maintained intact at £1,100,000 as the result of applying the provisions of the Act.

Workings (£000):

	Case a	Case b
Nominal value of shares redeemed	100	100
Less: Proceeds of new issue	50	75
Shortfall transferred from distributable profit to capital redemption reserve	50	25

7.4.4 Purchase by a Company of Its Own Shares

The Act allows a company to purchase its own shares, subject to certain conditions, whether or not they are redeemable. This ability benefits both public and private companies. Public companies are able, for example, to return to members any funds in excess of requirements and avoid the need for a capital reduction exercise, and to revise more easily their capital structures to bring them into line with current requirements. This procedure has also been used by quoted companies, especially in the USA, to increase the share price by reducing the number of shares on the market: this also has the effect of leaving fewer shares between which profits are to be shared and so increases the value of earnings per share. The main advantage to owners of shares in private companies is the ability to realize their investment by selling their shares to the company, thereby overcoming any difficulty that would previously have been experienced in transferring their shares. For instance, close control of family companies may be retained by using the company's resources to acquire the shares of a member who dies or retires. However, the company is not bound to purchase its own shares, and can do so only if it has the resources available.

The conditions that a company must satisfy to purchase its own shares are largely similar to those which apply to redeemable shares. The conditions are:

- The shares to be purchased must be fully paid.

- The terms of acquisition must include cash payment on purchase.

- The purchase may be made only out of distributable profits of the company or out of the proceeds of a fresh issue of shares made for the purpose of the acquisition.

- Any premium payable on purchase must be provided out of distributable profits.

- A transfer to a 'Capital Redemption Reserve' must be made in the following manner:

  (i) Where the purchase is made entirely out of profits, a sum equal to the nominal value of the shares purchased must be transferred from profit to the capital redemption reserve.

  (ii) Where the purchase is made wholly or partly out of a new issue, the sum to be transferred from profit to the capital redemption reserve is the amount, if any, by which the nominal value of the shares purchased exceeds the proceeds of the new issue.

- The shares purchased cannot be held by the company as an investment; they must be cancelled.

- The company must be authorized to purchase its own shares by its Articles of Association.

- Shares may not be purchased if, as a result of the purchase, the company would have only redeemable shares in issue.

- After the purchase the company must have at least two members.

- Public companies must have an allotted share capital in excess of the 'authorized minimum', which was set in the Act at £50,000. The purchase of its own shares must not reduce the allotted shares of a public company to below the authorized minimum.

Example 7.7

The following is the summarized balance sheet of Beacons Ltd, a long-established family company, at 31 March 20X0:

	£000
Ordinary shares of £1 each	300
Revaluation reserve	150
Profit and loss account	400
Net assets including cash	850

90% of the shares are owned by the directors, the balance being held by their distant relatives. The directors wish to concentrate ownership of the company in their own hands and, as the company has surplus cash, have made an offer for the company to purchase the shares held by the distant relatives. The offer values each share at £2.50.

The offer has been accepted by all the shareholders concerned, and was put into effect on 1 April 20X0.

Required:
(a) State the value of Beacons Ltd's permanent capital at 31 March 20X0.

(b) Prepare the balance sheet of Beacons Ltd on 1 April 20X0 immediately after it has purchased its own shares.

(c) State the value of Beacons Ltd's permanent capital at 1 April 20X0 after the purchase has been completed.

Solution (£000)

(a) The permanent capital is:
£450 (300 share capital + 150 revaluation reserve)

(b)
Ordinary shares of £1 each	270(W1)
Revaluation reserve	150
Capital redemption reserve	30
Profit and loss account	325(W2)
Net assets including cash	775

Workings:
W1 300 (original share capital) – 30 (capital redeemed 10% x 300)

W2 400 (original balance) – 30 (transfer to Capital Redemption Reserve – 45 (premium on redemption)

(c) The permanent capital is:
£450 (270 shares + 150 revaluation reserve + 30 capital redemption reserve).

7.5 FAILURE, LOSSES AND CAPITAL EROSION

It is a fact that some companies fail and then have to be liquidated. Management and owners are often unwilling to face the likelihood of failure and attempt to struggle on until they are forced to accept the reality of the situation by, for example, the appointment of a receiver. Companies in financial difficulties need to obtain further finance, and the bank manager is often the first person approached for these resources. The optimistic attitude typically displayed by business management, often with little regard to the actual circumstances, is that the firm's position will improve and failure will be avoided provided it can survive for a further short period of time. It is therefore in the interests of banks, and all other potential providers of finance, to be able to judge which companies are merely going through a period of temporary difficulty and which companies are going to fail. It is important to ensure, as far as possible, that too pessimistic an assessment is not made, because the withdrawal of an existing financial provision by the bank may cause the failure of a company which would otherwise have recovered. Success or failure cannot be forecast with certainty, but there are a number of indicators which have been observed in failed companies and which can be looked for in companies suffering from financial difficulties in order to see whether they too are likely to fail.

7.5.1 The Causes of Failure

The prime factor that causes companies to fail is inadequate management, which may misjudge costs, prices or markets, or base decisions on insufficient or out of date information. These shortcomings eventually cause the company to become insolvent and force it into liquidation. The causes of failure are therefore the factors that erode the liquidity of the company and leave it unable to attract further external finance or generate sufficient internal finance to continue in operation. When a bank manager is approached by a company with a request for an overdraft, an increased overdraft, or some other form of financial assistance, and the company's accounts reveal a poor liquidity position, the causes of the low liquidity ratio must be sought. If the causes are of a permanent nature, the provision of additional finance will merely postpone liquidation because the company will suffer another liquidity crisis as soon as the new funds have been used up. The causes of liquidity problems may be complex, but can be sought in such areas as:

1. Finance Costs

Interest charges on debt represent a fixed cost. They do not vary with the rate of output. A company with a high proportion of debt finance has to meet substantial interest payments, and it is possible for these to prove too great a burden, especially if there is a downturn in trading profit. Small companies often rely heavily on overdrafts for finance, and an increase in the rate of interest charged, particularly if it coincides with a fall in trading profits, can cause great difficulties.

2. Operating Costs

The high fixed costs associated with capital-intensive production methods can prove an excessive drain on resources, particularly if there is a fall in the level of activity. Fixed costs do not respond to changes in the level of output, and may be completely outside the control of management; for example, local authorities collect rates from the occupiers of business premises and these must be paid by businesses irrespective of their profitability. Also, the variable cost per unit of output may rise, for example, as the result of a pay increase granted to employees. If a firm cannot increase its selling price to recover increased operating costs, its profit margins are eroded, or even converted into losses, thereby reducing the level of cash flow into the businesses.

3. Over-trading

A company may be profitable, but management takes the unwise step of financing long-term developments with short-term funds, that is, they use money needed to meet operating costs to acquire fixed assets or to fund long-term activities such as research (see 10.8.2 for a fuller explanation of over-trading).

4. Market Failure

It is possible for a company to be efficient and, initially, to have a correctly balanced capital structure. However, it will still fail if it cannot sell its product at a price high enough to cover costs. The inability to charge an adequate price may be due to competitors having lower prices, or simply the fact that there is no longer a demand for the company's particular product.

5. Adverse currency movements

When the value of the home currency of an exporter rises relative to other currencies, the value of its sales in overseas markets falls when the proceeds are remitted, unless it is able to raise its prices overseas. For example, a company based in Upland, where the currency is the U, exports goods to Lowland, where the currency is the L. The customers in Lowland pay a price stated in Ls and, in both 20X0 and 20X1, the company collected L 100,000 from sales in Lowland. In 20X0 the exchange rate was $4L = 1U$; in 20X1 the U strengthened and the rate became $5L = 1U$. When exchanged, the 20X0 sales yielded $100,000/4 = U25,000$ while the 20X1 sales produced only

$100,000/5 = U20,000$. The company has to pay its costs in Us, and the reduced receipts may not be sufficient.

Where symptoms such as those described above are shown by a company, a decision must be made whether they can be rectified in sufficient time and at a small enough cost to enable the company to continue in existence. If it is fairly certain that the company is going to fail, commercial losses are minimized by injecting no further finance. The likelihood of a firm, which appears to be failing, avoiding eventual liquidation depends to a large extent on the ability of management. To have reached the position where failure is a distinct possibility can be evidence of poor management, and a condition of financial help could be the injection of new managerial expertise. The bank's evaluation of the prospects of survival is likely to be based on forecasts made by management, and these must therefore be checked carefully for realism and compared with past results to see if they are consistent. Future sales of a product are unlikely to be substantially higher than in the past unless there is a convincing explanation for an anticipated upturn. Expectations should be expressed in the form of accounting reports, the contents of which can then be scrutinized. It is important not to accept management's statements without question; enough investigation should be carried out to reach an informed opinion on their reliability.

7.5.2 Losses and Capital Erosion

Losses are caused by the failure to recover all costs through sales, and the solution lies in the company's ability to raise prices, cut costs, or produce a new product that can be sold profitably. It is unusual for companies to sell only one product, and diversification makes it more likely that poor results in one area will be offset by good results in others. The accounting system of a company should enable the identification of those lines that are being sold at a loss so that remedial action can be taken, but simply ceasing to trade in items that show a loss may not be the correct solution if they make a contribution to overhead costs. A successful company must be able to adapt to changes in the market, and should always be developing new improved lines to replace those that are likely to experience a fall in demand in the future. Both the time taken to develop and market a new product and the associated costs involved can be substantial, and so the process must be started well in advance and appropriate finance arranged. A firm whose current products are not in demand and which has no new developments to put into production is likely to fail.

A company that makes losses suffers an erosion of capital, which produces a corresponding reduction in net assets. The impact of losses on the viability of a company depends on their size relative to the company's resources, and on their duration. A relatively small annual loss is unlikely, in itself, to have a significant effect; the company still has a positive cash flow from trading if its depreciation charge is greater than the loss. The accumulation of a series of losses, even if individually small, has a more serious impact in the longer term; in these circumstances the cash flow represented by depreciation is used to finance running costs and the firm will probably be unable to attract finance when it is time for plant replacement. A company that continually makes losses is heading for likely failure; the size of the losses merely determines how long the process takes. The effect of large significant losses is more immediate and precipitates the crisis more quickly.

Example 7.8 – The Effects of Losses

The balance sheet of Going Ltd at 31 December 20X0 is:

	£000
Fixed Assets at written down value	400
Working Capital	350
	750
Share Capital	500
Profit and Loss Account	250
	750

The fixed assets are expected to last a further five years, and to keep pace with inflation it is forecast that £20,000 per year must be invested in additional working capital.

Required:
Prepare the balance sheet of Going Ltd at 31 December 20X5 on the alternative assumptions that in each of the next five years it makes a loss of:
(a) £20,000

(b) £60,000

Solution

	(a) £000	(b) £000
Fixed Assets at written down value	–	–
Working Capital	450	450
Surplus Cash	200(W1)	– (W2)
	650	450
Share Capital	500	500
Profit and Loss Account	150	(50)
	650	450

Workings (£000):

	5 years' losses	+	5 years' depreciation	−	5 years' addtional working capital	=	Surplus cash 31 December 20X5
W1	−100	+	400	−	100	=	200
W2	−300	+	400	−	100	=	0

No dividends have been paid throughout the five years, and in neither case does Going Ltd have enough cash at the end of 20X5 to replace the exhausted fixed assets. The continual losses make it most unlikely that new external finance can be obtained. In case (b) the losses have eroded the book value of the share capital, while annual losses in excess of £60,000 would deplete working capital and therefore reduce the volume of trade the company is able to undertake.

The Act requires any director who becomes aware of the fact that, as a result of business losses, the company's net assets are worth half or less of its called up share capital to call an extraordinary general meeting. The meeting must be convened within 28 days of the loss becoming known and must be held within 56 days. This meeting is instructed to consider whether any, and if so what, measures should be taken to deal with the situation. For this purpose, the 'net assets' of a company are defined as 'the aggregate of its assets less the aggregate of its liabilities' and so their value is revealed by the balance sheet. The speed with which the erosion becomes apparent will therefore depend on the frequency of preparation of balance sheets.

The objective of this provision is to make the shareholders aware of the fact that the company has suffered major losses; once this has been done, they are able to meet to consider possible courses of action to prevent the accumulation of further losses. However, the legal requirement to call a meeting may give rise to problems. The fact that a meeting has been called may cause a withdrawal of finance by, for example, banks and trade creditors, thereby bringing about a failure which might have been averted. Assets are valued for accounting purposes on the assumption that the business is a going concern; in the circumstances that lead to the calling of a meeting under the Act, the liquidation basis may be more appropriate. The use of liquidation values would, although prudent, possibly reinforce the assumption that the company is bound to fail and hasten its end.

7.6 LIQUIDATION
This is usually caused by a company being unable to pay its debts as they fall due. In determining the company's ability to pay its debts, the Act requires all contingent and

prospective liabilities to be taken into account. Therefore, a company may currently be solvent, but may be forced into liquidation if it is apparent that it will be unable to meet some future obligation. When a company goes into liquidation, the administration of its affairs passes from the board of directors to an official known as a 'liquidator'. It is the duty of the liquidator to realize the asset of the company for as much as possible and use the proceeds to pay its creditors and members in a specified order. The order of repayment is as follows:

- Debts secured with a fixed charge on an asset have first priority, and are repayable out of the proceeds received from the sale of that asset. It is unlikely that the realized value of the asset will be exactly equal to the amount of the debt, and any surplus is used by the liquidator to meet the company's other liabilities. Great care must be exercised when there is a deficit, that is, the value of the secured asset is less than the debt. In these circumstances, the secured debt effectively divides into two separate parts; the first is covered by the secured asset to the extent of its value, and the second part ranks alongside, and therefore is added to, the unsecured creditors.

- The costs of liquidation.

- Preferential debts, which include certain taxes and sums due to employees.

- Debts that carry a floating charge, that is, they are secured on the company's assets in general.

- Unsecured creditors.

- Shareholders. The priority for repayment where there exist different classes of shares is determined by the terms on which the shares were issued. Preference shares are normally repaid in full before the ordinary shares, while the Act gives priority, within their particular class, to redeemable shares and any which the company has agreed to purchase, but has not acquired by the time of liquidation.

Each category listed above must be paid in full before the next group receives any payment whatsoever. Thus, all preferential debts must be paid before creditors with floating charges receive anything, and they in turn must be fully settled before any payment is made to unsecured creditors. A company that is insolvent when it is wound up is unlikely to be able to pay the full amount due to all of its creditors and classes of shareholders; some receive less than the amount due, and others receive nothing. Within the class where the liquidator runs out of money, the debts abate equally, that is, each creditor or class of shareholder receives the same proportional payment.

Example 7.9 – Abatement

The liquidator of Gone Ltd has sold all of the company's assets for £250,000 in cash.

The sums to be met from this are:

	£000
Cost of liquidation	30
Preferential debts	20
Debts with floating charges	100
Unsecured creditors	200
Ordinary shareholders	250

Required:
(a) Calculate how much is received by each class of creditor and shareholder, showing clearly the order of priority.

(b) Calculate the sum received by an unsecured creditor owed £2,500.

Solution

(a) The funds available are distributed as follows:

	Order of Priority	£000
	Received from sale of assets	250
1.	*Less*: Cost of liquidation	30
		220
2.	*Less*: Preferential debts	20
		200
3.	*Less*. Debts with floating charges	100
4.	Available for unsecured creditors	100
	Unsecured creditors are owed £200,000 and each receives 50 pence in the pound.	
5.	Ordinary shareholders receive nothing.	

(b) An unsecured creditor owed £2,500 receives 50 pence x 2,500=£1,250.

There are two circumstances in which a lender may be interested in a company that is threatened with liquidation:

•   Where the lender is owed money by a company, the maximum amount it can expect to recover if the company fails is the sum due on liquidation. The extent of the lender's potential loss is then the difference between the sum lent and the receipts expected on liquidation.

- The lender may hold shares in a company as security for a loan, in which case the sum receivable on the shares in a liquidation gives the value of the shares as a security.

Example 7.10

A bank's customer, Jeremiah, has deposited 6,000 shares in Eastgate Ltd as security for a personal bank overdraft on which £2,460 is at present outstanding. You have heard that, at a meeting between the directors and creditors of Eastgate Ltd held on 20 April 20X1, it was decided to liquidate that company. Certain facts and estimates were examined by the meeting. These included:

(i) *Balance Sheet of Eastgate Ltd at 19 April 20X1*

	£	£
Goodwill at cost		22,000
Freehold property at cost		45,000
Plant and machinery at cost less depreciation		48,000
		115,000
Quoted investments (market value £16,000)		12,000
Current assets		
Stock	108,000	
Debtors	194,000	
	302,000	
Current liabilities		
Creditors	209,000	
Bank overdraft	68,000	
	277,000	
Working capital		25,000
		152,000
12% Debenture		50,000
		102,000
Share capital (£1 shares)		100,000
Reserves at 31 December 20X1	70,000	
Loss for 20X1 to date	(68,000)	
		2,000
		102,000

(ii) *The following asset values were considered to be relevant in a liquidation:*

	£
Plant and machinery	10,000
Stock	47,000
Debtors	160,000

There was significant disagreement regarding the likely value of freehold property. The majority accepted a valuation of £60,000 recently obtained from a firm of surveyors. A minority argued that, in view of development potential in the area where this property was located, a sale figure of £150,000 was likely to be much nearer the mark.

(iii) Eastgate Ltd's bank holds a fixed charge on the freehold property as security for the overdraft.

(iv) Of the £209,000 creditors, £57,000 were estimated as being preferential.

(v) The debenture is secured by a floating charge over the assets of Eastgate Ltd, other than the freehold property. There are no arrears of debenture interest.

(vi) Liquidation expenses are estimated at £6,000.

Required:
(a) Calculations of the amounts which would be received by each of the providers of finance, assuming that the majority view regarding the value of the freeholds is correct and that the other information proves accurate. You should show clearly the order of priority for repayment.

(b) An indication of the effect on the findings under (a) if the minority view regarding the value of the freeholds proves to be correct.

Note:
Ignore taxation.

Solution

(a)	*Assets are expected to realize:*	£000	£000
	Freehold property		60
	Less: Bank overdraft secured thereon		68
	To unsecured creditors		8
	Quoted Investments		16
	Plant and Machinery		10
	Stock		47
	Debtors		160
			233

Priority Repayment

1	Liquidation expenses		6
			227
2	Preferential creditors		57
			170
3	Debenture with floating charge		50
			120
4	Unsecured creditors:		
	Bank overdraft residue	8	
	Other creditors (209-57)	152	
			160

Unsecured creditors therefore receive 75 pence in the pound

In total the bank receives £60,000 + (.75 x 8,000)	66
Unsecured creditors receive £152,000 x .75	114

5   Shareholders receive nothing.

(b) If the property sells for £150,000, the bank will recover the full overdraft of £68,000 out of its security and the non-preferential creditors will be repaid in full, £152,000. The amount available for the shareholders will be:

	£000
Increase in expected selling price of property	90
Less: additional amount due to bank and creditors	40
	50

Shareholders receive $\dfrac{£50,000}{100,000}$ = 50 pence per share.

A 'receiver' may be appointed to enforce the terms of a secured debt if a company defaults in the payment of interest or capital when due, or behaves in a manner that threatens secured assets. The receiver takes control of the assets covered by the charge and realizes them to provide funds to satisfy the terms of the loan. If the company remains solvent after the receivership is completed, management reverts to the directors. However, the appointment of a receiver is usually an indication that the company is failing and so liquidation, under the control of the liquidator, normally follows receivership.

7.7 CAPITAL RECONSTRUCTION

Liquidation is not the inevitable outcome of a company's insolvency. It may be worthwhile to attempt a rescue where the insolvency is due to specific, curable factors. For example, a company may have overtraded, and, if it is basically profitable, an injection of additional capital may save it; alternatively, a company may need time and finance to cease the production of unprofitable lines and bring to the market new, profitable products. In these circumstances, meetings of creditors and members are called to consider the acceptance of variations in their rights; to be acceptable it is anticipated that the proposed reconstruction must be more attractive to all parties than the alternative of liquidation.

7.7.1 The Variation of Rights

The objective of a reconstruction scheme is to enable the company to continue as a going concern by the removal of the burden of immediate debts, the attraction of additional funds and the creation of a viable financial structure. The reconstruction can be carried out by altering the rights of creditors and members in the existing company, or the activities of the old company may be taken over by a newly established corporate entity which accepts revised obligations to the old company's creditors and members, with the old company being wound up or dissolved. It is possible to vary rights in a number of ways on reconstruction:

- The nature of the debt may be changed, for example, debentures may be converted to share capital or creditors to secured loans.

- The value of the liability may be changed; for example, the nominal value of ordinary shares, which are likely to be of little or no value on liquidation, can be greatly reduced, or creditors may agree to forego part of their debt.

- The return on the debt may be varied. Trade creditors could be offered interest to delay their claims, or debenture holders given higher interest to extend the term of the debenture.

- A combination of the three points above can be applied. 8% debentures with a face value of £100,000 repayable in one year's time may be cancelled in exchange for £75,000 ordinary shares of £1 each and £50,000 debentures carrying 12% interest and repayable in ten years' time.

The rights of creditors and members cannot be varied in an arbitrary manner; the Companies Act provides for meetings of all classes to be called, and, if each of these approves of the proposed arrangement by a majority of at least 75%, then, with the sanction of the court, it becomes binding on all the interested parties.

7.7.2 Implementation of a Scheme of Reconstruction

When a company is reconstructed it is common to revalue the assets at realistic amounts and eliminate the debit balance on the profit and loss account, if any. When the reconstruction does not involve the creation of a new company, a Resconstruction Account is opened to complete the book-keeping double entries for the adjustments on reconstruction. This account is debited with reductions in the value of assets, the adverse profit and loss account balance, and the creation of liabilities; it is credited with reductions in liabilities and increases in the value of assets.

The corresponding entries are in the appropriate asset or liability account.

Example 7.11 – The Reconstruction Account

The following is the balance sheet of File Ltd on 31 December 20X1:

	£000	£000
Fixed Assets at written down value		180
Goodwill		50
Stock	90	
Debtors	85	
	175	
Trade Creditors	85	
Bank Overdraft	40	
	125	
Working Capital		50
		280
8% Secured Debentures repayable 31 December 20X8		130
		150
Ordinary Shares of £1 each		250
Profit and Loss Account		(100)
		150

The company's activities have been partially reorganized and a number of loss-making branches closed. It is forecast that profits will be made in the future, but reconstruction is necessary to enable the company to raise further equity capital needed to complete the reorganization. The following scheme has been accepted by all interested parties:

1. The assets are to be written down to realistic current values:

	£000
Fixed Assets	80
Goodwill	–
Stock	70
Debtors	80

2. The debit balance on the profit and loss account is to be eliminated.

3. The existing 8% debentures are to be cancelled. In return the debenture holders are to receive 12% debentures with a nominal value of £90,000 and 35,000 ordinary shares of £1 each fully paid.

4. The trade creditors are to be reduced by £25,000, and they agree, in return for an interest payment, to wait two years for their money.

5. Each existing ordinary share of £1 is to be written down to two pence. The two pence shares are to be consolidated into shares with a nominal value of £1 each. The ordinary shareholders agree to subscribe in cash for 60,000 shares of £1 each at par.

Required:
(a) Prepare the Reconstruction Account of File Ltd to put the scheme into effect.

(b) Prepare the Balance Sheet of File Ltd after the scheme has been effected.

Solution

Reconstruction Account

	£000		£000
Fixed Assets (1)	100	8% Debentures (3)	130
Goodwill (1)	50	Creditors (4)	25
Stock (1)	20	Ordinary Shares (5)	245
Debtors (1)	5		
Profit and Loss Account (2)	100		
12% Debentures (3)	90		
Ordinary Shares (for debenture holders) (3)	35		
	400		400

Note:
The number in ( ) after each entry in the above account refers to the step in the reconstruction scheme given in the question.

Balance Sheet after Reconstruction

	£000	£000
Fixed assets		80
Current assets		
Stock	70	
Debtors	80	
Cash (W2)	20	
		170
		250
Less: liabilities due in more than 1 year		
12% Debentures	90	
Creditors deferred for 2 years	60	
		150
		100
Financed by:		
Ordinary share capital (WI)		100

Workings:

W1 *Ordinary Share Capital*	£000
Issued to Debenture holders	35
Ordinary shareholders (reduced)	5
Issued for cash	60
	100

W2 *Cash*	
Overdraft	(40)
Cash from issue of shares	60
	20

In the above example the amounts written off assets together with the removal of the accumulated loss were exactly balanced by adjustments to the claims from various providers of finance. The credit balance, which sometimes remains on the reconstruction account after the adjustments have been made, is a capital reserve and is shown in the balance sheet as part of equity.

In questions on reconstruction, care must be taken to show how the revised figures in the balance sheet after reconstruction have been computed. The following example shows this need clearly, because the value of ordinary shares in the new company's balance sheet involves a fairly complex calculation. Failure to show detailed workings may make it impossible for the examiner to detect the nature of particular errors and give due credit for calculations correctly made.

Example 7.12

Arches Ltd has incurred trading losses during each of its last three accounting periods and is now in severe financial difficulty. The company's balance sheet at 31 March 20X0 is as follows:

Balance Sheet

	£	£
Fixed assets at cost less depreciation		239,000
Goodwill		37,000
Current assets		
Stock	90,000	
Trade debtors	64,000	
	154,000	
Current liabilities		
Trade creditors	93,000	
Bank overdraft (secured)	67,000	
	160,000	
Working capital		(6,000)
		270,000
12% Debenture stock		100,000
		170,000
Ordinary shares (£1 each)		200,000
Profit and loss account		(30,000)
		170,000

A reorganization of the company's activities during March 20X0 resulted in a transfer of resources from loss-making to profitable product lines.

A meeting of all parties involved is held on 2 April 19X0 to consider a scheme of reconstruction under the Companies Acts. The proposal made by the directors is that a new company called Arches (20X0) Ltd be formed to take over the assets, liabilities and business activities of Arches Ltd. It is estimated that the annual trading profits of Arches (20X0) Ltd, for the foreseeable future, will be £43,500 before charging debenture interest (see below). After debenture interest has been deducted 50 per cent of the balance remaining is to be paid out as dividends.

Arches (20X0) Ltd would take over the fixed assets at their depreciated replacement cost, estimated at £156,000; stock, trade debtors, trade creditors and the bank overdraft would be transferred at the figures appearing in the above balance sheet.

Arches (20X0) Ltd would issue 20p ordinary shares and 15 per cent debenture stock as follows:

(1) The existing debenture holders of Arches Ltd would receive £10 of 15 per cent debenture stock for every £20 of 12 per cent debenture stock presently held. They would also receive the number of 20p ordinary shares which causes the dividend plus debenture interest receivable from Arches (20X0) Ltd to be equal to the amount of debenture interest previously received from Arches Ltd.

(2) The issued share capital of Arches (20X0) Ltd would consist of 500,000 ordinary shares of 20p each. After the issue of ordinary shares referred to above, the balance of the 500,000 shares would be issued on a pro rata basis in exchange for the ordinary shares held in Arches Ltd.

If the reconstruction proposal is accepted the existing ordinary shareholders of Arches Ltd have agreed to subscribe in cash for an additional 400,000 ordinary shares of 20p each at par. The proceeds would be used primarily to repay the bank overdraft.

Required:
The opening balance sheet of Arches (20X0) Ltd assuming the proposed reconstruction is adopted and put into effect. The balance sheet should show clearly the number of ordinary shares issued to the debenture stock holders of Arches Ltd and the number of shares issued to the ordinary shareholders of Arches Ltd distinguishing those paid for in cash.

Notes:
(i) Ignore taxation and any arrears or accruals of dividends or interest.

(ii) Assume that no changes have occurred since the balance sheet date.

Solution

Balance Sheet of Arches (20X0) Ltd

	£	£
Fixed Assets at valuation		156,000
Stock	90,000	
Trade Debtors	64,000	
Bank (80,000-67,000)	13,000	
	167,000	
Less: Trade Creditors	93,000	
		74,000
		230,000
Less: 15% Debenture Stock		50,000 (WI)
		180,000

Financed by.
Ordinary shares:

Issued to debenture holders	45,000 (W2)
Issued to shareholders for cash	80,000 (W3)
Issued to shareholders on reconstruction	55,000 (W3)
900,000 shares at 20 pence each	180,000

Workings:
WI 15% Debentures issued: 10/20 x 100,000 = £50,000
W2 Interest payable on new debentures: 15% x £50,000 = £7,500

	£
Debenture holders of Arches Ltd received interest of	12,000
Less: Interest on new debentures in Arches (20X0) Ltd	7,500
Balance to be received as dividends	4,500

Calculation of Dividends:	
Forecast profit before finance charges	43,500
Less: Finance Charge	7,500
	36,000
Dividend (50% x £36,000)	18,000
Profit retained	18,000

Shares issued to debenture holders of Arches Ltd are therefore:

$$\frac{4,500}{18,000} \times 900,000 = 225,000 \text{ shares}$$

225,000 at 20 pence = £45,000

W3 Shares issued to shareholders of Arches Ltd:
For cash: 400,000 at 20 pence = £80,000
On reconstruction: 500,000 – 225,000 (W2) = 275,000 at 20 pence
= £55,000

7.7.3 The Evaluation of Reconstruction Schemes

The providers of finance, when asked to participate in a scheme of reconstruction, should weigh the benefits they might obtain from its implementation with the alternative, which is usually liquidation. A first step in the review of any scheme is to consider the rights of each class on liquidation and reconstruction. The likely outcomes must be based on forecasts, and so cannot be guaranteed as accurate, but because liquidation is more immediate its results are open to less doubt. Presentation and assimilation of the outcome of liquidation and reconstruction, as alternatives, is achieved by the use of a tabular format. Such an analysis for Arches Ltd (Example 7.12), on the assumption that in a liquidation its fixed assets would be worth their depreciated replacement cost, is:

Provider of Finance	Position on Liquidation	Position on Reconstruction
Shareholders	Receive £50,000 (WI) less liquidation expenses	Receive £55,000 shares and buy £80,000. This entitles them to expected dividends of £13,500. They own 75% of the company.
Debenture Holders	Receive £100,000 cash	Receive £50,000 of debentures and £45,000 of shares. No reduction in income occurs. They own 25% of the company.
Creditors	£93,000 received	£93,000 received. Future custom.
Bank	£67,000 received	£67,000 received. Future custom.

WI (£000) Assets 310 (156 + 90 + 64) – liabilities 260 (100 + 93 + 67).

Provided that the profit forecast is accurate, it appears that all parties are left no worse off, or indeed benefit, from the reconstruction of Arches Ltd.

The timing of any prospective payments is also important when assessing the merits of a reconstruction scheme. For example, if the creditors of Arches Ltd in Example 7.12 were asked to wait a year before payment, they would expect some compensation for this delay. On liquidation they would be paid in the near future, and the cash received could be invested; to wait a year they would require reimbursement for the interest foregone, plus perhaps an additional amount for the risk of leaving their money in a company which has been on the brink of failure. When the payment of sums of money is offered on different dates, an adjustment for interest is needed to enable comparison. For example, if funds can be invested at 10% per annum and a creditor is offered the choice between £1,000 on immediate liquidation or £1,050 in one year's time, liquidation is preferable since £1,000 could be invested for a year at 10% to give £1,100 at the end of the year.

Some of the costs and benefits associated with reconstruction schemes are intangible, and hence difficult to quantify; they should be considered nevertheless. For example, a bank may wish to avoid unfavourable publicity which might result from putting a customer into liquidation. The social consequences of liquidation, such as unemployment, should also be considered, together with the benefit of future custom which will come from the firm's continued existence.

An important matter to investigate is whether the factors that produced the need for a reconstruction are eliminated by the proposed scheme. If they are not, reconstruction is not worthwhile. For example, if the underlying fact is that there is no demand for a company's product, then a reconstruction will not create a demand; the losses will continue unless there are new, profitable products ready to be marketed. In addition, a check should be made that the reconstructed company will at least start off in a viable condition; a forecast balance sheet will reveal if it will have an acceptable level of liquidity and working capital, and whether the proposed gearing is satisfactory.

Example 7.13

Sutherland Ltd is a private company. Three quarters of the issued share capital is held by the directors or members of their families. The company's draft balance sheet as at the end of 20X5 was as follows:

BALANCE SHEET AT 31 DECEMBER 20X5

Fixed Assets	£	£
Intangible assets: Development costs		85,000
Goodwill		60,000
Tangible assets:　Land and buildings		270,000
Plant and machinery		326,000
		741,000
Current Assets		
Stocks	426,000	
Debtors	531,000	
	957,000	
Creditors falling due within one year		
Creditors	393,000	
Bank loans and overdrafts	687,000	
	1,080,000	
Net current liabilities		(123,000)
Total assets less current liabilities		£618,000
Capital and Reserves		
Called up share capital (800,000 shares of £1 each)		800,000
Share premium account		50,000
Profit and loss account		(232,000)
		£618,000

Bank loans and overdrafts consist of a 10% loan of £400,000 repayable in 20X6 carrying a fixed charge on the company's land and buildings, and an unsecured overdraft of £287,000.

The demand for the company's products fell drastically owing to the import of high-quality and cheaper products from south-east Asia. The development costs appearing in the balance sheet above relate to a new product which has been perfected to a marketable stage, and for which there is believed to be a strong demand. The costs have been properly capitalized in accordance with the provisions of SSAP13. The company is in urgent need of capital to meet existing liabilities and the necessary new investment in plant and working capital.

A scheme for financial reorganization has been drawn up for the consideration of shareholders and creditors. The terms are as follows:

(i)   The shares of £1 each are to be written down to 20p per share and subsequently every five shares of 20p each are to be consolidated into one fully paid share of £1.

(ii) The existing shareholders are to subscribe for a rights issue of two new £1 ordinary shares, at par, for every share held after the proposed reduction and consolidation.

(iii) A major supplier agrees to exchange a debt of £180,000, included in creditors, for 180,000 ordinary shares of £1 each fully paid.

(iv) In full satisfaction of the £687,000 owing, the bank agrees to accept an immediate payment of £87,000 and to consolidate the balance of £600,000 into a loan, carrying interest of 13% per annum, repayable in five equal annual instalments commencing 31 December 20X7. The loan is to be secured by a fixed charge on the land and buildings and a floating charge on the company's remaining assets.

(v)   The credit balance on the share premium account and debit balances on the profit and loss account and goodwill, considered valueless, are to be written off.

(vi) The assets listed below are to be restated at the following amounts:

	£
Plant and machinery	125,000
Stock	210,000
Debtors	500,000
Land and buildings	320,000

A group of dissatisfied shareholders plan to oppose the scheme on the following grounds: 'We have to bear the whole burden of the reorganization whereas the bank loses nothing.'

The company has received a cash offer of £1,120,000 for its fixed and current assets.

Required:
(a)   The revised balance sheet of Sutherland Ltd at 1 January 20X6 giving effect to the proposed scheme for reorganizing the company.

(b)   A report for the group of dissatisfied shareholders explaining whether they should accept or oppose the scheme.

(c)   A report for the bank explaining the matters to be taken into account in deciding whether it would be better to support the scheme or press for immediate liquidation of the company.

Note:
Assume you are making the calculations and writing the reports on 1 January 20X6 and that no other changes occur.

Solution

(a) *Revised Balance Sheet at 1 January 20X6*

	£000	£000
Fixed Assets		
Intangible assets: Development costs		85
Tangible assets: Land and buildings		320
Plant and machinery		125
		530
Current Assets		
Stock	210	
Debtors	500	
Bank balance (£320,000 – £87,000)	233	
	943	
Creditors falling due within one year		
Creditors	213	
Net Current Assets		730
		1,260
Creditors falling due after one year		
13% Bank loan		600
		660
Capital and Reserves		
Called up share capital		660 (W1)
Wl Called up share capital:		
Original shares (reduced by 80%)	160	
Rights issue	320	
Issued to major supplier	180	
	660	

(b) The report for shareholders should cover the following points:

(i) The holders of ordinary shares own the equity of the company; they benefit from any increase in the value of the concern as the result of trading, and must in turn bear the losses.

(ii) If the company is liquidated, liabilities totalling £1,080,000 must first be met out of the 'cash offer'. This leaves just £40,000 for the shareholders, which is far less than the nominal value of the shares allocated to them on reconstruction.

(iii) The shareholders are required to make a substantial cash injection, which they will do only if they are confident about the company's future prospects.

(iv) Provided prospects are sound the shareholders will benefit from the reorganization because they retain ownership of nearly three-quarters of the equity shares and this entitles them to a similar proportion of future profits.

(v) Past losses are eliminated and so the company can pay dividends as soon as profits are made.

(c) The report for the bank should cover the following points:

  (i) On liquidation the bank would receive the full amount due because the cash offer exceeds total liabilities by a sum which is probably sufficient to meet liquidation expenses.

  (ii) If the scheme is given effect, the bank will receive £87,000 immediately, but the remaining £600,000 will be recovered over a five-year period.

  (iii) The bank will receive a higher interest rate and better security to help to compensate for the need to wait longer for its money.

  (iv) The social and financial effects of liquidation, such as the loss of a customer and the associated publicity, must be assessed.

  (v) Adequate security should be arranged; a fixed charge on the land and buildings and a floating charge on the remaining assets would be appropriate.

  (vi) Prospects need to be sound for the bank to support the scheme.

7.8 FURTHER READING
Lewis, R. and Pendril, D. (2000), *Advanced Financial Accounting*, sixth edition, Pitman, Chapter 12.

7.9 QUESTIONS

Question 7.1

The summarized 'balance sheet of Kylsant Ltd as at 31 March 20X7 is as follows:

SUMMARIZED BALANCE SHEET AS AT 31 MARCH 20X7

	£
Ordinary shares of £1 each	200,000
8% convertible preference shares of £1 each	100,000
Share premium account	60,000
Retained profits (all distributable)	685,000
	1,045,000
Fixed and net current assets	1,045,000

The company's freehold property, currently included in the balance of fixed and net current assets at £300,000, has been professionally valued at £620,000.

Required:
Starting from the summarized balance sheet above, prepare five revised balance sheets which take separate account of each of the following schemes:

(a) The freehold property to be recorded and reported at the new valuation.   [3]

(b) The company to make a bonus issue to existing ordinary shareholders of three new ordinary shares, fully paid, for each share currently held.   [3]

(c) The company to make a rights issue of one new ordinary share at £3.00 per share for every ordinary share currently held.   [3]

(d) The preference shareholders to exercise their right to exchange their shares for 80,000 ordinary shares of £1 each.   [5]

(e) 50,000 of the ordinary shares are redeemable. The company to redeem these at a price of £1.50 per share. The shares were issued at par some years ago.   [6]

[Total marks – 20]

Question 7.2

The following information is provided for Palmer plc:

Summarized Balance Sheet as at 31 December 20X5

	£000
Ordinary share capital	1,000
Redeemable shares of £1 each	500
Share premium account	300
Distributable profit	1,400
	3,200
Net assets	3,200

The company intends to redeem the 500,000 redeemable shares.

Required:

(a) Define ' permanent capital', and calculate the permanent capital of Palmer plc at 31 December 20X5 using relevant information from the balance sheet above. [5]

(b) List FOUR conditions that must be met where a public limited company wishes to redeem share capital. [4]

(c) Prepare separate balance sheets to show the effect of the proposed redemption in each of the following alternative circumstances:

(i) The shares were issued and redeemed at par;

(ii) The shares were issued at par and redeemed at £1.60 per share;

(iii) The shares were issued at par and redeemed at £1.40 per share. The redemption is to be partly met by a new issue of 120,000 £1 ordinary shares at a premium of 50p per share. [11]

[Total marks – 20]

Question 7.3

Lee Ltd is a well-established company owned by its three directors. It traded successfully until the early 1990s but has lost much of its market in recent years as the result of competition from overseas. The leading competitor has now redirected its activities to another area of the world and the directors are confident that profitability will be restored in the year 2000.

The following information is provided relating to the company's financial position on 31 December 1999.

Balance Sheet as at 31 December 1999

	£000	£000
Fixed assets at cost less depreciation		500
Current Assets		
Stock at cost	1,020	
Debtors	650	
	1,670	
Creditors falling due within one year		
Creditors	410	
Taxation	470	
Bank overdraft	220	
Loan from Jenkins plc	400	
	1,500	
Net current assets		170
		670
Share capital and reserves		
Share capital (ordinary shares of £1 each)		800
Accumulated loss		−130
		670

It is estimated that £200,000 of the debtors are bad but that, if the company continues as a going concern, the stock and fixed assets are worth their book value. The bank overdraft and the loan from Jenkins plc, Lee's main supplier, are both unsecured. The preferential creditors of Lee Ltd comprise the taxation liability and £50,000 of the figure for creditors.

The following proposals were prepared for consideration by a meeting of creditors held on 1 January 2000.

Immediate liquidation of the company
Under this option, the saleable value of certain items of stock that cost £400,000 would be just £80,000 and the fixed assets would realize only £30,000. Liquidation expenses would amount to £170,000.

Reconstruction
This would involve the following arrangements:

- The existing shareholders to accept 666,000 new ordinary shares of £1 each in exchange for those presently held.

- The directors to subscribe in cash for a further 600,000 ordinary shares of £1 each.

- The preferential creditors to be repaid immediately.

- The non-preferential creditors to reduce their claims by 20%, postpone repayment until 31 December 2000, and waive their right to interest during that period.

Required:

(a) A calculation of the amounts that the bank and that Jerkins plc would receive under the liquidation option. [7 marks]

(b) The revised balance sheet of Lee Ltd if reconstruction takes place. [7 marks]

(c) An examination of the relative merits of the two options from the viewpoint of:

(i) Jenkins plc; and

(ii) the bank. [6 marks]

Notes:

1. Assume the calculations are being made on 1 January 2000 and that either of the proposals can be put into effect immediately.

2. Under the reconstruction option, the present bank overdraft would be frozen and a new bank account opened for subsequent transactions.

3. Assume that the cost of capital for Jenkins plc and the bank is 11%.

[Total – 20 marks]

Question 7.4

Carpet Ltd is a family company owned by the directors. The company traded profitably until the late 1980s, but has suffered a succession of losses during recent years because cheap foreign imports have taken away the market for some of its goods. The balance sheet of the company as at 21 October 1996 contains the following information:

Balance Sheet as at 21 October 1996

	£000	£000
Freehold land and buildings at book value		18
Machinery at book value		<u>164</u>
		182
Current assets:		
Stocks	282	
Debtors	<u>150</u>	
	<u>432</u>	
Current liabilities:		
Creditors including preferential creditors	300	
Overdraft with Midtown Bank plc	<u>100</u>	
	<u>400</u>	
Net current assets		<u>32</u>
Total assets minus current liabilities		214
12% debentures (secured on freeholds)		<u>50</u>
		<u>164</u>
Financed by:		
Ordinary share capital (£1 shares)		100
Accumulated profit		<u>64</u>
		<u>164</u>

The bank overdraft carries a second charge on the freehold land and buildings.

In response to the succession of losses, and in recognition of growing financial problems, the directors have called a meeting of shareholders and creditors to consider the following options

OPTION 1
Immediate liquidation. It is estimated that the freehold land and buildings would realize £95,000, the machinery could be sold for £35,000 and the stocks for £171,000. The debtors would pay up in full. There are preferential creditors amounting to £105,000 and liquidation costs are estimated at £51,000.

OPTION 2
Reorganization and reconstruction. The directors of Carpet Ltd. have drawn up a plan which will involve closing down the unprofitable lines with immediate effect and restoring the company to profitability in the forthcoming year.

Under this option, the assets will be restated in the accounts at liquidation values The existing shares will be written down to lp per share and then consolidated into £1 shares. The debenture holders, bank and creditors of the company, other than the preferential creditors, will each be asked to accept an equivalent value of ordinary shares of £1 each, at par, in satisfaction of 60% of the amount owing to them.

The directors will subscribe for an additional 200,000 £1 ordinary shares at par, and this amount will be paid into a new 'A' account with Midtown Bank plc. The following payments will be made out of the 'A' account: the £20,000 remaining due to the debenture holders; the £40,000 remaining due to Midtown Bank plc; and the amount due to the preferential creditors. Under this option, future annual profits are estimated at £100,000 for the foreseeable future, with one-half of those profits paid out as dividends.

OPTION 3
Sale as a going concern. Fittings plc has made an offer for the entire business of Carpet Ltd. The terms of the offer involve the bank receiving 25% of the amount due immediately, with the remainder payable after twelve months. No interest would be paid on the balance outstanding under this option.

You may assume that any of the above options could be given immediate effect. Assume that Midtown Bank plc earns 10% interest on all its lending.

Required:
(a) Calculations of the amounts that would be received by each of the providers of finance under the immediate liquidation option (Option 1). You should show clearly the order of priority of repayment.   [10]

(b) The revised balance sheet of Carpet Ltd at 21 October 1996 under the reorganization and reconstruction option (Option 2).   [8]

(c) A numerical analysis of the financial implications of each of the three options from the viewpoint of Midtown Bank plc.   [6]

(d) A discussion of the merits of the three options from the viewpoint of Midtown Bank plc.   [6]

[Total marks – 30]

Note:
Ignore taxation.

Question 7.5

Kimberley Ltd has suffered a series of losses and is close to its overdraft limit. The current balance sheet contains the following information:

Balance Sheet of Kimberley Ltd at 23 October 20X5

	£000	£000
Freehold property at cost		800
Goodwill		400
Current assets		
Stock at cost	1,260	
Debtors	620	
	1,880	
Current liabilities		
Sundry creditors	1,310	
Bank overdraft secured on freehold property	1,600	
	2,910	
Net current liabilities		(1,030)
		170
Financed by:		
Share capital		200
Accumulated loss		(30)
		170

The directors have analysed the company's position and concluded that there are two alternative courses of action:

Plan 1

The directors sell the assets individually and liquidate the company. The following estimates have been made of the value of the assets in a piecemeal liquidation:

	£000
Freehold property	1,000
Goodwill	–
Stock	530
Debtors	500

It is estimated that liquidation expenses would amount to £20,000. Preferential creditors, included in sundry creditors, amount to £ 110, 000.

Plan 2

The directors mount a rescue operation by injecting a further £1,000,000 from private resources into the company. The bank would be repaid £600,000 immediately, with the remainder used to reduce trade creditors to an acceptable level. The bank would be asked to accept a debenture carrying interest at 13% in exchange for the balance due. The debenture would be repayable in five annual instalments, commencing 23 October 20X6, with interest due for the preceding year paid on the same date.

Assume that:
1. The bank's current average rate of interest on all borrowing is 11%.

2. Either plan (1 or 2) could be put into effect immediately.

Required:
(a) Prepare a numerical analysis of both plans from the viewpoint of the company's bank.   [12]

(b) Discuss the advantages/disadvantages of the two plans from the viewpoint of the bank.   [8]

Table of factors for the present value of £1 at 11%

Year	Factor
0	1.00
1	0.90
2	0.81
3	0.73
4	0.66
5	0.60

Note:
Make all calculations to the nearest £000.   [Total marks – 20]

Question 7.6

Limperg Ltd is a long-established company which has been trading at a loss in recent years. The company's balance sheet as at 31 December 20X7, together with certain other financial information, is set out below:

Balance Sheet	£000	£000
Fixed assets at written down value		
Freehold land (Note 1)		1,000
Plant and equipment (Note 2)		1,200
		2,200
Current assets		
Stock (Note 2)	400	
Debtors (Note 2)	800	
	1,200	
Current liabilities		
Creditors (Note 3)	760	
Overdraft (Note 4)	880	
	1,640	
Net current assets (– = liabilities)		– 440
		1,760
Creditors due in more than one year		
Debentures (Note 5)		800
		960
Financed by		
Ordinary shares of £1 each		2,000
Profit and loss account		–1,040
		960

Note 1.
The freehold land does not, at present, have planning permission for development, but it may be possible to obtain such permission. The freehold land has therefore been valued on alternative bases:

	£000
Market value with planning permission	2,400
Market value without planning permission	640

Note 2.
On liquidation, the plant and equipment could be sold for £800,000; the stock would raise £300,000; £100,000 of the amount owed by debtors is considered to be bad.

Note 3.
The value of creditors in the balance sheet includes £200,000 that would rank as preferential creditors on liquidation.

Note 4.
The overdraft is secured by a fixed charge over the company's plant and equipment.

Note 5.
The debentures are repayable on 31 March 20X9 and carry a fixed charge over the company's freehold land.

Note 6.
Liquidation expenses would amount to £120,000.

Required:
(a) Identify and discuss two potential causes of corporate failure.   [4 marks]

(b) Prepare a statement which shows how much each of the providers of finance to Limperg Ltd would receive on liquidation on the alternative assumptions that the freehold land is sold for:
   (i) £2,400,000;
   (ii) £640,000.   [10 marks]

(c) Examine the matters to be taken into account when deciding whether to arrange for a capital reconstruction of Limperg Ltd rather than place the company in liquidation.   [6 marks]

[Total – 20 marks]

8

SHARE AND
BUSINESS
VALUATION

8.1 INTRODUCTION

The financial interest of ownership in a company is shown in the capital section of the balance sheet, and is equal to the recorded value of the net assets, that is, the value of the assets less all non-ownership liabilities. The figure for capital is produced by using accounting concepts and conventions to value assets and liabilities, and is most unlikely to reflect the current value of the company as a whole. For example, fixed assets are shown at their historical cost less accumulated depreciation, but the historical cost of an asset does not represent its current value, and accumulated depreciation does not accurately reflect the value lost during the period of ownership.

A theoretical present-day value for a business can be obtained by using any one of a number of techniques, but the true price can be established only when a buyer and seller agree to an actual transaction. The available valuation techniques are applicable to all business forms, sole traders, partnerships and limited companies, but this chapter concentrates on the valuation of shares in limited companies. To a large extent each company is unique, with its own individual blend of such factors as management, assets, products and potential, and the theoretical approaches to valuation give only a guide to the value to be placed upon the entity. The circumstances where valuation is required are:

1. Taxation

Inheritance Tax is levied on the open market value of shares that belonged to the deceased. When shares for which a market value is not readily available are inherited (i.e. unquoted shares), a theoretical valuation must be undertaken.

A liability to Capital Gains Tax arises on all disposals of chargeable assets. The gift of shares in an unquoted company is deemed to be a chargeable disposal which gives rise to the need for a theoretical market valuation at the time of giving so that the capital gain can be calculated.

2. Private Sale of Existing Shares (including the purchase by a company of its own shares)

The owner of shares in an unquoted company may wish to sell all or part of this holding; in these circumstances, price is determined by negotiation between the prospective buyer and seller, but the theoretical valuation of the shares provides a useful basis for the discussions which take place. A common misconception which may be noted at this stage is that the sale of shares already in issue provides additional funds for the company. This is wrong; the only entry needed in the company's books records the change of ownership of the traded shares in the register of members.

3. Private Issue of New Shares

A company may decide to raise finance by the issue of additional shares, and, unless these are purchased by the existing members as a 'rights issue', the price must be set so as not to dilute the value of the existing shares.

Example 8.1 The Determination of Issue Price for Shares

The Newcash Company Ltd wishes to raise £150,000 by the issue of shares with a nominal value of £1 each for cash. Prior to the issue, the balance sheet fairly reflects the current value of net assets.

Newcash Company Ltd Balance Sheet Prior to Issue

	£000
Net Assets	300
	300
Ordinary Shares of £1 each	200
Profit and Loss Account	100
	300

Although the nominal value of each share is £1, its asset value is

$$\frac{£300,000}{200,000} = £1.50$$

and so the new shares should be issued at £1.50 each; £1 is the nominal value and 50 pence is the share premium.

Newcash Company Ltd Balance Sheet after Issue

	£000
Net Assets	300
Cash	150
	450
Ordinary Shares of £1 each	300
Share Premium	50
Profit and Loss Account	100
	450

All shares, both original and newly issued, are worth $\frac{£450,000}{£300,000} = £1.50$ each.

The issue would not be taken up if the price had exceeded £1.50, which is the underlying value per share, while to price shares at less than £1.50 effectively transfers value from the existing to the new members. For example, 150,000 shares would have been issued if they were priced at £1, and the value of the old and new shares would become:

$$\frac{£450,000}{350,000} = £1.29$$

It is most unlikely that the balance sheet reflects the fair current value of the business, which is assumed in Example 8.1, and so in practice the issue price of the shares must be determined theoretically.

4. Flotation of Shares on the Stock Market

A market on the Stock Exchange for the shares of a company may be created either by owners selling their existing shares, or by the company issuing new shares. In either instance the shares must not be over- or underpriced. In the former case the shares would not be purchased, while the latter would create excessive demand and result in the vendor losing potential receipts. The price at which the flotation is made must be set carefully and, again, valuation techniques give a guide to the appropriate level.

5. Business Amalgamations

The need for valuation arises where one company wishes to take over or merge with another. In a takeover, the price offered for the shares of the company to be acquired must be decided: too low an offer will cause the bid to fail; too high an offer will result in overpayment. When two companies merge, valuation is required to determine the relative interest in the combined entity to be given to each set of shareholders.

6. Security

Shares may be used as security for a loan, and the lender will wish to ensure that they represent adequate cover. Unless the shares are quoted on the stock market, and therefore have an ascertainable price, the valuation must be made on a theoretical basis.

7. Alternative Investments

The owner of unquoted shares may wish to value them to see whether they are providing an adequate return and whether the funds obtained from their sale could be more profitably employed elsewhere.

8.2 MARKETS FOR BUYERS AND SELLERS

The ease with which an ownership interest can be sold depends on the type of business involved. A sole trader is free to dispose of his business in any way, but a partners cannot sell their share of the partnership without the agreement of the other partners. The freedom to transfer shares in a private limited company can be restricted by its Articles of Association, and the public cannot be invited to subscribe for shares. A public limited company has no restriction on the number of shareholders, and can invite the public to subscribe for shares; its shares may also be listed, that is, traded on a recognized stock exchange.

Where markets exist they provide contact between prospective buyers and sellers of shares, and the price established for each share equates supply and demand. The price of a share rises when demand exceeds supply and stabilizes when equilibrium is restored as the result of demand being depressed, more sellers offering their shares on the market, or a combination of both these factors. Conversely, prices fall when supply exceeds demand. The causes of a change in the price of a particular share may be related to the individual company, the market as a whole, or a combination of both. The prospects of a single company may be reappraised in the light of new information, such as the announcement of profits that are better than expected, and the price of its shares will react accordingly. A share price index shows the state of the market as a whole and reflects the general demand for equity shares which can be affected by a single occurrence, such as a cut in interest rates or a fall in the rate of inflation. Therefore, the price of an individual share is determined both by the state of the market as a whole and the prospects of the company itself. Nevertheless, the price of a share may fall while the market index is rising, for example, as the result of the company's own dismal prospects outweighing the beneficial effect of a fall in interest rates, or it may rise when there is a general fall in share prices.

The value of quoted shares is readily available in the financial press, but it must be appreciated that the prices quoted relate to the relatively small proportion of total share capital which is sold and purchased at a particular time. Therefore, although the capitalized market value of a company is often calculated by multiplying the number of shares in issue by the quoted price per share, this is not the amount it would cost to acquire all of the share capital. An attempt to buy all of the shares of a company represents an increase in demand, drives up the price, and thereby increases the capitalized market value. Therefore, a reliable estimate of the value of the whole company is more likely to be obtained by the use of theoretical valuation techniques than by simply using the quoted price which results from trading in a small proportion of the company's shares.

It is more difficult for prospective buyers and sellers to meet when a company's shares are not traded in the market. A buyer may identify the area of activity in which it is desired to invest, actively seek an appropriate company and then approach its owners with an offer. In this exercise the buyer often seeks guidance from financial advisers who may carry out the procedure on the purchaser's behalf. Sellers are also likely to seek advice from the same sources, and so a point of contact is created. Alternatively, contact may be established through advertising, personal acquaintance, or trade connections. The identification and bringing together of a buyer and seller is only the first requirement, and, if the transaction is to take place, must be followed by the negotiation of an acceptable price. Theoretical valuations of the company provide a useful basis for negotiation, but the size of the stake to be acquired must be borne in mind; the price per share is higher where the purchase of the whole company is contemplated than if only a minority holding is to be acquired.

The various methods of valuation are examined in 8.3 and 8.4.

8.3 BREAK-UP VALUATION

This valuation technique looks on a business as a collection of assets which may be sold off piecemeal, with the owners receiving any residue after all other contributors of finance have been reimbursed (for the order of repayment on liquidation, see 7.6).

The steps used to calculate the break-up value of the owner's interest in a business are:

1. Estimate the sales proceeds of the individual assets.

2. Estimate the liquidation costs and identify the liabilities.

3. Find the value of the ownership interest by deducting 2 from 1.

The value of an individual share is found by dividing the total value of the ownership interest by the number of shares in issue.

Example 8.2 Valuation on the Break-up Basis

The summarized balance sheet of Vend Ltd at 31 December 20X1 is as follows:

Vend Ltd Balance Sheet at 31 December 20X1

	£000	£000
Fixed Assets:		
Freehold Premises		1,000
Plant and Machinery		750
		1,750
Current Assets:		
Stock	250	
Debtors	125	
Cash at bank	25	
	400	
Less: Current Liabilities	150	
Working capital		250
		2,000
Less: 10% Debentures Repayable 20X1		500
		1,500

Financed by:

Ordinary Shares of £1 each		600
Retained Profits: Brought forward	650	
For 20X1	250	
		900
		1,500

It is estimated that in a forced sale on liquidation the expenses would be £50,000 and the assets would realize:

	£000
Premises	1,350
Plant and Machinery	700
Stock	300
Debtors	125
	2,475

Required:

(a) Calculate the break-up value of the owner's interest in Vend Ltd.

(b) Calculate the break-up value of one share in Vend Ltd.

Solution

(a) The break-up value of the owner's interest is:

		£000	*£000*
Step 1	Estimated proceeds from sale of assets		2,475
	Cash at bank		25
			2,500
Step 2	*Less*: Liquidation Expenses	50	
	Debentures	500	
	Current Liabilities	150	
			700
Step 3	Value of Ownership Interest		1,800

(b) On liquidation the break-up value of each share is:

$$\frac{£1,800,000}{600,000} = £3$$

Liquidation values are based on the assumption of a forced sale of individual assets in the second-hand market. This approach ignores the possibility that the assets together may be worth more than the sum of their individual values because of the particular manner in which the company uses them. Furthermore, when applied to a going concern, the assumption that the company is to be liquidated is contrary to the facts. Many factors indicate that Vend Ltd, in Example 8.2, is a viable company: it has a healthy working capital and liquidity position; the capital structure is balanced; there is no pressure from imminent debenture repayment; and enough profit was made in 20X1 to add substantially to reserves. Another weakness is that the values placed on the costs and assets are estimates. The values of items such as cash and debtors may be assumed with confidence, but the sale value of premises and plant and machinery can only be truly ascertained in an actual sale. When liquidation is considered, it is also necessary to take into account any consequential costs that result from that course of action, such as redundancy payments or liabilities for breach of contract.

The break-up value of a business does, however, have some relevance for prospective buyers and sellers. It represents, for the seller, the minimum value at which the transaction should take place, especially if pessimistic valuations are applied to the assets. This is illustrated if the position of the owner of 95% of the equity shares of Vend Ltd is considered, as a holding of this size gives the owner power either to sell the business as a going concern or to liquidate it. The owners of the remaining 5% of the shares cannot on their own exercise such a choice. No offer to acquire the company at less than £3 per share is acceptable because it is estimated that at least this sum would be received on liquidation. The buyer has a bargain if the vendor is ignorant of the break-up value of the company and accepts less than £3 per share, a possibility exploited by 'asset strippers' who, after acquisition, sell off the assets to realize a profit.

It is possible for the shares of a company listed on the Stock Exchange to be traded at less than break-up value, but the volume of shares dealt in to determine this price would not give control and so the buyer could not enforce the sale of the assets. A bid to acquire full control has to be made under Stock Exchange rules, and the directors will inform shareholders of the underlying asset value if they wish to oppose the bid. In the past, shareholder ignorance of the current value of the asset backing for their shares largely stemmed from the use of historical cost for reporting purposes. The inclusion of more up-to-date valuations in the Directors' Report now keeps members better informed.

The break-up value also gives ownership an indication of the minimum amount of capital which could be obtained from the business for investment elsewhere. For example, if the valuations are accurate, the majority shareholder in Vend Ltd would receive in cash, on liquidation, 95% x 600,000 x £3 = £1,710,000, and it might be possible to place this in a safe fixed-interest investment to yield, say, a 7% return, that is, £119,700 per annum. This possible return can then be weighed against that expected to be received from the investment in Vend Ltd in the form of dividends and capital growth. The majority shareholder would be expected to retain the shares only if they produced a sufficiently high return to compensate for the additional risk of an equity investment. As Vend Ltd is profitable, sale as a going concern is likely to yield a greater sum for alternative investment than liquidation and would also protect the interests of other people dependent on the company, such as employees and suppliers.

8.4 GOING CONCERN VALUATION

A company is a collection of assets which has been brought together with the aim of producing a profit which accrues to ownership. It also provides a return for those who input other factors, such as employees and providers of debenture or overdraft finance, who are rewarded by earned income and interest, respectively. To value an entity as a going concern assumes that it will continue to operate with substantially the same combination of assets, employees and management as previously. A number of possible approaches are examined in sections 8.4.1 to 8.4.6.

8.4.1 Book Value

An undertaking's book value is calculated from its balance sheet, which contains the values of assets and liabilities as shown in the books of account. The entries in the books are normally made at historical cost, less accumulated depreciation in the case of fixed assets other than freehold land.

Example 7.3 Calculation of Book Value

The summarized balance sheet of Hist Ltd, a trading company at 31 December 20X1 is as follows:

Hist Ltd Balance Sheet at 31 December 20X1

	£000	£000
Fixed Assets:		
Land and Buildings: at cost	500	
less: depreciation	150	
		350
Vehicles: at cost	300	
less: depreciation	75	
		225
		575
Current Assets:		
Stock	400	
Debtors	150	
	550	

Less: Current Liabilities:		
Trade Creditors	125	
Overdraft	50	
	175	
Working Capital		375
		950
Less: 10% Debentures Repayable 20X7		150
		800
Financed by:		
Ordinary Shares of £1 each		350
Share Premium		150
Retained Profits		200
		700
8% Preference Shares		100
		800

The company belongs to the owners of the ordinary shares, and the book value of their investment is £700,000 in total, or £2 per share. The book value is calculated either as the total of ordinary share capital plus reserves, or as fixed assets plus working capital less non-equity debts, that is: (£000) 575 + 375 – 150 – 100 = 700.

The argument for the use of book value calculations is that the figures are factual, because they are based on historical cost; they are also easily obtainable because they come from routinely produced reports. However, there are serious deficiencies in this technique and these must be appreciated whenever it is applied.

The historical cost of an asset is the amount paid for it at the time of acquisition, and this is not relevant to a current valuation. A company that has been established for a number of years has, in its books, assets that have been purchased at various times throughout its life and they are recorded at cost. The impact of inflation means that, in general, historical cost is not an accurate measure of current value, and becomes less accurate the longer an asset is held. The effects of inflation have called into question the relevance of accounts prepared on the historical cost basis and so their use for valuation purposes must also be doubted. Even in the absence of price movements, the written-down value of fixed assets does not measure their current value. Accumulated depreciation is deducted from the historical cost of fixed assets, other than freehold land, in order to recognize their decline in value while in use by the business. The depreciation charge is an arbitrary apportionment of the cost of an asset over its estimated life, and its written down value is not intended to reflect an asset's value in exchange. Moreover, due to errors when estimating the lives of fixed assets, it is common for firms to hold in their books items that are fully depreciated, but are still providing useful service, and so must have a value greater than zero.

The book value of stock is also unlikely to reflect its current value, both because the cost figures are out of date and because a market valuation would include an element of profit. However, the discrepancy is not so great, as stocks are held for a shorter period of time than fixed assets and the historical cost is more recent. On the other hand, the debtors figure in a properly prepared set of accounts is acceptable as the amount to be received (assuming that adequate provision has been made for bad debts). The values of non-equity liabilities in the balance sheet are shown at the amount of cash owed and so accurately reflect the indebtedness of the business.

A further criticism of the book value basis of valuation is that it ignores the possible existence of intangible assets such as goodwill (see further discussion in 6.4.3).

8.4.2 Replacement Cost

To make a more useful asset-based valuation, assets must be valued at their replacement costs. A person who considers buying an existing business has the alternative option of assembling an identical collection of assets. Ignoring intangible assets for the moment, the maximum price the buyer will be willing to pay is calculated by ascertaining, in physical terms, the assets owned by the company and then, possibly with expert advice from a professional valuer, estimating their replacement cost. In most cases the identification of assets can be achieved only with the cooperation of the company, although sometimes the major assets may be clearly visible, such as the shops owned by a retailing company, which may even advertise a list of branches.

Example 8.4 Replacement Cost Valuation

The share capital of Shelf Ltd, a profitable company, is owned in equal proportions by four brothers who are also the company's directors. The brothers are nearing retirement age and wish to sell the company as a going concern. Two of the brothers consider that the values shown in the balance sheet should be used to calculate the price at which to offer to sell the company, while the other two feel that the replacement cost is appropriate. The following information is available:

(i) *Shelf Ltd Balance Sheet at 31 December 20X1*

	£000	£000
Fixed Assets		
Freehold Premises		100
Plant and Machinery at written down value		200
		300

	£000	£000
Current Assets:		
Stock	75	
Debtors	50	
Cash	10	
	135	
Less: Current Liabilities	65	
Working Capital		70
		370
Less: Secured Loan		100
		270
Financed by:		
Ordinary Shares of £1 each		100
Retained Profits		170
		270

(ii) *The replacement costs of the assets, based on expert advice, are:*

	£000
Freehold Premises	250
Plant and Machinery	500
Stock	80

Required:
(a) Calculate the value of the business as a whole and the value of an individual share on the basis of:
    (i) book value;

    (ii) replacement cost.

(b) Advise the brothers which valuation basis is most appropriate.

Solution

(a) (i) Book Value: £270,000 or £2.70 per share
    (ii) Replacement Cost

	£000	£000
Freehold Premises		250
Plant and Machinery		500
Stock		80
Debtors		50
Cash		10
		890
Less: Current Liabilities	65	
Secured Loan	100	
		165
		725

The total replacement cost of the company is £725,000 or £7.25 per share.

(b) It is clear that the replacement cost value of £7.25 per share is far higher than that based on the book value, of £2.70. To sell the company for £270,000 charges the buyer the same amount, in cash terms, for the assets as was paid by the company, less depreciation on plant and machinery. It would cost a prospective purchaser £890,000 to acquire a similar set of assets, which would be reduced to an outlay of £725,000 if the same contribution is obtained from loans and current liabilities. In these circumstances, it is fair to expect a buyer to meet the replacement costs of the assets. However, earnings valuations (see 8.4.3 to 8.4.6) are even more relevant to a profitable company such as Shelf.

The assets of a company may be included in its balance sheet at a more current valuation than their original historical cost. Where a group of companies is being valued on the basis of its consolidated accounts, the assets of the subsidiary companies will be included at their fair values at the time when the holding company acquired the shares in its subsidiaries. Alternatively, a company may have a policy of revaluing its fixed assets and including the revised values in its accounts. Both of these cases provide a more up-to-date value for the assets, but it is still not totally current at the point in time when the valuation exercise for the company as a whole is being carried out. Where the assets are depreciated, the accumulated depreciation does not necessarily reflect the amount by which their value has declined since the revaluation. Therefore, revaluations overcome some of the drawbacks of historical cost, but not all of them.

The above example provides a current valuation of the company's tangible assets, but does not recognize the possible existence of intangible assets such as goodwill. A set of tangible assets identical to those used by an existing profitable company could be assembled, but the owner would not necessarily make a similar profit. It may not be possible to attract a similar skilled work force, establish trading contacts, or obtain a management team with the same ability. Where a business earns a profit in excess of the opportunity cost of the inputs of ownership valued at replacement cost, it possesses goodwill: so the use of replacement cost of only the tangible assets results in undervaluation. However, even goodwill can be created, at a cost, for instance, by means of advertising and special offers to attract customers who must then be retained by providing an efficient service. Other intangible assets may also be owned which are not recorded in the balance sheet, such as the value of research work, the cost of which has been written off as incurred to comply with SSAP13 (see 5.2).

In different circumstances replacement cost may overvalue a company (see Question 8.1). For instance, it is possible that a company fails to earn an adequate profit, but, because the investment in fixed assets represents a 'sunk' cost, it continues to trade.

The trading conditions and expectations that existed when the firm was established may not have transpired, and yet the nature of the assets gives rise to a high current replacement cost. The acquisition of the present combination of business assets would not be repeated, however, because they could not be used to yield an adequate return.

Valuations based on assets (see 8.4.1 and this section) measure the resources possessed by companies, but the purpose of owning these is to produce income. When a company is bought, the purchaser acquires not just a collection of assets, but their earning potential, and, therefore, the techniques of valuation discussed in sections 8.4.3-8.4.6 are generally considered more relevant.

8.4.3 Earnings Yield Valuation

Companies use assets in conjunction with other inputs, such as labour, to earn profits, and when a company is sold as a going concern the new owner acquires the right to the profits made after the date of purchase. The return made by a company can be expressed as the 'Earnings Yield' which relates the profit to the amount invested. For example, if a company has a value of £16 million and makes an annual profit of £2.4 million, its earnings yield is $(2.4/16) \times 100 = 15\%$. The value of a company on the earnings-yield basis is the value of the stream of profit, or earnings, which the company is expected to generate. Calculation of an earnings yield value involves three steps:

1. Predict the future maintainable profits (annual earnings) of the company being valued.

2. Identify the required earnings yield by reference to the results of similar companies.

3. Apply the earnings yield to future profits using the formula:

$$\frac{\text{Annual Earnings (from step 1)}}{\text{Required Earnings Yield (from step 2)}}$$

Example 8.5 Earnings Yield Valuation

A company is expected to generate future profits of £24,000 per annum. What is its value based on its earnings yield if investments of this type are expected to give an annual return of 12%?

Solution

Step 1   Annual Earnings: £24,000.

Step 2   Required Earnings Yield: $12\% = \dfrac{12}{100} = 0.12$.

Step 3   Value: $\dfrac{£24,000}{0.12} = £200,000$.

The buyer could be expected to pay £200,000 to obtain the right to receive annual profits of £24,000, representing a return of 12%.

The profit made by a company is given in its profit and loss account. However, this figure relates to a past accounting period, whereas the earnings yield value of a company should be based on its ability to make profits in the future. To predict likely future earnings, information from past years is a useful starting point, but it must be adjusted to take account of any factors that cause distortions and any changes that are anticipated in the future.

Example 8.6 Profit Adjustment

The directors of Chair Ltd, who also own the company, have been approached in 20X4 by Table plc with a takeover offer. The directors of Table plc suggest that the price is the capitalized value of the expected future earnings of Chair Ltd on the assumption that the takeover is completed. This is agreed by the directors of Chair Ltd who consider that the average of the last three year's profits after adjustment is appropriate and produce the following information:

(i)   Profit and Loss Account Extracts:

	20X1	20X2	20X3
	£000	£000	£000
Net profit	300	281	261
Directors' remuneration	70	80	90
Overdraft interest	20	15	10
Depreciation	100	100	100

(ii) A provision was made in 20X0 against a single doubtful debt of £50,000, but this did not materalize and the provision was written back in 20X1.

(iii) Directors' remuneration does not reflect their market value; if it acquires the company, Table plc would reduce the cost to £60,000 per annum.

(iv) The equipment of Chair Ltd is old and Table plc would soon have to replace it at an estimated cost of £2 million. The expected life of the new plant is ten years.

(v) Table plc is the holding company of a large group and would give Chair Ltd access to group financial resources. This would enable the overdraft to be repaid, but an annual intra-group charge of £12,000 would be made for treasury services.

Required:
(i) Calculate the average profit of Chair Ltd for the past three years after making any adjustments considered necessary to reflect the company's likely future earnings if taken over by Table plc.

(ii) Capitalize the adjusted average profit at an earnings yield of 17% per annum.

Solution

(i) *Profit Adjustment*

	20X1 £000	20X2 £000	20X3 £000
Net profit before adjustment	300	281	261
Bad debt written back 20X1	(50)	–	–
Reduction in directors' remuneration	10	20	30
Increase in depreciation	(100)	(100)	(100)
Finance charge adjustment	8	3	(2)
Adjusted annual profit	168	204	189

Summary:

20X1	168
20X2	204
20X3	189
	561

Average profit: $\dfrac{561}{3} = £187,000$

(ii) *Earnings Yield Valuation*

$$\frac{\text{Earnings}}{\text{Yield}} = \frac{187,000}{0.17} = £1,100,000$$

Many of the details required for the earnings yield valuation, such as the imminence of plant replacement and consequent change in depreciation charge, are accurately ascertainable only with the help of the business being valued. Therefore, the ability of the valuer to prepare an accurate forecast depends on access to relevant information, and this is determined by the relationship between the valuer and the business. Cooperation exists where the valuation is undertaken at the instigation of the company itself, but no help would be given to a valuer working for a competitor who is preparing an unwelcome takeover bid. Even where full assistance is given, the forecast of future earnings is an estimate which is unlikely to prove accurate, and, the greater the uncertainty attached to achieving targets, the greater is the risk associated with the investment. Results achieved in the past do not necessarily reflect the future earnings of a business; ideally the estimate of future earnings should be derived from budgets based on detailed forecasts of activity, costs and revenues, although these are still liable to error.

The value of the business bears an inverse relationship to the earnings yield used for capitalization. For instance, an earnings stream of £10,000 per annum capitalized at 10% is worth £100,000; capitalized at 20% the value is £50,000. This places great importance on the determination of the appropriate yield, and, in general, the higher the risk attached to an income stream, the greater is the earnings yield required and hence the lower the capitalized value. The earnings yield of a listed company is calculated from its quoted market price and its most recently reported profit, and this may be used as the basis for an earnings yield valuation of an unlisted company. Care must, of course, be taken to use the earnings yield of a listed company which approximates, so far as is possible, to the unlisted company in terms of size, trade and risk.

The market price of the listed company, or companies, used to calculate the earnings yield is influenced by general economic factors that affect the individual share, a sector of the market, or the market as a whole. Similarly, the profit figures used for the calculation may be distorted because of exceptional circumstances. To avoid the selection of an unrepresentative earnings yield, the average of a number of measurements taken at different times for a number of companies may be used. Alternatively, an anticipated earnings yield can be agreed on as part of overall discussions on valuation, although these are still likely to be based on yields observed in the market.

8.4.4 Price/Earnings (P/E) Ratio Valuation

The P/E ratio is calculated for listed companies, and relates the market price of a company's share capital to its most recently reported earnings. It is calculated by using the formula:

$$\text{P/E ratio} \ = \ \frac{\text{Market Price of One Share}}{\text{Earnings per Share}}$$

The market price of a share is found in the Stock Exchange Daily Official List published after each day's trading on the stock market, and the value of earnings per share, which is based on profits after tax, must be given in the published accounts of listed companies. For example, a company with five million issued shares and earnings of £1.2m has an earnings per share of £1.2m/5m = 24 pence. If its market price per share is 180 pence, then it has a P/E ratio of 180/24 = 7.5, that is, the value of each share is 7.5 times the earnings related to that share.

There is the following direct link between the P/E ratio and the earnings yield of a company:

$$\text{Earnings Yield} \ = \ \frac{1}{\text{P/E ratio}} \ \text{x} \ 100$$

This can be illustrated by the use of the figures given above:

$$\text{Earnings Yield} = \frac{24}{180} \ \text{x} \ 100 \ = \ 13.3\%; \text{ or } \frac{1}{7.5} \ \text{x} \ 100 = 13.3\%$$

The P/E ratio is therefore the inverse of the earnings yield, and they produce exactly the same company valuations. For example, the value of the company for which details are given above can be calculated in either of the following ways:

Valuations based on:

P/E Ratio:	7.5 (P/E Ratio) x £1.2m (Earnings)	= £9m
Earnings Yield	$\dfrac{£1.2m \ (\text{Earnings})}{0.133 \ (\text{Earnings Yield})}$	= £9m

An unlisted company can therefore be valued by multiplying its earnings by the P/E ratio of a similar, but listed, company. To give consistency, the earnings of both companies must be measured on the same basis, and adjustment made for the impact on Earnings per Share of any exceptional items. Distortions that arise from the use of a single company's result are avoided by the calculation of an average ratio for a number of similar companies over a number of years.

Example 8.7 Valuation by P/E Ratio

The directors of Door Ltd in 20X4 wish to value the company on the basis of the P/E ratios of similar, listed, companies. The average annual earnings of Door Ltd for the previous three years are £150,000 after tax and adjustments considered necessary by the directors. The P/E ratio of the listed companies to be used for the calculations are:

	20X1	20X2	20X3
Glass plc	6.4	7.1	6.9
Rock plc	5.5	5.8	6.1
Stone plc	6.9	6.6	7.2

Each of the three companies is considered to be comparable to Door Ltd in terms of size, type of business, etc.

Required:
Calculate the value of Door Ltd on the basis of a single average P/E ratio.

Solution

The P/E ratios of the three listed companies are averaged as follows:

	Average PIE Ratio *20X1 – 20X2 – 20X3*
Glass plc	6.8
Rock plc	5.8
Stone plc	6.9
	19.5

The average P/E ratio is $\dfrac{19.5}{3} = 6.5$

The value of Door Ltd is: 150,000 x 6.5 = £975,000.

The apparent precision of the P/E Ratio and Earnings Yield as a basis for company valuation must not be allowed to mask their limitations. A major matter to consider is the extent to which the listed companies used for valuation truly compare with the company to be valued. Listed companies offer significant advantages to their members because their shares are marketable and their large size gives them an element of stability: these advantages make their shares more desirable, and therefore more highly priced, than those of an unlisted company. The P/E ratio of an unlisted company is expected to be less than that for a corresponding listed company, and so the use of unadjusted quoted ratios can result in overvaluation.

Consideration must also be given to the size of the holding valued. The price of shares in a listed company is set to equate supply and demand, but in routine trading only a small proportion of a listed company's share capital changes hands. A bid to buy control of a listed company has to be well above the market price to attract those shareholders reluctant to sell at the current rate. The P/E ratio of a company increases with a rise in price, and so the ratio calculated with the day-to-day market price is less than would result from the use of the price needed to buy enough shares to give control. To value the whole of an unlisted company's share capital with a P/E ratio derived from transactions of non-controlling holdings gives rise to undervaluation.

8.4.5 Dividend Yield Valuation

Ownership of shares in a company entitles the holder to receive any dividends that are declared. For an individual member to be able to influence the size of a company's dividend, enough shares must be held to enable significant voting power to be wielded; the owner of less than 50 per cent of the equity shares can always be out-voted by the remainder, although significant influence may be exerted by the holder of a large, but non-controlling, block of shares when the remainder are spread over a large number of small investors. When valuing a small shareholding (which cannot influence the proportion of earnings to be distributed), the calculation should be based on the dividends, rather than earnings, per share.

The dividend yield of a listed company is expressed as a percentage, i.e.:

$$\frac{\text{Dividend for the year (pence per share)}}{\text{Quoted market price (in pence)}} \times 100$$

The dividend for the year includes any interim dividend as well as the final dividend.

If a company pays an interim dividend of 5 pence per share, declares a final dividend of 10 pence and has a quoted share price of 130 pence, 'cum div', its dividend yield is:

$$\frac{10 + 5}{130 - 10} \times 100 = \frac{15}{120} \times 100 = 12.5\%$$

As long as the share price remains 'cum div', a buyer of the shares acquires the right to receive the final dividend. Once this dividend is paid the price falls to the share's underlying capital value, in this instance 120 pence: it is then termed 'ex dividend' and will be quoted 'ex div' or 'xd' in the financial press.

The dividend of the unlisted company is capitalized using the yield of a listed company in the following manner:

1. Identify the annual dividend of the company being valued.

2. Identify the required dividend yield.

3. Apply the dividend yield to the annual dividend using the formula:

$$\frac{\text{Annual dividend (from step 1)}}{\text{Required dividend yield (from step 2)}}$$

Example 8.8 Dividend Yield Valuation

Mill Ltd has an issued share capital of 100,000 ordinary shares of 50 pence each, the ownership of which is concentrated in the hands of the directors, although some members of their families hold small numbers of shares. The company has regularly paid a total annual dividend of £25,000, and expects to maintain this level of distribution in the future.

The average dividend yield for listed companies in the same line of business is 11.2%.

Required:
Calculate the value of 250 shares in Mill Ltd on the dividend yield basis.

Solution

1.
$$\text{Dividend per share} = \frac{£25,000}{100,000} = 25 \text{ pence.}$$

2. Dividend Yield = 11.2%.

3.
$$\text{Value of one share} = \frac{25}{0.112} = 223.2 \text{ pence.}$$

Value of 250 shares = 250 x 223.2 = £558.

The use of the dividend yield to value shares in an unlisted company rests on the assumption that the relationship between value and dividend is the same as for the listed company, or companies, chosen for the calculation. This assumption is questionable. In practice the private company is likely to distribute a smaller proportion of its earnings, with the result that it is undervalued by this technique. This difference is compensated to some extent by the fact that more risk may be deemed to attach to the dividends of small companies and so they are expected to offer a higher yield on the shareholders' investments.

The disparity between the dividend policies of unlisted and listed companies is caused by a number of factors. The listed company tries to prevent falls in its share price that leave it vulnerable to a takeover bid and unable to attract additional investment; a generous dividend policy helps to maintain a high share price. Unlisted companies, and especially private companies, find it more difficult to attract external funds, for example, because they are not so well known, and are reliant on retained earnings to finance development. The need to plough back into the business a large proportion of earnings leaves limited amounts available for distribution.

One drawback of the dividend yield valuation of an unlisted share is that it is usually based on past dividends, and these may not be representative of future expectations, which should help to determine the current price. A company may pay small current dividends, but still be able to justify a high share price if it is retaining a large proportion of its earnings to finance profitable developments leading to a higher level of future distributions. Care must be taken to use the dividend yield of a listed company in the same area of trade, and, to avoid the application of undue weight to a single observation, the average dividend yield may be calculated for a number of companies over a number of years.

8.4.6 Valuation Based on Cash Flows

The most theoretically acceptable method of valuation is to examine the cash flows which result from the acquisition of the whole, or part of, a business. The valuation takes place as follows:

Step 1   Predict the prospective buyer's annual cash flow on the assumption that the acquisition does not take place.

Step 2   Predict the prospective buyer's annual cash flow on the assumption that the acquisition does take place.

Step 3   Calculate the difference between the cash flows found in Steps 1 and 2 and reduce it to a present value.

The value of the company under consideration is taken to be the present value of the additional cash flow resulting from its acquisition found in Step 3 above.

The complexity of Step 2 compared with Step 1 depends on the size of the holding acquired. A minority holding yields only dividends whereas total ownership gives access to the cash flow measured by earnings plus depreciation and adjusted for acquisitions and disposals of fixed assets, taxation and capital redemptions. In the latter case, the forecasts are very difficult to make with sufficient accuracy for an adequate number of years, especially if access to the company's records is denied. Also, in both cases, it is difficult to determine the rate at which to discount the cash flows to present values.

Example 8.9

River Ltd is a long-established company with a steady record of results; in each of the last three years it has generated a cash surplus of £100,000, and expects this to continue for the foreseeable future. In December 20X2 the directors were approached by the owners of a competitor, called Tributary Ltd, who are willing to sell their entire business for £165,000.

The directors of River Ltd consider that only the results for the next five years should be considered and obtain the following information:

1. It is expected that Tributary Ltd will make a profit of £50,000 in each of the next five years, after charging annual depreciation of £10,000.

2. Tributary Ltd has to repay a debenture of £30,000 on 31 December 20X4 and will have to replace plant at a cost of £55,000 on 31 December 20X6.

3. If it takes over Tributary Ltd, River will carry out a rationalization scheme and by 31 December 20X3 will be able to dispose of property to realize £45,000 and reduce the combined working capital by £10,000. It will also make annual cost savings of £5,000. 4. The appropriate discount rate to be applied to this acquisition is 25%.

Required:
Advise the directors of River Ltd on whether the acquisition of Tributary Ltd at the stated price should be undertaken.

Note:
Assume cash flows take place on the last day of the year in which they arise.
Table of Factors for the Present Value of £1 at 25%

Year	Factor
1	0.800
2	0.640
3	0.512
4	0.410
5	0.328

Solution (£000)

	20X3	20X4	20X5	20X6	20X7
Step 1					
Cash flow without acquisition	100	100	100	100	100
Step 2					
Cash flow with acquisition:					
River:					
Cash generated	100	100	100	100	100
Cost savings	5	5	5	5	5
Tributary:					
Profit	50	50	50	50	50
Depreciation	10	10	10	10	10
Sale of property	45				
Reduction in working capital	10				
Debenture repaid		(30)			
Plant purchased				(55)	
Cash flow	220	135	165	110	165
Step 3					
Deduct Step 1 cash flow	100	100	100	100	100
Cash flow from acquisition (A)	120	35	65	10	65
Present value factor (B)	0.800	0.640	0.512	0.410	0.328
Present value of cash flows (A x B)	96.0	22.4	33.3	4.1	21.3

The total present value is $96.0 + 22.4 + 33.3 + 4.1 + 21.3 = 177.1$

The present value of the forecast cash flows exceeds the price being asked by the owners of Tributary Ltd, and so the acquisition would be worthwhile. However, a lot of the cash inflow comes from the rationalization which River is able to carry out and so might not be available to other prospective purchasers. This explains why the asking price is below the value to River Ltd, as only River can unlock the surplus assets. It might be worthwhile to see if a lower price can be negotiated, but the directors of River have ignored cash flows after 20X7 which, if positive, would add to the desirability of purchasing Tributary.

8.5 THE VALUATION OF MINORITY AND MAJORITY INTERESTS

The relevance of particular business valuation techniques to individual circumstances is determined, in part, by the extent of control given by the holding to be valued. There exists a number of classes of share capital, and not all of them carry equal voting rights. For example, there are non-voting ordinary shares, and preference shares usually bestow no say in how the business is run so long as dividends are paid. A majority holding of shares is defined, for the purpose of this section, as one which gives the owner over 50% of the votes, and hence control; a minority holding is less than 50%. Where a number of minority shareholders, who together own more than 50% of the votes, act in concert for valuation purposes, the considerations appropriate to a single majority shareholder apply.

Ownership of a majority shareholding gives control over the company, including its distribution policy and whether it is to be liquidated. The fact that the management of companies is the responsibility of the directors is irrelevant as the board can be changed by a majority shareholder with whose wishes it does not comply. A majority interest in a going concern can, therefore, be valued on the basis of the earnings yield, or the P/E ratio, as the disposition of earnings between distribution and retention is at the owner's discretion. The liquidation basis of valuation is appropriate where it cannot be assumed that the business is a going concern, or the majority shareholder wishes to ascertain the minimum value of the investment. The replacement cost basis, including an allowance for goodwill, is the maximum a buyer would pay; the price is likely to be agreed somewhere between these two extremes. Dividend yield valuation is not relevant in circumstances where the level of dividend is effectively set by the majority shareholder, as such control gives access to the company's earnings and assets.

The owner of a minority interest is the passive recipient of dividends and is unable to influence their size without support from other members. Accordingly, the dividend yield approach to valuation is appropriate for small blocks of shares. However, a higher price may be achieved where the buyer needs the small holding to establish, together with shares already owned, a majority interest. Valuations based on earnings and assets are of little relevance to minority shareholders becuase they are not able to gain access to them for the purpose of enhanced distributions.

8.6 NEGOTIATION AND PRICE FIXING
The application of the various techniques of valuation produces a range of values, and each is likely to be given different weight by the parties engaged in negotiations to decide a price. A seller wants to receive as much as possible, while the buyer wants to minimize the price, and so each favours the valuation that supports their position. In practice arguments may be advanced at various dates, in favour of different valuations for the same shares: a low one for the calculation of inheritance tax, a high one when a holding is sold. However, neither of the parties to negotiations can select a valuation and insist on its acceptance. The essence of negotiation is that agreement should result from compromise on both sides. Where an offer to buy or sell is at a totally

unacceptable price, and there is no chance of movement, there is nothing to be gained from negotiation and the sale does not take place.

A factor that may affect the negotiations is the availability of information. For example, a director who owns shares in an unlisted company has access to the full range of management information, whereas a prospective buyer starts with only the data that is published. In the course of negotiations for a substantial holding, the gap in knowledge often narrows. The purchaser may request authority to carry out independent investigations within the company, and this request is usually granted, since refusal of access may well deter the buyer from proceeding.

Interpretation of information is important because it affects the view of the future. For example, both sides may agree on the number of units of output likely to be sold, but have different views on the price of each unit, or, where exports are concerned, on the rates of foreign currency exchange. A pessimistic seller faced with an optimistic buyer may agree a price less than the buyer would be willing to pay. The taxation implications of the transaction for the buyer and seller must also be considered.

The valuation procedures described in this chapter do not make it possible to predict the outcome of negotiations, but they do indicate the reasonable boundaries within which negotiations are likely to take place.

8.7 FURTHER READING
Lewis, R. and Pendrill, D. (2000), *Advanced Financial Accounting*, sixth edition, Pitman, Chapter 14.

8.8 QUESTIONS

The following questions examine the valuation techniques covered in this chapter.

Question 8.1 Overvaluation by Replacement Cost

Down Ltd is entirely financed by Ordinary Share Capital and owns only one asset, a building, for which it collects an annual rent of £14,000. The company's expenses are £2,000 per annum, and these would have to be met by any owner of this building or a similar one. The rent is lower than expected as a result of a general lack of economic activity.

The historical cost of the building is £100,000 and its current replacement cost is £200,000. Funds can be invested currently with a similar element of risk to give a return of 10%.

Required:
Discuss, with numerical analysis, what a reasonable value for the company might be.

Question 8.2

Falkus plc plans to diversify its activities and has under consideration the possible acquisition of a number of different private companies. One such company is Fanshawe Ltd, in respect of which the following information has been obtained:

(1) *Profit and Loss Appropriation Account for 20X0*

	£
Net profit	72,000
Less: dividends	18,000
Retained profit	54,000

Balance Sheet as at 31 December 20X0

	£
Freehold property at cost less depreciation	29,000
Machinery at cost less depreciation	125,000
Stocks	63,000
Net monetary assets	17,000
	234,000
Financed by:	
Share capital (£1 ordinary shares)	100,000
Reserves	134,000
	234,000

(2) The freehold property is estimated to be currently worth £150,000. The machinery and stocks might be expected to sell for £50,000 and £52,000, respectively, in a forced sale. The cost of replacing each of these assets is put at: machinery £180,000; stocks £75,000.

(3) Shares in quoted companies operating in the same line of business as Fanshawe have an average price/earnings ratio of 10 and a dividend yield of 6%.

Required:
(a) Calculations of the value to be placed on one £1 ordinary share in Fanshawe Ltd based on the

information provided above. You should summarize the results of your calculations in the following manner:

		Valuation of one £1 ordinary share	
(i)	Break-up basis	....	
(ii)	Replacement cost basis	....	
(iii)	Dividend yield basis	....	
(iv)	Price/earnings basis	....	[10]

(b) Discuss the meaning and significance of EACH of the four valuations and comment on their relevance in the light of the proposed takeover by Falkus plc. [10]

Note:
Ignore taxation. [Total marks – 20]

Question 8.3

Peter Lubbock has recently sold his business to a multinational company and he is keen to invest the proceeds in Graig Security Systems Ltd, a recently established company which installs and monitors sophisticated surveillance systems for domestic and business use. The formation of this company involved a heavy capital investment, but the fixed assets acquired are sufficient to support a significant increase in the level of operations.

The following information is provided relating to Graig Security Systems Ltd:

(1) BALANCE SHEET AT 30 JUNE 20X9

	£000
Fixed assets	580
Working capital	20
	600
Share capital (£1 ordinary shares)	400
16% loan	200
	600

(2) The profits of the company for the year to 30 June 20X9, after deducting loan interest, amounted to £130,000. It is the directors' policy to pay out the entire profits each year in the form of dividends, and this policy is expected to continue for the foreseeable future.

(3) The fixed assets are highly specialized. It is estimated that it would cost £760,000 to replace them, but their break-up value is put at no more than £230,000. Goodwill is estimated to be worth £200,000.

(4) Peter Lubbock has been invited to acquire 120,000 ordinary shares in the company at a price of £2 per share. The proceeds would be used to repay immediately the loan and to provide much needed working capital requirements.

(5) An earnings yield of 18% is considered appropriate for companies in this line of business.

Required:
(a) Calculations of the value to be placed on one £1 ordinary share in Graig Security Systems Ltd, based on the information provided. You should summarize the results of your calculations in the following manner:

	Valuation of £1 ordinary share
(i) Break up basis	
(ii) Replacement cost basis	
(iii) Earnings yield basis	

[8]

(b) Discuss the relevance of each of these three valuations to Peter Lubbock in deciding whether to make the share purchase. Make (and show) any other calculations you consider appropriate. [12]

Notes:
(i) Ignore taxation.

(ii) Assume you are making the calculations on 30 June 20X9. [Total marks – 20]

Question 8.4

The directors of Pantheon Ltd have under consideration the acquisition of shares in Purley Ltd. The following information has been extracted from the recent published accounts of Purley Ltd:

Year to 30 September	*20X5*	*20X6*	*20X7*	*20X8*
	£	£	£	£
Directors' remuneration	85,000	102,000	33,000	37,000
Depreciation	25,000	25,000	25,000	25,000
Net profit	157,000	127,000	119,000	103,000
Dividends	50,000	50,000	50,000	50,000

The following further information is provided in respect of Purley Ltd:

(1) It is discovered that stock was overvalued by £20,000 on 30 September 20X5 and £36,000 on 30 September 20X8.

(2) It is discovered that a provision of £28,000 was made for debts considered to be doubtful on 30 September 20X4. The debts were paid in full during December 20X4.

(3) It is thought that the services provided by the directors have a fair market value of £60,000 per annum.

(4) The machinery of Purley is old and will need to be replaced immediately at a cost of £400,000. The new machinery is expected to have a useful life of ten years and then a zero residual value.

(5) Purley's £200,000 15% debentures were repaid on 1 October 20X6 using cash surplus to business requirements.

(6) Private companies in a similar line of business to Purley have recently changed hands at prices which represent a dividend yield of 6% or a price/earnings ratio of 12.

(7) The share capital consists of 500,000 ordinary shares of £1 each.

Required:
(a) The valuation to be placed on one £1 ordinary share in Purley Ltd on the dividend-yield basis. [2]

(b) The valuation to be placed on one £1 ordinary share in Purley Ltd using the price/earnings ratio. For this purpose the maintainable profits for each of the years 20X5, 20X6, 20X7 and 20X8 are to be 'weighted' 1, 2, 3 and 4 respectively. [12]

(c) An assessment of the relevance of each of the above valuations on the alternative assumptions that Pantheon will purchase:

(i) a majority interest in Purley,

(ii) a minority interest in Purley. [6]
Note:
Ignore taxation. [Total marks – 20]

Question 8.5

Peter Rice owns 30,000 ordinary shares in Drysgol Ltd. He is in need of cash and has received an offer of £54,000 for the shares. He knows that you are studying accountancy and approaches you for advice. The balance sheet of Drysgol Ltd at 30 September 1999 contained the following information:

	£1000
Fixed Assets	
Freehold property at book value	360
Goodwill	240
	600
Current Assets	
Stock	252
Debtors	234
Cash	24
	510
Current Liabilities	210
Net current assets	300
	900
Financed by:	
Issued ordinary share capital (£1 shares)	600
Retained profit	300
	900

The following additional information is obtained:

• The average annual profits of Drysgol Ltd in recent years have amounted to £120,000.

• An annual dividend of 12 pence per share is paid on the issued ordinary shares.

- The following resale values are provided in respect of the company's tangible assets if sold individually:

	£1000
Freehold property	810
Stock	294

- All the debtors are thought to be recoverable and the goodwill is considered to be valueless in a forced sale.

- In the event of liquidation, liquidation costs are estimated at £30,000.

- The shares in comparable companies are sold at prices which give an earnings yield of 12% and a dividend yield of 6%.

Required:
(a) Valuations of the entire shareholding of Peter Rice presented in the following format:

Valuations

1. Book value basis	_____	
2. Liquidation (break up) basis	_____	
3. Earnings yield basis	_____	
4. Dividend yield basis	_____	[10 marks}

(b) Explain the relevance to Peter Rice of each valuation. [10 marks]

Note:
Assume you are making the calculations on 30 September 1999. Ignore taxation. [Total marks – 20]

Question 8.6

The following balance sheet relates to the financial affairs of Haworth Ltd as at 31 December 20X4.

Balance Sheet as at 31 December 20X4

	£	£
Land at cost		35,000
Other fixed assets at cost	100,000	
Less: Accumulated depreciation	40,000	60,000
		95,000
Net current assets (working capital)		70,000
Total assets less current liabilities		165,000
15% secured loan		40,000
		125,000
Share capital		80,000
Retained profit at 31 January 20X4	25,000	
Profit for 20X4	20,000	45,000
		125,000

The directors of Denholme Ltd are keen to diversify their company's activities and are considering the possible acquisition of Haworth Ltd, which would then be operated as a separate division. The directors of Haworth Ltd would be willing to sell 'at the right price' and have made their books and records available to enable Denholme Ltd to carry out a full financial appraisal. The following facts have been established and plans made:

Facts
(1) The fixed assets are four years old and are being depreciated on the straight-line basis.

(2) Assuming no changes are made to the nature of Haworth's activities, the profit generated in 20X4 will be repeated for the foreseeable future.

(3) Denholme Ltd will carry out a rationalization scheme on Haworth during the financial year 20X5. This will enable Denholme to dispose of the land for £90,000 on 31 December 20X5 and reduce the investment in working capital at that date by £20,000. A further expected effect of the rationalization scheme will be a reduction in annual operating costs of £8,000, commencing with the financial year 20X6.

(4) Denholme will proceed with the acquisition only if it can be reasonably expected that the investment will yield an internal rate of return (DCF yield) of at least 20%.

Plans
(1) For the purpose of assessing the acquisition, it is to be assumed that Haworth will be wound up when the fixed assets reach the end of their expected useful life.

(2) Haworth Ltd will repay the secured loan on 31 December 20X7.

Required:
(a) A calculation of the maximum price that the directors of Denholme Ltd should offer for the business of Haworth Ltd. [14]

(b) Identify any other factors that might be considered by the directors of each company when deciding whether to proceed with the business transfer. [6]

Notes
(1) Assume all cash flows take place on the last day of the year in which they occur.

(2) Assume you are making the calculations on 1 January 20X5.

(3) Ignore taxation and dividends.

(4) Table of factors for the present value of £1 at 20%:

Year	Factor
1	0.83
2	0.69
3	0.58
4	0.48
5	0.40
6	0.33
7	0.28
8	0.23
9	0.19
10	0.16

[Total marks – 20]

9

INTERPRETATION OF ACCOUNTS: TRADITIONAL RATIO ANALYSIS

9.1 PRINCIPLES OF RATIO ANALYSIS

9.1.1 Objective

The accounts published annually by companies constitute an important source of information for external users, and their form and content are carefully regulated (see Chapters 3-6) with the intention of ensuring that they are a helpful and reliable guide to corporate progress. Often the banker is not restricted to published financial information as the basis for reaching decisions, such as whether to increase an overdraft facility, although the amount of additional data that companies are willing to provide does vary considerably. In general, large public companies are reluctant to provide detailed trading figures, although there are always useful indicators of what is happening in the chairman's report and the Operating and Financial Review; in small private companies there are no such indicators, but the accounts submitted to the bank nearly always include a full breakdown of trading results. The amount of useful information which can be gleaned from the profit and loss account and balance sheet, however, is severely limited, even when a detailed breakdown of trading results is provided. For example, the profit and loss account might show that purchases amount to £500m and the balance sheet might disclose trade creditors totalling £21m but, taken in isolation, it is impossible to assess whether these amounts are satisfactory or unreasonable.

Ratio analysis has been developed to help to translate the information contained in the accounts into a form more helpful and readily understandable to users of financial reports. The ratios do not appear in the accounts, however, and the user must calculate and interpret them himself or employ someone with the necessary skill to do the job. Due to the banker's particular relationship with the customer, that is the ability to insist on the regular provision of up to date financial information for the duration of the advance, ratio analysis can be used to follow through the underlying commercial business, establish the reasons for unexpected variations in performance, and make a fair assessment of the degree of risk involved at periodic intervals. No other user of accounting reports, except management, is in a better position to make this analysis.

9.1.2 Calculation

Accounting ratios are calculated by expressing one figure as a ratio or percentage of another with the objective of disclosing significant relationships and trends that are not immediately evident from the examination of individual balances appearing in the accounts. The ratio which results from a comparison of two figures possesses real significance, however, only if an identifiable commercial relationship exists between the numerator and the denominator. For example, one would expect there to be a positive relationship between net profit and the level of sales. Assuming that each item sold produces a profit, one would expect a higher sales figure to produce more profit. So mere observation of the fact that profit is £5m, is not particularly illuminating. What is of greater interest is net profit expressed as a percentage of sales. If sales are found to be £25m, the net profit percentage could be calculated as follows:

$$\text{Net profit percentage} = \frac{\text{Net profit}}{\text{Sales}} \times 100 = \frac{5}{25} \times 100 = 20\%$$

9.1.3 Interpretation

The significance of an accounting ratio is enhanced by comparison with some yardstick of corporate performance. There are three options available, namely comparison with:

- results achieved during previous accounting periods by the same company (trend analysis);

- results achieved by other companies (inter-firm comparisons);

- predetermined standards or budgets.

The advantage of making comparisons is that it enables users to classify a company's performance as good, average or poor in certain key areas.

Example 9.1 (illustrates the first two types of comparison)

For 19X0 Bradford Ltd reported net profit and sales figures respectively of £50,000 and £400,000. In 19X1 net profit increased to £90,000 and sales for the year amounted to £900,000. The net profit percentage earned by Bingley Ltd, which carries on trade in competition with Bradford, was 14% in 19X1.

Required:
Calculate and comment on the net profit percentages of Bradford for 19X0 and 19X1.

Solution

Net profit percentages: 19X0   19X1

$$\frac{50,000}{400,000} \times 100 =   12.5\%$$

$$\frac{90,000}{900,000} \times 100 =   10\%$$

The company's accounts report a significant increase in net profit, but the accounting ratios show that net profit expressed as a percentage of sales has declined and, moreover, is significantly below the return earned by a similar business. We cannot make a definitive assessment of Bradford's progress on the basis of a single accounting ratio, but it does point to the need for further investigation to determine why the ratio has fallen and why the margin earned by its competitor has not been achieved. (The net profit percentage is examined further in section 9.5.2.)

There are attractions and limitations attached to each of the three bases for comparison listed above. Last year's results are readily available, but observed changes over time are not necessarily significant. A comparison may show that there is an improvement in the net profit percentage, but last year's results may have been disastrous. Problems with inter-firm comparisons include the difficulty of finding a company engaged in a similar range of business activities, while differences in accounting policies might detract from the significance of any findings. It is, however, important to discover how a company is faring in relation to its competitors since this should throw a great deal of light on the efficiency of management and the long-term prospects of the concern. A comparison of actual results with predetermined budgets should, in theory, be the best test of whether the work force has achieved a reasonable level of efficiency. There is, however, the problem and cost of establishing standards. Also, it is little consolation to discover that work is being carried out efficiently if, due to the existence of a declining market, profit is falling. In practice management rarely publishes forecasts of future results and so external users of accounting reports, other than the bank manager, usually have to confine their attention to trend analysis and inter-firm comparisons.

9.2 CLASSIFICATION OF ACCOUNTING RATIOS

A meaningful accounting ratio is calculated by comparing balances between which there exists some identifiable economic relationship, but there are certain balances between which there exists no apparent link, e.g. accumulated depreciation and trade creditors. In many cases, however, a significant relationship does exist and the large number of financial totals appearing in the accounts produce numerous combinations which form the basis for the calculation of a relevant accounting ratio. Many of these ratios duplicate one another, whereas others are of limited significance and can probably be ignored without detracting from the value of the analysis. The authors believe that the following representative list of fourteen ratios is adequate for most purposes:

1. Working capital (current) ratio

2. Liquidity (quick) ratio

3. Proprietorship ratio

4. Interest cover

5. Rate of stock turnover

6. Rate of collection of debtors

7. Rate of payment of creditors

8. Fixed asset turnover

9. Total asset turnover

10. Gross profit margin

11. Net profit percentage

12. Rate of return on gross assets

13. Rate of return on shareholders' equity

14. Debt:equity ratio

The procedure followed below is to use the detailed final accounts of Ludlow Ltd, for 19X1 (see Figure 9.1), to illustrate the calculation and significance of the above ratios. There is a legal requirement for published accounts to give corresponding figures for the previous year, and these are used for comparative purposes to help to develop the analysis. The aim is to build up a corporate profile by describing Ludlow Ltd's performance during 19X1 and comparing it with the performance achieved a year earlier. It is unlikely that all the ratios will produce the same conclusions regarding the company's performance; we may find that in certain areas results have improved whereas elsewhere the performance is less satisfactory than in the previous year. This emphasizes the importance of not attaching too much attention to individual accounting ratios, and the overall assessment of Ludlow Ltd's progress requires us to balance carefully the relative significance of the ratios that are calculated. The limitations of ratio analysis are examined more fully in section 9.8.

Figure 9.1

Towards the end of 19X0 the directors of Ludlow Ltd, a firm of wholesale merchants, decided to raise additional capital in the form of a debenture of £800,000 to facilitate expansion of the business.

The annual accounts for the year ended 31 December 19X1, together with corresponding figures for 19X0, are set out below:

Trading and Profit and Loss Account

	19X0		19X1	
	£	£	£	£
Sales: Credit		5,500,000		6,600,000
Cash		500,000		400,000
		6,000,000		7,000,000
Less: Opening stock	1,340,000		1,360,000	
Purchases (on credit)	4,700,000		5,670,000	
Closing stock	(1,360,000)		(1,500,000)	
Cost of sales		4,680,000		5,530,000
Gross Margin		1,320,000		1,470,000
Expenses: Administration	270,000		275,000	
Selling	395,000		400,000	
Warehouse & distribution	280,000		325,000	
Depreciation	30,000		35,000	
		975,000		1,035,000
Operating profit		345,000		435,000
Less: Debenture Interest		–		80,000
Net profit		345,000		355,000
Corporation tax		172,500		177,500
Net profit after tax		172,500		177,500

Statement of Retained Earnings

	19X0	19X1
Reserves at 1 January	655,000	750,000
Add: Net profit after tax	172,500	177,500
	827,500	927,500
Less: Dividends proposed	77,500	77,500
Reserves at 31 December	750,000	850,000

Balance Sheet

	19X0		19X1	
	£	£	£	£
Fixed Assets:				
Cost		700,000		900,000
Accumulated depreciation		150,000		185,000
		550,000		715,000
Current Assets:				
Stock	1,360,000		1,500,000	
Trade debtors	960,000		1,560,000	
Cash at bank	20,000		120,000	
	2,340,000		3,180,000	

Less: Current liabilities				
Trade creditors	562,500		667,500	
Dividends payable	77,500		77,500	
	640,000		745,000	
Working capital		1,700,000		2,435,000
		2,250,000		3,150,000
Less: Debentures		—		800,000
		2,250,000		2,350,000
Financed by:				
Share capital		1,500,000		1,500,000
Reserves		750,000		850,000
		2,250,000		2,350,000

The following additional information is provided:

1. At 1 January 19X0 trade debtors amounted to £800,000, gross assets to £2,710,000 and shareholders' equity to £2,155,000.

2. The product range and buying prices were unchanged over the period 1 January 19X0 to 31 December 19X1.

3. The debenture loan was received on 1 January 19X1 and additional warehouse facilities became available on that date at a cost of £200,000.

4. No fixed assets were purchased during 19X0.

The 14 accounting ratios listed previously are illustrated in the following sections of this chapter:

- 9.3 ratios measuring solvency and financial strength (1-4);

- 9.4 asset turnover ratios (5-9);

- 9.5 profit ratios (10-13);

- 9.7 gearing ratio (14).

9.3 RATIOS MEASURING SOLVENCY AND FINANCIAL STRENGTH

The ratios illustrated in this section may be further classified into those that examine short-term solvency and those that investigate the longer-term financial strength of the concern.

SHORT-TERM SOLVENCY

9.3.1 Working Capital (Current) Ratio

Working capital is defined as the excess of current assets over current liabilities, and an adequate surplus is normally interpreted as a reliable indication of the fact that the company is solvent. The working capital ratio is calculated as follows:

$$\text{Working capital ratio} = \frac{\text{Current assets}}{\text{Current liabilities}} : 1$$

The purpose of the ratio is to shed further light on the short-term solvency of the company and, more specifically, on its ability to pay debts as they fall due by calculating the relationship between current assets and current liabilities. A question which students and businesspeople often ask is 'What is a correct working capital ratio?' Textbooks often quote a ratio of 2:1 but, although this is often a useful guideline, it must be used with care. The analyst must familiarize himself with the rate at which current assets are converted into cash and how quickly current liabilities must be paid. This, in turn, very much depends on what is normal practice within the industry. For example, a retailer who sells goods for cash normally operates with a much lower ratio than a manufacturer who sells goods on credit. In the case of the retailer resources are converted directly from stocks into cash, whereas in the manufacturing firm goods sold are probably 'tied-up' as debts outstanding for six to eight weeks before cash becomes available. Then again, the period for which stocks are held varies from one industry to another. A manufacturer of small-value metal products is likely to convert raw materials into finished goods and sell them much more quickly than a construction company, and in the latter case stocks are likely to comprise a much higher proportion of current assets to reflect the relatively slower rate of stock turnover. For these, and other reasons (see section 9.8), readers should be on their guard against always accepting accounting ratios at face value, and should assess their significance only after carefully considering the economic facts which lie behind them.

Ludlow Ltd is a firm of wholesale merchants, and we can see from its accounts that most of its sales are made on credit and that the company also receives credit from its suppliers. The company therefore requires a working capital ratio sufficiently in excess of 1:1 to accommodate the large quantity of resources tied up in stocks. This is because the company is likely to allow customers roughly the same amount of credit that it receives from suppliers, and so resources tied up in stocks will not be converted into cash in time to pay trade debts as they fall due. It is on the assumption that one half of all current assets are invested in stocks that a working capital ratio of 2:1 is often regarded as a reasonable 'rule of thumb'.

Calculations for Ludlow Ltd are:

$$19X0 \quad \frac{2,340,000}{640,000} : 1 = 3.7:1$$

$$19X1 \quad \frac{3,180,000}{745,000} : 1 = 4.3:1$$

We do not know what type of wholesaler Ludlow Ltd is, but a ratio of about 1.5:1 is quite common in that sector of the economy, and so the calculated figures suggest that the company is financially stable. The high ratio may, however, have unfavourable implications for the profitability of the firm, because resources unnecessarily tied up in stock, cash and debtors are not earning a return. In business there is often a conflict between profitability and financial stability, and managerial policies that place an excessive amount of emphasis on financial stability may cause profits to be unduly depressed.

9.3.2 Liquidity (Quick) Ratio

The purpose of the liquidity ratio is also to examine solvency. It is calculated in a similar manner to the working capital ratio, but with one important difference: the liquidity ratio concentrates attention more directly on a company's prospect of paying its debts as they fall due by excluding current assets that will not be converted into cash within the next couple of months. It is for this reason that the calculation is often colourfully described as the 'quick ratio' or 'acid test of solvency'.

It is necessary to examine carefully current assets in order to decide which items should be included or omitted. Stocks should be excluded, unless they are expected to be sold quickly for cash, as should any trade debts not receivable within the next few months, e.g. because the sales price is payable on an instalment basis spread over a year. Marketable securities held as a temporary means of employing surplus funds should be included, whereas prepayments should technically be excluded though the amount involved is usually immaterial.

The normal approach is to include all current liabilities irrespective of their payment dates. Trade creditors and proposed dividends are, of course, usually payable within a relatively short timespan, but this is not necessarily the case with taxation payable.

Companies pay tax nine months after the end of the accounting year, and so a strong case could be made for excluding this item from the calculation. It might also be argued that, for many companies, the bank overdraft is a revolving source of finance which is unlikely to be withdrawn without advance warning, although much may depend on the company's financial position and the general economic climate. It is probably because accountants are inclined to favour conservative measures of corporate progress that all current liabilities are usually included in the calculation of the liquidity ratio. We shall comply with this convention, but bear in mind the limitation that this places on the significance of the ratio that results.

Calculations for Ludlow Ltd (the fact that a small proportion of sales is for cash is ignored and all stocks are excluded) are:

$$19X0 \quad \frac{980,000}{640,000} :1 = 1.5:1$$

$$19X1 \quad \frac{1,680,000}{745,000} :1 = 2.3:1$$

A liquidity ratio of 1:1 is desirable; a ratio significantly below unity usually causes a company to encounter great difficulty in meeting its debts as they fall due, while a ratio in excess of unity indicates that the company is in possession of cash resources surplus to requirements. At the end of 19X0 Ludlow Ltd's ratio is more than adequate, and a year later it has 'improved' even further. While there is no doubt that the company is solvent, there must be some doubt whether it is making the best use of available resources.

The liquidity ratio is of major importance to the banker, particularly in times when the customer is in financial difficulty. For this reason the bank normally requests customers to provide the information on which the calculation is based, namely cash, debtor and creditor levels, on a regular basis from the management accounts.

LONGER-TERM FINANCIAL STRENGTH

9.3.3 Proprietorship Ratio

The total assets belonging to a company are financed by a combination of resources provided by shareholders and creditors. The proportion of business assets financed by the shareholders is measured by the proprietorship ratio which is conventionally calculated by expressing the shareholders' investment, or equity, in the company as a percentage of total sources of finance.

$$\text{Proprietorship ratio} = \frac{\text{Shareholders' equity}}{\text{Total sources of finance}} \times 100$$

This ratio, conventionally expressed as a percentage, is a measure of financial stability, since the larger the proportion of business activity financed by shareholders the smaller are the creditors' claims against the company. This produces two advantages:

- Equity finance is normally repaid only when the company is wound up, and even then repayment occurs only if sufficient cash remains after all other providers of finance have been refunded the amounts due to them. Where an excessive proportion of total finance is provided by short-term creditors, management is likely to be under continuous pressures to finance repayments falling due. In these circumstances any withdrawal of, or reduction in, a source of finance causes the company acute financial embarrassment.

- Dividends are payable at the discretion of management whereas interest payable on loan capital is a legally enforceable debt. A company with a large proportion of equity finance is therefore more able to survive a lean period of trading than a highly geared company (see section 9.7) which is legally obliged to make interest payments irrespective of profit levels.

It is difficult to specify an appropriate percentage because this depends a great deal upon trading conditions within the industry. In general, a higher percentage is expected in those industries where there are large fluctuations in profitability. This is because reliance on overdraft and loan finance gives rise to heavy interest charges which a company may find it difficult to pay when results are poor. In any event, one normally expects shareholders to provide at least half the finance, and the implications of significant changes from one year to the next should receive careful investigation.

The proprietorship ratio, viewed from the creditors' standpoint, provides a useful indication of the extent to which a company can stand a fall in the value of its assets before the creditors' position is prejudiced. Book values are not the same as current values, of course, but a proprietorship ratio of say 75% would indicate that there exists a significant cushion for creditors, and the resale value of assets would have to fall to less than one-quarter of their book value before the creditors' position on liquidation would be jeopardized.

Calculations for Ludlow Ltd are:

$$19X0 \quad \frac{2,250,000}{2,250,000+640,000} \times 100 = 78\%$$

$$19X0 \quad \frac{2,350,000}{3,150,000+745,000} \times 100 = 60\%$$

Shareholders provide a healthy 78% of total finance at the end of 19X0, but there is a decline to 60% by the end of the following year. The main reason for this change is the debenture issue which had a significant effect on the financial structure of the company. Shareholders remain the dominant source of funds, but there is now much greater reliance on external finance and a corresponding need to meet heavy annual interest payments.

9.3.4 Interest Cover

The fact that a company is legally obliged to meet its interest charges was referred to when examining the proprietorship ratio (see section 9.3.3). There is no legal restriction on the sources of cash that may be employed by management to meet its interest payments, and it may even make an additional share issue with the intention that part of the proceeds should be used for that purpose. Nevertheless, interest payments are a business expense and, in the long run, all such costs must be met out of sales revenue if the company is to remain viable. 'Interest cover' stresses the importance of a company meeting its interest charges out of revenue, and it does this by expressing net profit before interest charges (operating profits) as a multiple of the interest charged.

$$\text{Interest cover} = \frac{\text{Net profit before interest and tax}}{\text{Interest charged}}$$

The purpose of this calculation is to indicate the ease with which a company meets its fixed interest obligations out of profit. A low figure indicates that interest payable imposes a heavy burden on the company's finances, thereby increasing the risk of insolvency. It should be recognized, however, that interest cover would be expected to fall immediately following a loan issue. For example, debentures are often raised with two/three years' capital requirements in mind, but a full utilization of the additional resources made available is unlikely to be achieved straight away. In this situation, current earnings have to bear the full weight of the additional charges but the extra revenue, which is expected to result from an expansion programme, takes longer to materialize.

Interest cover is a ratio which receives a significant amount of attention from analysts in general, and bankers in particular. This is because traditional measures of asset utilization and asset cover for advances are of little relevance in service-based industries where tangible assets are at a low level. In these circumstances, it is particularly important to measure the ability of companies to generate enough revenue to cover finance charges and leave a sufficient balance over for dividends and to finance eventual loan repayments. The ratio of earnings to finance charges helps a great deal in this direction.

Calculations for Ludlow Ltd are:

19X0   No interest charged

19X1 $\dfrac{435,000}{80,000}$ = 5.4 times

The interest cover for Ludlow Ltd appears adequate.

9.4 ASSET TURNOVER RATIOS

The four ratios calculated in this section are designed to examine how fully management is utilizing the resources placed at its disposal by shareholders and creditors. These ratios help to explain any improvement or decline in the solvency of a business; they also provide clues to the reasons underlying changes in profitability which are measured by the accounting ratios contained in section 9.5.

9.4.1 Rate of Stock Turnover

The term 'ratio' is used loosely in accountancy to cover all the calculations that measure the relationship between two financial totals. We have already seen that net profit is conventionally expressed as a percentage of sales and that interest cover is presented as a simple multiple, i.e. 'N' times. The rate of stock turnover, which measures the speed with which a company turns over its stock, may also be expressed as a single figure. The calculation is made as follows:

$$\text{Rate of stock turnover} = \frac{\text{Cost of goods sold}}{\text{Average stock level}}$$

Regarding the above formula, two typical queries raised are as follows: why use cost of goods sold rather than sales, and why use the average stock level rather than closing stock? The reason is to ensure that both the numerator and denominator are computed on a comparable basis. Stocks, which make up the denominator, are valued at cost for accounting purposes, and the numerator must be computed on a similar basis. The sales figure can be used to produce a ratio that enables users to make helpful inter-period comparisons, when cost of sales figures are not available, but there is a risk that wrong conclusions will be drawn when there are changes in the gross profit margin from one accounting period to another.

Turning to the reason for using average stock levels: the numerator measures the cost of goods despatched to customers during an accounting period, and the denominator must therefore represent the investment in stocks during the same time period. In practice, stock levels are likely to fluctuate a great deal; they are often built up during relatively quiet times and subsequently run down when the level of activity increases. For this reason it is important to calculate the average investment in stocks rather than use the stock level at a particular point in time. The average is usually based on opening and closing stock figures; a more precise calculation makes use of stock levels at various dates during the year, perhaps at the end of each month (for similar reasons, average figures are used in a number of other ratios calculated below).

Many analysts prefer to present this ratio in terms of the number of days that elapse between the date that goods are delivered by suppliers and despatched to customers, i.e. the stock holding period. This is done by modifying the formula so as to achieve the desired result in a single step:

$$\text{Rate of stock turnover, in days} = \frac{\text{Average stock}}{\text{Cost of goods sold}} \times 365$$

Companies strive to keep the stock holding period as low as possible in order to minimize associated costs. An increase in the stock holding period from, say, 30 days to 60 days causes the investment in stocks to double. Extra finance then has to be raised, handling costs increase, and the potential loss from stock damage and obsolescence is much greater. But although management aims to keep stocks to a minimum, it must, at the same time, ensure there are sufficient raw materials available to meet production requirements (in the case of a manufacturer) and enough finished goods available to meet consumer demand. It is therefore management's job to maintain a balance between conflicting objectives.

Calculations for Ludlow Ltd are:

$$19X0 \quad \frac{\frac{1}{2}(1{,}340{,}1\,000 + 1{,}360{,}000)}{4{,}680{,}000} \times 365 = 105 \text{ days}$$

$$19X1 \quad \frac{\frac{1}{2}(1{,}360{,}000 + 1{,}500{,}000)}{5{,}530{,}000} \times 365 = 94 \text{ days}$$

There has been a significant reduction in the average period for which stocks are held, and this suggests that the management has streamlined the purchasing, selling and distribution functions. A comparison of the two balance sheets reveals an increase in the figure for stocks, but this is to be expected because there has been a significant increase in the level of sales during the year. Indeed, a higher level of business activity normally calls for an equivalent increase in stocks to ensure that additional consumer requirements can be met without delay. It is because Ludlow's management has succeeded in increasing sales without a commensurate increase in stock that resources, which would otherwise be tied up in stock, remain available for use elsewhere in the business.

The above presentation of the rate of stock turnover produces a satisfactory measure for wholesalers and retailers, but only a rough approximation for manufacturing companies. This is because manufacturers have three different categories of stocks, namely raw materials, work in progress and finished goods. Ideally each of these should be accounted for separately to compute the total stock holding period. The calculations are demonstrated in section 9.4.4, where the 'cash operating cycle' is examined.

9.4.2 Rate of Collection of Debtors

The period of credit taken by customers varies between industries but, as a general rule, companies extract the maximum amount of credit from suppliers since, in the absence of discounts for prompt payment, accounts unpaid represent a free source of finance. At the same time undue delays should be avoided because these have a harmful long-run effect on the company's credit standing. In practice it is quite usual for customers to take from six to eight weeks to pay their bills.

The rate of collection of debtors is calculated, in days, as follows:

$$\text{Rate of collection of debtors, in days} = \frac{\text{Average trade debtors}}{\text{Credit sales}} \times 365$$

It should be noted that the denominator is confined to credit sales, since only these give rise to debts outstanding. Where the split between cash and credit sales is not given, the total sales figure may be used to calculate a ratio which gives useful comparative information provided there is no significant change in the proportion of total sales made for cash.

Calculations for Ludlow Ltd are:

$$19X0 \quad \frac{\frac{1}{2}\,(800{,}000 + 960{,}000)}{5{,}500{,}000} \times 365 = 58 \text{ days}$$

$$19X1 \quad \frac{\frac{1}{2}\,(960{,}000 + 1{,}560{,}000)}{6{,}600{,}000} \times 365 = 70 \text{ days}$$

It takes Ludlow Ltd on average nearly two weeks longer to collect its debts in 19X1. The result is that a disproportionate amount of money is tied up in trade debts: these resources are yielding no return and also losing value during a period of inflation. The reasons for the change should be investigated, e.g. it may be the result of a conscious policy decision to offer customers additional credit to make the company's products more attractive. This can be a sound business tactic, particularly when credit is tight, but management must make arrangements to finance the much higher level of trade debtors that result. An alternative explanation for the slower rate of debt collection may be slackness in the credit-control department, whose functions include confirmation of new customers' creditworthiness before goods are supplied and the task of following up overdue accounts. Failure to discharge both these duties efficiently results in an unduly large figure for trade debtors and a substantial increase in bad debts.

9.4.3 Rate of Payment of Creditors

This ratio measures the average period of time taken by companies to pay their suppliers. The result must be interpreted with particular care since not all suppliers grant similar terms of credit, but, provided there are no significant changes in the 'mix' of trade creditors, the average payments period should remain stable.

$$\text{Rate of payment of suppliers, in days} = \frac{\text{Average trade creditors}}{\text{Credit purchases}} \times 365$$

We are not given Ludlow's balance for trade creditors at the beginning of 19X0 and so we cannot make the above calculation for that year. We can make the calculation for 19X1, but, without a comparative figure for 19X0, this is of little interpretive value.

Comparable figures may be obtained, however, by basing each year's calculation on the closing figure for trade creditors rather than the average figure for the year. This tells us the approximate numbers of days' purchases represented by the closing balance of trade creditors. It does not of course follow that a similar credit period was obtained throughout the year unless purchases were made at a uniform rate.

Calculations for Ludlow Ltd based on closing trade creditor balances are:

$$19X0 \quad \frac{562,500}{4,700,000} \times 365 = 44 \text{ days}$$

$$19X1 \quad \frac{667,500}{5,670,000} \times 365 = 43 \text{ days}$$

A change in the rate of payment of suppliers may well reflect an improvement or decline in a company's liquidity. For instance, if a company is short of cash it is likely that creditors will have to wait longer for the payment of amounts due to them. This may be an acceptable short-term strategy, particularly where suppliers are familiarized with their customer's 'temporary' predicament. Management should, however, take prompt steps to arrange for additional finance; otherwise supplies of goods will eventually be curtailed. The solvency ratios calculated in 9.3.1 and 9.3.2 show that Ludlow Ltd has no cash problems and, as might therefore be expected, the average period of credit taken from suppliers remains fairly stable at just over six weeks.

9.4.4 The Cash Operating Cycle

A period of time elapses between the payment for goods or raw materials received into stock and the collection of cash from customers in respect of their sale. The gap is known as the 'Cash Operating Cycle' and, during this period of time, the goods acquired, together with the value added in the case of a manufacturer, must be financed by the company. The shorter the length of time between the initial outlay and ultimate collection of cash, the smaller is the value of working capital to be financed. To estimate the length of the cash operating cycle it is necessary to:

1. Calculate the time that the product spends in each stage of its progression from acquisition to sale and subsequent cash receipt.

2. Deduct from the length of time found in step 1 the period of credit received from suppliers.

The various elements in the calculation are described below and illustrated in Example 9.2. For a trading company which buys and sells goods without processing them, omit stages 1(a) and 1 (b).

1. Stocks. Items are purchased or produced, held for a period of time, and then used or sold. We have seen in section 9.4.1 that estimates of the length of time for which various categories of stock are held must be based on a comparison of the average stock levels with the withdrawals from stock during the period under consideration. In the case of a manufacturing company, separate calculations must be made for each of the following three categories of stock:

   (a) *Raw Materials.* These are acquired, held in stock, and then transferred to production. Stocks of raw materials are related to raw materials consumed to find the average length of time for which they are held.

   (b) *Working in Progress.* Raw materials are taken from stock and processed, which involves additional manufacturing costs. The average production time is found by relating the stock of work in progress to the cost of goods manufactured.

   (c) *Finished Goods.* When production is complete, the finished goods are transferred from the factory to the warehouse. (In the case of a trader, finished goods, stored in the warehouse, are purchased from outside.) The average length of time for which items are held is found by relating the stock of finished goods to the cost of goods sold during the accounting period.

2. Debtors. The average age of debts is found from the values of debtors and sales (see section 9.4.2).

3. Creditors. These finance the production and selling cycle from the time raw materials or goods are received into stock until they are paid for. The period of credit is found from the values of creditors and purchases (see section 9.4.3).

The length of the cash operating cycle is obtained by aggregating the periods of time calculated for each of the above items; note that item 3 is negative.

Example 9.2

The cash balance of Wing Ltd has declined significantly over the last twelve months. The following financial information is provided.

Year to 31 December	19X0	19X1
	£	£
Sales	573,000	643,000
Purchases of raw materials	215,000	264,000
Raw materials consumed	210,000	256,400
Cost of goods manufactured	435,000	515,000
Cost of goods sold	420,000	460,000

Balance at 31 December	19X0	19X1
	£	£
Debtors	97,100	121,500
Creditors	23,900	32,500
Stocks: Raw materials	22,400	30,000
Work in progress	29,000	34,300
Finished goods	70,000	125,000

All purchases and sales were made on credit.

Required:
(a) An analysis of the above information, which should include calculations of the cash operating cycle (i.e. the time lag between making payment to suppliers and collecting cash from customers) for 19X0 and 19X1.

(b) A brief report on the implications of the changes that have occurred between 19X0 and 19X1.

Note:
1. Assume a 360-day year for the purpose of your calculations, and that all transactions take place at an even rate.

2. All calculations are to be made to the nearest day.

Solution

(a) Cash Operating Cycle

	19X0 days		19X1 days	
Raw material stock	$\frac{22,400}{210,000} \times 360$	38	$\frac{30,000}{256,400} \times 360$	42
Credit from suppliers	$\frac{23,900}{215,000} \times 360$	(40) $\overline{(2)}$	$\frac{32,500}{264,000} \times 360$	(44) $\overline{(2)}$

Production period	$\dfrac{29,000}{435,000}$ x 360	24	$\dfrac{34,300}{515,000}$ x 360	24
Finished goods stocks	$\dfrac{70,000}{420,000}$ x 360	60	$\dfrac{125,000}{460,000}$ x 360	98
Credit to customer	$\dfrac{97,100}{573,000}$ x 360	61	$\dfrac{121,500}{643,000}$ x 360	68
Cash operating cycle		143		188
Gross profit%		26.7		28.5

(b)   The cash operating cycle has increased by 45 days or 31.5%. This is reflected in an increased investment in working capital, calculated as follows:

	£	£
Stocks	121,400	189,300
Debtors	97,100	121,500
Less: Creditors	(23,900)	(32,500)
	194,600	278,300

The increased period for which raw material stock is held has been balanced by an equivalent increase in the period of credit taken from suppliers. Furthermore, the production period has remained constant at 24 days, suggesting no change in the efficiency with which resources are moved through the factory. The areas of concern are the significant increase in the period of credit taken by customers and the massive increase in the holding of finished stock which has grown from the equivalent of two months' sales at the end of 19X0 to more than three months' sales at the end of 19X1.

The company has achieved a significant growth in its gross profit percentage; more information is needed in order to discover whether any resulting increase in profit sufficiently compensates the likely cost of the increase in capital employed.

9.4.5 Fixed Asset Turnover

A new company first needs to arrange for the provision of accommodation and the installation of any necessary plant and equipment. It is unusual for these facilities to be immediately used to their full capacity, but, as business builds up, the level of utilization increases. The ratio which measures the degree of fixed asset utilization is computed as follows:

$$\text{Fixed asset turnover} = \frac{\text{Sales}}{\text{Average fixed assets}} \quad :1$$

The ratio is likely to reveal excess capacity from time to time during the life of a business, and it may be unavoidable. Possible reasons include:

- Temporary inconveniences such as a strike or a fire which destroys essential equipment.

- The collapse in demand for a product line, unless steps are promptly taken to dispose of the equipment or transfer it to an alternative use.

- The acquisition of additional fixed assets. The point is eventually reached where existing fixed assets are used to their full capacity, and a further increase in business activity first requires the acquisition of additional plant. It is some while before demand increases sufficiently to absorb the extra capacity, however, and meanwhile fixed asset turnover declines.

Example 9.3

During 19X0 Rhyl Ltd operated at full capacity and 1,000 units of output were produced and sold for £50 each, using plant which cost £20,000. On 1 January 19X1 management purchased for £20,000 additional plant with a capacity to produce a further 1,000 units. Output for the years 19X1-19X3 is as follows:

19X1	1,200 units
19X2	1,500 units
19X3	2,000 units

The selling price remained unchanged at £50 per unit.

Required:
Calculate the fixed asset turnover ratio for each year, ignoring depreciation.

Solution

Fixed asset turnover ratio:

$$19X0 \quad \frac{50,000}{20,000} = 2.5:1 \qquad 19X2 \quad \frac{75,000}{40,000} = 1.875:1$$

$$19X1 \quad \frac{60,000}{40,000} = 1.5:1 \qquad 19X3 \quad \frac{100,000}{40,000} = 2.5:1$$

The new plant is working at only 1/5th of its capacity during 19X1, and the result is that fixed asset turnover declines to 1.5:1. Only when both new and old plant are working at full capacity, in 19X3, is the ratio restored to 2.5:1.

Calculations for Ludlow Ltd are:

$$19X0 \quad \frac{6,000,000}{\frac{1}{2}\,(580,000 + 550,000)} \quad :1 = 10.62:1$$

$$19X1 \quad \frac{7,000,000}{\frac{1}{2}\,(750,000^* + 715,000)} \quad :1 = 9.56:1$$

*The additional warehouse facilities become available on 1 January 19X1 at a cost of £200,000.

The ratio has declined which suggests that the additional warehouse facilities may not have been used to their full capacity during 19X1.

9.4.6 Total Asset Turnover

It is management's job to make the fullest use of available resources, because only if this objective is achieved will profits be maximized. The stock turnover, fixed asset turnover and debt collection ratios are designed to measure management's ability to control the level of investment in certain selected areas, whereas 'total asset turnover' has the broader aim of assessing the extent to which management utilizes all available resources. It is computed as follows:

$$\text{Total asset turnover} \; = \frac{\text{Sales}}{\text{Average total assets}} \quad :1$$

A high ratio indicates that management is using the assets effectively to generate sales; most probably the company is working at near full capacity. A decline in the ratio suggests that assets are underutilized and should either be used more fully or sold. One drawback of the calculation is that it benefits companies using older assets. This is partly the effect of inflation, but also because company accounts show fixed assets at net book value which declines each year.

Calculations for Ludlow Ltd are:

$$19X0 \quad \frac{6,000,000}{\frac{1}{2}\,(2,710,000 + 2,890,000)} \quad :1 = 2.14:1$$

$$19X1 \quad \frac{7,000,000}{\frac{1}{2}\,(3,690,000^* + 3,895,000)} \quad :1 = 1.85:1$$

*Assets at the end of 19X0 totalled £2,890,000 but cash of £800,000 was received from a debenture issue made on 1 January 19X1. This is included in the opening balance for the purpose of computing average total assets during 19X1.

The ratio may be expressed either in the above form or as an amount of sales per £1 invested, i.e. sales were £2.14 per £1 invested in 19X0 and £1.85 per £1 invested in 19X1. It is therefore apparent that a significant reduction in asset utilization has occurred, and earlier calculations suggest that this is principally due to the much longer period of credit allowed to customers in 19X1.

9.5 PROFIT RATIOS

The purposes of profit ratios are to help to assess the adequacy of profits earned by the company and to discover whether profitability is increasing or declining. A proper appreciation of the significance of the gross profit margin and the net profit percentage (examined in sections 9.5.1 and 9.5.2 below) is dependent upon a thorough understanding of the different ways in which business costs respond to changes in the levels of production and sales. It is for this reason that readers are referred to Chapter 11 which contains a discussion of fixed and variable costs.

9.5.1 Gross Profit Margin

The calculation is made as follows:

$$\text{Gross profit margin} = \frac{\text{Gross profit}}{\text{Sales}} \times 100$$

The popular view that the gross profit margin should remain unchanged, irrespective of the level of production and sales, is based on the assumption that all costs deducted when computing gross profit are directly variable with sales.

Example 9.4

Chester is a trader who purchases 'frame' tents for £40 each and sells them, through a mail-order catalogue, at a price of £50. During 19X0 and 19X1 sales amounted to 1,000 tents and 2,000 tents respectively. There is no opening or closing stock.

Required:
Prepare Chester's trading accounts for 19X0 and 19X1, and calculate the gross profit margin for each year.

Solution

Trading Account

	19X0	19X1
Sales	50,000	100,000
Less: Cost of goods sold	40,000	80,000
Gross profit	10,000	20,000
Gross profit margin	20%	20%

Sales have doubled in 19X1 and, because costs debited to the trading account are directly variable with sales, the gross profit is also twice the 19X0 level. A gross profit of 10 per unit continues to be earned, however, and the gross profit margin therefore remains unchanged at 20%.

A stable gross profit margin is quite usual for a trader, like Chester, and also for a retailer, but less likely for a manufacturer. This is because the cost of goods sold figure, for a manufacturing company, includes fixed costs such as factory rent and rates, and semi-variable costs such as factory lighting and heating. Except in highly capital-intensive industries, variable costs will nevertheless remain dominant and large fluctuations in the gross profit margin would be unexpected. A stable gross profit margin is therefore the 'norm' and variations, which call for careful investigation, may be caused by any of the following events:

- *Price cuts.* A company may need to reduce its selling price to achieve the desired increase in sales. For instance, assuming Chester had to reduce the selling price to £48 to sell 2,000 tents in 19X1, the revised trading account would be as follows:

Trading Account 19X1	£
Sales	96,000
Less: Cost of goods sold	80,000
Gross profit	16,000
Gross profit margin	16.7%

- *Cost increases.* The price which a company pays its suppliers, during a period of inflation, is likely to rise, and this reduces the gross profit margin unless an appropriate adjustment is made to the selling price. Assume Chester had to pay £44 for his tents in 19X1 and he keeps his selling price at £50.

Trading Account 19X1	£
Sales	100,000
Less: Cost of goods sold	88,000
Gross profit	12,000
Gross profit margin	12%

- *Changes in mix.* A change in the range or mix of products sold causes the overall gross profit margin to vary, assuming individual product lines earn different gross profit percentages.

- *Under- or overvaluation of stocks.* If closing stocks are undervalued, cost of goods sold is inflated and profit understated. An incorrect valuation may be the result of an error during stock-take or it may be due to fraud. For instance, a businessperson might intentionally undervalue stocks to reduce the amount of tax payable. It must, of course, be remembered that the closing stock of one period is the opening stock of the next, and so the effect of errors cancels out unless repeated.

Calculations for Ludlow Ltd are:

$$19X0 \quad \frac{1,320,000}{6,000,000} \times 100 = 22\%$$

$$19X1 \quad \frac{1,470,000}{7,000,000} \times 100 = 21\%$$

The reduction from 22% to 21% appears small, but the effect is to reduce gross (and net) profit by 1% of £7,000,000, i.e. £70,000. The reason for the decline is implied by note 2 to the accounts which tells us that the product range and buying price were unchanged over the period 1 January 19X0 to 31 December 19X1. Assuming stock was properly valued, the lower margin may therefore be attributed to lower selling prices. Whether the policy of reducing prices, presumably to increase sales and profit, is successful, can be investigated using the further profit ratios calculated below.

9.5.2 Net Profit Percentage
The ratio is calculated as follows:

$$\text{Net profit percentage} = \frac{\text{Net profit before interest and tax}}{\text{Sales}} \times 100$$

This ratio is designed to focus attention on the net profit margin arising from business operations. In many banks the convention is to express profit after tax and interest as a percentage of sales. A drawback is that the percentage which results varies depending on the sources employed to finance business activity; interest is charged 'above the line' whereas dividends are deducted 'below the line'. It is for this reason that net profit (i.e. earnings) before interest and tax (sometimes abbreviated to EBIT) is used in this chapter. Both ratios may of course be calculated, but a choice has been made to avoid unnecessary duplication. Attention is focused on profit after tax and interest when calculating the rate of return on shareholders' equity considered in section 9.5.5.

When examining the gross profit margin we saw that an increase in sales is expected to produce an equivalent increase in gross profit, and that gross profit expressed as a percentage of sales normally remains stable. Similarly, net profit increases with sales but, in this case, the increase occurs also as a percentage of sales. The different response of the two profit balances to an increase in sales is explained by the fact that, whereas most of the costs debited to the manufacturing and trading accounts are variable, the majority of the costs debited to the profit and loss account are fixed. The result is that an increase in sales causes cost per unit to decline because the fixed costs are spread more thinly over a larger volume of output. It is often useful to express each item of cost as a percentage of sales to help to illustrate changes in their relative impact over time.

Example 9.5

Assume the same facts as for Example 9.4. In addition Chester pays rent and rates of £3,000 each year while other overhead expenses, including the salary of a part-time employee, stationery and electricity, amount to £4,000 in 19X0 and £6,000 in 19X1.

Required:
Prepare Chester's trading and profit and loss accounts for 19X0 and 19X1, and express costs and profit balances as a percentage of sales.

Solution

Trading and Profit and Loss Account

	19X0		19X1	
	£	%	£	%
Sales	50,000	100	100,000	100
Less: Cost of goods sold	40,000	80	80,000	80
Gross profit	10,000	20	20,000	20
Less: Rent and rates	3,000	6	3,000	3
Other overhead expenses	4,000	8	6,000	6
Net profit	3,000	6	11,000	11

The net profit percentage has risen from 6% to 11 % because of the reduced impact of fixed costs as sales increase; the rent and rates have remained unchanged and therefore fallen from 6% to 3% of sales, while other overhead expenses have increased by just 50% and fallen from 8% to 6% of sales. The point will eventually be reached where output cannot be increased further without incurring a significant addition to fixed costs. For instance, if Chester's business grows further he may have to rent new premises thereby causing a large increase in overhead costs. This will cause a temporary reduction in the net profit percentage until full use is made of the increased capacity.

Calculations for Ludlow Ltd are:

$$19X0 \quad \frac{345,000}{6,000,000} \times 100 = 5.75\%$$

$$19X1 \quad \frac{435,000}{7,000,000} \times 100 = 6.2\%$$

There has been a small increase in the net profit percentage, but rather less than might have been expected in view of the fact that sales increased by one-sixth and expenses debited to the profit and loss account were kept under tight control (this could be confirmed by expressing the expenses individually or in total as a percentage of sales). The main problem is the fall in the gross profit margin, because this caused gross, and consequently net, profit to be approximately £70,000 lower (see 9.5.1) than would have been the case if the 22% margin achieved in 19X0 had been repeated in 19X1.

9.5.3 Rate of Return on Gross Assets

The rate of return on gross assets is often alternatively described as the rate of return on capital employed. The problem with the latter description is that the term capital employed is used, in accountancy, to signify three different financial totals:

- shareholders' equity;

- long-term capital employed (shareholders' equity plus long-term loans);

- gross assets.

To avoid potential confusion, the term 'rate of return on capital employed' is normally avoided in this text. Depending on the version of capital employed under investigation, we use the term: rate of return on shareholders' equity; or rate of return on long term capital; or rate of return on gross assets. This section focuses on the rate of return on gross assets, which is calculated as follows:

$$\text{Rate of return on gross assets} = \frac{\text{Net profit before interest}}{\text{Average gross assets}} \times 100$$

It is management's job to ensure that the most effective use is made of available resources; the rate of return on gross assets measures the extent to which this objective has been achieved and, for this reason, is often described as the 'primary accounting ratio'.

Calculations for Ludlow Ltd are:

$$19X0 \; \frac{345,000}{\frac{1}{2} \, (2,710,000 + 2,890,000)} \times 100 = 12.3\%$$

$$19X1 \; \frac{435,000}{\frac{1}{2} \, (3,690,000 + 3,895,000)} \times 100 = 11.5\%$$

The reason for the decline in the ratio is examined in the following section.

9.5.4 Relationship between Accounting Ratios

An analysis of corporate performance made by students, and even by trained accountants, is often unsatisfactory, and a common weakness is the failure to explore the relationship between the various ratios that have been calculated. A particularly important relationship is expressed in the following so-called 'du Pont' formula:

SECONDARY RATIOS		PRIMARY RATIO
Total asset turnover	x Net profit percentage	= Rate of return on gross assets

Management endeavours to maximize the return earned on gross assets, and it can accomplish this objective in two ways: it can increase the net profit percentage and/or it can achieve a higher rate of asset utilization. It may well happen that greater asset utilization, for instance more sales, can be achieved only by lowering prices, and management has to judge whether the larger volume of activity is sufficient to justify the lower gross and net margins that result from implementing a policy of price reductions.

Example 9.6

Holly and Head run separate businesses in different geographical areas, marketing a similar product for which there exists a ready market. They meet at a conference and are interested to discover that, whereas Holly keeps prices low in order to keep her business operating at full capacity, Head supplies goods only at 'normal prices for the industry'. They decide to compare their results and extract the following information from recently published accounts:

	Holly £	Head £
Net profit before interest	50,000	100,000
Sales	600,000	750,000
Average gross assets	200,000	500,000

Required:
Calculate and comment on the 'primary' ratio and 'secondary' ratios of Holly and Head.

Solution

Applying the formula:

		Total asset turnover	X	Net profit percentage	=	Rate of Return on gross assets
Holly	=	$\dfrac{600,000}{200,000}$	X	$\dfrac{50,000}{600,000}$ x 100	=	$\dfrac{50,000}{200,000}$ x 100
		3	X	8.3%	=	25%
Head	=	$\dfrac{750,000}{500,000}$	X	$\dfrac{100,000}{750,000}$ x 100	=	$\dfrac{100,000}{500,000}$ x 100
		1.5	X	13.3%	=	20%

The above calculations show that Holly achieves the greater asset utilization (£3 of sales per £1 invested as compared with the £1.50 achieved by Head) but her business' net profit percentage is lower (8.3% compared with Head's 13.3%). Overall Holly's policies seem to be more successful, i.e. the greater asset utilization more than compensates for the lower margins, and she achieves a rate of return on gross assets of 25%.

The formula may also be used to shed further light on the performance of Ludlow Ltd by extracting, from sections 9.4.6, 9.5.2 and 9.5.3, the following ratios previously calculated:

	SECONDARY RATIOS			PRIMARY RATIO
	Asset utilization		Profit margin	Rate of return on gross assets
19X0	2.14	X	5.75%	= 12.3%
19X1	1.85	X	6.2%	= 11.5%

The asset utilization is much lower in 19X1, and the explanation for this is that much of the money raised through issuing an £800,000 debenture has been absorbed by increasing the period of credit allowed to customers by nearly two weeks. The directors have, however, succeeded in increasing the net profit percentage. Sales have been increased and, although price cuts have reduced the gross margin by one point to 21%, overhead expenses have been kept under tight control and a small reduction in the total cost per unit has been achieved. The higher net profit margin does not sufficiently compensate for the lower asset utilization, however, and the primary ratio suffers a significant decline.

9.5.5 Rate of Return on Shareholders' Equity
The factor that motivates shareholders to invest in a company is the expectation of an

adequate rate of return on their funds and, periodically, they will want to assess the rate of return earned in order to decide whether to continue with their investment. There are various ways of measuring the return earned including the earnings yield and dividend yield which are examined in Chapter 8. Another useful measure is the rate of return expressed as a percentage of the book value of shareholders' equity:

$$\text{Rate of return on shareholders' equity} = \frac{\text{Earnings* for equity shareholders}}{\text{Average shareholders' equity}} \times 100$$

*The ratio may be computed on either a pre- or post-tax basis but, whichever basis is used, any preference dividends payable must be deducted since they reduce profits available for ordinary shareholders. An argument for using the pre-tax basis is that the resulting ratio can be related more meaningfully to the other calculations demonstrated in this chapter. On the other hand corporation tax must be deducted to arrive at the balance available for distribution to shareholders and the post-tax basis implies full recognition of this fact.

Calculations for Ludlow Ltd are:

Pre-tax

$$19X0 \quad \frac{345,000}{\frac{1}{2}(2,155,000 + 2,250,000)} \times 100 = 15.7\%$$

$$19X1 \quad \frac{355,000}{\frac{1}{2}(2,250,000 + 2,350,000)} \times 100 = 15.4\%$$

Post-tax

$$19X0 \quad \frac{172,500}{\frac{1}{2}(2,155,000 + 2,250,000)} \times 100 = 7.8\%$$

$$19X1 \quad \frac{177,500}{\frac{1}{2}(2,250,0W + 2,350,000)} \times 100 = 7.7\%$$

There has been a modest decline in the return earned for shareholders, but rather less than might have been expected in view of the fairly sharp decline in the primary ratio from 12.3% to 11.5% (see section 9.5.3). The reason for this difference is that the return earned for shareholders is dependent on three key factors:

- profit margins;

- asset utilization;

- capital structure.

We saw in 9.5.4 that the rate of return on gross assets is a function of profit margins and asset utilization, but it takes no account of the company's capital structure (this can be confirmed by observing the fact that the numerator comprises net profit before deducting any interest charges). The significance for the equity shareholders of financing a part of a company's activities with loan capital is examined in section 9.7.

9.6 EARNINGS PER SHARE

The basic purpose of the earnings per share (EPS) calculation is to discover the amount of profit accruing to the holder of one share in a company. EPS is widely used due to:

- The belief that earnings are an important determinant of share price. They set an upper limit for dividends and, by comparing earnings with dividends, a measure of likely future growth from retained earnings can be obtained;

- The popularity of the Price/Earnings Ratio as an indicator of financial performance and also a method of business valuation (see Chapter 8); and

- The determination of financial commentators to reduce the complexities of corporate activity to a single figure.

9.6.1 Definition of Earnings per Share

The nature, purpose and calculation of EPS is dealt with in FRS 14 entitled 'Earnings per share'. EPS may be defined as the earnings, in pence, attributable to each equity share, and is calculated using the formula:

$$EPS = \frac{\text{Earnings}}{\text{Number of equity shares in issue}}$$

Where:

Earnings is the profit (or in the case of a group the consolidated profit) of the period after tax, minority interests and extraordinary items and after deducing preference dividends and other appropriations in respect of preference shares

Shares: are the number of equity shares in issue and ranking for dividend in respect of the period

Further points to note:

- FRS 14 applies only to listed companies

- When a loss is suffered, the EPS is a negative figure

- The importance attached to EPS is reflected by the requirement for the current year's figure, together with the comparative for the previous year, to be displayed on the face of the profit and loss account. That is, it cannot be 'tucked away' in the notes to the accounts

9.6.2 Earnings per Share and FRS 3

Extraordinary items are defined by FRS 3 (Reporting Financial Performance – see Chapter 3) as 'extremely rare as they relate to highly abnormal events or transactions that fall outside the ordinary activities of a reporting entity and which are not expected to recur' (para 48). We have seen in Chapter 3 that, if an extraordinary items occurs, it must be reported 'below the line' in order to comply with FRS 3. They must nevertheless be taken into account in arriving at the earnings figure for the purpose of the EPS calculation. FRS 3 was designed to stamp out the use of extraordinary items because of the tendency of management to argue, successfully, that major losses were extraordinary items and should therefore be reported below the line in order to avoid the full glare of publicity. In view of their extreme rarity – they have been likened to the likelihood of walking along the street and meeting 'a man from Mars' – no examples of extraordinary items are offered by FRS 3. The standard setters have proved successful in their desire to abolish extraordinary items which are, as a result, instead shown in the accounts as 'exceptional'. Exceptional items are:

> *Material items which derive from events or transactions that fall within the ordinary activities of the reporting entity and which individually or, if of a similar type, in aggregate, need to be disclosed by virtue of their size or incidence if the financial statements are to give a true and fair view.* (FRS 3, para. 5)

The EPS may fluctuate from year to year due to the impact of such exceptional items. Therefore, companies are allowed, in addition, to present alternative measures of EPS. The alternative measure, which is quite likely to be based on profit before exceptional items (particularly when the exceptional item is a loss!), must be given prominence no greater than that of the compulsory figure and must be accompanied by a reconciliation and explanation of the adjustments.

9.6.3 Calculation of Earnings per Share

We start with the basic calculation where no shares have been issued during the year.

Example 9.7

The following information is provided for A plc in respect of 20X1:

	£000	£000
Profit before taxation		300
Taxation (30%)		90
		210
Dividends:		
Ordinary shares	100	
Preference shares	35	
		135
Retained profit		75

The company has in issue £1,000,000 ordinary shares of 50p each and £500,000 7% preference shares.

Required:
Calculate the EPS for 20X1

Solution

$$EPS = \frac{(£210,000 - £35,000) \times 100}{£1,000,000 \times 2} = 8.75p$$

9.6.4 Share Issues During the Year

We now introduce the complication of a share issue being made during the current year. There are three possibilities: issue at full market price; bonus issue during the year; and rights issue during the year.

Issue at full market price

This increases the number of shares in issue and the earnings capacity of the company. The earnings for the period must therefore be spread over the increased number of shares in issue. However, where the issue takes place part of the way through the year, it is necessary to calculate the average number of shares in issue during the year, on a weighted time basis, because the extra shares increase earnings only after they have been issued.

Example 9.8

A plc (see Example 9.7) issues a further 600,000 ordinary shares on 1 May 20X2. Profits after tax for 20X2 are £280,000.

Required:
Calculate the EPS for 20X2

Solution

$$EPS = \frac{(£280,000 - £35,000) \times 100}{(£1,000,000 \times 2) + (600,000 \times 2/3)} = 10.2p$$

Bonus issue

We have seen earlier (Chapter 7) that a bonus issue produces no cash and so will not increase the available resources nor affect earnings capacity. The effect of the issue, therefore, is to spread the earnings over a greater number of shares. Because the bonus issue does not increase earnings capacity, there is no need to calculate a weighted average for the shares in issue during the year. However, it is necessary to restate the comparative EPS figure, for the previous year, in order to place it on a 'like' basis.

Example 9.9

The results of A Ltd for 20X1 are as in Example 9.7. During 20X2, A Ltd makes a bonus issue of one additional ordinary share for every two shares presently held. Profits after tax for 20X2 are £250,000.

Required:
(a) Calculate the EPS for 20X2

(b) Calculate the revised EPS for 20X1

Solution

(a) Calculation for 20X2:

$$EPS = \frac{(£250,000 - £35,000) \times 100}{(£1,000,000 \times 2) \times 3/2} = 7.2p$$

(b) Revised calculation for 20X1: EPS = 8.75 x 2 ÷ 3 = 5.8p

Rights issue

This occurs when new shares are issued to existing shareholders, usually at below the existing market price. This increases the number of shares in issue, but does not increase the earning capacity of the company proportionally. After a rights issue, the market price should therefore fall. The dilution in the value of pre-rights issue share capital, in such circumstances, can be demonstrated as follows:

	£
4 shares in circulation before rights issue at a market price of £2 each:	8.00
Rights issue of, say, 1 for 2 at an artificially low price of 50p each for illustrative purposes:	1.00
6 shares then in issue will have theoretical post-rights issue worth of:	9.00
Theoretical ex-rights price will be £9 ÷ 6 shares	1.50

Diluted post-rights equivalent of pre-rights issue shares:
4 shares worth £2 each (pre-issue) = 4 x (£2 ÷ £1.5) = 5.3 shares (post-issue)

Proof:	£
4 shares at pre-issue market price of £2:	8.00
5.3 shares at theoretical ex-rights price of £1.5:	8.00

The above adjustments are incorporated in the calculation of EPS in the following manner:

1. Calculate total value of equity before rights issue: market price x number of shares

2. Calculate proceeds of new issue

3. Calculate theoretical price after issue:

$$\frac{1 + 2}{\text{Number of shares after rights issue}}$$

4. Calculate the post-issue equivalent of the number of shares outstanding pre-issue:

$$\text{Number of shares } x \ \frac{\text{Actual pre-issue price}}{\text{Theoretical post-issue price}}$$

5. Calculate the number of shares in issue during the year on the weighted average basis

6. Compute EPS

7. Obtain corresponding comparative figure for previous year:

$$\text{Last year's EPS} \ \times \ \frac{\text{Theoretical post issue price}}{\text{Actual pre-issue price}}$$

Example 9.10

The following information is provided for B Ltd.

- B plc has earnings of £16,640 for 20X4

- There were 120,000 ordinary shares in issue at the start of the year

- 40,000 further shares were issued on 31 August 20X4 at £1.50 each

- The market price of each share immediately before the rights issue was £2

Required:
Calculate the EPS for 20X4

Solution

Procedure to calculate EPS
1. Calculate total value of equity before issue: market price x number of shares

   £2 x 120,000 = £240,000

2. Calculate proceeds of new issue

   £1.50 x 40,000 = £60,000

3. Calculate theoretical price after issue:

   $$\frac{£240,000 + £60,000}{120,000 + 40,000} = £1.875$$

4. Calculate the post-issue equivalent of the number of shares outstanding pre-issue:

   $$120,000 \ \times \ \frac{2}{1.875} = 128,000$$

5. Calculate the number of shares in issue during the year on the weighted average basis

   (128,000 x 2/3) + (160,000 x 1/3) = 138,667

6. Compute EPS

   $$\frac{16,640 \times 100}{138,667} = 12p$$

9.6.5 Possible Future Changes in Share Capital

A company may grant someone (e.g. a director) the right to take up ordinary shares at some future date at a predetermined price. Quite obviously this option will be exercised only if the offer price is lower than the prevailing market price. In such circumstances, however, the existing shareholders will suffer a dilution in the value of their investment which can be illustrated in the following manner.

Assume that a company has only one share in issue which has a market price of £1,000 representing the value of the company. If someone has an option to purchase one further share at £600, and this option is exercised, the total value of the business now becomes £1,600 (£1,000 + £600), and the value of each share becomes £1,600 divided by two, i.e. £800.

FRS14 therefore requires the potential effect of any such option to be calculated and reported in the accounts where it would result in a material dilution (greater than 5%) in the EPS. For the purpose of computing the potential effect, it is assumed that the option is exercised on the first day of the accounting period under review.

A second example of a share option concerns the right to convert either loan stock or preference shares into equity. In these cases, interest or preference share dividend will not be payable once the relevant securities are converted. Therefore, when calculating EPS, such interest (net of any tax effect) or preference dividend must be added back to reported earnings for the year.

The calculation of fully diluted earnings per share is illustrated in Example 9.11 and Example 9.12.

Example 9.11

The following information is provided for C Ltd.

- 400 ordinary shares in issue

- £100 10% loan stock in issue, convertible into 80 ordinary shares any time on or after 1 January 20X7

- Profit before interest for 20X5, £110.

Ignore taxation

Required:
Calculate the basic and fully diluted EPS for 20X5

Solution

$$\text{Basic EPS} \quad \frac{110\text{-}10 \text{ [interest]}}{400} \text{ x } 100 \quad = 25\text{p}$$

$$\text{Fully diluted EPS} \quad \frac{110 \text{ x } 100}{400 + 80} \quad = 22.9\text{p}$$

Example 9.12

Assume the same facts as Example 9.7. In addition, the company has £200,000 of 6% convertible loan stock, convertible on 1 January 20X4 at the rate of 10 shares for every £4 of loan stock.

Required:
Calculate the fully diluted EPS for 20X1

Solution

$$\text{Fully diluted EPS} = \frac{(£175,000 + £12,000^1 - £3,600^2) \text{ x } 100}{2,000,000 + (200,000 \text{ x } 10/4)} = 7.3\text{p}$$

[1] Interest saved
[2] Additional tax at 30%

The dilution is >5% and must be disclosed in each case. Taking Example 9.12 for illustration purposes, the dilution from 8.75p to 7.3p is 16.6%.

This significant dilution occurs because the holder of £1 of debenture stock currently gets a return of 12p which is far less than the return accruing to an equivalent (post conversion) holding of 2.5 shares presently attracting a total return of 21.9p (8.75p x 2.5).

9.7 GEARING

Capital is derived from two sources: shares and loans. It is quite likely for shares to be issued only when the company is formed, but loans are invariably raised at some later date. There are numerous reasons for issuing loan capital. For instance, the owners might want to increase their investment but avoid the risk which attaches to share capital, and they can do this by making a secured loan. Alternatively, management might require additional finance which the shareholders are unwilling to supply, and so a loan is raised instead. In either case, the effect is to introduce an element of gearing or leverage into the capital structure of the company. There are numerous ways of measuring gearing, but the debt:equity ratio is perhaps most commonly used. For the purpose of calculating this ratio, debt may be calculated in either of two ways:

(a) Debt defined as long-term loans.

$$\text{Debt:equity ratio} \quad \frac{\text{Long-term loans*}}{\text{Shareholders' equity}} \times 100$$

*Includes any preference shares outstanding.

(b) Debt defined as total borrowings.

The banker, when assessing risk, wants to examine total borrowing in relation to the equity base. For this reason it is often found useful to extend the definition of debt for the purpose of calculating the debt:equity ratio:

$$\text{Total debt:equity ratio} = \frac{\text{Total financial debt*}}{\text{Shareholders' equity}} \times 100$$

*Includes loans from directors and bank overdrafts which, although technically for the short-term, are a permanent source of financing for many businesses.

The use of debt capital has direct implications for the profit accruing to the ordinary shareholders, and expansion is often financed in this manner with the objective of increasing, or 'gearing up', the shareholders' rate of return. This objective is achieved, however, only if the rate earned on the additional funds raised exceeds that payable to the providers of the loan.

Example 9.13

The directors of Conway Lid are planning to undertake a new project which calls for a total investment of £1m in fixed assets and working capital. The directors plan to finance the investment with a long-term loan bearing interest at 12% per annum, and the financial controller forecasts an annual profit, before finance charges, of £150,000 from the new project.

Required:
Calculate the 'surplus' profit, if any, expected to accrue to shareholders from the new project. Ignore tax.

Solution

	£
Additional profit contributed by new project	150,000
Less: Interest charge, 12% of £1m	120,000
Surplus	30,000

The existing shareholders benefit from the project, to the extent of £30,000, because the new venture yields a return of 15% whereas providers of the required finance have contracted for interest at the lower rate of 12%. Profit may, of course, not come up to expectations, and if it is less than £120,000 the introduction of gearing will be detrimental to the ordinary shareholders whose rate of return will suffer.

Returning to the case of Ludlow Ltd, calculations of the debt/equity ratio are as follows:

19X0 Zero gearing (no loans)

$$19X1 \quad \frac{800,000}{2,350,000} \times 100 = 34\%$$

A significant element of gearing was introduced in 19X1 by the issue of an £800,000 debenture to finance an expansion of operations. The policy was not entirely successful and the rate of return on total assets declined from 12.3% to 11.5%. The shareholders' return suffered only a modest decline, however (see section 9.5.5) and this suggests that, assuming 19X0's results would otherwise have been repeated, the additional activity produced a return only marginally below the 10% interest payable on the debenture.

The shareholders of a highly-geared company reap disproportionate benefits when earnings before interest and tax increase. This is because interest payable on a large proportion of total finance remains unchanged. The converse is also true, and a highly-geared company is likely to find itself in severe financial difficulties if it suffers a succession of trading losses. It is not possible to specify an optimal level of gearing for companies but, as a general rule, gearing should be low in those industries where demand is volatile and profits are subject to fluctuation. The effect of profit fluctuations on the rates of return earned by companies with different levels of gearing is demonstrated in Example 9.14.

Example 9.14

Ponty Ltd and Pop Ltd are established companies engaged in similar lines of business. Trading conditions change significantly from year to year, and an analysis of past results achieved by companies in the same line of business as Ponty and Pop shows that operating profit, before deducting interest charges, can fluctuate by up to 50% above or below the following estimated results for the forthcoming year:

	Ponty £000	Pop £000
Ordinary share capital (£1 shares) at 1 June 20X4	1,500	3,200
Revaluation surplus at 1 June 20X4	500	1,000
Capital redemption reserve at 1 June 20X4	–	800
14% debentures at 1 June 20X4	4,000	1,000
Operating profit before interest 20X4/5	840	840

It is the policy of each company to pay out its entire profits in the form of dividends.

Required:
(a) For each company, calculations of the estimated:

    (i)   rate of return on shareholders' equity;

    (ii) gearing (debt:equity) ratio.

(b) A discussion of the relative merits of the capital structures of each of the two companies from the shareholders' point of view. The discussion should include calculations of maximum possible variations in the return on shareholders' equity.

Note:
Ignore taxation.

Solution

(a)

	Ponty £000	Pop £000
Operating profit	840	840
Interest charge	560	140
Net profit	280	700
Equity	2,000	5,000
ROCE	14%	14%
Debt:equity (4,000:2,000)	2:1	
(1,000:5,000)		1:5

(b)

	Ponty		Pop	
	+50% £000	−50% £000	+50% £000	−50% £000
Operating profit	1,260	420	1,260	420
Interest	560	560	140	140
	700	(140)	1,120	280

Ordinary share capital	1,500		3,200	
Revaluation surplus	500		1,000	
Capital redemption reserve	–		800	
Equity	2,000	2,000	5,000	5,000
ROCE	35%	(7%)	22.4%	5.6%

The capital structure of Ponty Ltd is highly geared, which means that there is a high ratio of debt to equity finance.

The main advantage of gearing is that the return to shareholders will be 'geared up' when there is a rise in profits. This is because all additional profits accrue to the equity shareholders.

This can be seen above with an increase in profits of 50% causing the return on capital employed to increase by 1½ times to 35%.

Conversely, when profits decline the return on equity falls quickly due to the fact that the fixed interest charges, in the case of Ponty £560,000, must still be paid.

A fall in operating profit of 50% results in a figure for operating profit that is insufficient to cover interest charges and there is a reduction in shareholders' equity to the tune of £140,000.

The capital structure of Pop, by way of contrast, is low geared with a debt:equity ratio of 1:5.

A 50% rise in profits results in an increase in the return on capital employed but the rise is more modest to 22.4%.

Conversely, a fall in profits is not so detrimental to the equity shareholders who continue to receive a return of 5.6% on their investment.

A further drawback of a high level of gearing is that the company may face acute financial embarrassment if there is a significant fall in profits. Whereas dividends can be reduced when profits are low, if necessary to zero, interest charges are a legal obligation which must be paid irrespective of profit levels.

9.8 LIMITATIONS OF ACCOUNTING RATIOS

The various calculations illustrated in this chapter suffer from a number of limitations which should be borne in mind by anyone attempting to interpret their significance. The main limitations are:

- Accounting ratios can be used to assess whether performance is satisfactory, by means of inter-firm comparison, and also whether results have improved, worsened or remained stable, by comparing this year's results with those achieved last year. The ratios do not, however, provide explanations for observed changes, and the external users' ability to obtain further information varies considerably. The shareholder may ask questions at the annual general meeting, while the lending banker may demand extra information when an advance is requested, but only management has direct access to the information needed to provide the right answer.

- A deterioration in an accounting ratio cannot necessarily be interpreted as poor management. For example, a decline in the rate of stock turnover initially appears undesirable, but further investigation might reveal the accumulation of scarce raw materials which enable the plant to continue working when competitors are forced to suspend production.

- Too much significance should not be attached to individual ratios, e.g. a rate of return on gross assets of 30% might indicate that all is well, but this conclusion might be unjustified if further analysis revealed a liquidity ratio of 0.4:0.

- Changes in many ratios are closely associated with one another and produce similar conclusions, e.g. the ratio of total debt to total assets (not illustrated in this chapter) and the debt:equity ratio. Care should therefore be taken when selecting ratios to be used as the basis for the analysis; a representative selection should be made and duplication avoided.

- Company financial statements are usually based on historical cost and, therefore, accounting ratios based on these figures would be expected to improve, irrespective of efficiency, during a period of rising prices, e.g. a total asset turnover of £3 per £1 invested might be computed from historical cost accounts, whereas a figure of £1.80 per £1 invested might be obtained if assets were restated at current values.

- Differences in accounting policies may detract from the value of inter-firm comparisons, e.g. the valuation of stock on the LIFO basis rather than the FIFO basis would probably produce a much lower working capital ratio.

- Financial statements and accounting ratios can be distorted as the result of 'one off' large transactions such as the credit purchase of plant, which will significantly increase current liabilities until payment is made, or a profit on the sale of a fixed asset. Analysts should similarly be on their guard for evidence of 'window dressing', perhaps designed to conceal a deteriorating financial position.

- Where a company undertakes a mix of activities, it is important to calculate separate ratios for each section wherever possible.

- Particular care must be taken when interpreting accounting ratios calculated for a seasonal business. Where sales are high at a particular time during the year, e.g. at Christmas, stock might be expected to increase and cash to decline in the months leading up to the busy period. In these circumstances, deteriorations in both the liquidity ratio and the rate of stock turnover are not necessarily causes for concern.

- Consideration must be given to variations in commercial trading patterns when assessing the significance of accounting ratios computed for particular companies. For example, a retail chain of supermarkets would be expected to have a much lower liquidity ratio and a much higher rate of stock turnover than a constructional engineering firm. In this context, accepted 'norms' such as a working capital ratio of 2:1 must be used with care.

9.9 FURTHER READING

Alexander, D. and Britton, A. (1999) *Financial Reporting*, fifth edition, London: International Thomson Business Press, pp. 569-83 and Chapter 28.

Bloor, G. (1999) 'Understanding earnings per share', *ACCA Students' Newsletter*, August, pp. 58-60.

Davies, Mike, Ron Paterson and Allister Wilson (1999), *Generally Accepted Accounting Practice in the United Kingdom*, sixth edition, Croydon: Butterworth Tolley, Chapter 23.

Elliott, B. and Elliott, J. (2000) *Financial Accounting and Reporting*, fifth edition, Hemel Hempstead: Prentice Hall, Chapters 23 and 25.

Lewis, Richard and David Pendrill (2000), *Advanced Financial Accounting*, sixth edition, Pitman, Chapters 13 and 14.

9.10 QUESTIONS

Question 9.1

The following financial information is provided in respect of Elton Lid, a trading company.

Year to 31 December	1998	1999
	£000	£000
Sales	24,000	30,000
Purchases	18,000	24,500

Balances at 31 December	1998	1999
	£000	£000
Trade debtors	4,667	6,250
Trade creditors	3,000	4,900
Stocks	4,500	6,500
Bank balance (overdraft)	600	(900)

The stocks of Elton Ltd at 1 January 1998 amounted to £4,500,000

Required:
(a) The following calculations for 1998 and 1999:

    (i)   Gross profit percentage

    (ii) Cash operating cycle in days

    (iii) Current (working capital) ratio   *[8 marks]*

(b) A critical assessment of financial development at Elton Ltd based on the above information
    provided and your calculations under (a).   *[12 marks]*

Notes:
Assume a 360-day year for the purpose of your calculations and that transactions accrue at an even rate
during the year.

Calculations to the nearest day or, in the case of ratios and percentages, one decimal point.

[Total – 20 marks]

Question 9.2

Brooksbank plc and Beltz plc trade in the same industry but in different geographical locations. The following data is taken from the 1997 annual accounts:

	Brooksbank £m	Beltz £m
Turnover	200	300
Total operating expenses	180	275
Average total assets during 1997	150	125

Required:
(a) Calculate the following ratios for each company, and demonstrate the numerical relationship between them:

    (i)   the rate of return on the average total assets for each company;

    (ii) the net profit percentage; and

    (iii) the ratio of turnover to average total assets.   *[8 marks]*

(b) Comment, insofar as the information permits, on the relative performance of the two companies.   *[8 marks]*

(c) Indicate what additional information you would require to decide which company is the better proposition from the viewpoint of:

    (i)   potential shareholders; and

    (ii) potential loan creditors.   *[4 marks]*

Note:
Ignore taxation

       [Total – 20 marks]

Question 9.3

The following information is provided for Brownlee plc:

Profit and Loss Account Extracts, 20X4

	£000
Profit before taxation	5,600
Corporation tax	1,680
	3,920
Dividends: Ordinary shares	2,000
Preference shares	800
Retained profit for the year	1,120

Balance Sheet Extracts at 31 December 20X4

	£000
Issued share capital (£1 shares)	5,000
Retained profit	26,100
	31,100
8% Preference shares	10,000
Shareholders' funds	41,100

Required:

(a)   Define 'earnings per share' and explain the purpose of this calculation.   [3]

(b)   Calculate the earnings per share of Brownlee plc for 20X4 based on the above information. [4]

(c)   (i)   Explain the nature and purpose of a bonus (capitalization) issue of ordinary shares.   [4]

     (ii)   Produce revised balance sheet extracts as at 31 December 20X4 for Brownlee plc, assuming that a bonus issue of five fully paid ordinary shares was made at that date for every ordinary share previously held.   [2]

(d)   Recalculate the earnings per share of Brownlee plc for 20X4, assuming that the bonus issue referred to under (c) had been made. Indicate the adjustment required to the corresponding figure for 20X4 which was reported in the previous year's accounts at 54p per share, and explain the reason for the adjustment.   [7]

[Total – 20]

Question 9.4

The following information is provided relating to the affairs of two companies engaged in similar trading activities:

	Ouse plc	Tyne plc
	£m	£m
Ordinary share capital	400	250
14% debentures	100	250

Each company earned an operating profit before finance charges of £44 million in 1995 and £88 million in 1996.

You may assume that corporation tax is charged at 30% on the operating profits after finance charges have been deducted.

Ouse and Tyne each pays out its entire after-tax profits as dividends.

Required:

(a)   Summary profit and loss accounts, dealing with the results of each of the two companies' activities during 1995 and 1996, so far as the information given above permits.   *[8 marks]*

(b)   Calculations for each company, for each year, of:
    (i)   return on long-term capital employed; and

    (ii)   post-tax return on shareholders' equity.   *[4 marks]*

(c)   An examination of the relative performance of Ouse and Tyne from the viewpoint of their shareholders during each of the years 1995 and 1996, based on your calculations under (a) and (b). *[8 marks]*

[Total – 20 marks]

Question 9.5

Alban and Lamb are partners in a firm called Alban Lamb & Co which acts as agents for the sale of commercial premises and domestic dwellings and also manages properties on behalf of clients. Alban deals entirely with the sale of commercial and domestic dwellings and spends time equally on these two activities, while Lamb, who works part time, is client property manager. The partners share profits equally after allowing for salaries which appear in the revenue account below.

The following information is provided for the year to 30 June 20X1 together with some comparative figures for the previous financial year.

	20X1 £	20X0 £
Revenue		
Commissions received: commercial properties	36,000	
domestic properties	63,000	
managed properties	29,500	
	128,500	123,000
Expenditure		
Advertising: commercial properties	14,200	
domestic properties	15,500	
Rent collection costs	4,100	
Cleaning managed properties	3,700	
Salary of: Alban	24,000	
Lamb	10,800	
Other salaries	22,500	
Finance charges (20X0, £2,500)	3,200	
General administration costs	33,000	
	131,000	102,400
Surplus (deficit)	(2,500)	20,600

BALANCE SHEET AS AT 30 JUNE

	20X1 £	20X0 £
Assets		
Freehold premises	85,000	20,000
Furniture and equipment	9,400	5,100
Debtors	11,100	6,000
Bank balance	–	4,200
	105,500	35,300
Financed by:		
Capital: Alban	36,450	5,200
Lamb	34,250	3,000
Trade creditors	9,300	5,900
Value added tax (VAT) outstanding	3,400	1,200
Bank overdraft	2,100	–
Loan from financial institution	20,000	20,000
	105,500	35,300

It is discovered that the freehold premises, previously stated at cost, were revalued during the year to

30 June 20X1 and that the figure for trade creditors, at 30 June 20X1, includes £2,500 in respect of a recently acquired photocopier. It is estimated that the staff, other than Alban and Lamb, spend an equal amount of time on each of the three areas of activity.

Alban and Lamb have approached your bank and requested an increase in the firm's overdraft limit from £7,500 to £15,000 for a six month period. They point out that the overdraft shown in the balance sheet is very modest when compared with total balance sheet assets of £105,500 including a freehold property valued at £85,000.

Required:
(a) A report for the bank on the financial progress and position of the firm in the light of the request for an increased overdraft facility. The report should be based on the accounting ratios listed below, an analysed revenue account showing the results of each activity, and any other calculations you consider relevant.

Accounting ratios:

(i) Net profit percentage (margin).

(ii) Interest cover.

(iii) Rate of return on partners' capital investment.

(iv) Liquidity (quick) ratio.

(v) Gearing ratio.   [25]

(b) Identify FIVE limitations of ratio analysis. You should illustrate the limitations, where possible, by reference to the information you have given in answer to (a) above.   [5]

Note:
A recommendation on whether to grant the overdraft is NOT required.

[Total marks – 30]

Question 9.6

Sikka plc and Willmott plc are engaged in a similar range of business activities in different geographical areas, with Sikka approximately twice the size of Willmott by most financial and physical measures relating to their business operations. Their draft accounts for the year ended 31 March 2000 contain the following information.

Profit and Loss Accounts for the Year ending 31 March 2000

	Sikka Note	Willmott £000	£000
Turnover		50,100	25,000
Cost of goods sold	1	−23,000	−11,110
Depreciation of plant	2	−1,050	−368
Administration, selling and distribution expenses	3	−23,000	−11,530
Development expenditure	4	−500	−120
Operating profit		2,550	1,872
Actuarial surplus	5	−	630
Interest charge	6	−320	−
Net Profit		2,230	2,502
Retained profit at 1 April 1999		6,770	4,068
Retained profit at 31 March 2000		9,000	6,570

Balance Sheets at 31 March 2000

	Note	Sikka £000	Willmott £000
Tangible fixed assets			
Freehold property at cost or valuation	7	9,500	800
Property in course of construction	6	2,000	1,150
Plant at cost	2	5,000	2,500
Less: Accumulated depreciation	2	2,550	736
		2,450	1,764
		13,950	3,714
Development expenditure	4	−	600
Stock	1	7,200	4,150
Debtors, net of bad debt provision	3	3,800	2,450
Pension prepayment		−	630
Other current assets/liabilities		50	26
		25,000	11,570
Share capital and reserves			
Ordinary share capital (£1 ordinary shares)		10,000	5,000
Revaluation reserve		6,000	−
Retained profit		9,000	6,570
		25,000	11,570

Notes:
The following further information is provided.

1   Sikka values its stocks using the weighted average cost basis whereas Willmott uses first in, first out. The stock valuations of Willmott on each basis are as follows:

	FIFO	*WAC*
	£000	*£000*
At 1 April 1999	2,200	2,000
At 31 March 2000	4,150	3,600

2   Each company possesses plant with an estimated useful life of six years. Their expected residual values at the end of their useful life are: Sikka, £584,000; Willmott, £292,000. For each company, the plant is, on average, one-third of the way through its estimated useful life at 31 March 2000. Willmott employs straight-line depreciation and Sikka the reducing-balance basis applying a rate of 30%.

3   Both companies have a similar history of bad debts. Sikka has made a general provision for bad debts for the year of 5% and Willmott a general provision of 2%. The provisions are included in administration, selling, and distribution expenses.

4   Sikka writes off all development expenditure as soon as it is incurred whereas Willmott amortizes such expenditure over its estimated period of benefit to the company. The movement on Willmott's development expenditure account during the year to 31 March 2000 was as follows:

	£000
Balance at 1 April 1999	470
Incurred during the year	250
Written off	−120
Balance at 31 March 2000	600

5   Both companies operate defined benefit pension schemes which were the subject of an actuarial revaluation on 31 March 2000. Sikka showed a surplus of £1,220,000 and Willmott a surplus of £630,000. Sikka has decided to utilize the surplus by taking a pension holiday over the forthcoming three years; Willmott has chosen to credit the entire surplus to the profit and loss account for the current year.

6   Each company began to construct new premises financed by borrowing during the current year. Sikka has charged the interest relating to the borrowing to the profit and loss account; Willmott includes the interest charge of £150,000 as part of the cost of construction.

7   Sikka revalued its freehold property on 31 March 2000. The freehold property of Willmott continues to be shown at cost (£1,000,000) less accumulated depreciation (£200,000). The freehold property of Willmott is estimated to have been worth £3,800,000 on 31 March 2000.

Required:
(a)   Redraft the above accounts of Willmott, as necessary, in order to adopt the same accounting policies as those employed by Sikka to account for each of the items 1-7 above.   *[17 marks]*

(b) Calculate the following ratios and percentages for each company on the basis of the accounts supplied in the question and those prepared in order to comply with requirement (a).

- Rate of return on shareholders' equity

- Net asset turnover

- Net profit percentage   *[3 marks]*

(c) Discuss fully the implications of the calculations made under (a) and (b).   *[10 marks]*

(d) Consider the extent to which uniformity in accounting policies between companies is achievable or desirable, particularly in relation to the issue of creative accounting.

You should include in your discussion the identification of any two financial reporting standards issued in the last three years which might be expected to bring about a significant improvement in the comparability of accounting information between companies.   *[10 marks]*

Notes:
1. Ignore taxation.

2. Calculations to the nearest £000.

3. Assume all figures to be material.   *[Total – 40 marks]*

10

INTERPRETATION OF ACCOUNTS: CASH FLOW

10.1 INTRODUCTION

The balance sheet and profit and loss account are important accounting statements, but they do not contain a sufficiently wide range of information to enable users to make a full assessment of a company's performance. More specifically, an important gap is left because the profit and loss account provides financial information relating to only a limited range of financial transactions entered into during an accounting period, namely those that impinge on the calculation of reported profits, i.e. revenues and expenditures. Other transactions involving flows of cash, such as an issue of shares or debentures or the purchase of a fixed asset, are not reported in the profit and loss account since these are capital transactions as opposed to revenue transactions. The view gradually developed that capital inflows and outflows, which often involve large amounts of money, should be reported to investors and the cash flow statement was devised to provide this information. FRS 1, entitled 'Cash Flow Statements', makes publication a requirement. The statement must contain full details of the cash inflows and outflows that have taken place during an accounting period, and it is thought that the information it contains, when used in conjunction with other details in the corporate report, will help bankers and other users when they assess:

- An enterprise's ability to generate positive future net cash flows.

- Whether an enterprise is likely to be able to meet its financial obligations, such as the payment of dividends and the need to repay external funding.

- The effect on the enterprise's financial position of investments undertaken during the accounting period.

- The reasons for differences between profits and cash flows arising from normal operating activity.

- The value of a business because the statement provides a useful input for business valuation models based on estimates of likely future cash flows.

Before we examine how the cash flow statement can be used in this way, it is useful to examine the sources of cash available to a business and the various ways in which it may be spent.

10.2 SOURCES OF CASH
The cash available to a company is conveniently classified into the following two basic sources: internal and external.

10.2.1 Internal
This is obtained by a company either reducing its investment in business assets or generating finance from business operations.

1. Reducing the investment in business assets
A company may be able to raise cash by reducing the level of stocks or debtors where these are excessive in relation to business needs. Alternatively, a company may be in possession of fixed assets or investments, surplus to operating requirements, which can be sold. Where outright sale is not feasible, there are other schemes which may be used to release cash tied up in business assets. In this context, 'sale and leaseback' has become a fairly popular device in recent decades. The procedure followed is for the company to sell the freehold property which it occupies, perhaps to an insurance company, and then to lease the property back for an agreed number of years. The company benefits from a substantial injection of much needed cash, but drawbacks include the obligation to pay an annual rental, the loss of an asset which might have been expected to appreciate in value (and which could have been used as security for

further loans), and perhaps also the need to move out and find new accommodation when the lease expires.

'Debt factoring' is another scheme for releasing cash tied up in business assets. It can take a number of different forms: one version is for the company to invoice the customer in the usual way, while the 'factor' maintains accounts for each debtor and takes responsibility for collecting the cash. The factor then makes guaranteed payments to the company at specific intervals after the goods have been invoiced. Depending on the terms of the agreement, the company may obtain cash more quickly than if it had to wait for the customer to pay. The company also benefits from a more predictable cash flow, while the cost of operating a debt-collecting department is avoided. The charges made by the factor are substantial, however, and must be compared with the cost of alternative sources of finance.

2. Finance generated from business operations

This is made up of the following main items:

Profit adjusted for changes in stock, debtors and creditors	XXX
Add: Depreciation	XXX
Finance generated from operations	XXX

The reason for including depreciation as part of the finance generated from operations requires further comment. During the course of trading activity a company generates revenue, principally in the form of sales proceeds, and incurs expenditure comprising a wide range of different outlays. These outlays can be divided into two categories for the purpose of this chapter: those that produce an outflow of cash in the accounting period under review and those that do not. Most outlays fall into the first category, e.g. payments to suppliers, wages, salaries and rent. There is, however, a small number of items (the most important of which is depreciation) which is charged against profit but does not result in an equivalent outflow of resources during the accounting period under review. Depreciation is charged against profit to reflect the fact that the business has benefited from using a fixed asset, acquired in a previous accounting period, to help to provide goods or services. The asset declines in value as the result of business use, but no corresponding cash outlay occurs. It is therefore necessary to add back the depreciation charge to the adjusted profit figure to arrive at the total for finance generated from operations. The extent to which finance represented by the depreciation charge is available for investment purposes is examined in Section 10.7.1.

10.2.2 External

The ability of a company to raise finance from external sources depends upon a number of factors. These include:

- The nature of the business: whether it is a sole trader, a partnership or a registered company. Only the last of these can issue shares.

- The size of the business. For example, all public limited companies may offer shares to the general public, but the high fixed costs involved mean that this is only a feasible proposition for a large public company.

- The personality of the directors. This may be a particularly important factor in the company's relationship with its bank.

The main external sources of cash available to businesses are:

- unsecured loans (long-term and short-term);

- debentures;

- shares (sole traders and partnerships are unable to issue shares, and access to certain other sources of finance is often difficult due to their inability to provide adequate security).

It is a part of management's job to make sure that the finance raised is appropriate for the intended purpose. As a general rule, long-term investments should be financed from long-term sources, while short-term sources and applications are often linked together in a similar manner (the reasons for this are examined in Section 10.7). It is therefore necessary to consider the likely duration for which the above types of finance are normally made available, so that we can assess, in due course, whether outgoings have been properly financed.

Unsecured loans can be raised for varying durations, while debentures and share capital are long-term sources. Debentures are, however, normally repayable at some future date, while share capital is redeemable in certain circumstances (see Chapter 7). As the redemption date for unsecured loans and debentures gets nearer, the relevant amounts must be viewed as medium-term finance and ultimately be classified as amounts falling due for repayment within one year. For creditors falling due for payment after one year, the Companies Acts require registered companies to disclose, by way of note, amounts repayable within five years. For the purpose of this chapter, we shall regard amounts repayable between one and five years of the balance sheet date as medium-term finance.

10.3 APPLICATIONS OF CASH

The way in which cash raised is employed reflects the priorities of management at a particular point in time. Basically there are three alternatives:

1. Distribute

A company normally pays an annual dividend, both to ensure that the share price remains at an acceptable level, and to increase the likelihood of the company being able to raise further finance from shareholders when required. The dividend is normally declared out of the current year's profit but, if this is insufficient, retained profits brought forward from previous years may be used. In the latter case, the cash payment cannot be financed out of the current year's profits, and the cash flow statement helps to identify the source which has been used instead. More often, profits for the year exceed dividends, and the excess is available for either of the purposes identified below.

2. Invest

Each year a company is likely to purchase fixed assets in order to maintain its present level of business activity, and sometimes also to put into operation a programme of expansion. In the latter case, an additional investment in working capital is also called for. Where management wishes to increase the scale of business operations by external growth (see Chapter 6), cash is required for the purpose of acquiring either the assets of, or the shares in, another company.

3. Reduce external finance

The directors may choose to use available cash to repay the bank or providers of loan capital and, in certain circumstances (see Chapter 7), share capital. This course may be adopted because repayment is due, or because management takes the view that the company is excessively reliant on external finance, or because it is the most profitable use for available funds, i.e. a reduction of interest charges increases profit by more than any other option available.

10.4 THE CASH FLOW STATEMENT

The cash flow statement sets out, in an orderly and meaningful manner, the sources from which cash has been derived and how it has been spent during an accounting period. FRS 1 requires businesses to analyse their cash flows under (up to) nine main headings. The outline format of the cash flow statement is set out in figure 10.1

Figure 10.1

Specimen Cash Flow Statement for the year

		£000
1	Net cash flow from operating activities	x
2	Returns on investment and servicing of finance	x
3	Taxation paid	x
4	Capital expenditure and financial investment	x
5	Acquisitions and disposals	x
6	Equity dividends paid	x
	Cash flow before management of liquid resources and financing	x
7	Management of liquid resources	x
8	Financing cash flows	x
9	Movement in cash balance	x

The numbered headings contained in Figure 10.1 are discussed further below. The profit and loss account and balance sheet of Lisvane Ltd for 19X1 is first set out in Figure 10.2.

Figure 10.2

Lisvane Ltd: Accounting Reports for 19X1

PROFIT AND LOSS ACCOUNT FOR THE YEAR TO 31 DECEMBER 19X1

	£000	£000
Sales		3,620
Less: Opening stock	224	
Purchases	1,760	
Closing stock	(293)	
Cost of goods sold		1,691
Gross Profit		1,929
Less: Depreciation	104	
Net loss on disposal of plant and investments	25	
Administration expenses	1,136	
Distribution costs	275	
		1,540
Operating profit		389
Interest received	26	
Interest paid	(10)	16
Profit on ordinary activities before tax		405
Tax on profits on ordinary activities	90	
Transfer to deferred taxation account	30	120
		285
Dividends: Paid	45	
Proposed	180	225
Retained profit for the year		60

BALANCE SHEET AS AT 31 DECEMBER 19X1

	19X1 £000	19X0 £000
Fixed Assets		
Plant and machinery at book value, 1 Jan.	945	1,000
Additions	530	20
Disposals at book value (cash proceeds £5,000)	(40)	–
Depreciation charged	(104)	(75)
	1,331	945
Current Assets		
Stocks	293	224
Debtors	508	407
Temporary investments	78	142
Cash at bank and in hand	–	53
	879	826
Creditors: Amounts falling due within one year		
Bank overdraft	171	–
Trade creditors	181	156
Proposed dividend	180	120
Mainstream corporation tax	90	117
	622	393
Net current assets	257	433
Total assets less current liabilities	1,588	1,378
Creditors: Amounts falling due after more than one year		
Debentures	–	(200)
Provision for liabilities and charges		
Deferred taxation	(90)	(60)
Net Assets	1,498	1,118
Capital and Reserves		
Called-up share capital	1,200	1,000
Share premium account	120	–
Profit and loss account	178	118
	1,498	1,118

Note:
Investments costing £64,000 were sold during the year for £74,000.

The calculation of relevant balances for inclusion in the cash flow statement, under the headings identified in Figure 10.1, are illustrated based on the contents of Figure 10.2.

1. Net cash flow from operating activities

This comprises the cash effects of transactions and other events relating to operating or trading activities reported in the profit and loss account. The conversion of the operating profit, appearing in the profit and loss account, to net cash flow from operating activities should disclose, separately, non-cash expenses, profits and losses relating to capital flows, and the movements in stocks, debtors and creditors. The reconciliation may either appear adjoining the cash flow statement or as a separate note. The calculation starts with operating profit and is derived below from the contents of Figure 10.2.

	£000
Operating profit	389
Depreciation charge	104
Loss on sale of tangible fixed assets	35
Profit on sale of investments	(10)
Increase in stocks	(69)
Increase in debtors	(101)
Increase in trade creditors	25
Net cash flow from operating activities	373

2. Returns on investments and servicing of finance

These are receipts, such as interest received, resulting from the ownership of investments, and payments made to providers of finance (e.g. preference dividends), other than equity finance. It includes, where appropriate, the interest element of payments made under finance leases. The relevant items from Figure 10.2 are:

	£000
Interest received	26
Interest paid	(10)
	16

3. Taxation

This comprises payments made to the tax authorities, less any tax rebates or returns in respect of overpayments. The relevant items from Figure 10.2 are:

	£000
Corporation tax	(117)

4. Capital expenditure and financial investment

This covers cash flows in respect of the purchase or sale of fixed assets, including long-term investment made in the shares or debentures of other companies (unless the acquisition of another company is involved, in which case see next heading) and their eventual sale or repayment. The relevant items from Figure 10.2 are:

	£000
Payment to acquire tangible fixed assets	(530)
Receipts from the sale of tangible fixed assets	5
	(525)

5. Acquisitions and disposals

These are the cash flows that result from buying or selling an associated company, a joint venture, or a subsidiary undertaking. There are no entries to be made under this heading for Lisvane Ltd.

6. Equity dividends

This comprises the amount paid out in dividends in respect of equity shares. The relevant items from Figure 10.2 are:

	£000
Interim dividend for 19X0	(45)
Final dividend for 19X1	(120)
	(165)

7. Management of liquid resources

This is made up of current asset investments held as readily disposable stores of value. It covers investments that are readily convertible into known amounts of cash at close to their carrying amount or investments traded in an active market. It therefore includes treasury bills and shares quoted on the stock exchange held as temporary investments. The relevant item from Figure 10.2 is:

	£000
Sale of investments	74

8. Financing cash flows

These are receipts from and repayments to providers of long-term finance, principally shareholders and debenture holders. The heading also covers, where appropriate, the capital element of payments made under finance leases. The relevant items from Figure 10.2 are:

	£000
Issue of shares (£200,000 share capital + £120,000 premium)	320
Repayment of debentures	(200)
	120

9 Movement in the cash balance

Cash is defined as cash in hand and at the bank, deposits repayable on demand without penalty, less any overdrafts repayable on demand. The relevant items from Figure 10.2 are:

	£000
Opening cash balance	53
Closing bank overdraft	171
Movement in cash balance	(224)

We are now able to assemble the above calculations in the form of a cash flow statement for Lisvane Ltd. The information is set out in Figure 10.3

Figure 10.3

Specimen Cash Flow Statement for Lisvane Ltd for the year 19X1

		£000	£000
	Reconciliation of operating profit to net cash inflow from operating activities		
	Operating profit		389
	Depreciation charge		104
	Loss on sale of tangible fixed assets		35
	Profit on sale of investments		(10)
	Increase in stocks		(69)
	Increase in debtors		(101)
	Increase in trade creditors		25
1	*Net cash flow from operating activities*		373
2	*Returns on investment and servicing of finance*		
	Interest received	26	
	Interest paid	(10)	16
3	*Taxation paid*		(117)
4	*Capital expenditure and financial investment*		
	Payment to acquire tangible fixed assets	(530)	
	Receipts from the sale of tangible fixed assets	5	(525)
6	*Equity dividends paid*		
	Interim dividend for 19X0	(45)	
	Final dividend for 19X1	(120)	(165)
	Cash outflow before use of liquid resources and financing		(418)
7	*Management of liquid resources*		
	Sale of investments		74
8	*Financing cash flows*		
	Issue of shares (£200,000 share capital + £120,000 premium)	320	
	Repayment of debentures	(200)	120
9	*Decrease in cash*		(224)

10.5 INTERPRETATION OF THE CASH FLOW STATEMENT

The preparation of the Cash Flow Statement is not, of course, an end in itself. Its purpose is to help users assess business development. It is therefore relevant to review the information contained in Figure 10.3 to see what messages it contains.

- Lisvane has a substantial net cash flow from operations, and the reconciliation helps to explain the extent to which this differs from operating profit. We can see that cash from operations represented by operating profit, depreciation charge and the loss on sale of tangible fixed assets accounts for the 'lion's share' of cash generated. A proportion of this cash has been used to finance the increase in stocks and debtors, to the extent that this has not been covered by the increase in trade creditors, but there remains a healthy residual balance of £373,000.

- The entry for 'Returns on investment and servicing of finance' show some minor cash flows resulting in a modest net cash inflow of £16,000.

- Taxation. This shows that nearly one-third of net cash flow from operating activities has been absorbed in the form of corporation tax payments.

- Capital expenditure and financial investment. A substantial outlay has been made during the current accounting period. This is the single largest item in the Cash Flow Statement and is mainly responsible for a net cash outflow before 'use of liquid resources and financing' of £418,000.

- Management of liquid resources. The sale of some of Lisvane's temporary investments has made a modest contribution towards the substantial investment that has taken place during the year.

- Financing. The company has made a significant share issue which has been substantially absorbed in meeting the cost of repaying the debentures, leaving a balance of only £120,000 to help to defray net investment during the current accounting period.

- The net result is a substantial decrease in cash and cash equivalents of £244,000.

The overall impression is of a significant expansion which appears to have put a considerable strain on the company's liquidity position. It would of course be necessary to examine the company's profitability and financial position in greater depth based on other information in the accounts – an appraisal which would call for the calculation of relevant accounting ratios (see section 10.8) before reaching any balanced conclusions concerning the performance of Lisvane Ltd during 19X1.

10.6 SOME PROBLEM AREAS

10.6.1 Non-Cash Items

We have seen above that there are a number of accounting entries made by companies which neither use nor provide cash. These require further consideration, and, to explain their significance for the cash flow statement, it is useful to classify them on the basis of whether or not they affect the level of reported profit before tax.

- Non-cash items that affect pre-tax profit. The most important item falling into this category is depreciation which, as we have seen above, is added to profit. A loss arising on the sale of a fixed asset is accounted for in the same way, since its purpose is to equate total depreciation actually charged with the amount which should have been charged. By way of contrast, a profit on the sale of a fixed asset (or on the sale of a temporary investment, as demonstrated above), which has been credited to the profit and loss account, must be deducted, since the entire sales proceeds are shown separately elsewhere in the cash flow statement under the heading 'investing activities'.

- Non-cash items that do not affect pre-tax profit. The most common adjustments are transfers to reserves, a transfer to the deferred tax account, a bonus issue of shares and the revaluation of fixed assets. Since these adjustments do not represent either a cash inflow or outflow, they do not affect the resources available to the company.

10.6.2 Gross Changes

Where examination questions require candidates to prepare a cash flow statement, many of the figures can be obtained directly from the profit and loss account or balance sheet or from a straightforward comparison of the balances appearing in successive balance sheets. The latter procedure does not work, however, where a number of transactions have occurred, during the year, some increasing and others decreasing the opening balance. The inclusion of 'net' figures does not provide a complete view of financial developments, and so 'gross' changes must be computed. Students often find it helpful to use either ledger accounts or a tabular format to build up the gross figures. The latter approach is used to identify movements on a fixed asset account in Example 10.1.

Example 10.1

The following information is provided in respect of Stanmore Ltd's plant and machinery:

Balances at 31 December	*19X0*	*19X1*
Plant and machinery at cost	206,500	317,800
Less: Accumulated depreciation	104,200	123,500
	102,300	194,300

During 19X1 the company sold plant, which cost £26,000 some years ago, for £7,000. Accumulated depreciation, at the date of sale, was £16,000.

Required:
Calculate the figures for 'additions to plant' and the 'depreciation charge' for 19X1 using the tabular format.

Solution

Figures for 'additions to plant' and the 'depreciation charge' are calculated, as the balancing items, using the following tabulations:

	Cost £	*Accumulated Depreciation* £
Opening balances	206,500	104,200
Sale of plant	(26,000)	(16,000)
Additions to plant (balancing item)	137,300	
Depreciation charge (balancing item)	–	35,300
Closing balances	317,800	123,500

10.7 FINANCING BUSINESS INVESTMENT

When making an assessment of a particular company's financial developments, and of the financial policies pursued by management, it is normally useful to start by considering whether the investment has been financed correctly. The appropriate source for financing particular types of business investment must therefore be considered.

Companies invest in projects with widely different lifespans; for example, a surveyor may decide to purchase a property in a dilapidated condition with the intention of renovation and resale. If events go according to plan, perhaps only six months elapse between the dates when the initial investment is made and the property is resold. An investment may be made for an even shorter duration; a retail trader may be given the opportunity to purchase a considerable quantity of fire-damaged stock at an extremely low price and, although this may be additional to his normal trading activity, he seizes the opportunity for a quick profit and resells the stock, within days, at a favourable price. Often, however, investment decisions tie up resources in a project for years rather than weeks or months. The purchase of a lathe and the construction and operation of an oil rig are examples of long-term investments, although there is a tremendous difference between the quantity of resources committed to each of these two projects.

The guiding factor, when making a decision concerning the type of finance to use, is the duration of the investment. It is perfectly reasonable to finance a short-term investment with equivalent finance. The surveyor may finance his project out of a bank overdraft, while the retailer may be able to resell the damaged stock before he is obliged to pay his supplier who therefore finances the whole transaction. Long-term investments, on the other hand, should normally be paid for out of long-term sources of finance, because the funds committed to them are recovered over a much longer time period.

Example 10.2

Complex Ltd is an established company with a wide range of activities. It plans to invest in a new project. It is estimated that the project requires an initial investment of £100,000, and that cash generated from the project, before deducting finance charges, will amount to £25,000 for each of the next ten years. The project is to be financed by a £100,000 bank loan, at a 10% annual rate of interest, repayable in three years' time.

Required:
(a) An assessment of the new project, taken in isolation from Complex's other activities. You should support your assessment with relevant numerical calculations.

(b) A discussion of further possible considerations if the assumption that the project is to be undertaken in isolation is relaxed.

Note:
Ignore the time value of money.

Solution

(a)	*Overall results*		*£000*
	Cash from project		250
	Less: Initial investment		100
	Available for interest and profit		150

		£000	*£000*
	Results over first 3 years		
	Loan		100
	Less: Annual cash flow	25	
	Interest payable on loan	(10)	
	Available for repayment of loan 3 x	15	45
	Shortfall		55

The project appears highly remunerative, but if the company is committed to repay the £100,000 at the end of year 3, acute financial embarrassment may result. Perhaps it will be possible to raise the shortfall of £55,000 from elsewhere, at that stage, but the risk will not necessarily be one which management wishes to take; at least some long-term finance should therefore be raised, by Complex Ltd, at the outset. An extreme course of action would be to finance the entire project out of a 10-year loan, in which case the company would not be obliged to repay the finance until it had received the full benefit of resources generated from the project. Such a cautious option need not be followed; finance is generated throughout the life of the project and it would be perfectly feasible to employ a combination of medium-term and long-term finance.

(b) If we relax the assumption that the project is being undertaken in isolation, account may be taken of the financial implications of the other activities of Complex Ltd. Although it is usually prudent to finance long-term investments substantially out of long-term sources of finance, this is not an inviolable rule; for instance Complex Ltd may have built up its cash resources in anticipation of this new project. If such a course has been followed, the balance sheet of Complex Ltd, immediately prior to the investment being undertaken, would probably include a large balance of working capital reflected in the existence of a working capital ratio significantly in excess of 2:1. It is perfectly reasonable, in these circumstances, to finance at least some of the expansion out of working capital and, as a result, reduce the working capital ratio to a more conventional level. Furthermore, any finance which it is necessary to raise, at the outset, may be repaid not only out of cash generated by that particular investment but also out of cash generated from the other activities in which the company is engaged.

10.7.1 Depreciation as a Source of Finance

The two main components of cash generated from operations are profit and depreciation. The depreciation charge acknowledges the fact that the value of a fixed asset declines over its working life and earmarks, for retention within the company, a quantity of resources equal to the asset's original cost. Therefore, even if a company pays out its entire profit in the form of dividends, working capital will increase by the amount of the depreciation charged over the asset's useful life. The question arises whether these resources, as they arise, are available for investment purposes, or whether they should be set aside specifically to finance the replacement of the fixed asset when it is worn out.

In the distant past, management often took the precaution of setting aside, each year, a sum of money equal to the amount of the depreciation charge, either in a separate bank account or invested in readily realizable securities. This procedure is no longer common and, instead, the cash is usually reinvested in operating assets. Even then, there are a number of alternative uses from which management may choose. The resources may be invested in current assets, for instance raw materials may be purchased in large quantities to obtain the benefit of discounts for bulk purchases. This causes stock levels to rise but, when the date for replacing the fixed asset falls due, stocks can be restored to their former levels. Alternatively, the resources may be used to help to finance a programme of expansion which involves the acquisition of additional fixed assets. If this is done, it will not be possible to release the resources when replacement falls due, and it will be necessary for management to arrange an alternative source of finance. Section 2 of this chapter indicates the range of sources to which management may turn at this stage. For instance, it may well happen that replacements falling due in a particular accounting period will be partly or wholly financed out of funds earmarked for retention by the *total* depreciation charge made in respect of that accounting period.

Example 10.3

Goldcliffe Ltd owns ten machines. Each machine cost £5,000 and has a five-year life and zero residual value at the end of that period. Replacement machines cost £5,000. Each year two machines wear out and are replaced.

Required:
Calculate the total depreciation charge each year and the cost of replacements each year.

Solution

Total depreciation charge each year on the straight-line basis is: $\dfrac{£5,000}{5}$ x 10 = £10,000

Replacements each year: two machines at £5,000 = £10,000

Goldcliffe Ltd is able to finance replacements entirely out of the current year's depreciation charge.

A final point which should be emphasized, in this section, is that a company suffering losses still generates a positive cash flow from operations, provided losses (plus any net investment in stock plus debtors minus creditors) do not exceed depreciation (plus any other adjustments which do not involve an outflow of funds). For instance, a company which reports a loss of £1m, after charging depreciation of £4m, has generated cash from operations of £3m provided its levels of stock, debtors and creditors remain unchanged. This helps to explain how loss-making companies are able to carry on, at least in the short run, despite the fact that they find it impossible to issue shares or raise loans in view of their poor performance.

10.7.2 Working Capital Requirements

A decision to increase the level of turnover requires an additional investment in fixed assets only if the planned increase results in total output in excess of the current available capacity. A company's working capital requirements are likely to increase, however, irrespective of whether expansion requires an additional investment in fixed assets. This is because the level of stocks, debtors and creditors are closely related to the level of business activity.

Example 10.4

As the result of an advertising campaign, Overton Ltd, a trading company, expects sales to increase significantly in 19X2. The following facts and estimates are provided.

	Facts 19X1 £	Estimates 19X2 £
Turnover	600,000	800,000
Cost of goods, sold	450,000	600,000
Stocks	64,000	*
Trade debtors	80,000	*
Operating cash balance	6,000	*
Trade creditors	60,000	*
Working capital	90,000	*
Working capital ratio	2.5:1	*

*Management has not calculated its working capital requirements for 19X2, but expects that the stock-holding period and the periods of credit allowed to customers and obtained from suppliers will remain the same as in 19X1. The amount of cash required to finance operations is a function of the level of business activity.

Required:
A calculation of the additional working capital requirement of Overton Ltd for 19X2.

Solution

Turnover and cost of goods sold are each expected to increase by one-third. Stocks, debtors, cash and creditors are expected to increase by the same proportion, and so the estimated balances and additional working capital requirement are as follows:

	19X1 £	19X2 £
Stocks	$64,000 \times \frac{4}{3}$	85,333
Trade debtors	$80,000 \times \frac{4}{3}$	106,667
Operating cash balance	$6,000 \times \frac{4}{3}$	8,000
	150,000	200,000
Trade creditors	$(60,000) \times \frac{4}{3}$	(80,000)
Working capital	90,000	120,000
Less Existing requirement		90,000
Additional requirement		30,000

Expansion is expected to result in additional investments in stocks, debtors and cash totalling £50,000 (£200,000 – £150,000), of which £20,000 is financed by creditors. The remaining £30,000 must be provided from medium- or long-term sources to maintain a working capital ratio of 2.5:1. It therefore follows that it is not enough for an expanding company merely to arrange for an increase in its working capital; it must increase working capital by a sufficient amount to safeguard the existing ratios of stock + debtors + operating cash requirements:creditors. There are of course exceptions to this general rule; for instance, a less than proportionate increase in the working capital requirement is needed if the average stock-holding period can be reduced by improved stock-handling procedures. By way of contrast, a more than proportionate increase in the working capital requirement is needed if it is necessary to offer customers more credit in order to increase sales.

10.8 UNBALANCED FINANCIAL DEVELOPMENT

The successful development of corporate activity depends on the existence of a system of forward planning which examines the likely profitability and financial implications of investment proposals. Even the best laid plans may of course be thwarted and unforeseen events can render unprofitable a project which careful planning suggested would produce a highly satisfactory rate of return. Nevertheless planning is important, otherwise companies will embark upon projects which, even in the most favourable conditions, will yield an unacceptable return on the amount invested. Planning for the financial implications of an investment proposal is just as important.

When a new company is formed, it is management's job to ensure that sufficient long-term finance is raised to cover planned expenditure on fixed assets and make an adequate contribution towards the financing of current assets, with the balance provided by current liabilities, mainly in the form of trade credit and a bank overdraft. Throughout the life of the company, it remains management's job to maintain an appropriate balance between long-term, medium-term and short-term finance, and, within the first category, an acceptable relationship must exist between share capital and loan capital (see Chapter 9.8). When expansion occurs, additional long-term finance is needed to cover the cost of fixed assets and working capital requirements; while a reduction in the scale of a company's operations may permit the repayment of certain sources of finance. In practice, management often fails to achieve a balanced financial structure, either because it does not plan ahead or because unexpected events occur. It is possible to identify two main aspects of unbalanced financial development.

10.8.1 Overcapitalization

This occurs where management is unable to make full use of the capital available to it. For instance, it may not have proved possible to achieve the volume of activity anticipated at the outset, when the capital structure was decided upon. Alternatively, management may find itself in possession of surplus resources, for instance, as the result of selling a division of the company's activities. In these circumstances, it may be appropriate to return capital to the members either by purchasing or redeeming some of its shares or by reducing capital in accordance with the procedures described in Chapter 7.

10.8.2 Overtrading

This occurs when the volume of business activity is excessive in relation to the finance provided by the shareholders, with the result that there is undue reliance on external finance in the form of loan capital, bank overdrafts and trade credit. The situation arises because of significant errors in the financial policy pursued by management; often it occurs because management has expanded the volume of business activity beyond the level justified by the resources available to the company. In essence, management has attempted to do 'too much too quickly', with the result that the company is left with insufficient resources to meet its currently maturing liabilities, that is, the company finds it difficult to pay wages due to employees, debts due to suppliers, tax payable to the government and money owing to the bank. The financial signs of overtrading, which should be looked for in a balance sheet, are a decline in the ratios of debtors:creditors and current assets:current liabilities, a low figure for working capital, perhaps even a deficit, a high ratio of fixed assets to working capital and a severe shortage of cash.

Overtrading is a common cause of business failure, and is therefore of considerable interest to bankers. The following case study sets out some of the possible causes of over-trading and the potential remedies which are available.

Overtrading: A Case Study

The following financial information and facts are provided relating to the affairs of Elford Ltd., a manufacturing company which carries on its activities from rented accommodation.

Extracts from Profit and Loss Accounts

19X1 £000		19X2 £000
1,600	Turnover	1,800
80	Operating profit after interest	100
40	*Less*: Proposed dividend	40
40	Retained profit for the year	60
30	Retained profit at 1 January	70
70	Retained profit at 31 December	130

Balance Sheets at 31 December

19X1 £000		19X2 £000	£000
	Tangible Fixed Assets		
500	Plant and machinery at cost	800	
(220)	*Less*: Accumulated depreciation	296	
			504
20	Fixtures and fittings at cost	20	
(10)	*Less*: Accumulated depreciation	12	
			8
290			512
	Current Assets		
100	Stocks	154	
90	Trade debtors	130	
30	Cash at bank	–	
220		284	
	Less: Current liabilities		
80	Trade creditors	200	
40	Proposed dividend	40	
–	Bank overdraft	26	
120		266	
100	Net Current Assets		18
390			530
–	Loan repayable 19X5		60
390			470
	Financed by:		
320	Share capital (£1 ordinary shares)		336
–	Share premium account		4
70	Retained profits		130
390			470

Notes:

1. The additional plant was acquired on 1 March 19X2.

2. 16,000 shares were issued at a premium of 25p per share on 10 February 19X2.

3. Taxation is ignored.

4. £8,000 interest was paid during 19X2.

A casual examination of the above information indicates that 19X2 has been a year of rapid expansion. A particularly significant development was the additional investment of £300,000 in plant and machinery, implying an increase in productive capacity of approximately 60%. The information given also suggests that the expansion has been a success since turnover has increased by £200,000 and trading profit has increased from £80,000 to £100,000. Even larger increases in turnover and profit might have been expected in view of the significant increase in productive capacity, but it must be borne in mind that the additional plant and machinery was not acquired until 1 March, and the extra capacity it provided is unlikely to have been fully utilized immediately. The sources used to finance this investment must be examined, and the following cash flow statement helps to clarify the financial developments which occurred at Elford during 19X2.

Preparation

Cash flow statement for the year ended 31 December 19X2

	£000	£000
Net cashflows from operating activities (note 1)		212
Interest paid		(8)
Dividend paid		(40)
Payments to acquire tangible fixed assets		(300)
Net cash outflow before financing		(136)
Issue of shares	20	
Loan raised	60	
Net cash flow from financing		80
Decrease in cash		(56)

Note 1. Reconciliation of operating profit to net cash inflow from operating activities.

	£000
Operating profit	108
Depreciation charges (W1)	78
Increase in stocks	(54)
Increase in debtors	(40)
Increase in trade creditors	120
	212

W1 £76,000 (plant and machinery) + £2,000 (fixtures and fittings).

Interpretation

Students will generally find it useful to ask themselves the following two questions as the basis for interpreting the financial data contained in the cash flow statement.

Question 1: Has expansion, if any, been financed from the right sources? Elford has used three sources to finance expansion: cash generated from operations; share capital; and a loan. Of these, cash generated from operations and share capital are acceptable sources for financing long-term investment (see section 7 of this chapter), but the propriety of a medium-term loan is more doubtful. A medium-term loan may be used to finance part, or even the whole, of a long-term investment provided profit margins are sufficient to generate, and enable the company to retain, enough cash to repay the loan on its due date. Alternatively, where margins are lower, it may be acceptable to finance part of an investment on a medium-term basis, provided the remaining finance is long-term. Neither of these conditions appear to be fulfilled at Elford: profit has increased in 19X2, but margins are not exceptionally high; moreover, a significant portion of the investment (£120,000) has been financed by an increase in creditors.

Question 2: What has been the effect of financial developments, during 19X2, on Elford's solvency position? Working capital has declined from £100,000, on 1 January to £18,000 on 31 December, and the relevant solvency ratios are:

	19X1	*19X2*
Working capital ratio	1.8:1	1.1:1
Liquidity ratio	1:1	0.5:1

For a manufacturing company, these ratios are satisfactory at the beginning of the year; admittedly the working capital ratio is a little below the conventional norm, but, more important, the liquidity ratio shows that the company was capable of meeting its short-term obligations as they fell due for payment. The financial position appears far less acceptable at the end of 19X2. The working capital ratio is just 1.1:1 and more than half the current assets are tied up in stocks, while the liquidity ratio suggests that the company can pay only 50% of the current liabilities outstanding at the balance sheet date. Manufacturing capacity appears to have been increased by about 60%, judging from the increase in the balance sheet figure for plant and machinery, and the increases in stocks and debtors indicate that the company was operating at this level of activity by the end of the year. However, trade creditors at 31 December 19X2 are two-and-a-half times the corresponding figure a year earlier. This is a disproportionate increase and probably means that suppliers are being asked to wait a considerable period of time before their claims are met. They are unlikely to be satisfied with this state of affairs and are probably pressing for payment.

Conclusion

The directors have not succeeded in arranging satisfactory sources of finance for the investment programme undertaken in 19X2. They have overstretched the available resources and the totally inadequate solvency ratios prove that the company is in a critical financial position at the year end. Further unfavourable financial characteristics, which reveal evidence of overtrading, are the sharp increase in the ratio of fixed assets to working capital, the deterioration in the structure of the current assets which have become less liquid, and the decline in the ratio of debtors to creditors which has fallen from 1.1:1 to 0.65:1 during 19X2. It is important to realize that these financial difficulties have arisen despite the fact that the new project has been a success judged in terms of profitability. For example, the rate of return on the shareholders' equity investment in the company has increased as follows.

Rate of return on shareholders' equity:

$$19X1 \quad \frac{80,000}{390,000} \times 10 = 20.5\%$$

$$19X2 \quad \frac{100,000}{470,000} \times 100 = 21.3\%$$

An unbalanced financial position can of course produce disastrous consequences. The company is short of money and will find it difficult to pay its bills on their due dates. As a result, any goodwill built up in the past between the company and its suppliers will quickly disappear. Suppliers may refuse to deliver more goods until existing bills are paid and, if the bills continue to remain unpaid, it is probable that the creditors will take legal action to recover the amounts due to them. Failure, on the part of the company, to comply with the court's instruction to honour its obligations will result in its liquidation. This sequence of events need not necessarily occur; it is one of the purposes of financial information to draw the reader's attention to a declining financial position, and it is the job of management to heed the 'warning lights' and take the necessary steps to restore an acceptable measure of financial stability. This emphasizes the need for management to obtain up-to-date information as the basis for performance assessment and resource allocation decisions and, for this reason, quarterly and even monthly management accounts are prepared by many companies. Even this type of information may be made available too late to avoid unnecessary financial loss, however, and the preparation of forecast accounts to provide management with advance notice of the need to take remedial action is discussed in Chapter 13.

Prospects of Recovery

The company finds itself in financial difficulties because the directors have undertaken a heavy investment programme without due regard to the financial implications of such an expansionist policy. Clearly further investment is out of the question at this stage; a period of consolidation is needed, and management should concentrate its attention on the various ways in which the finances of the company might be improved. There are a number of possible courses of action which should be considered.

1. Raise additional external finance

The directors should consider the feasibility of issuing shares or raising a loan. In some respects, a further share issue would seem to be the better prospect. The company undertook a substantial investment in 19X2, and the shareholders were called upon to inject only £20,000. There is the additional fact that the shareholders have most to lose if the company goes into liquidation. The company is profitable, producing a return of over 20% on the book value of the shareholders' investment and paying regular dividends; whereas on liquidation the shareholders might lose most of their investment. The company seems viable, apart from the cash difficulties, and, provided this short-term problem is overcome, there is no reason why it should not prosper. An offer of shares to existing members in proportion to their present holdings, i.e. a 'rights issue', should be carefully considered.

The ability of the directors to attract further loans must be more doubtful. Whether the directors attempt to obtain further finance from the bank or look elsewhere to raise a loan, they are faced with the same major stumbling block, namely the financial position displayed in the balance sheet at 31 December 19X2. This document casts severe doubt on the financial capability of Elford's management; it shows clear evidence of a policy of expansion pursued without due consideration being given to its financial implications. Had management approached the bank at the outset, and produced budgeted financial information to support an application for a substantial loan, the prospects of success may well have been high, particularly as the project promised a good profit. An approach to the bank, early in 19X3, with a request for funds to help to overcome the financial problems which have now emerged, is quite a different proposition. The banker may well take the view that the directors have made bad errors in the past and may not be convinced that they will succeed in avoiding similar mistakes in the future. The absence of a satisfactory security for any loan request would reinforce this cautious attitude.

2. Economize on working capital

The directors should examine the possibility of releasing funds by cutting down on its holding of stocks and reducing the period of credit allowed to customers. The feasibility of these courses of action depends on whether or not the larger balances, at 31 December 19X2, are reasonable in relation to the higher level of business activity now undertaken by Elford. The systems of stock control and credit control should be examined carefully. It may then be discovered, for example, that management has offered its customers an extended period of credit to make its products more attractive. This is a sound business tactic, in certain circumstances, but it can tie up large amounts of money with very little real benefit. The possibility that stock levels were increased, in anticipation of an increase in sales which did not fully materialize, should also be examined.

Where companies are under severe financial pressure, management may decide to cut back the level of activity so as to reduce the working capital requirement and, perhaps, also remove the need for certain fixed assets which can then be sold. This is not likely to be a popular solution to a company's financial problems, since it reduces the scale of business activity and the level of funds generated from operations is therefore likely to diminish in the long run. It is, however, an option which remains available as the last resort, but it is unlikely to be needed in the case of Elford Ltd.

3. Utilize funds generated from operations

The company is profitable and, provided it is able to continue in business, it is likely to generate funds which can be used to help to correct the present financial imbalance.

Forecasts

To help assess the prospects of recovery the following facts and forecasts, for 19X3, have been prepared by Elford's management and checked by a firm of accountants:

(i) The company will benefit from using the new plant throughout 19X3 and forecast profits are £120,000, after charging depreciation of £80,000 (plant £78,000, fixtures £2,000) and interest of £9,000.

(ii) Plant which cost £90,000, and is now fully depreciated, will be replaced during 19X3 at a cost of £110,000. The old plant has no disposal value.

(iii) The dividend proposed for 19X2 will be paid, but no dividends will be paid in respect of 19X3.

(iv) Trade creditors will be reduced to £155,000.

(v) The investments in stocks and debtors are reasonable in relation to the level of business activities, and will remain unchanged.

(vi) The bank has agreed to provide overdraft facilities of up to £30,000 for a period of 12 months.

This information can be used to prepare an estimated cash flow statement and an estimated balance sheet.

Forecast cash flow statement for the year ended 31 December 19X3

	£000	£000
Net cash flows from operating activities (note 1)		164
Interest paid		(9)
Dividend paid		(40)
Payments to acquire tangible fixed assets		(110)
Increase in cash and cash equivalent		5

Note 1: Reconciliation of operating profit to net cash inflow from operating activities.

	£000
Operating profit	129
Depreciation charges	80
Decrease in trade creditors	(45)
	164

Estimated Balance Sheet, Efford Ltd, 31 December 19X3

Tangible fixed assets	£000	£000
Plant and machinery at cost (800+110-90)	820	
Less: Accumulated depreciation (296+78-90)	284	
		536
Fixtures and fittings at cost	20	
Less: Accumulated depreciation	14	6
		542
Current Assets		
Stock	154	
Trade debtors	130	
	284	
Current Liabilities		
Trade creditors	155	
Bank overdraft (26−5)	21	
	176	
Net Current Assets		108
		650
Loan repayable 19X5		60
		590
Financed by		
Share capital (£1 ordinary shares)		336
Share premium account		4
Retained profits (130 + 120)		250
		590

The estimated balance sheet, at 31 December 19X3, shows a significant improvement in the financial position of the company, compared with a year earlier, and this is reflected in the following solvency ratios:

	19X2 (actual)	*19X3 (estimated)*
Working capital	1.1:1	1.6:1
Liquidity	0.5:1	0.7:1

However, the estimated ratios remain well below the 31 December 19X1 levels and it will take more time to achieve those figures. The loan of £60,000 falls due for repayment in 19X5, and it will probably be the end of that year before the balance sheet appears as financially sound as it was at the end of 19X1. The recovery process is therefore gradual and depends on the achievement of forecast profit levels, further support from the bank and the continued tolerance of trade creditors. The balance due to creditors, at the end of 19X1, was £80,000. The 60% expansion, which we have assumed took place during 19X2, suggests that the balance outstanding to suppliers should not have increased beyond £130,000. At 31 December 19X2, creditors were owed £200,000. The estimates for 19X3 include plans for a reduction to £155,000 by the year end, but it will be well into 19X4 before a balance of £130,000 is achieved. The sympathetic support of creditors is therefore a crucial element in the success of this plan. If the directors are unwilling to rely heavily on creditors, they must look to alternative sources. One possibility would be to raise a modest amount of external finance to tide the company over the next three years, by which time sufficient funds should have been generated from trading operations to complete the recovery process. Elford's prospects of recovery appear hopeful, but this is mainly because the company has been profitable and it has been assumed, for the purpose of analysis, that this situation will continue in the future. If profit margins were narrower, the recovery period would be much more drawn out and the prospects of survival greatly reduced.

10.9 CASH-BASED ACCOUNTING RATIOS

The merits of cash-based financial reporting – for example, it is based principally on facts rather than problematic accounting measurements – have been known for many years. However, it was not until 1990 that the Accounting Standards Board issued FRS 1 (revised 1996) and made the publication of Cash Flow Statements a standard requirement for UK companies. FRS 1 tells us that the 'cash flow statement in conjunction with a profit and loss account and balance sheet provides information on financial position and performance as well as liquidity, solvency and financial adaptability'. Wise words, but what do they mean?

The usefulness of financial statements is enhanced by an examination of the relationship between them; also by comparisons with previous time periods, other entities and expected performance. We have seen that value can be further added through the calculation and interpretation of accounting ratios. An examination of accounting textbooks and the pages of accounting periodicals reveals an enthusiasm for rehearsing the potential of 'accounting ratios', demonstrated through calculations of the net profit margin, return on capital employed, current ratio and a host of other 'traditional' measures based on the contents of the profit and loss and balance sheet, such as those studied in Chapter 9 of this book and earlier in the present chapter. But where does the cash flow statement come into all this? We have seen that its publication was required by the ASB in order to improve the informative value of published financial information. Indeed, some laud it as the most important financial statement. One based on 'hard facts' which has helped to prevent financial machinations such as those that are believed to have occurred at companies such as Polly Peck in the 1980s.

The lack of attention to cash-flow based ratios in accounting textbooks is particularly surprising given their acknowledged role in credit-rating assessments and in the prediction of corporate failure. In these and other contexts, the traditional ratios suffer from the same defect as the financial statements (the profit and loss account and balance sheet) on which they are based. Such ratios are the result of comparing figures which have been computed using accounting conventions and 'guestimations'. Given the difficulty of deciding the length of the period over which a fixed asset should be written off, whether the tests which justify the capitalization of development expenditure have been satisfied, the amount of the provision to be made for claims under a manufacturer's twelve-month guarantee (to give just a few examples), ratios based on such figures are also bound to have limited economic significance. This is not to suggest that the traditional ratios are irrelevant. Clearly this is not so, because they reveal important relationships and trends that are not apparent from the examination of individual figures appearing in the accounts. However, given the fact that cash flow ratios contain at least one element that is factual (the numerator, the denominator or both), their lack of prominence in the existing literature is puzzling.

10.9.1 Early Recognition of Cash Flow Ratios

The importance of cash flow ratios was dramatically demonstrated, early on, by W. H. Beaver whose 1966 study showed that the most effective predictor of corporate failure was the ratio of cash flow to total debt. Indeed, one of his most surprising findings was that the current ratio proved to be one of the *least* useful ratios in predicting impending collapse. The importance of cash as an indicator of continuing financial health should not be surprising in view of its crucial role within the business. Colourfully described as a company's 'life-blood', a strong cash flow will enable a business to recover from temporary financial problems whereas future negative cash flow will cause even an apparently sound enterprise to move towards liquidation. Expressing the importance of cash differently: a company which descends into a loss making position often succeeds in making a comeback; one that runs out of cash is unlikely to have a second chance.

Another US-based writer, Yuji Ijiri, has noted the paradox between the way in which investment decisions are made by business and other entities and the way in which the results of those decisions are evaluated. The principal focus for informed investment decisions is cash flows, whether the capital project appraisal method is 'payback' or one of the more sophisticated discounted cash flow-based techniques, namely 'net present value' and 'internal rate of return' (see Chapter 12). Turning to performance evaluation, however, the emphasis usually shifts to techniques such as return on capital employed. The inconsistency between the two approaches is highlighted by the use of depreciation cost allocation for computing ROCE – a calculation that has no place whatsoever in the above project appraisal methods. Ijiri persuasively argues, therefore, the importance of making project appraisal and performance evaluation consistent.

Below are presented:

• Ratios that link the cash flow statement with the two other principal financial statements (section 10.9.2).

• Ratios and percentages based entirely on the contents of the cash flow statement (section 10.9.3).

To illustrate the calculations, the results of Tamari plc for 20X8 and 20X9 appear in Figure 10.4. For each ratio is presented both the calculation and a discussion of its significance. Inevitably, there will be some overlap in the messages conveyed by the various ratios presented. This may be due to similarities in the nature of the calculations or to the fact that the results of just one company are used for illustration purposes. The application of the same ratios to different financial facts might well yield additional valuable insights.

10.9.2 Ratios that Link the Cash Flow Statement with the Two Other Principal Financial Statements

Cash flow from operations to current liabilities

$$\text{Cash flow from operations to current liabilities} = \frac{\text{Net cash flow from operating activities}}{\text{Average current liabilities}} \times 100$$

Where:
Net cash flow from operating activities is taken directly from the cash flow statement published to comply with FRS 1.

Average current liabilities are computed from the opening and closing balance sheet.

This ratio examines the liquidity of the company by providing a measure of the extent to which current liabilities are covered by cash flowing into the business from normal operating activities. The ratio is thought, by some, to be superior to balance sheet-based ratios such as the liquidity ratio as a measure of short-term solvency. This is because balance sheet ratios are based on a static positional statement (the 'instantaneous financial photograph') and are therefore subject to manipulation by, for example, running down stock immediately prior to the year end and not replacing it until the next accounting period. Balance sheet-based ratios may alternatively be affected by unusual events which cause particular items to be abnormally large or small. In either case, the resulting ratios will not reflect normal conditions.

Cash recovery rate

$$\text{Cash recovery rate (CRR)} = \frac{\text{Cash flow from operations}}{\text{Average gross assets}} \times 100$$

Where:
Cash flow from operations is made up of 'net cash flow from operating activities' together with any proceeds from the disposal of long-term assets.

Gross assets is the average gross value (before deducting accumulated depreciation) of the entity's assets over an accounting period.

Assets are required to generate a return which is ultimately, if not immediately, in the form of cash. The CRR is, therefore, a measure of the rate at which the company recovers its investment in fixed assets. The quicker the recovery period, the lower the risk. You may have noticed that the CRR is thus the reciprocal of the payback period used for capital project appraisal purposes (see Chapter 12.3) assuming projects have equal (or roughly equal) annual cash flows.

Cash flow per share

$$\text{Cash flow per share} = \frac{\text{Cash flow}}{\text{Weighted average no. of shares}}$$

There are two versions of cash flow reflecting different applications of the cash flow per share calculation:

Version I
Where cash flow = operating profit plus non-cash adjustments such as depreciation and the amortization of fixed assets.

This version provides a measure of the amount of cash that a company generates from operating activities, exclusive of working capital changes. It draws attention to the important role of non-cash adjustments in this process. A company may be operating at a low profit or even a loss and still be capable of generating a significant amount of 'cash flow'.

Version II

Where cash flow = net cash flow from operating activities +/- returns on investments and servicing of finance – taxation and dividends paid.

This version recognizes the fact that cash is available for long-term investment only after working capital requirements, tax and dividends have been met. It indicates the ability of the company to fund long-term investment out of resources generated internally.

In either case, the number of shares used as the denominator should be the weighted average of the number in issue during the year. However, the average needs to be weighted only if there is an issue of shares involving an inflow of resources; in the case of a bonus issue (where no extra resources are generated), the number of shares post bonus issue should be used without weighting and the number in issue the previous year made comparable.

Capital expenditure per share

$$\text{Capital expenditure per share} = \frac{\text{Capital expenditure}}{\text{Weighted average no. of shares}} \times 100$$

Where:
Capital expenditure = net investment (purchases less sales proceeds) in fixed assets.

This ratio, in conjunction with cash flow per share (version II) can be used in order to obtain a broad indication of whether a business is a net generator of cash or whether it is 'cash hungry'.

Debt service coverage ratio

$$\text{Debt service coverage ratio (DSCR)} = \frac{\text{EBITDA}}{\text{Annual debt repayments and interest}}$$

Where:
EBITDA = Earnings before interest, tax, depreciation and amortization.

The purpose of this ratio is to help to assess the ability of a company to meet debt repayments and interest out of cash flow generated from operations. A feature of this ratio is that it is forward looking with the denominator representing expected future cash flows. (If available, the numerator should also be prospective.) It is seen to be superior to traditional methods used by banks to analyse risk of exposure to debt finance such as interest cover. A drawback of interest cover is that, as conventionally applied, it is backward looking. Also, it takes no account of the level of capital repayments which, of course, can vary considerably depending on the period of the loan repayment.

Cash flow adequacy ratio

$$\text{Cash flow adequacy ratio (CFAR)} = \frac{\text{Annual net free cash flow (NFCF)}}{\text{annual debt repayments}}$$

Where
NFCF = EBITDA minus capital expenditure, interest, tax and preference dividends.

This is a measure widely used in the United States which, in common with the DSCR, attempts to redress some of the weaknesses of traditional analytical ratios through taking a dynamic view of a company's credit quality by capturing the extent and direction of future financial changes. The calculation of the ratio is conventionally based on estimates for the forthcoming five years, where such data are available. Working capital changes and equity dividends are not adjusted in computing NFCF on the grounds that management has considerable discretion, in the short term, concerning working capital levels and dividend policy. The outflows included in NFCF are, therefore, those that are judged to be unavoidable. The company has no option but to pay interest, tax and preference dividends; also, it must incur capital expenditure in order to maintain its competitive position.

The significance of the ratio is as follows: the higher the CFAR, the more financial pressure the company is able to withstand before its financial stability and therefore its credit rating is eroded.

Figure 10.4 – Published accounts of Tamari plc for year ended 31 December 20X9

Cash Flow Statement	*20X9*	*20X8*
	£000	*£000*
Operating profit	501	420
Depreciation charges	660	600
(-)Increase/decrease in stocks	−305	250
(-)Increase/decrease in debtors	−184	220
Increase in trade creditors	420	120
Net cash flows from operating activities	1,092	1,610
Returns on investment and servicing of finance		
Interest paid	−150	−50
Taxation paid	−130	−110
Capital expenditure and financial investment		
Purchase of tangible fixed asset	−1,620	−900
Equity dividends paid	−160	−160
Cash outflow before financing	−968	390
Financing		
Issue of loan	1,000	100
Increase in cash	32	290

Profit and Loss Account extracts	*20X9*	*20X8*
	£000	*£000*
Operating profit for 20X9	501	420
Interest paid	150	50
Profit before tax	351	370
Taxation:	125	115
Profit after tax	226	255
Dividends paid and proposed	175	175
Retained profit for 20X9	51	80
Profit and loss account balance 31 December 20X8	282	202
Profit and loss account balance 31 December 20X9	333	282

Balance Sheet at 31 December	*20X9*	*20X8*
Tangible Fixed Assets	*£000*	*£000*
Cost	5,220	3,600
Accumulated depreciation	2,360	1,700
	2,860	1,900
Current Assets	1,893	1,372
Creditors falling due within one year		
Loan repayment due	150	–
Other current liabilities including dividends and taxation	1,270	840
	1,420	840
Net current assets (liabilities)	473	532
Total assets less current liabilities	3,333	2,432
Creditors: Amounts falling due after more than one year		
10% Loan repayable 20X-10-20X-19	1,350	500
	1,983	1,932
Capital and Reserves		
Called up share capital (£1 ordinary shares)	1,400	1,400
Share premium account	250	250
Profit and loss account	333	282
	1,983	1,932

Note:
Tamari raised a loan of £1 million during 20X9; this together with the already existing loan is repayable by ten equal instalments over the period 20X-10 to 20X-19.

We can now apply some of the above cash-based accounting ratios to the information provided for Tamari plc in Figure 10.4 together with the following information for 31 December 20X7: fixed assets at cost, £2,700,000; current assets, £1,802,000; creditors falling due within one year, £838,000; called-up share capital, £1,400,000. Cash flow per share (version I), which is of limited interest in this case, given Tamari's profit record, is not calculated. Neither do we calculate CFAR because the necessary forecast information is not provided.

Ratio	Calculation	20X9	Calculation	20X8
Cash flow from operations to current liabilities	$\dfrac{1,092}{\frac{1}{2}[1,420+840]}$	96.6%	$\dfrac{1,610}{\frac{1}{2}[840+838]}$	191.9%
Cash recovery rate	$\dfrac{1,092}{\frac{1}{2}[7,113+4,972]}$	18.1%	$\dfrac{1,610}{\frac{1}{2}[4,972+4,502]}$	34.0%
Cash flow per share (version II)	652/1,400 x 100	46.6p	1,290/1,400 x 100	92.1p
Capital expenditure per share	1,620/1,400 x 100	115.7p	900/1,400 x 100	64.3p
DSCR*	[501+660]/[150+150]	3.9x	1,020/150	6.8x

* Forecast EBITDA unavailable so historical used

Cash flow from operations to current liabilities
There has been a startling decline in this ratio between 20X8 and 20X9, falling to one half of the previous level. This has been caused by a combination of a reduction in the operating cash flow and a rise in average current liabilities. Nevertheless, the current liabilities (which include taxation and proposed dividends not payable until well into the year) remain adequately covered by cash flow on the assumption that this aspect of Tamari's financial affairs is repeated in the year 20X-10.

Cash recovery rate
This has also fallen to about one-half of the figure of the previous year. The implication is that the company is now recovering its investment in business assets over twice the period that was previously the case. It should be borne in mind, however, that the 20X8 ratio benefited from the release of investment in working capital which was not, and probably could not, be repeated in 20X9.

Cash flow per share (version II) and Capital expenditure per share
There is a marked decline in cash flow per share reflecting, again, the significant disinvestment in working capital that occurred in 20X8. The capital expenditure per share has risen dramatically and it is patently obvious that the company has had to look elsewhere to fund a much greater proportion of that investment in 20X9 (115.7p – 46.6p = 69.1p per share) compared with 20X8.

DCSR

The DCSR for 20X8 is a strong, with EBITDA 6.8x based on the prospective interest charges for 20X9; there is no loan repayment in that year. For 20X9, the ratio declines to 3.9x but still shows debt commitments to be comfortably covered out of internally generated cash flow. The multiple also suggests that there is surplus cash available to meet working capital requirements and for capital expenditure, tax and dividend payments.

10.9.3 Ratios and Percentages Based Entirely on the Contents of the Cash Flow Statement

Figure 10.5 sets out the relationship between the various numbers in Figure 10.4. 'Net cash flow from operating activities' is given an index of 100 and becomes the pivotal figure for each of the other calculations. The presentation of calculations in Figure 10.5 is analogous to the expression of expenses in the profit and loss account as a percentage of sales.

Figure 10.5

Cash Flow Statement	20X9	20X8
	%	%
Net cash flows from operating activities	100.0	100.0
Returns on investment and servicing of finance		
Interest paid	−13.7	−3.1
Taxation paid	−11.9	−6.9
Capital expenditure and financial investment		
Purchase of tangible fixed asset	−148.4	−55.9
Equity dividends paid	−14.6	−9.9
Cash outflow before financing	−88.6	24.2
Financing		
Issue of loan	91.6	6.2
Increase in cash	3.0	18.0

The following observations may be made concerning the content of Figure 10.5, focusing principally on the numbers for 20X9.

- Interest, taxation and dividends each absorbs a relatively small proportion of cash generated by Tamari from its business operations – no more than 14.6% in any one case. In total, just 40.2% of internally-generated funds are applied to service obligations to the government and suppliers of long-term finance.

- There has been a heavy investment in tangible fixed assets with 59.8% of the cash flow from operations (100% – 40.2%) used for this purpose. However, with the investment in fixed assets represented by an index of 148.4, the directors of Tamari have had to look elsewhere for the bulk of the funding. These financial relationships may be contrasted with the previous year when the entire capital investment was funded from internal sources, and a significant proportion (24.2%) of cash flow from operating activities remained available to increase the cash balance.

- The balance of long-term expenditure was entirely funded by the issue of a loan, leaving a small amount over to increase cash available at the end of 20X9 compared with a year earlier.

It is possible to add to the interpretative value of the cash flow statement by expressing some of the financial totals contained in the cash flow statement presented in Figure 10.4 as ratios of one another. As is always the case with ratio analysis, the validity of a ratio depends on the existence of an expected relationship between the financial magnitudes being compared. A number of valid ratios could be computed and two are presented below as illustrative of the possibilities available.

1. The internal:external finance ratio
The relationship between internal and external debt finance may be examined by expressing profit before non-cash expenses as a ratio of external financing. A low ratio shows that the company is increasing its reliance on external funding, perhaps for the purpose of further investment, and a deterioration in the gearing position of the company would be likely to result. The calculations for Tamari are as follows:

		20X9		20X8
Internal:external finance ratio	1,161:1,000 =	1.2:1	1,020:100 =	10.2:1

We can see that Tamari placed very little increased reliance on external finance in 20X8, but this has changed dramatically during 20X9 with amounts generated internally and externally roughly equal. This will be reflected in a revision of the long-term capital structure of the company which could be interrogated further by computing leverage ratios based on the contents of the balance sheet.

2. The shareholder funding ratio
The extent to which the equity shareholders have funded business investment during the year can be examined by expressing free cash flow available to shareholders

(internal cash flow after taxation, interest and dividends) as a percentage of expenditure on fixed assets and net current assets.

	20X9		20X8
Shareholder funding ratio	721:1,689 =	0.43:1	700:310 =	2.3:1

The shareholders of Tamari comfortably funded the entire business investment in 20X8, leaving a significant surplus to improve the company's liquidity position. In 20X9, by way of contrast, the directors have decided to rely heavily on debt to fund the substantial investment programme undertaken during the year.

The purpose of the cash flow statement is to improve the informative value of published financial reports. The lack of prominence given to cash flow-based accounting ratios as a means of improving the interpretative value of this data is particularly surprising given the enormous amount of space usually devoted to traditional accounting ratios in text books on financial accounting, management accounting and corporate finance. This section of Chapter 10 has demonstrated the contribution of three types of calculation: ratios that link the cash flow statement with key related items appearing in the balance sheet; the expression of each item in the cash flow statement as a percentage of net cash flow from operating activities; and the calculation of ratios to explore the interrelationship between items within the cash flow statement.

As usual, it should be noted that different ratios are expressed in different ways, as percentages, as multiples, or in pence, as well as in the classic form.

The interpretative value of individual ratios will depend upon the nature of the financial developments at a particular business. Given the content of Figure 10.4, for example, the cash flow per share (version I) ratio was not seen to possess any interpretative value and was not calculated. It is also the case that the messages conveyed by certain ratios may be similar for a particular company covering a particular year, but in a different time and place the same ratios may yield different insights.

Finally, one must remember the importance of not attaching too much weight to any single ratio but to use a representative range of ratios (including cash flow ratios!) to build up a meaningful business profile.

10.9 FURTHER READING

Alexander, D. and Britton, A. (1999) *Financial Reporting*, fifth edition, London: International Thomson Business Press, pp. 569-83 and Chapter 27.

Davies, Mike, Ron Paterson and Allister Wilson (1999), *Generally Accepted Accounting Practice in the United Kingdom*, sixth edition, Croydon: Butterworth Tolley, Chapter 26.

Elliott, B. and Elliott, J. (2000) *Financial Accounting and Reporting*, fifth edition, Hemel Hempstead: Prentice Hall, Chapter 24.

Lewis, Richard and David Pendrill (2000), *Advanced Financial Accounting*, sixth edition, Pitman, Chapter 11

Mills, J and Yamamura, H. (1998) 'The power of cash flow ratios', *Journal of Accountancy*, October.

Saksida, M. (1999) 'Subject to interpretation' *Management Accounting*, July/August, p.73

10.10 QUESTIONS

Question 10.1

The following are the Profit and Loss Account of Oakworth Ltd. for the year to 31 December 1998 and the Balance Sheets at the end of 1997 and 1998:

Profit and Loss Account for 1998

	£000	£000
Sales		3,500
Opening stock	240	
Purchases	1,700	
Closing stock	−400	
		1,540
		1,960
Depreciation	200	
Administration expenses	1,100	
Distribution costs	300	
		1,600
		360
Profit on sale of land	25	
Interest received	30	
Interest paid	−14	
		41
Net profit		401
Corporation tax		110
		291
Proposed dividend		180
Retained profit		111

Balance Sheets

	31 December 1998		31 December 1997	
	£000	£000	£000	£000
Net assets				
Land at cost		–		60
Other fixed assets at cost		1,500		1,000
Accumulated depreciation		700		500
		800		500
		800		560
Stock	400		240	
Debtors	526		390	
Cash	–		50	
	926		680	
Creditors	120		140	
Corporation tax	110		90	
Dividend	180		120	
Overdraft	115		–	
	525		350	
Net current assets		401		330
		1,201		890
Debenture loan		200		–
		1,001		890
Capital and Reserves				
Ordinary shares of £1 each		600		600
Retained profit		401		290
		1,001		890

Required:
(a) Prepare a Cash Flow Statement for Oakworth Ltd for the year to 31 December 1998 which complies with FRS1 entitled 'Cash Flow Statements'. *[12 marks]*

(b) Identify and discuss four significant financial developments that have occurred during 1998 based on the content of the cash flow statement prepared under (a). *[8 marks]*

[Total –20 marks]

Question 10.2

Mr Thornton's accountant has recently prepared the accounts of Thornton & Co. including the following balance sheet:

Balance Sheet of Thornton & Co. at 30 April

	1995		1994	
	£	£	£	£
Plant and machinery at cost	10,000		10,000	
Less: Accumulated depreciation	6,750	3,250	5,500	4,500
Motor vehicles at cost	62,000		45,000	
Less: Accumulated depreciation	37,000	25,000	22,000	23,000
		28,250		27,500
Current Assets				
Stocks	18,600		12,500	
Debtors and prepayments	17,100		13,350	
Bank balance	–		1,640	
	35,700		27,490	
Current Liabilities				
Creditors and accruals	13,200		10,350	
Bank overdraft	562		–	
	13,762		10,350	
Net current assets		21,938		17,140
Total assets less current liabilities		50,188		44,640
Loan repayable 1997 (repaid 1 May 1994)		–		8,000
		50,188		36,640
Capital		50,188		36,640

Mr Thornton tells you that the accounts must be wrong:

> 'The profit and loss account shows that sales are up by one-third and that, during the year, I made my best profit ever of £44,798. 1 have kept my drawings down to £2,000 each month, although I did have to take out of the business a further £7,250 to pay demands for income tax and national insurance. I cannot understand how a healthy bank balance at the start of the year could have been turned into an overdraft.'

Required:
(a) Identify the main differences between a cash flow statement and a profit and loss account. [4]
(b) Prepare a cash flow statement for Thornton & Co. for the year ended 30 April 1995. The statement should be presented in accordance with the provisions of FRS1. You should provide a reconciliation of operating profit with net cash flow from operations, but other notes to the cash flow statement are not required. [8]
(c) Calculate the liquidity ratio and the gearing ratio at 30 April 1994 and 1995. [2]
(d) Prepare a report for Mr Thornton on the main financial developments during the year and their impact on the financial position of the company. Your report should be based on your calculations under (b) and (c) above. [6]

Note:
There were no sales of fixed assets during the year to 30 April 1995. [Total – 20]

Question 10.3

The following cash flow statement has been prepared for Cowton Ltd for 1999.

Cash Flow Statement for the year ended 31 December 1999

	£m	£m
Reconciliation of operating profit to net cash inflow from operating activities.		
Operating profit		19
Depreciation charges		31
Net increase in stocks, debtors and trade creditors		−7
Net cash flows from operating activities		43
Returns on investment and servicing of finance		
Preference dividend paid	7	
Interest element of finance lease rental payments	4	−11
Taxation paid		−13
Capital expenditure and financial investment		
Purchase of tangible fixed assets		−23
Equity dividends paid		−18
Cash outflow before use of liquid resources and financing		−22
Financing		
Issue of shares	39	
Capital element of finance lease rental payments	−25	14
Decrease in cash		−8

One of your customers, who owns shares in Cowton Ltd, has raised the following queries:

1 . The figure for depreciation is added to operating profit in order to compute the net cash inflow from operating activities, and the customer cannot understand how charging deprecation can generate cash.

2. Payments in respect of the lease rental of £29 million are split between two sections of the cash flow statement.

3. The tax charge in the profit and loss account amounts to £17 million compared with the figure of £13 million in the cash flow statement.

4. The preference dividend paid and the equity dividend paid are shown in separate sections of the cash flow statement.

5. The figure for ordinary share capital in the balance sheet has gone up by just £26 million compared with the figure of £39 million in the cash flow statement.

Required:
Set out in detail how you would respond to the queries raised by your customer.   *[20 marks]*

Question 10.4

The balance sheet and statement of movement of fixed assets of Poulet plc for 1997 contained the following information.

Balance Sheet at 31 December 1997

	1997 £000	1996 £000
Tangible fixed assets		
Freehold land and buildings	1,160	1,200
Plant and machinery	1,700	700
	2,860	1,900
Current Assets		
Stocks	1,020	715
Debtors and prepayments	826	590
Government securities	–	52
Cash at bank and in hand	47	15
	1,893	1,372
Creditors: Amounts falling due within one year		
Trade creditors	940	520
Current corporation tax	45	130
Proposed dividend	105	90
	1,090	740
Net current assets (liabilities)	803	632
Total assets less current liabilities	3,663	2,532
Creditors: amounts falling due after more than one year		
10% Debentures repayable 2010	1,500	500
Provisions for liabilities and charges		
Provision for deferred taxation	180	100
	1,983	1,932
Capital and Reserves		
Called up share capital (£1 ordinary shares)	1,400	1,400
Share premium account	250	250
Profit and loss account	333	282
	1,983	1,932

Statement of Movement of Fixed Assets

	Freehold land buildings	*Plant and machinery*	*Total*
	£000	*£000*	*£000*
Cost at 1 January 1997	2,000	1,600	3,600
Additions	–	1,620	1,620
Cost at 31 December 1997	2,000	3,220	5,220
Depreciation at 1 January 1997	800	900	1,700
Provided during the year	40	620	660
Depreciation at 31 December 1997	840	1,520	2,360
Net book amount at 31 December 1997	1,160	1,700	2,860

The following additional information is provided:

1. Additional debentures were issued on 1 January 1997. Interest is payable on 31 December.

2. The company sold its temporary investment in government securities for £59,000 on 1 January 1997.

3. An interim dividend for 1997 of £70,000 was paid on 1 August 1997.

4. A significant expansion of the company's operations took place in the autumn of 1997 to meet rapidly rising consumer demand.

Required:
(a) Reconstruct the profit and loss account of Poulet plc for 1997, insofar as the information permits, to enable the identification of the figure for operating profit before interest. *[6 marks]*

(b) The cash flow statement of Poulet plc for 1997 complying with the provisions of FRS 1. A reconciliation of operating profit to net cash inflow from operating activities should be prepared, but other notes to the cash flow statement are not required. *[12 marks]*

(c) Discuss the financial developments at Poulet plc during 1997, its financial position at the year-end and its prospects for 1998. Your discussion should be based on the information provided in the question together with that prepared under (a) and (b) and relevant traditional accounting ratios. *[12 marks]*

[Total – 30 marks]

11

BUSINESS
DECISION MAKING:
COST BEHAVIOUR

11.1 INTRODUCTION

The assumption of the rational economic person is at the basis of accounting techniques designed to analyse the financial consequences of alternative courses of action. This assumption leads to the inevitable conclusion that the options chosen will be those that help to achieve the corporate objective of profit maximization. In practice, however, the option that appears financially most beneficial is not always selected, and there are a number of possible explanations for what appears to be an irrational decision. These include: unacceptable social consequences, such as the need to lay off workers and significantly increase local unemployment; environmental hazards; the failure to correspond with the overall corporate plan; and a high level of risk which cannot be precisely measured in financial terms.

Despite these constraints the science of management accounting has been developed to enable information to be generated which is relevant for the interrelated purposes of planning, decision making and control. Within this framework:

- *Planning* involves the identification of corporate objectives, and the collection and analysis of data in order to enable alternative courses of action to be ranked in terms of their expected financial merit.

- *Decision making* involves choosing, and implementing, the financially most favoured alternative, bearing in mind the possible constraints identified above.

- *Control* involves monitoring actual results and evaluating performance by comparison with earlier expectations. This information provides the necessary 'feedback' which enables corrective action to be taken when a plan is not fulfilling expectations, and helps to build up experience which can be 'tapped' when future plans are subjected to financial scrutiny.

This chapter concentrates on the decision making stage of the management accounting process and, more specifically, the study of cost behaviour to analyse available opportunities.

11.2 COST BEHAVIOUR AND ANALYSIS

Sales revenue is the product of the number of units sold and the price per unit, but the number of units sold is, in turn, influenced by price; if the unit price rises, fewer units are sold; if it falls, more are sold. It is management's job to select the unit price and, thereby, the quantity sold and total revenue, so as to maximize profit. To measure profit at any forecast level of output, the related costs must also be estimated. This requires a clear understanding of the fact that different costs behave in different ways when output changes. It is therefore useful to analyse costs into different categories, each of which contains costs which respond in a similar manner. The categorization is unlikely to be completely accurate, but the impact of any error is reduced by the fact that the information is used to help to predict future results, and this exercise must necessarily contain an element of uncertainty. One useful classification of costs is fixed and variable (see 11.2.1 and 11.2.2); another is marginal cost and sunk cost (see 11.5).

11.2.1 Fixed Costs

Certain costs are incurred irrespective of an enterprise's rate of activity. For example, once the decision has been made to rent a factory, the full rent must be paid irrespective of whether the occupier uses all, or just a small proportion, of the available floor area. Such costs are known as 'fixed costs' because they remain fixed over a limited range of output. Up to a certain level of activity, a company can expand its output without the need to incur additional fixed costs. However, once full capacity is reached, any further expansion will require the company to incur an additional set of fixed costs. Other examples of fixed costs are administrative salaries and straight-line depreciation charges.

11.2.2 Variable Costs

These vary with the rate of activity; the greater the output of a company, the higher are its total variable costs. For example, when a shop makes extra sales it has to purchase additional stock, and this is a variable cost. In manufacturing, examples of variable costs are the direct labour and direct material costs. It is usual to assume that the variable cost per unit is constant, that is, each extra unit of throughput causes the company to incur the same additional cost. This relationship may not hold in practice; the unit cost of labour may rise with an expansion of output, as overtime is worked, while the unit material cost may fall as the result of receiving increased discounts on bulk purchases (see Chapter 9, Examples 4 and 5, for simple illustrations of the effect of changes in the level of activity on costs and, therefore, profit margins).

Example 11.1

The summarized profit and loss account of Merrill Ltd, a company which manufacturers a single product, is as follows:

PROFIT AND LOSS ACCOUNT, YEAR ENDED 30 JUNE 19X2

	£	£
Sales (25,000 units)		1,000,000
Less: Manufacturing costs – variable	500,000	
– fixed	180,000	
Cost of goods sold		680,000
Gross profit		320,000
Less: Running costs		200,000
Net profit		£120,000

There is strong demand for the company's product, but there is also keen competition from other suppliers. The directors of Merrill Ltd believe that if the sales price remains unchanged, at £40 per unit, turnover will amount to only 23,000 units in the year to 30 June 19X3. Further estimates show that turnover of 25,000 units could again be achieved if the price were reduced to £39, while a reduction in sales price to £38 would cause turnover to increase to 35,000 units. Variable manufacturing costs per unit and fixed manufacturing costs per annum are expected to remain unchanged whichever of the three options is chosen by the company's directors. At 23,000 units, running costs will fall to £165,000 whereas at 35,000 units they will rise to £320,000.

Required:
(a) Forecast profit and loss accounts of Merrill Ltd for the year ended 30 June 19X3, under each of the alternatives indicated above.

(b) Calculations of the net profit ratio (net profit as a percentage of sales) under each of these alternatives.

(c) An indication of the alternative that you would favour. You should explain your choice and also refer to any further information which might help the decision making process.

Note:
Assume for the purposes of this question that your calculations are being made on 1 July 19X2.

Solution

(a) *Forecast Profit and Loss Accounts*

	23,000 units		25,000 units		35,000 units	
	£000	£000	£000	£000	£000	£000
Sales		920		975		1,330
Less: Manufacturing costs:						
Variable	460		500		700	
Fixed	180		180		180	
Cost of goods sold		640		680		880
Gross profit		280		295		450
Less: Running costs		165		200		320
Net profit		115		95		130

(b) Net profit ratio   12.5%   9.7%   9.8%

(c) The choice between the three options depends on which measure of performance is considered more relevant for the purpose of the decision which must be made, net profit or the net profit ratio.

Applying the former criterion, it would seem that the sales price should be reduced to £38 in order to enable production and sales to increase to 35,000 units. This results in a profit of £130,000 which is significantly higher than the net returns arising under the other two alternatives.

The net profit ratio is higher where sales amount to 23,000 units. This is because the smaller gross margin accruing to the reduced output is substantially offset by lower running costs.

Each of the above measures provides helpful guidelines but should be used in conjunction with other information and estimates. The amount of additional investment required to enable output to be increased to 35,000 units should be established and, when this information is obtained, the return on capital employed can be calculated. An estimate of the likely demand pattern after the expiration of the forthcoming twelve months is also needed.

11.2.3 Contribution Costing

A useful approach to the study of cost behaviour is that based on the 'contribution' which each unit sold makes towards fixed costs. Analysis based on this approach assumes that the revenue from each unit is first applied to meet its related variable costs, and any surplus, the contribution, is then set against fixed costs. Once the fixed costs have been completely recovered, the contribution of each additional unit sold adds to profit. The contribution of each unit is calculated by the formula:

$$\text{Contribution per Unit} = \text{Selling Price per Unit} - \text{Variable Cost per Unit}$$

Example 11.2

Starling Ltd manufactures a single product called 'Tibber'. The manufacturing costs of a single unit of Tibber are:

	£
Materials	5.00
Wages	4.50
Variable expenses	1.50

Annual fixed manufacturing expenses are £238,000.

Required:
Calculate the contribution made by each unit of Tibber if its selling price is:
(a) £18;
(b) £15.

Solution

The total variable cost per unit is:

	£
Materials	5.00
Wages	4.50
Variable expenses	1.50
	11.00

(a) Contribution = £18 − £11 = £7
(b) Contribution = £15 − £11 = £4

The use of 'Contribution' as a management aid is now examined in the context of Breakeven Analysis (11.3) and Limiting Factors (11.4).

11.3 BREAKEVEN ANALYSIS

Breakeven analysis examines the behaviour of costs in response to changes in the level of output; it compares the total cost, that is, fixed plus variable costs, with sales revenue to determine the profit or loss. The point at which the firm breaks even is when it makes neither profit nor loss as total costs are exactly equal to sales revenue. Breakeven analysis is useful both to discover the level of output required to achieve various profit targets and also to compare the likely results of different techniques of production. It is often possible to interchange fixed and variable costs; for example, a method of production can be capital intensive or labour intensive.

This section shows how to calculate the breakeven point in straightforward circumstances (11.3.1), then examines its evaluation (11.3.2 and 11.3.3) and finally considers the effect of introducing the more complicated situations likely to be met in the real world (11.3.4 to 11.3.7).

11.3.1 Calculation of the Breakeven Point

The numerical approach to breakeven analysis is based on the 'contribution' (see 11.2.3). The breakeven point, i.e. where neither a profit nor loss results, is reached when sufficient units have been sold to cover fixed costs exactly; below this point a loss is made, and above it a profit. The breakeven point, in terms of units, is calculated with the formula:

$$Q = \frac{F}{C}$$

Where: Q = units sold
F = fixed costs
C = contribution

$Q \times S$ gives the breakeven point in terms of sales revenue.

Where: S = selling price per unit.

Target profit If it is desired to find the level of sales necessary to achieve a given level of profit, the formula is:

$$Q = \frac{F + P}{C}$$

Where P = the desired profit, and the other items are as given above.

Example 11.3

Bevan Ltd is considering two alternative methods to manufacture a new product it intends to market. The two methods each have a maximum output of 50,000 units and produce identical items with a selling price of £25 each. The costs are:

	Method I (Labour intensive) £	Method II (Capital intensive) £
Variable cost per unit	15	10
Fixed costs	100,000	300,000

Required:
(a) Calculate the breakeven point of each method in terms of both units and sales revenue.

(b) Calculate the level of sales, in terms of both units and revenue, required under each method to produce a profit of £30,000.

(c) Calculate the profit of each method at full capacity.

Solution

(a) *Breakeven point*

	Method I	Method II
Selling price per unit	25	25
Variable cost per unit	15	10
Contribution	10	15

$$\frac{\text{Fixed cost}}{\text{Contribution}} =$$

	Method I	Method II
	$\frac{100,000}{10}$	$\frac{300,000}{15}$
	= *10,000 units*	= *20,000 units*
Sales revenue:	10,000 x £25	20,000 x £25
	= *£250,000*	= *£500,000*

(b) Target Profit £30,000

Method I
$$\frac{100,000 \text{ (fixed cost)} + 30,000 \text{ (target profit)}}{10 \text{ (contribution)}} = 13,000 \text{ units}$$

13,000 (units sold) x £25 (unit price) = *£325,000*

Method II
$$\frac{300,000 \text{ (fixed cost)} + 30,000 \text{ (target profit)}}{15 \text{ (contribution)}} = 22,000 \text{ units}$$

22,000 (units sold) x £25 (unit price) = *£550,000*

(c) *Profit at full capacity*

	Method I	*Method II*
Contribution	50,000 x 10 = £500,000	50,000 x 15 = £750,000
Less: Fixed costs	100,000	300,000
Profit	£400,000	£450,000

The method of production appropriate for Bevan Ltd depends on the expected level of sales. More units have to be sold to reach breakeven point under Method II, and it carries the risk of greater loss, which at zero output is equal to fixed costs. At low levels of output, Method I is therefore preferred. Once fixed costs have been recovered, the profit grows more quickly with each additional unit sold under Method II as its contribution is greater. At maximum output, Method II produces the higher profit.

The relationship between costs, profit and volume can be clearly demonstrated using a graph (see Figure 11.1 based on the information given in Example 11.3). The horizontal axis measures units of output, while the vertical axis measures the value of sales revenue and business costs. Revenues and costs relating to individual projects are represented by the following straight lines on the graph.

Sales: When no sales are made the revenue is zero. The revenue at maximum output is plotted, R, and these two points are joined, O-R.

Fixed Costs: These are the same at all levels of output up to maximum capacity, and so the line is horizontal. For Method I, fixed costs are £100,000 and are represented by the line FCI.

Variable Costs: When no output is produced, these are zero. The variable cost at maximum output is plotted, VCI for Method I, and the two points are joined, O-VCI.

Total Cost: This is the total of fixed and variable costs, represented by the line TCI for Method I.

The breakeven point is where the total cost line crosses the revenue line; the profit or loss at any point is represented by the gap between these lines. The rate at which the width of the gap changes shows how quickly profits and losses respond to changes in output.

Figure 11.1

The breakeven graph for both Methods I and II using the information given in Example 11.3 above for Bevan Ltd is:

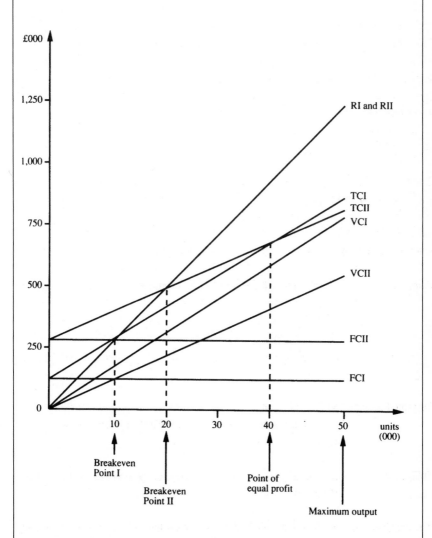

Notes:
1. For ease of interpretation the variable cost lines may be omitted.
2. Study the rate of growth of profit under each of the methods.

11.3.2 Profit Equilibrium

It is possible to find the point of output at which two alternative methods of production achieve the same profit. This is the level at which total costs are the same under each plan. It is found using the formula:

$F_I + V_I Q = F_{II} + V_{II} Q$
Where: F = fixed costs
V = variable cost per unit
Q = units sold
I and II signify different methods of production

For Bevan Ltd (Example 11.3), equal profits are earned when:

$$100,000 + 15Q = 300,000 + 10Q$$
$$5Q = 200,000$$
$$Q = 40,000 \text{ units}$$

This is shown on the graph in Figure 11.1 as the point where the total cost lines cross.

11.3.3 Margin of Safety

To emphasize the extent of vulnerability to changes in output, it is useful to calculate the 'Margin of Safety', which shows how far sales can fall before a loss is incurred. It is calculated, either in terms of units or value, by the formula:

$$\frac{\text{Anticipated Sales} - \text{Sales at Breakeven Point}}{\text{Anticipated Sales}}$$

For example, if Bevan Ltd (Example 11.3) anticipated sales of 30,000 units, the margin of safety for each method is:

	Method I		*Method II*	
Units:	$\dfrac{30,000 - 10,000}{30,000} = \dfrac{2}{3}$	$= 67\%$	$\dfrac{30,000 - 20,000}{30,000} = \dfrac{1}{3}$	$= 33\%$
OR				
Value:	$\dfrac{750,000 - 250,000}{750,000} = \dfrac{2}{3}$	$= 67\%$	$\dfrac{750,000 - 500,000}{750,000} = \dfrac{1}{3}$	$= 33\%$

These calculations show that under Method I sales can fall by 67%, from forecast levels, before a loss is made, while under Method II a loss occurs after a fall of only 33%. Therefore, Method I has the greater margin of safety.

11.3.4 Stepped Costs

The analysis of costs into fixed and variable is a useful step in financial analysis, but constraints imposed by 'time' and 'output' must also be considered.

In the short run virtually no costs (other than perhaps material inputs) are variable, and must therefore be classified as fixed for decision-making purposes. By way of contrast, in the long run all costs become variable, in the sense that it becomes possible to discontinue the use of plant which has reached the end of its useful life, surrender a lease and, even, close down the entire business. Between these extremes exists the more usual situation where some costs, such as rent, rates, straight-line depreciation and directors' remuneration, may be treated as fixed costs, and others, such as material costs, labour costs and salesman's commission behave as variable.

Looking more closely at variable costs, very few are smoothly variable, in the sense that a very small increase in activity results in a corresponding, and proportional, increase in costs incurred. More usually costs are incurred in indivisible lump sums which may be either large or small. These possibilities are demonstrated in Figure 11.2 in which the 'steps' represent the costs incurred by a manufacturing company which has to employ one additional operative to obtain the capacity to produce an additional 5,000 units of output and is able to rent, at equal cost, premises which provide a capacity of 40,000 units of output. An examination of the information contained in Figure 11.2 shows that the classification of a cost as fixed or variable depends on the possible range of expected output. This is referred as the 'relevant range'.

1. Relevant range of output: 1-40,000 units. Rent is a fixed cost and the operatives' wages a variable cost.

2. Relevant range of output: 11,000-14,000 units. Both types of cost are fixed between these points.

3. Relevant range of output: 1-50,000 units. Both categories of cost show variation.

11.3.5 Curvilinear (or Semi-Variable) Costs and Revenues

Even though variable costs usually increase in short steps, it is perfectly reasonable to represent such a cost function by a straight line which closely approximates actual cost behaviour. A separate problem which must be recognized is that the behaviour of variable costs may well begin to depart quite dramatically from the straight-line approximation after a particular level of activity is reached. Figure 11.3 depicts the possibility of rising labour costs per unit which might occur because of, for example,

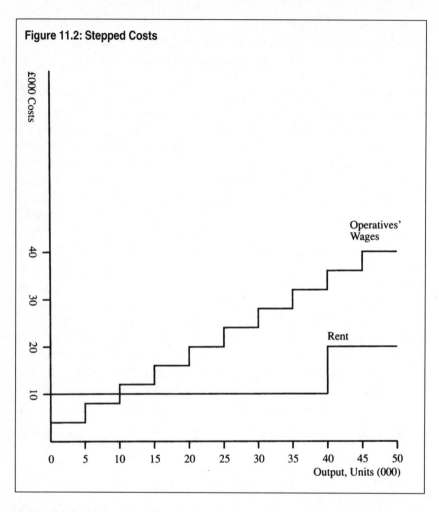

Figure 11.2: Stepped Costs

the need to pay overtime. The cost is no longer represented by a straight line and becomes what is described as a 'curvilinear'. In a similar vein, it is possible that material costs per unit will decline as purchases increase due to a company's ability to negotiate more favourable trade discounts.

Management must also remain aware of the fact that the demand for their product is extremely unlikely to be inelastic when forecasting possible future results. Selling price is usually inversely related to the level of output. Where this occurs the curvilinear revenue function will broadly take the form also represented in Figure 11.3.

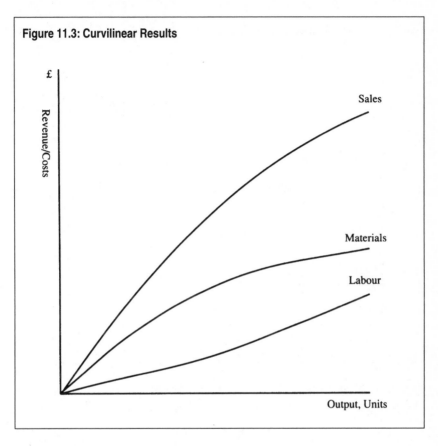

Figure 11.3: Curvilinear Results

11.3.6 Multiple Breakeven Points

Figure 11.1 shows a single breakeven point for each method of production, and the clear implication of the graph is that at increased levels of activity a higher profit will always be made. However, the fact is that, in the real world, revenues, costs and profits respond to increases in activity in a more complicated manner. The possibility of rising output accompanied by falling profits may be caused by any or all of the following: the need to incur an additional set of fixed costs, a rise in variable costs per unit, or the need to charge a lower price to achieve additional sales.

The existence of more than one breakeven point therefore also becomes a possible outcome of which management needs to be aware. Figure 11.4 shows that the project breaks even at point Ob but, if the company is to extend activity beyond Oc, an additional set of fixed costs must be incurred which results, initially, in a loss being suffered. The

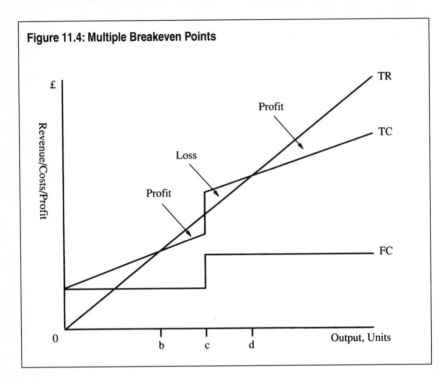

Figure 11.4: Multiple Breakeven Points

company will therefore not make this investment unless it is reasonably confident that a level of activity significantly in excess of Od can subsequently be achieved.

Example 11.4

The following information is provided for a product produced by Variation Ltd.

Fixed costs: output	1-100,000 units = £80,000. 100,000-250,000 units = £160,000.
Variable costs:	1-100,000 units = £1 per unit. Thereafter £1.60 per unit.
Revenue: Sales	1-100,000 units = £2.20 per unit. Thereafter £2 per unit.

Required:
(a) A flexible budget showing cost, revenues and profit at 25,000 intervals of output, commencing at zero up to a maximum of 250,000.

(b) A graphical presentation of the results prepared in answer to (a).

Solution

(a)

Output £000	FC £000	VC £000	TC £000	TR £000	P £000
0	80	–	80	–	(80)
25	80	25	105	55	(50)
50	80	50	130	110	(20)
75	80	75	155	165	10
100	80	100	180	220	40
125	160	140	300	270	(30)
150	160	180	340	320	(20)
175	160	220	380	370	(10)
200	160	260	420	420	–
225	160	300	460	470	10
250	160	340	500	520	20

(b)

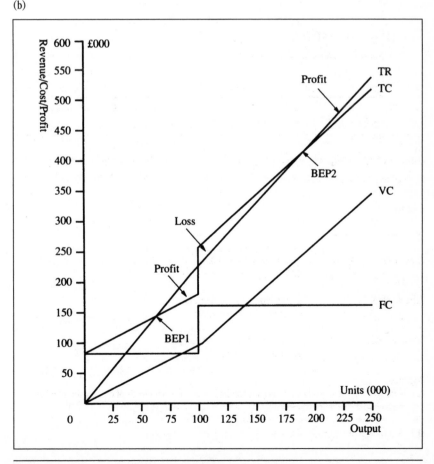

11.3.7 Multi-Product Firms

Further problems may arise because of the fact that most firms deal in more than one product. In such circumstances it is usually sensible for management to produce a separate breakeven chart for each product so that its financial implications can be individually assessed. Difficulties occur where there exist joint products and/or common fixed costs. For joint products – i.e. where the production and/or sale of one product is inextricably linked with that of another – the usual solution is to assess them as a single item. If breakeven analysis is used, their financial effects will be displayed on a single graph. In the case of common costs – i.e. costs that cannot be directly associated with a particular product – the appropriate treatment is to exclude such costs from the financial assessment of individual products. Common costs must not of course be forgotten, and should be deducted from the combined 'contributions' made by individual product lines in order to determine the overall results of the business.

11.4 LIMITING FACTORS

The total output of a firm or department, especially in the short term, may be constrained by the amount available of a particular essential input, such as labour or machinery. The item that restricts the firm's output is known as the 'Limiting Factor'. It takes time to train additional labour or acquire a new machine, and so, where a company manufactures and sells a number of different products, all of which require this scarce resource, it is necessary to select the mix of items which maximizes the firm's overall profit. Different products made by a firm are likely to use different amounts of the limiting factor, and, to maximize profit, it is necessary to concentrate on the products that give the greatest contribution to fixed costs per unit of the limiting factor consumed.

Example 11.5

A department of Noste Ltd has the ability to produce three products termed A, B and C; the department's annual fixed costs are £5,000. Each of the products uses a specialized type of labour which is in limited supply.

The following information is provided:

Product	A	B	C
Selling price per unit £	10.00	15.00	20.00
Variable cost per unit £	7.60	10.00	12.20
Hours of specialized labour per unit	3.0	2.5	6.0
Maximum annual sales – units	1,600	2,200	500

Required:
Advise management which products it should make and calculate the department's profit if the annual total hours of specialized labour available are:
(a) 8,020
(b) 9,100

Solution

Workings

Product	A	B	C
	£	£	£
Selling price per unit	10.00	15.00	20.00
Variable cost per unit	7.60	10.00	12.20
Contribution per unit (A)	2.40	5.00	7.80
Hours of specialized labour per unit (B)	3.0	2.5	6.0
Contribution per hour of labour (A/B)	0.8	2.0	1.3
Ranking*	3	1	2
Maximum annual sales – units (C)	1,600	2,200	500
Usage of limiting factor at maximum sales – hours (C x B)	4,800	5,500	3,000

*It is not possible to satisfy the full demand for all three products. The demand for product B will be met first, then product C, and finally product A.

(a) The hours of the limiting factor available are 8,020. The full demand for B can be met, and the remaining 2,520 hours (8,020-5,500) will be used to produce 420 (2,520 hours available/6 hours per unit) units of C.

The profit will be:

	£
Contribution from B	
(2,200 output x £5 contribution)	11,000
Contribution from C	
(420 output x £7.8 contribution)	3,276
	14,276
Less: Fixed costs	5,000
Profit	9,276

(b) The hours of the limiting factor available are 9,100. The full demand for B and C can be met, and the remaining 600 hours (9,100- 5,500-3,000)) will be used to produce 200 (600 hours available/3 hours per unit) units of A.

The profit will be:

	£
Contribution from B	
(2,200 output x £5 contribution)	11,000
Contribution from C	
(500 output x £7.8 contribution)	3,900
Contribution from A	
(200 output x £2.4 contribution)	480
	15,380
Less: Fixed costs	5,000
Profit	10,380

11.5 MARGINAL COSTS AND SUNK COSTS

Marginal cost is the increase in costs caused by an increase in activity of one unit; for analytical purposes the unit may be, for example, a single article, a batch, an order, or a whole department. In the context of breakeven analysis the marginal cost of producing one extra unit is its variable cost, but the approach has wider applications as it may be applied to, for example, an increase in productive capacity which also involves additional fixed costs. Unlike breakeven analysis, marginal costing does not assume that each additional unit imposes the same extra variable cost; each marginal unit is considered separately. To aid decision making, the marginal cost is compared with marginal revenue and, if there is an excess of revenue over cost, the activity is undertaken because it adds to the aggregate profit.

Sunk costs are those resources that have already been invested in a particular project, and they are ignored when the marginal cost approach is used to aid a decision between alternative courses of action, such as, whether to replace an existing machine or retain it in use. For example, a company which has a machine, still in working order, with a book value of £1m and a scrap value of zero should disregard its written down value when assessing the offer of a new, technically improved machine at an annual hire charge of £200,000. If the new machine can produce savings in excess of £200,000 per annum it should be hired and the old machine scrapped; the £1m at which the old machine is held in the books is a sunk cost and no outflow of resources will occur if it is replaced by the new machine, then scrapped, and the balance written off.

Consideration of marginal cost is particularly relevant when prices are determined by the market, especially where separate markets can be differentiated or bids have to be made to obtain work. The marginal cost is the minimum that can be accepted as a selling price, since below this the activity does not recover even its out-of-pocket expenses. Provided that a sale is made at above marginal cost, some contribution is made to fixed costs and profit. The alternative is to use a full-cost approach which attempts to recover in each sale its full share of overhead costs, but this approach might result in orders being lost which would be beneficial to the company.

Example 11.6

Home Ltd has a maximum productive capacity of 60,000 units but can sell only 50,000 units per year in the home market at a price of £10 each. The variable cost per unit is £6 and the company's annual fixed costs are £150,000. The company has been approached by an exporter who wishes to place an order of 15,000 units a year at a price of £8 each.

Required:
Prepare a financial statement on which the management of Home Ltd can base a decision on whether, from the point of view of profitability, the export order should be accepted. No increase in productive capacity is to be made.

Solution

	Without Export Order		£000	*With Export Order*		£000	£000
Variable Cost	50,000 x £6	=	300	60,000 x £6	=		360
Fixed Cost			150				150
Total Cost			450				510
Revenue	50,000 x £10	=	500	45,000 x £10	=	450	
				15,000 x £8	=	120	
							570
Profit			50				60
Average Total Cost	$\dfrac{450,000}{50,000}$	=	£9	$\dfrac{510,000}{60,000}$	=		£8.5

In both cases the average total cost per unit is greater than the export price. However, acceptance of the export order increases overall profit because its marginal cost (£6 per unit) is less than its marginal revenue (£8 per unit).

11.6 FURTHER READING

Arnold, J. and Turley, S. (1996) *Accounting for Management Decisions,* London: Prentice Hall, Chapter 8.

Drury, C. (1997) *Management Accounting for Business Decisions*, London: International Thomson Business Press, Chapter 3.

Idowu, S. (1998) 'The concept of breakeven analysis in decision making', *ACCA Students' Newsletter,* April, pp. 62-4.

Weetman, P. (1999) *Management Accounting. An Introduction*, London: Pitman, Chapter 9.

11.7 QUESTIONS

Question 11.1

The directors of Mattessich Ltd have under consideration the supply of a new product, designated ZZ, for which the maximum possible demand is estimated to be 8,000 units per annum. ZZ can be produced employing either of two production methods, and the following costs and related data have been assembled by the estimating department:

	Method A	Method B
Plant: cost	£6,200,000	£3,700,000
useful economic life	6 years	6 years
estimated residual value	£200,000	£100,000
Initial working capital requirement	£1,000,000	£1,000,000
Variable costs per unit	£900	£1,200
Fixed costs other than depreciation	£2,000,000	£600,000
Unit selling price of ZZ	£1,500	£1,500

Required:
(a) For Methods A and B, separate calculations of:

    (i) the breakeven point;

    (ii) the level of sales required to produce a return of 25% per annum on the original investment. *[8 marks]*

(b) The identification of the range of sales activity at which it would be financially beneficial to:

    (i) produce ZZ using method A;

    (ii) produce ZZ using method B. *[4 marks]*

(c) Discuss the limitations of breakeven analysis and outline how these might be overcome. *[8 marks]*

[Total – 20 marks]

Question 11.2

The following forecast information is provided for Russell Ltd, which manufactures four different types of metal containers, in respect of 1999.

1.
Container	A	B	C	D
Capacity (litres)	3	8	10	20
Selling price per unit	£60	£100	£110	£200
Variable cost per unit	£30	£60	£80	£100
Annual demand for containers	3,000	5,000	4,000	1,800

2. The amount of metal required to produce each of the containers is as follows:

Container	Metal required, per unit (kilograms)
A	10
B	20
C	30
D	40

3. The directors of Russell Ltd estimate that they will be able to acquire 100,000 kilograms of the appropriate type of metal in 1999.

4. The fixed costs are expected to amount to £120,000 in 1999.

Required:
(a) Define the term 'limiting factor' and explain its significance in relation to production decision making. *[4 marks]*

(b) On the assumption that the directors' policy is one of profit maximization, prepare the following for Russell Ltd based on the information provided above:

(i) a production plan for 1999; and

(ii) an estimated profit calculation for 1999. *[11 marks]*

(c) Explain how the production plan that you prepare results in the most effective use of the limited quantity of metal estimated to be available. *[5 marks]*

[Total – 20 marks]

Question 11.3

The following costs and other information are provided relating to product Zed.

1. Plant costing £100,000 to be purchased on year one, day one. The plant is expected to have a four-year life and zero residual value.

2. A contract to be entered into on year one, day one for the rental of premises at a cost of £12,000 per annum for four years. The premises may be vacated at any stage but a penalty equal to the rental outstanding for the four-year period must then be paid.

3. Other fixed costs to amount to £6,000 per annum.

4. The variable cost of producing product Zed to amount to £5 per unit.

Required:
(a) Explain the difference between total costs, marginal costs and sunk costs.   *[5 marks]*

(b) Assuming that the project has not yet commenced, calculate the minimum price that must be charged for Zed in order to break even if planned production is 10,000 units per annum.   *[5 marks]*

(c) Assuming that contractual obligations have been entered into relating to items 1 and 2, calculate the minimum price that must be charged for Zed in order to cover any remaining marginal and variable costs if planned production is 10,000 units per annum.   *[3 marks]*

(d) Distinguish between fixed and variable costs, and explain why the classification of a particular cost as fixed must be conditional on the level of activity within the business entity.   *[4 marks]*

(e) Calculate the breakeven level of sales per annum in terms of quantity and value, assuming product Zed is to be sold for £8 per unit.   *[3 marks]*

Notes:
Ignore the time value of money.
Ignore taxation.   *[Total – 20 marks]*

Question 11.4

The directors of Pylon plc have under consideration two methods of manufacturing a new product which they intend to bring to the market on 1 January 20X4. The following information is provided:

1.		Method A	Method B
	Variable costs per unit	£	£
	Materials	60	60
	Labour	100	60
	Expenses	20	20
	Cost of plant	500,000	1,000,000
	Working capital requirements	400,000	400,000
	Fixed operating costs per annum		
	(other than depreciation)	200,000	300,000

2. The plant to be acquired for the purposes of methods A and B is, in each case, expected to have a useful economic life of 5 years and a zero residual value at the end of that time.

3. The company plans to finance the investment in plant and working capital from available cash resources which would otherwise be invested in securities expected to yield an annual return of 10%.

4. The new product will sell for £300 per unit and the planning department has forecast annual sales of 7,000 units.

Required:
(a) For method A and method B separate calculations of.

    (i)   the level of sales, in units and value, required to break even;

    (ii)   the level of sales, in units and value, at which profits earned under each plan are equal;

    (iii) profit at the forecast level of sales;

    (iv) the margin of safety.   [16]

(b) A graph (not necessarily to scale) which shows the level of sales at which profits earned under each method are equal. You should indicate on the graph the levels of activity at which profits are higher under method B.   [6]

(c) A full discussion of the relative merits of the two methods of manufacture based on your answers to (a) and (b). Explain which method you would favour.   [8]

Notes:
1. Ignore the time value of money.

2. Ignore taxation.   [Total marks – 30]

Question 11.5

Carburton Ltd manufactures a standard product, designated XL, which sells for £70 per unit. The company normally produces and sells 16,000 units per annum, representing 80% of total available capacity. The cost forecasts for the twelve months commencing 1 June 20X2, set out below, have been prepared on the assumption that the company operates at its normal level of activity throughout that period. The estimated costs at full capacity are provided for the purpose of comparison.

Level of activity	80%	100%
Costs	£	£
Direct materials	480,000	600,000
Direct labour	80,000	100,000
Production overheads	260,000	300,000
Administration costs	220,000	220,000

The production overheads contain both fixed and variable costs.

The demand for XL has recently weakened, and the sales manager is doubtful whether it will be possible to operate at much more than 60% of full capacity during the forthcoming year.

From time to time Carburton Ltd also manufactures specialist machinery, SM, for which it holds a registered patent. The SM machine is constructed by workers, specifically engaged for that purpose, in a part of the factory which otherwise remains vacant. An SM machine has been completed for a customer, for an agreed price of £50,000, at a cost of £42,000. The customer has since gone into liquidation and is unable to proceed with the planned acquisition. The sales manager has produced three possible schemes for the disposal of the SM machine. These schemes have the following financial implications:

Scheme 1
Sell the SM machine, as it stands, to Roche Ltd at a 20% discount on the price of £50,000.

Scheme 2
An offer of £56,000 has been received from Renishaw Ltd for the SM machine, provided it is re-designed to meet Renishaw's specifications. It is estimated that the following additional costs will be incurred during the conversion process: direct materials, £7,000; direct labour, £4,000.

Scheme 3
Convert the SM machine to a general-purpose model which the sales manager is confident can be sold for £54,000. The conversion costs in this case are: direct materials, £6,000; direct labour, £1,500. Under this option, advertising costs will be incurred amounting to £1,000.

Required:
(a) Prepare:

    (i)   A calculation of the contribution arising from the sale of each unit of XL.   [6]

    (ii) An operating statement which sets out the expected revenues, costs, contribution and profit at:
           • 60% of total capacity – the sales manager's estimate;
           • 80% of total capacity – the normal level of output.   [5]

(iii) A calculation of the breakeven point, in units, for the sale of product XL. [4]

(iv) Calculations of the relevant (marginal) costs and revenues for each of the three possible schemes for dealing with the SM machine. [5]

(b) Advise Carburton's management on the financial implications of your calculations under (a) above. [10]

Note:
There are no stocks of XL at either the beginning or the end of the year. [Total marks – 30]

Question 11.6

Manningham Ltd manufactures 'grummits' for sale in England and Wales at a uniform price of £60 per unit. The activities of Manningham are organised as follows: the head office is located in Reading; factories are located in Southampton, Cardiff and Lancaster.

The following estimates were prepared, in March 20X3, for the forthcoming year to 30 June 20X4.

FACTORY OUTPUT: YEAR TO 30 JUNE 20X4

Southampton	25,000 units
Cardiff	45,000 units
Lancaster	60,000 units
	130,000 units

FORECAST OPERATING STATEMENT: YEAR TO 30 JUNE 20X4

	Head Office £000	South-ampton £000	Cardiff £000	Lancaster £000	Total £000
Turnover	–	1,500	2,700	3,600	7,800
Factory costs					
Variable manufacturing costs	–	1,095	1,890	2,520	5,505
Depreciation	–	60	108	144	312
Other fixed costs	–	220	400	530	1,150
Head office costs					
Administration – all fixed	300	–	–	–	300
Re-allocated	(300)	100	100	100	–
Total costs	–	1,475	2,498	3,294	7,267
Net profit	–	25	202	306	533

The board of directors examined the above estimates when they were prepared in March 20X3, and was particularly disappointed with the forecast results of the Southampton factory. A sub-committee was appointed to consider ways of improving overall performance; its report contained the following findings and recommendations:

Findings

1. The variable costs of each factory will increase or decrease in direct proportion to the level of output.

2. There is no spare capacity at the Cardiff factory, but capacity available at Lancaster is sufficient for the production of 80,000 grummits in total.

3. An increase in Lancaster's output to 80,000 units will result in its fixed factory costs, other than depreciation, rising to £650,000.

4. Additional costs of £5 per unit would be incurred to transport grummits manufactured in Lancaster to the former customers of the Southampton factory.

5. A Scottish company, Thorpe Lid, is keen to market its own grummits in England and Wales. It would be possible to enter into a contract for Thorpe to supply some, or all, of Manningharn's customers previously supplied from the Southampton plant. Thorpe would pay a commission to Manningham of £8 per unit.

6. If production is discontinued at any of the factories, steps can be taken to eliminate 'other fixed costs' because these are incurred locally.

Recommendations

The board to consider the financial implications of each of the following schemes:

1. The closure of the Southampton factory.

2. The closure of the Southampton factory and the expansion of output at Lancaster.

3. The closure of the Southampton factory and a contract with Thorpe Lid to supply Southampton's former customers.

4. The implementation of scheme 2 (above) and a contract with Thorpe Lid to supply, as necessary, Southampton's former customers.

Required:

(a) Redraft the forecast operating statement given in the question so as to identify the contribution expected to be made by each department towards sunk costs. [6]

(b) Explain the lower level of forecast profits at Southampton compared with the other two factories. [2]

(c) Prepare separate financial statements which demonstrate the financial implications of each of the four schemes (1-4 above) recommended by the sub-committee. The financial statements should indicate clearly the overall increase or decrease in contribution which results from implementation of each of the schemes. [16]

(d) Examine the relative merits of each of the four schemes and advise management which scheme should be adopted, assuming that the principal criterion is profit maximization. [6]

[Total marks – 30]

12

BUSINESS
DECISION MAKING:
INVESTMENT
APPRAISAL

12.1 INTRODUCTION

Corporate management has funds at its disposal that should be invested to give the maximum return. This investment usually involves the outlay of substantial sums of money to acquire productive capacity or maintain existing capacity in working condition. The aim is that the investment will generate an inflow of cash sufficient both to repay the capital invested and to give a satisfactory surplus of profit. Management has to decide which investment projects to undertake, and the manner in which they are to be carried out. Examples of the types of project that may be considered are:

- *Expansion*. This involves the acquisition of additional fixed assets and the associated working capital. The intention is to generate extra profit from a greater volume of sales, possibly involving the introduction of a new product.

- *Modernization*. Modern equipment is acquired with the aim of generating additional profit from the same volume of sales by reducing unit costs; this may in turn allow demand to be stimulated by enabling prices to be cut. The adoption of modern equipment and techniques may also involve reorganization costs, such as redundancy payments, but can give rise to an offsetting reduction in working capital requirements.

- *Production Technique.* Management has to decide how to meet an identified demand when there are alternative possibilities, for example, whether to adopt labour- or capital-intensive production techniques.

- *Repair or replace.* When a vital machine is in need of repair, management should compare the cost of repair with that of replacing the asset, possibly with a more efficient modern equivalent.

- *Lease, buy or hire purchase.* There are a number of ways in which the acquisition of fixed assets can be financed, the main alternatives being to buy them outright, to acquire them under a hire purchase agreement, or to lease them. Immediate purchase involves the outlay of the full purchase price, whereas leasing and hire purchase commit the company to a number of smaller payments spread over a period of time. All three methods of finance secure the services of the fixed assets for the company, and management has to decide which involves the least overall cost.

- *Capital Repayment.* Companies have to pay interest on loans and dividends on share capital. The most profitable use of funds may be to repay loans or redeem capital so as to avoid the outflows of cash caused by the payment of interest and dividends.

Faced with a number of alternative investments, management has to decide which projects to select, and this decision should be based on the following criterion: which best fulfil the firm's objective of maximizing profit? It is important that the correct investment decisions are made because, once the investment has been undertaken, the funds are a sunk cost which must be recovered from the profitable use of the assets acquired. An unsuccessful investment will produce undesirable consequences of variable effect depending on the extent of the failure. Where the investment shows little or no return, it will not generate the internal funds required to support a policy of expansion. Moreover, the poor results reported will make it difficult to attract external funds as an alternative source for financing planned further developments.

Finally, a project that produces heavy losses will erode the company's capital base and perhaps even cause it to be liquidated.

The selection of poor investment projects has implications not only for the individual company, but also for the economy as a whole. The total of funds available in the economy for investment is limited, and so the selection of one project precludes the adoption of another. If a project which is a commercial failure is undertaken, while one which would have been a success is rejected, the economy receives no stimulus from the creation of additional resources to provide funds for further developments.

This chapter examines a number of techniques which have been developed to help management to choose the most appropriate projects, but it must be noted that these techniques are an aid to the decision-making process and do not provide the sole basis of selection. The decisions are based on assumptions about the future which are most unlikely to prove accurate, and managerial skill must be exercised to decide what weight to give to alternative possible outcomes and appraisal techniques. The level of risk must also be included in the evaluation, because, the greater the risk involved, then the greater the return that is required as compensation. Tax effects are ignored throughout this chapter and will not be examined in questions set on investment project appraisal.

12.2 WORKING CAPITAL
Investment projects often involve changes in working capital requirements for stock, debtors and creditors, and these changes have an impact on cash flows. The initial investment in working capital causes a cash outflow, while, at the end of the project's life, the cash tied up in working capital is recovered as stocks are run down, amounts due from debtors are collected and creditors are paid. It is normal, and consistent with the idea of prudence, to assume that only a proportion of working capital will be recovered because bad debts and unusable stocks may materialize. In examination questions, full recovery of working capital can be assumed unless information to the contrary is given. Where changes in working capital requirements take place during the life of a project, the cash effect must be shown in the forecast.

Example 12.1

The directors of Tin Ltd, a trading company, are considering an investment project which will last for seven years and requires, on 1 January 19X1, the following initial investment in working capital:

	£000
Stock	70
Debtors (net of profit element*)	100
	170
Less: Creditors	60
	110

*In terms of cash flow, the investment consists of the cost of the goods supplied to customers. It is forecast that the price of stock purchased will rise by 10% in June 19X4. In the final year of the project's life it is expected to recover 90% of the value of stock and 95% of the value of debtors.

Required.
Calculate for each of the years 19X1 to 19X7 inclusive the net cash flows which result from the movements in working capital of Tin Ltd.

Solution

	Stock £000	Debtors £000	Creditors £000	Net Cash Flows £000
19X1	(70)	(100)	60	(110)
19X2	–	–	–	–
19X3	–		–	–
19X4	(7)	(10)†	6†	(11)
19X5	–		–	–
19X6	–	–	–	–
19X7	69.3	104.5	(66)	107.8

† the cost rises by 10%, then so will the investment in debtors and the value of creditors unless the credit periods are varied.

12.3 PAYBACK

There are three main methods of investment appraisal: payback, accounting rate of return, and discounted cash flow. This section deals with payback, while accounting rate of return and discounted cash flow are covered in sections 12.4 and 12.5.

The payback technique of investment appraisal is based on the length of time taken by a project to recover its initial investment. It can be operated in two ways: either a company may specify that any project that recovers its capital investment within a given period of time should be accepted, or, when a choice has to be made between projects, the one that has the shortest payback period is selected.

The steps necessary to carry out an appraisal by means of payback are as follows:

1. Calculate the cash flows of each project.

2. Find the length of time for which each project has to operate to recover its initial investment.

3. Select those projects which pay back the initial investment within the specified time, unless there is some restriction on choice, in which case the project with the shortest payback period is selected.

Example 12.2

The directors of Tape Ltd are considering the following three investment projects:

	Project 1 £000	Project 2 £000	Project 3 £000
Initial Capital Outlay	1,000	1,800	2,000
Cash Inflows, Year: 1	100	400	1,000
2	200	400	1,000
3	300	1,200	–
4	400	600	
5	500	–	
6	500	–	–
Total	2,000	2,600	2,000

Required:
(a) Calculate the payback period for each project.

(b) Which projects would be selected if the company specifies the payback must be completed within three years?

(c) Which project would be selected if only one of the three can be undertaken?

Note:
Assume cash inflows occur at a uniform rate each year.

Solution (£000)

(a) Project 1: 4 years (W 1)

Project 2: 2 years 10 months (in year 3 the monthly inflow is 100) (W 1)

Project 3: 2 years (W 1)

W1	Project 1	Project 2	Project 3
	£	£	£
Capital outlay	1,000	1,800	2,000
Less: Inflows:			
Year 1	100	400	1,000
	900	1,400	1,000
Year 2	200	400	1,000
	700	1,000	–
Year 3	300	1,200	
	400	(200)	
Year 4	400		

(b) Projects 2 and 3 are undertaken because they recover their costs within three years.

(c) Project 3 because it has the shortest payback period.

The advantages claimed for payback are:

- It involves simple calculations and is easy to understand.

- The projects selected, because they are chosen to recover their costs rapidly, leave the company at risk for the shortest period of time. The initial capital investment reduces the company's cash resources, and so the selection of projects with short payback periods ensures a prompt restoration of liquidity, which may be of critical importance to a company with liquidity problems.

- The technique implicitly acknowledges that the further into the future predictions are made, the less reliable they are.

The criticisms of payback are:

- It ignores receipts expected to arise after the end of the payback period; for instance, in Example 12.2 above, project 1 eventually creates a total cash inflow equal to 200% of the investment and is rejected, whereas project 3 is accepted although it only recovers its cost.

- No account is taken of the timing of receipts, yet, the further into the future cash is expected to arise, the lower is its current value (see Section 12.5.1).

- The selection of the time period within which an acceptable project must recover its cost is arbitrary.

- The technique does not take profitability into consideration. In Example 12.2, project 3, on the basis of payback, is chosen, even though it gives no surplus.

- Payback cannot be used to reach decisions where there are no cash inflows, for example, when deciding whether to lease or buy an asset.

In conclusion, the payback technique emphasizes the need for projects to recover their costs in a reasonable period of time, but it is not satisfactory if used as the sole criterion. Its results should be assessed in conjunction with the findings from other, more acceptable, methods of investment appraisal.

12.4 ACCOUNTING RATE OF RETURN

The ratio 'Return on Capital Employed' has been discussed previously (see Chapter 9.5.3, 'Rate of Return on Gross Assets' and 9.5.5, 'Rate of Return on Shareholders' Equity'). A similar measure, the 'Accounting Rate of Return' can be used for investment project appraisal. This ratio relates the return, or profit, expected from a project to the amount of capital it employs, and, although there are a number of possible measures, the usual formula for its calculation is:

$$\frac{\text{Average Annual Return}}{\text{Average Capital Invested}} \times 100$$

The average annual return is found by dividing the project's total expected profits by the number of years over which they accrue. The average capital invested is the value of working capital plus half the cost of the initial investment in fixed assets. This is because the investment in working capital has to be maintained throughout the life of the project, while the value of fixed assets is depreciated and reduced to zero by the end of the project; the cash flow represented by depreciation is not required by the project and so is available for alternative investment. Where the split of the initial investment between working capital and fixed assets is not given, it is usual to take half of the value of the whole investment.

Projects are chosen that have an accounting rate of return in excess of a pre-determined level, or, where a choice has to be made between projects, the one with the highest accounting rate of return is preferred.

The steps to carry out the appraisal of an investment project by means of the Accounting Rate of Return are as follows:

1. Calculate the average capital invested in the project.

2. Determine the profits generated by the project.

3. Find the average annual profit of the project.

4. Express the average annual profit (from step 3) as a percentage of the average capital invested (from step 1).

5. Accept projects that have a rate of return in excess of the required level, or, where choice is restricted, select the project with the highest rate of return.

Example 12.3

The following information relates to two investment projects which are under consideration by the directors of Case Ltd:

	Project A £000	Project B £000
Investment in: Working Capital	500	400
Fixed Assets	1,000	1,600
Anticipated Profit: Year 1	540	200
Year 2	440	300
Year 3	330	400
Year 4	130	600
Year 5	–	600
Total	1,440	2,100

Required:
(a) A calculation of the accounting rate of return for each project.

(b) Which of the projects would be accepted if the required accounting rate of return is 30%?

(c) Which project would be accepted if they are mutually exclusive, that is, only one of them can be undertaken?

Solution (£000)

(a)	Project A	Project B
Working capital investment	500	400
Fixed asset investment x ½	500	800
Average capital invested (Step 1)	1,000	1,200
Total profit (Step 2)	1,440	2,100

Average annual profit (Step 3) $\dfrac{1,440}{4} = 360$ $\dfrac{2,100}{5} = 420$

Accounting rate of return (Step 4) $\dfrac{360}{1,000} \times 100 = 36\%$ $\dfrac{420}{1,200} \times 100 = 35\%$

(b) Both projects, A and B, would be undertaken because their accounting rates of return exceed the required minimum.

(c) Project A would he undertaken because it has the higher accounting rate of return.

The advantages of the accounting rate of return as a technique of investment project appraisal are:

- It brings into consideration the profits earned over the whole life of the project.

- It allows the comparison of projects that require different amounts of initial capital investment.

- The idea of the return on capital employed is generally understood, and this aids the comprehension of the accounting rate of return.

- The minimum required rate of return can be set with reference to the cost of the finance used by the company plus the additional return it requires for its own profit.

The main disadvantage of this appraisal technique is that the timing of profit arising from alternative projects is ignored; for instance, in Example 12.3 the technique is indifferent to the fact that project A has high early profits which reduce over the life of the project whereas project B earns the majority of its profit towards the end of its life.

12.5 DISCOUNTED CASH FLOW (DCF)

Disadvantages of the payback and accounting rate of return methods of investment appraisal include the facts that payback ignores cash flows arising after the payback period, while the accounting rate of return takes no account of the timing of cash flows. DCF techniques provide a means of overcoming these problems by expressing all cash flows in terms of a common point in time. To carry out a DCF appraisal, it is necessary to:

1. Prepare an annual cash forecast for each project under consideration (see Chapter 13).

2. Develop a means of expressing monetary flows, which take place over a period of time, on a common basis; this is done by calculating the time value of money, which is now considered.

12.5.1 The Time Value of Money

A person who invests money in a bank deposit account expects to receive interest; for example, if £100 is deposited for one year at 10% interest, at the end of the year £110 is available to be withdrawn; the additional £10 is compensation for parting with £100 for one year. To the person willing to make this investment, £100 today is worth £110 in one year's time; this shows that money has a time value. Moreover, the longer the investor has to wait to withdraw the deposit, then the greater the compensation required. The rate of interest will also vary with the amount of risk attached to the investment; the greater the risk, then the greater the return required.

As well as calculating the amount to which a present sum will grow in the future, as a result of interest being added, it is possible to express sums receivable in the future in terms of their present value. This can provide useful information for all kinds of decisions. For example, an individual might want to know how much to set aside now in order to produce £1,000 which she intends to give to her daughter on her eighteenth birthday in one year's time. If she can invest money at 12%, she must set aside $\frac{£1,000 \times 100}{12}$ = £893.

In one year's time she will receive back her £893 plus interest of £893 x 12% = £107 to give the required total of £1,000.

The examples given so far have only dealt with time periods of one year; to accommodate periods of two years or more it is necessary to use compound interest which, each year, adds interest to the initial sum deposited plus accumulated interest at the beginning of the year. For example, at 10% interest a sum of £100 will grow to £133.1 after three years:

Initial deposit: 1.1.19X1	100
Interest: 19X1	10
Accumulated sum: 31.12.19X1	110
Interest: 19X2	11
Accumulated sum: 31.12.19X2	121
Interest: 19X3	12.1
Accumulated sum: 31.12.19X3	133.1

Alternatively, the present value of £133.1 receivable in three years' time, at 10% interest, is £100.

The computation of a present value, given a sum of money receivable some years in the future and a rate of interest, is a complicated process, and so discount tables have been developed which show the present value of £1 receivable at various times in the future and at different rates of interest. An example of such a table is given in Appendix B. (There are also tables available which ease the calculation of future values.)

The discount table is used to calculate the present value of sums receivable or payable in the future, by identifying the appropriate 'interest rate' column and then finding the factor relating to the future date on which the money is to be received. Continuing the example of £133.1 receivable in three years' time at 10% interest, the relevant factor is 0.751 (see Appendix B) and the present value of £133.1 is £133.1 x 0.751=£100. In this way the present value of any future sum can be determined, provided that the required rate of interest is known.

12.5.2 The Cost of Capital

The rate of interest applicable to a company's investment projects has to be decided upon to enable the use of discounting techniques. The appropriate interest rate is the cost of the finance provided to the company by shareholders and other investors, as investment projects have to earn a return at least sufficient to pay the interest on the funds they utilize. The main sources of finance and their costs to the company are:

- *Ordinary Shares*. Shareholders receive a return on their investment in the form of dividends, and so the cost of equity finance is found by the formula:

$$\frac{\text{Dividends for the year (interim plus final)}}{\text{Shareholders' equity}} \times 100$$

- *Preference Shares.* These carry a fixed rate of dividend, and this is their cost.

- *Debenture and Other Loans.* The rate of interest on these is fixed, and this is their cost.

- *Overdrafts.* These carry a rate of interest, but the calculation of the amount payable may be complicated because the interest rate and/or the level of overdraft fluctuates.

12.5.3 Net Present Value (NPV)

This technique of investment project appraisal takes the cash flows that are expected to result from the adoption of a proposal and expresses them in terms of present value by the application of discount factors based on the company's required rate of return. For this purpose, the initial investment, assuming it takes place immediately, is already expressed in terms of its present value and does not need to be discounted. Future cash flows are discounted by applying factors which assume they arise at the end of the year in which they take place. This is an artificial assumption, but, it must be remembered, the calculations are intended only to provide a guide for decision-making and do not claim to be precise. The sum of the present values, including the initial investment which is a negative figure, is the NPV of the project.

The steps to carry out the appraisal of an investment project by means of NPV are as follows:

1. Determine the rate at which the project's cash flows are to be discounted, i.e. the cost of capital.

2. Identify the cash flows relevant to the project.

3. Select the appropriate discount factors from the table provided with the examination question or by using a suitable calculator.

4. Discount the cash flows (from step 2) using the appropriate discount factors (from step 3).

5.   The project is accepted if it has a positive NPV, unless choice is restricted, in which case the project with the highest NPV is chosen (see below).

Example 12.4

An investment project involves an initial investment of £0.9m and produces an annual inflow of £0.5m for three years. The appropriate discount rate is 10%.

Required:
Calculate the project's Net Present Value.

Note:
Table of factors for the present value of £1 appears in Appendix B.

Solution

Step 1: The discount rate is given as 10%.

The calculation of the NPV is usually undertaken in a tabular format:

| | Step 2 | Step 3 | Step 4 (Step 2 x Step 3) |
| | Cash Flow | Discount | NPV |
Year	(£000)	Factor	(£000)
0	(900)	1.000	(900)
1	500	0.909	455
2	500	0.826	413
3	500	0.751	375
			343

Step 5: The project has a positive NPV of £0.343m and is accepted.

Note.
An element of rounding of figures is acceptable in DCF techniques because it is based on a number of assumptions and forecasts. To work to the nearest pound or fraction of a pound suggests an accuracy that does not exist.

The significance of a positive NPV is that it shows the project is expected to generate a surplus, expressed in terms of present value, after all of its costs, including interest and the amount invested, have been recovered.

Where a choice has to be made between alternative projects that involve similar investments, the one with the greater positive NPV is selected. However, if the projects involve different capital outlays, then it is useful to calculate the 'Profitability Index' as a guide to reaching an investment decision. This index shows, for each project, the present value generated by each £1 invested, and is calculated using the formula:

$$\text{Profitability Index} = \frac{\text{Present Value of Cash Inflows}}{\text{Capital Invested}}$$

Example 12.5

A company, with a cost of capital of 13%, is considering three projects which have the following cash flows (£m):

Project	A	B	C
Initial Investment	2.0	2.0	3.0
Cash Inflows: Year 1	0.6	1.0	1.3
Year 2	0.7	0.9	1.8
Year 3	0.8	0.9	1.6

Required:
Calculations to indicate which project the company should undertake if it is able to adopt only one of them.

Note:
Table of factors for the present value of £1 appears in Appendix B.

Solution (£m)

Year	Discount Factor (Figure 1)	Project A Cash Flow	Project A Present Value	Project B Cash Flow	Project B Present Value	Project C Cash Flow	Project C Present Value
1	0.885	0.6	0.531	1.0	0.885	1.3	1.151
2	0.783	0.7	0.548	0.9	0.705	1.8	1.409
3	0.693	0.8	0.554	0.9	0.624	1.6	1.109
			1.633		2.214		3.669
Initial Investment			2.000		2.000		3.000
NPV			(0.367)		0.214		0.669
Appraisal on basis of NPV			Reject		Accept		Accept
Profitability index					$\frac{2.214}{2} = 1.11$		$\frac{3.669}{3} = 1.22$

Project C is accepted as it has the higher profitability index as well as the higher NPV.

The NPV technique can also be used where a company is faced with alternative ways of achieving the same objective, for example, whether to rent or buy a piece of equipment. Since this type of decision gives rise to cash outflows, but not cash inflows, the procedure is to reduce the cash outflows to their present values, and the option with the smallest total present value is chosen.

Example 12.6

Sorter Ltd requires some new equipment to help to manufacture a product for a period of four years, commencing 1 January 19X3. The accounts of Sorter Lid are prepared on the calendar year basis. At the end of four years, demand for the product will collapse and the company will be unable to make any further use of the equipment.

The equipment required by Sorter Ltd. can be obtained in any one of three ways:

(i)   the equipment could be purchased for cash on 1 January 19X3;

(ii) the equipment could be acquired under a hire purchase contract which requires a deposit to be paid on 1 January 19X3, and three further instalments at annual intervals following the date of the initial deposit;

(iii) the equipment could be rented, commencing 1 January 19X3.

You are given the following financial information and facts relevant to an assessment of the three alternatives:

1.   The cash price of the equipment is £50,000.

2.   The equipment will have no resale value at the end of the four-year period.

3.   The deposit required under the hire purchase contract is £26,000.

4.   The annual instalments payable under the hire purchase contract are £13,000.

5.   The annual rental of the equipment, payable in arrears each year, is £20,000.

6.   Sorter Ltd's estimated cost of capital over the four-year period is 15 per cent per annum.

Required:
(a) Calculations showing the best method of acquisition on the basis of the available information.

(b) A brief discussion of any further matters which might be taken into consideration when making a decision.

Notes:
Ignore taxation.

Table of factors for the present value of £1 appears in Appendix B.

Solution

(a) (i) *Cash Purchase*

Year	Purchase price £	Discount factor £	Present value £
0	50,000	1.000	50,000

(ii) *Hire Purchase*

Year	Payments £	Discount factor £	Present value £
0	26,000	1.000	26,000
1	13,000	0.870	11,310
2	13,000	0.756	9,828
3	13,000	0.658	8,554
			55,692

(iii) *Rent*

Year	Rentals £	Discount factor £	Present value £
1	(20,000)	0.870	17,400
2	(20,000)	0.756	15,120
3	(20,000)	0.658	13,160
4	(20,000)	0.572	11,440
			57,120

On the basis of the above analysis, the cash purchase option would be selected as it has the lowest NPV.

(b) Points for consideration:

1. Availability of cash. Option (i) has the lowest present value but requires an immediate outlay of £50,000.

2. Costs of maintaining and repairing the equipment. If these are borne by the lessor, option (ii) may be relatively more attractive.

3. Certainty of demand for the product continuing over the four-year period. Renting may give the option of returning the equipment if demand does not come up to expectations.

Where the cash flows arising from a project are the same each year, it is not necessary to discount them separately. The present value factors for the years in which the cash flows occur are added together, and the annual cash flow is multiplied by the aggregate factor which results. Relevant tables of factors are given in Appendix B.

For example:

- If a project is to be appraised at 12% and produces an annual cash inflow of £0.5m for five years, the present value of the inflow is £0.5m x 3.605 = £1.8m.

- If a project with a life of six years is to be appraised at 12% and produces an annual cash inflow of £0.75m for the first three years of its life and £0.45m for the last three years, the present value of the inflow is: (£0.75m x 2.402) + (£0.45m x (4.112 – 2.402)) = £2.57m.

12.5.4 DCF Yield or Internal Rate of Return (IRR)

The IRR of a project is the rate of return at which its cash flows must be discounted to give an NPV of zero. Again, it is assumed that the cash flows, other than the initial investment, take place at the end of the year in which they arise. Projects are accepted if their IRR is greater than the company's cost of capital, or, where the number of projects to be undertaken is restricted, the projects with the greatest IRR are chosen. The IRR can be found by trial and error using a variety of different interest rates. This is a laborious process, and a reasonable estimate can be obtained if the results for two rates of interest are available, one of which gives a negative and the other a positive NPV.

The steps to appraise a project by the IRR method are:

1. Find the project's cash flows.

2. Calculate the project's NPV at two discount rates, one of which gives a positive and the other a negative result.

3. Compute, by interpolation, the discount rate which gives an NPV of zero. This is the IRR of the project.

4. Accept the project if its IRR is in excess of the company's cost of capital. Where choice is restricted, the project with the highest IRR is selected.

Example 12.7

The expected cash flows of an investment project which requires an initial investment of £2.8m are:

Year	£m
1	0.7
2	0.8
3	0.9
4	0.8
5	0.7

Required:
Calculate the internal rate of return of the project.

Solution

Steps 1 and 2:

Year	Cash Flow (£m)	10% Discount Factor	NP V (£m)	15% Discount Factor	NPV (£m)
1	0.7	0.909	0.636	0.870	0.609
2	0.8	0.826	0.661	0.756	0.605
3	0.9	0.751	0.676	0.658	0.592
4	0.8	0.683	0.546	0.572	0.458
5	0.7	0.620	0.434	0.497	0.348
			2.953		2.612
Initial Investment			(2.800)		(2.800)
NPV			0.153		(0.188)

Step 3:
The information found from the above can be represented diagrammatically:

	←	5% →	
%	10	IRR	15
NPV	0.153	0	(0.188)[1]
	←	0.341 →	

The IRR of this project lies between 10% and 15%, at a discount rate which produces a zero NPV. The two discount rates used as reference points produce NPVs that differ, in total, by £0.341m (0.153 + 0.188). Since a 10% discount rate gives a positive NPV of £0.153m, the IRR is above 10%.

The general formula for this calculation is:

$$IRR = A + \left[\frac{a}{a+b} \times (B - A) \right]$$

where: A = Discount rate for positive NPV
B = Discount rate for negative NPV
a = positive NPV, found using A
b = negative NPV, found using B (ignore the negative sign)

In this example:

$$\text{IRR} = 10 + \left[\frac{0.153}{0.153 + 0.188} \times (15 - 10)\right] = 12.24\% \ (12\% \text{ to the nearest whole number})$$

Step 4:
If the project's cash flow forecast is discounted at 12%, it is found to have an NPV of zero, and so the project is accepted if the company's cost of capital is 12% or less.

Often examination questions requiring the calculation of the IRR also require candidates to compute the NPV. In these circumstances, the NPV should be the first calculated, and the IRR can then be found by using these results together with one other NPV based on a different discount rate.

Example 12.8

The directors of Carter Ltd have decided to undertake a programme of expansion. They have under consideration two mutually exclusive five-year projects and intend to invest in the project which offers greater financial gain. Project I requires an initial capital investment of £140,000 and Project II an initial capital investment of £280,000. The annual net cash flows which are expected to arise from the projects are as follows:

Year	Project I	Project II
1	£30,000	£100,000
2	£60,000	£90,000
3	£60,000	£90,000
4	£60,000	£90,000
5	£24,155	£53,706

Required:
(a) Calculations of the net present value of each of the two projects, assuming a 12 per cent cost of capital.

(b) Calculations of the discounted cash flow yield (internal rate of return) of each of the two projects.

Notes:
1. The capital investment will be undertaken immediately and the annual cash flows may be assumed to arise at the year end.

2. Ignore taxation.

3. Table of factors for the present value of £1 appears in Appendix B.

Solution

(a) *Net Present Value*

		Project I			Project II	
Year	Cash Flow	Discount Factor 12%	Present Value	Cash Flow	Discount Factor 12%	Present Value
	£		£	£		£
0	(140,000)	1.000	(140,000)	(280,000)	1.000	(280,000)
1	30,000	0.893	26,790	100,000	0.893	89,300
2	60,000	0.797	47,820	90,000	0.797	71,730
3	60,000	0.712	42,720	90,000	0.712	64,080
4	60,000	0.636	38,160	90,000	0.636	57,240
5	24,155	0.567	13,696	53,706	0.567	30,451
			29,186			32,801

(b) *Internal Rate of Return*

		Project I			Project II	
Year	Cash Flow	Discount Factor 21%	Present Value	Cash Flow	Discount Factor 21%	Present Value
	£		£	£		£
0	(140,000)	1.000	(140,000)	(280,000)	1.000	(280,000)
1	30,000	0.826	24,780	100,000	0.826	82,600
2	60,000	0.683	40,980	90,000	0.683	61,470
3	60,000	0.564	33,840	90,000	0.564	50,760
4	60,000	0.467	28,020	90,000	0.467	42,030
5	24,155	0.386	9,324	53,706	0.386	20,731
NPV			(3,056)			(22,409)

Project I	Project II

IRR: $12\% + \left[\dfrac{29,186}{3,056 + 29,186} \times (21 - 12) \right]$ $12\% + \left[\dfrac{32,801}{22,409 + 32,801} \times (21 - 12) \right]$

    $= 20\%*$ $= 17\%*$

*To the nearest whole per cent.

Check:

	Project I			Project II		
Year	Cash Flow	Discount Factor 20%	Present Value	Cash Flow	Discount Factor 17%	Present Value
	£		£	£		£
0	(140,000)	1.000	(140,000)	(280,000)	1.000	(280,000)
1	30,000	0.833	24,990	100,000	0.855	85,500
2	60,000	0.694	41,640	90,000	0.731	65,790
3	60,000	0.579	34,740	90,000	0.624	56,160
4	60,000	0.482	28,920	90,000	0.534	48,060
5	24,155	0.402	9,710	53,706	0.456	24,490

When the two DCF techniques, NPV and IRR, produce different results, a further calculation may be made to help to reach a decision where the project requiring a lower investment produces a higher IRR. In these circumstances, it is necessary to calculate the incremental return earned on the additional investment required by the larger project and compare this with alternative investment opportunities. This calculation for Carter Ltd, based on the two projects presented in Example 12.8, is:

Year	Cash flow Project I	Cash flow Project II	Cash flow Project II-I	Discount factor 13%*	NPV
	£	£	£	£	£
0	(140,000)	(280,000)	(140,000)	1.000	(140,000)
1	30,000	100,000	70,000	0.885	61,950
2	60,000	90,000	30,000	0.783	23,490
3	60,000	90,000	30,000	0.693	20,790
4	60,000	90,000	30,000	0.613	18,390
5	24,155	53,706	29,551	0.543	16,046
					666

*Found by the IRR technique or by trial and error.

The additional cash flows that arise under Project II represent a return of approximately 13% on the additional initial investment. This shows that Project II produces the same return as Project I (20%) on an equivalent amount of funds and a return of 13% on the remainder, which is in excess of the cost of capital. Therefore, Project II would be undertaken if no other investment was available that yields a return in excess of 13%.

12.5.5 The Impact of Inflation

Where the relevant information is given in the question, inflation should be taken into account when appraising capital projects. The rate of return which a company has to pay to its investors, the 'money cost', comprises two elements: it gives them compensation for parting with their cash for a period of time, which is known as the 'real cost of capital', and also recompenses them for the erosion in value which the money they invest undergoes as a result of inflation. If, with inflation, selling prices rise at least as fast as costs, the future cash inflows available to meet the capital and interest commitments of the company, which were established at the start of the project, also increase. In order to calculate the present value of a project, it is therefore necessary to ensure that both the discount rate and the cash flows are computed on the same basis. That is, they must either both be computed on a 'real' basis, or on a 'money' basis. These two approaches are now described.

1 Use the real cost of capital

The cash flows of the project must be forecast at current prices, that is, on the assumption that there is to be no inflation. These amounts are then discounted at the real cost of capital, which is calculated by the formula:

$$\text{Real cost of capital} = \frac{m - i}{1 + i}$$

Where: m = money cost of capital
i = The rate of inflation

Example 12.9

A company has a money cost of capital of 19% and the expected annual inflation rate is 7%. It is considering an investment project which has a life of 5 years, costs £1m, and generates an annual cash inflow of £0.3m at prices ruling at the date the project is to be undertaken.

Required:
Calculate the company's real cost of capital.

Table of factors for the present value of £1 appears in Appendix B

Solution

The company's real cost of capital is $\dfrac{0.19\text{-}0.07}{1+0.07} = 11\%^*$

* To the nearest whole percentage

The NPV of the project is £-1m + (0.3m x 3.696) = £0.11m, and so the project is accepted.

Note: If the project is discounted at 19% (the money cost of capital), the NPV is £-1m + (0.3m x 3.057) = £-0.08m. The project would be rejected when, in fact, its cash flows will probably increase over the years because of inflation and so it will generate a surplus.

---

2 Prepare the Cash Forecast in Monetary Terms
The cash flows which are actually expected to take place are forecast, and these are discounted using the money cost of capital

Example 12.10

A company is considering an investment project which costs £2.3m and produces an annual cash inflow, at current prices, of £0.8m for 4 years. The company's money cost of capital is 15%, and the expected rate of inflation is 6%.

Required:
Compute the net present value of the project using the annual cash flows expressed in monetary terms.

Table of factors for the present value of £1 appears in Appendix B

Solution

Year	Cash Flow £m	Present Value Factor 15%	Net Present Value £m
0	-2.300	1.000	-2.300
1	0.848*	0.870	0.738
2	0.899*	0.756	0.680
3	0.953*	0.658	0.627
4	1.010*	0.572	0.578
			0.323

* Adjusted assuming an annual inflation rate of 6%.

The NPV is positive and the project is accepted.

Note: If the cash flows re not adjusted, the NPV is £-2.3m + (0.8 x 2.856) = £-0.015m and a potentially profitable project is rejected.

Remember that care must be taken to compare like with like, i.e. either match the real cost of capital with cash flows expressed in terms of prices current when the calculation is made, or match the money cost of capital with the amounts of cash expected to be received at future dates.

12.5.6 Conclusion

The various applications of DCF discussed above show that, compared with other methods of investment appraisal, DCF has the advantage of bringing into consideration all of the cash flows associated with a project and also takes account of the timing of the cash flows. Against these advantages must be weighed the complexity of the technique which makes it difficult to comprehend. There is a danger that, with their possible lack of understanding, managers will place too much reliance on its results. Like all investment appraisal techniques, it is based on estimates which are converted into numerical forecasts and are subject to error. The results of DCF analysis should be used by management as a guide, but should not be the sole criteria. Other, overriding, factors which may have to be taken into account are:

- The availability of cash. If a company is short of cash, it may have to lease an asset rather than purchase it, even if the latter is shown to be the better option on the basis of a DCF calculation.

- Corporate policy may favour acquiring assets from a particular supplier or country.

- Government policy may favour the acquisition of 'home' produced assets, and may even favour a particular supplier.

- The ready supply of spare parts may be assured for one machine while not for another. The former may be chosen for that reason, even if it is not the one indicated by DCF appraisal techniques.

- Some options which are acceptable on a DCF basis may not be acceptable to employees on, for example, the grounds of health and safety.

- When the replacement of individual machines is considered, it may be desirable to maintain compatibility with existing machines.

12.6 ERRORS IN FORECASTS

Management must recognize that the forecasts, on the basis of which investment appraisal is undertaken, will not be achieved precisely if the project is accepted. All aspects of the forecast are subject to error, for example:

- Errors in capital estimates:

    (a) The investment in fixed assets and/or working capital may be greater or smaller than expected.

    (b) The period of time needed to acquire the fixed assets may be forecast inaccurately. Any delay in the start of revenue inflows reduces their present values.

    (c) The life of the fixed assets may be misjudged.

- Errors in trading estimates:

    (a) The forecast volume of sales may not materialize.

    (b) The expected selling price per unit may not be achieved.

    (c) Costs may differ from forecasts.

    (d) Cash flows may arise earlier or later than expected.

    (e) The total life of the project may be misjudged.

- Government Policy:

    (a) A change in tax rates, structure or capital allowances can have a significant impact on a project's cash flows and their timing.

    (b) Governments may impose restrictions that affect the company's exports.

Prior to undertaking a project, the significance of likely errors can be investigated. Appraisal may be undertaken on the alternative assumptions that the best likely or worst likely results are achieved, or the technique of 'Sensitivity Analysis' may be used. This technique involves the calculation of how far each element, taken individually, of the forecast can differ from expectations before the project becomes unacceptable. As the effect of variation in each separate element is examined, the other variables are held constant. The amount of error which is acceptable before a project is rejected can be weighed against the expected accuracy of the forecasts, and sensitivity analysis shows the areas in which a project is particularly vulnerable.

Example 12.11

The directors of Shovel Ltd are considering the following investment project:

Capital Investment	£1.25m
Annual Cash Inflow	£0.45m
Life of Project	5 years

The directors are positive that the company's cost of capital is 12%, but are concerned that, in the past, forecasts have proved inaccurate.

Required:
Calculate the extent to which each variable can differ from the forecast before the project is rejected on the basis of an NPV appraisal.

Solution

The NPV of the project, based on the above forecasts is:

$$£-1.25m + (0.45m \times 3.605^*) = £0.372m$$

*From Appendix B.

The project will be rejected if the NPV is less than 0, so the amount of acceptable variation can be computed as follows:

1. *Capital Investment (CI)*
   The project remains acceptable provided that the capital investment does not rise above the level where $CI + (0.45m \times 3.605) = 0$.

   This occurs when capital investment is a negative figure which equals £0.45m x 3.605 £1.622m.

   Therefore, the amount of acceptable upward variation in the capital investment is:

   $$\frac{1.622 - 1.25}{1.25} = 30\%.$$

2. *Annual Cash Flow (CF)*
   The project remains acceptable provided that cash flow does not fall below the level where $£-1.25m + (CF \times 3.605) = 0$.

This occurs when CF = $\dfrac{£1.25m}{3.605}$ = £0.347m.

Therefore, the amount of acceptable downward variation in the annual cash flow is:

$\dfrac{0.45 - 0.347}{0.45}$ =23%.

3. *Life of Project*
   The project remains acceptable provided that CDF (representing the 12% cumulative discount factor) does not fall below the level where £-1.25m + (0.45 x CDF) = 0.

   This occurs when CDF = $\dfrac{1.25}{0.45}$ = 2.778.

   From the discount table in Appendix B, it can be found that the cumulative discount factor for three years at 12% is 2.402, and that for four years is 3.038.

   The shortest acceptable life is $4 - \dfrac{3.038 - 2.778}{3.038\text{-}2.402} = 3.6$ years.

   Therefore, the amount of acceptable downward variation in the life of project is:

   $\dfrac{5 - 3.6}{5}$ = 28%.

Once a project is undertaken, it is important that management establishes accounting systems to monitor its results. The resource flows that actually take place should be recorded under the same headings as were used for the project's appraisal so that their amount and timing can be compared with the forecast. This comparison will highlight deviations from the forecast, which enables management to take possible remedial action and also provides a useful contribution to current investment appraisals by indicating areas which have proved difficult to forecast accurately.

12.7 FURTHER READING

Arnold, J. and Turley, S. (1996) *Accounting for Management Decisions,* London: Prentice Hall, Chapters 10, 11.

Drury, C. (1997) *Management Accounting for Business Decisions*, London: International Thomson Business Press, Chapter 9.

Idowu, S. (2000) 'Capital investment appraisal', *ACCA Students' Newsletter,* August, pp. 26-29.

McGrath, G. (1998) 'Evaluation techniques for capital budgeting', *ACCA Students' Newsletter,* November, pp. 24-6, 50.

Weetman, P. (1999) *Management Accounting. An Introduction*, London: Pitman, Chapter 10.

12.8 QUESTIONS

Question 12.1

The directors of Iwata Ltd are considering two mutually exclusive investment projects in respect of which the following information is provided:

	Project A £000	Project B £000
Initial capital investment	1,000	1,000
Net cash inflows: Year 1	700	400
2	300	500
3	100	800
4	–	600

The initial outlay will occur immediately and you may assume that the net cash inflows will arise at the year end.

Iwata's estimated cost of capital over the four year period is 10%.

Required:
(a) Outline the main advantages and disadvantages of the 'payback' method of capital investment appraisal.   [6]

(b) State the way in which the net present value (NPV) method of investment appraisal overcomes the criticisms made of payback.   [4]

(c) Numerical assessments of the two projects above based on the following methods of capital project appraisal:

  (i)   payback;

  (ii) net present value (NPV).   [6]

(d) Your advice on which project should be adopted, giving reasons for your choice.   [4]

Note:
Table of factors for the present value of £1 appears in Appendix B

[Total marks – 20]

Question 12.2

Landore Ltd has two investment projects under consideration, each involving an initial outlay on plant (which will last for five years) of £240,000 and on working capital of £10,000. The company is able to arrange finance for one, but not both, of these projects.

The estimated net cash inflows for the two projects are as follows:

Year	Project 1 £000	Project 2 £000
1	80	60
2	80	200
3	90	90
4	100	10
5	50	15

Required:
(a) A numerical analysis of each of the two projects using the following methods of capital project appraisal:

   (i)   accounting rate of return;

   (ii) net present value (the appropriate discount rate is 15%).   [10]

(b) A discussion of the relative merits of the two methods of capital project appraisal used above. Advise the management of Landore Ltd which project should be chosen.   [10]

[Total marks – 20]

Notes:
1 .   Assume that the initial investment will be made at the beginning of year one, and that annual net cash inflows arise at the year end.

2.   Make your calculations to the nearest £000.

3.   Ignore taxation.

Note:
Table of factors for the present value of £1 appears in Appendix B.

Question 12.3

Porterfield Ltd powers its plant using electricity. The company has been offered two alternative tariffs by a supplier of electricity. The details of the arrangements are set out below:

The alternative tariffs are as follows:

Alternative	Fixed Annual Charge	Variable Charge
Tariff: Wye	29,000	0.5 per unit
Zed	5,000	1.8 per unit

The tariff selected will come into effect from 1 January 2000. The electricity supplier will invoice Porterfield Ltd at the year end (31 December) and the amount due will be paid immediately.

The contractual arrangement provides for the selected tariff to remain in operation for a minimum period of five years.

Porterfield Ltd estimates that its requirements for electricity will be as follows over the contractual period.

Year	Units
2000	10,000
2001	10,000
2002	10,000
2003	30,000
2004	40,000

The company's cost of capital is 14%.

Required:
(a) Calculate the total cash payments made under each of the two tariff alternatives over the contract period.   *[2 marks]*

(b) Calculate the net present value at 1 January 2000 of each of the two tariff alternatives. *[8 marks]*

(c) Explain to the management of Porterfield Ltd which of the two tariff alternatives should be adopted in the light of your calculations and any other relevant considerations.   *[10 marks]*

[Total – 20 marks]

Notes:
Assume that the annual net cash outflows arise at the year end. Ignore taxation.

Table of factors for the present value of £1 appears in Appendix B.

Question 12.4

The directors of Perkin plc have decided to undertake an expansion programme. They have under consideration two mutually exclusive three-year projects. Project A requires an initial capital investment of £200,000 and Project B an initial capital investment of £500,000. The annual net cash inflows over the three-year period are estimated to be the following:

Year	Project A	Project B
1	100,000	260,000
2	100,000	260,000
3	66,346	117,386

Required:

(a) Calculate the net present value of each of the two projects using a 13% cost of capital. *[6 marks]*

(b) Calculate the discounted cash flow yield (internal rate of return) of each of the two projects. *[8 marks]*

(c) Discuss the results of your calculations under (a) and (b) and outline any further factors which might be taken into account in deciding which project to select. *[6 marks]*

[Total – 20 marks]

Notes:
The capital investment will be undertaken immediately.
Assume the annual cash flows arise at the year end.
Ignore taxation.
Table of factors for the present value of £1 appears in Appendix B.

Question 12.5

The directors of Thames plc have under consideration a project in respect of which the following estimates have been made:

Capital investment	£2 million
Annual cash flow	£0.8 million
Life of project	4 years

The directors are aware of the fact that estimates prepared in the past have proved unreliable.

The company's cost of capital is certain to be 12%.

Required:

(a) Calculate the net present value of the above project. [3]

(b) Calculate the DCF yield (internal rate of return) generated by the above project. [3]

(c) Calculate the extent to which each of the following variables, taken individually, can differ from the estimate before the project yields a negative net present value:

    (i)   capital investment;

    (ii) annual cash flow; and

    (iii) life of project.   [8]

(d) In the light of your answers to (a), (b) and (c), what advice would you give to the directors of Thames plc with regard to whether to proceed with the project?   [6]

[Total marks – 20]

Note:
Ignore taxation.
Table of factors for the present value of £1 appears in Appendix B.

13

FORECASTS AND BUDGETS

13.1 FORECASTS

When management takes decisions, it is important that consideration is given to their likely effects, and this is achieved by the preparation of forecasts which set out the expected financial results of a proposed course of action. Even when there are no plans to implement fundamental changes, such as a major expansion project or a price-cutting campaign, forecast accounts should still be prepared to indicate what is expected to transpire and to alert management to any possible problem areas. It is most valuable to have advance notice of likely results so that alternative plans of action designed to meet a range of eventualities can be formulated. In some cases advance notice may be vital, for example, if a cash deficit is foreseen, appropriate sources of finance can be arranged to meet it in good time. To leave the search for funds until the company has a liquidity crisis may cause it to fail or be forced to obtain finance on disadvantageous terms.

The relationship between banker and customer is made more productive if the company's plans are discussed and its requirements for financial assistance and other services from the bank known in advance. The amount of detail required by the banker is likely to be less than that needed by management, but must be sufficient for an opinion to be formed on the reliability of the forecasts. It is, of course, open to the banker to ask for further details, and the bank's response to a request for help may be influenced by the readiness and ability of management to comply. For example, the banker may be satisfied by the information that a proposed expansion involves additional monthly expenditure on wages of £2,500, while management needs to know what gives rise to this figure in terms of employees and wage rates. The credibility of the whole forecast can be questioned if, in fact, the £2,500 transpires to be simply a rough guess and cannot be substantiated further.

The following are important links between accounting reports which deal with past results and forecasts relating to the future:

- The historical accounts can be used as a basis for preparing forecasts.

- The careful comparison of forecasts with actual previous results should prevent the acceptance of plans that reflect wild hopes rather than realistic expectations. For example, forecasts may show substantial future profits, but to achieve these it may have been assumed that the gross profit percentage will be much higher than in the past; the assumption would have to be justified fully to any external accounts user who is expected to base a decision on it.

- Actual results for a period of time can be compared with the forecasts for that period and deviations investigated. The results of this study should aid the understanding of current performance, indicate the reliability of the forecasts, and provide a useful input to the process of preparing further forecasts.

Comparisons are made easier if the formats of the forecast and the actual results are the same; to achieve this the data processing system of the company must be designed to produce information analysed in the appropriate way. For example, if sales are forecast for individual product lines or geographical areas, then the reports on actual sales should be prepared on the same basis and compared with the anticipated results.

Forecasts are prepared of cash flows, profit or loss and the financial position displayed in the balance sheet. These are now dealt with in turn.

13.1.1 The Cash Forecast

This shows the cash flows which are likely to result from the adoption of a particular plan. There are regular trading flows, such as result from sales and purchases, and irregular flows from, for example, the issue of shares or the purchase of plant. When a company is trading steadily at a profit the cash balance increases smoothly, but the occurrence of large irregular flows of cash causes distortions.

Before starting to prepare a cash forecast, a number of matters must be ascertained:

- The overall period of time to be covered. The end date may be specified, or it may depend on a certain condition being satisfied, such as the identification of the maximum overdraft.

- The detail to be contained in the forecast. Whether the figures should relate to weeks, months or years, and the extent of analysis of receipts and payments.

- The area of activity to be covered. The forecast may be for an existing company, a newly-established company, a new area of activity, or an existing company together with a new area of activity.

The time periods and detail contained in the forecast depend on the purpose for which it is prepared. Cash management needs frequent and detailed knowledge of the likely cash position of the company, and so it is usual to draw up forecasts on a monthly basis. It may even be desirable to draw up budgets covering periods shorter than a month where the cash position is of crucial importance. A year, without further analysis, is likely to be too long a period of time to aid cash management because within a year the balance can fluctuate significantly, although for purposes such as investment appraisal (see Chapter 12) annual forecasts are often adequate. The amount of detail contained in the forecast is largely conditioned by the time period it covers; the further it reaches into the future, the less detailed and accurate it can be. Management is not restricted in the number of forecasts it prepares, and may draw up details of expected weekly cash flows for, say, the next two months, monthly forecasts for two years and annual forecasts for ten years. As time passes, the longer-term forecasts are revised in the light of current expectations, which may change as a result of current knowledge.

Time can be saved when forecasts are prepared by using the columnar format which shows cash flows on one side and time periods on another. This layout is demonstrated in Example 13.1 below. Once the columnar layout has been prepared, it is then fairly straightforward to work through the information given in the question and insert the expected cash flows in the appropriate location.

The main items that appear in cash forecasts are:

1. Sales

A sale is an economic event which produces a cash inflow immediately, if it is a cash sale, or after some time has elapsed in the case of a credit sale. The amount expected to be received from cash sales is entered in the cash forecast against the time period when the sales take place. In the case of credit sales it is necessary to determine the time lag between the sale and the cash inflow; if debtors take discounts, the sums receivable must be reduced correspondingly. At any time, the sums uncollected from individual customers give, in total, the value of debtors.

Example 13.1

The accountant of Ceiling Ltd, a trading company, is preparing the company's cash forecast for the first six months of 19X7. Credit sales in November and December of 19X6 were £24,000 and £27,000 respectively; it is expected that sales, all on credit, for each of the first three months of 19X7 will be £30,000 and will then rise to £36,000 per month for the rest of the year. The company's policy is to allow customers two months' credit, and these terms apply to all sales up to 31 December 19X6.

Required:

I.   Prepare a forecast of Ceiling Ltd's monthly cash receipts for the first six months of 19X7 on the following alternative assumptions:

(a)   There is no change in the company's credit terms.

(b)   The company extends the period of credit on all sales made after 1 January 19X7 to three months.

(c)   A discount of 2% is offered for prompt payment if the debt is settled within one month; this is taken in respect of half the company's sales. If the discount is not taken, payment must be made within two months.

II.   Calculate the value of trade debtors at 30 June 19X7 under each of the three alternatives given above.

Assume that each month consists of four weeks.

Solution

I.

19X7	Sales £000	(a) £000	(b) £000	Cash Received wider assumption: (c) Not taking discount £000	Taking discount £000	Total £000
January	30	24	24	24	–	24
February	30	27	27	27	14.7	41.7
March	30	30	-	15	14.7	29.7
April	36	30	30	15	14.7	29.7
May	36	30	30	15	17.64	32.64
June	36	36	30	18	17.64	35.64
Total		177	141			193.38

Note:
The different credit policies affect the rate of cash inflows and the total of cash received during the six months. Option (b) causes no cash to be received in March, while (c), at the cost of the discount, accelerates receipts in February.

II. Credit Sales Uncollected at 30 June 19X7

	Debtors £000
(a) May and June: £36,000 x 2 =	72
(b) April, May and June: £36,000 x 3 =	108
(c) Half of May and all of June: £18,000 + £36,000, less discount on half of June of £360	53.64

As a general rule, it is best to prepare the calculations relating to sales first because these determine the level of activity on which other costs, such as purchases and direct wages, may depend.

2. Purchases

The volume of purchases is set by the company's stock policy, which determines the extent to which stock is held in anticipation of sales or production. If sales are expected to rise, additional stock is likely to be acquired, while stocks will be run down if a decline in sales is forecast. The purchasing pattern required to achieve the desired increase in stock level is superimposed on the regular purchases required to replace stock which has been sold. Once purchases have been calculated, they can be converted into cash outflows by allowing for any period of credit and prompt payment discounts given by suppliers. The value of trade creditors for purchases at any time is the amount of stock received but not paid for.

Example 13.2

It is the policy of Ceiling Ltd, the company whose sales forecast for the first half of 19X7 is given in Example 13.1 above, to calculate its selling price at cost plus 50%. On 31 December 19X6 the value of stock held was £40,000, representing purchases of £20,000 in the months of November and December 19X6.

Required:
I.   Calculate the monthly cash outflow in respect of purchases for the first six months of 19X7 on the alternative assumptions:

   (a) The company purchases stock each month sufficient to ensure that, at the end of the month, the level of stock is equal to the anticipated sales of the following two months. Suppliers allow the company one month's credit.

   (b) The purchasing policy is as given in (a) above, but in both 19X6 and 19X7 the company takes advantage of a 3% prompt payment discount on half of its purchases by paying within one month; the remaining creditors are paid within two months.

II. Calculate the value of creditors at 30 June 19X7 under both of the alternatives given in I. above.

Solution

I.

		(a)		*(b)*	
			No		
			Discount	Discount	
	Purchases	*Cash*	*Taken*	*Taken*	*Cash*
	£000	*£000*	*£000*	*£000*	*£000*
19X6					
November	20				
December	20				
19X7					
January	20	20	10	9.7	19.7
February	24 (W1)	20	10	9.7	19.7
March	24 (W1)	24	10	11.64	21.64
April	24	24	12	11.64	23.64
May	24	24	12	11.64	23.64
June	24	24	12	11.64	23.64

W1 Includes £4,000 increase in stock.

II. Purchases unpaid at 30 June 19X7

	Creditors
(a) June	24
(b) Half of May plus June	36*

*On the grounds of prudence, no discount is anticipated.

3. Other Variable Costs

The cost of these may depend on the level of sales, for instance commission paid to salesmen, or on the rate of production, for example direct manufacturing wages. Once determined, they are entered in the cash forecast with allowance for any payment in advance or arrears.

4. Regular Fixed Costs

These are independent of the level of sales and are entered in the forecast in accordance with any details given about their pattern of incidence during the period under review. It is usually assumed that they accrue evenly over time and are paid in equal instalments. Care must be taken to ensure that there is no element of depreciation in the fixed costs to be entered in the cash forecast as depreciation is a non-cash expense.

5. Irregular Flows

Information may be given about cash flows in respect of such items as the issue or redemption of shares or debentures, sales and acquisitions of fixed assets, and dividend payments. In some cases the value of the flow may have to be calculated, and it is then entered in the appropriate time period in the forecast.

Example 13.3

Regent, a trader, has been in business for a number of years. The summarized trading and profit and loss account for 19X1 was as follows:

SUMMARIZED TRADING AND PROFIT AND LOSS ACCOUNT 19X1

	£	£
Sales (all on credit)		240,000
Less: Variable costs: purchases	180,000	
Fixed costs: general expenses, etc.	42,000*	222,000
Net Profit		£18,000

*General expenses include depreciation of £12,000 on fixed assets.

Regent believes that profits can be improved by increasing the sales of his product for which there exists a strong demand. The following plans and estimates are made:

(1) In January 19X2 Regent will issue a circular informing customers that the period of credit allowed will be increased from one to two months on all sales from 1 February.

(2) The more favourable credit terms will produce an increase in monthly sales, over 19X1 levels, of 10% for February to June 19X2, and 20% thereafter.

(3) The period of credit received from suppliers will remain unchanged at one month.

(4) It is Regent's policy to maintain stocks at a level equivalent to expected sales over the forthcoming two months. Stocks at 31 December 19X1 were £30,000.

(5) General expenses accrue evenly during the year and, depreciation apart, are paid for on a monthly basis.

At 31 December 19X1 Regent's bank balance stands at £3,000. Regent's bank has agreed to provide overdraft facilities up to a limit of £13,000 for the forthcoming twelve months.

Required:
(a) A cash budget showing the forecast bank balance or overdraft at the end of each month during 19X2.

(b) Comments, in the light of your calculations under (a), on the bank's requirement that the overdraft should not exceed £13,000.

Notes:
1. Assume that 19X2 consists of twelve months of equal length.

2. Trading transactions occurred at an even rate during 19X1.

Solution

(a)

Month	Opening balance £000	Sales £000	Purchases Replacements £000	Purchases Stockpiling £000	General expenses £000	Closing balance £000
January	3.0	20	15.0		2.5	5.5
February	5.5	20	15.0	3.0(W1)	2.5	5.0
March	5.0	-	16.5		2.5	(14.0)
April	(14.0)	22	16.5		2.5	(11.0)
May	(11.0)	22	16.5		2.5	(8.0)
June	(8.0)	22	16.5	1.5(W2)	2.5	(6.5)
July	(6.5)	22	16.5	1.5(W3)	2.5	(5.0)
August	(5.0)	22	18.0		2.5	(3.5)
September	(3.5)	24	18.0		2.5	-
October	-	24	18.0		2.5	3.5
November	3.5	24	18.0		2.5	7.0
December	7.0	24	18.0		2.5	10.5

Workings

		£000
WI	Estimated cost of goods sold: February	16.5
	March	16.5
	Stock level required at 31 January	33.0
	Stock level 1 January	30.0
	Additional January purchases, paid February	3.0

	W2	W3
W2 and W3	£000	£000
Estimated cost of goods sold: June	16.5	
July	18.0	18.0
August		18.0
Required stock level: 31 May	34.5	
30 June		36.0
Stock level at: 1 May	33.0	
1 June		34.5
Additional purchases: May, paid June	1.5	
June, paid July		1.5

(b) The maximum overdraft is exceeded only in March but, if the plans are fulfilled, there will be a healthy balance at the bank by the end of December. Regent could comply with the bank's requirement by delaying, for a couple of months, the build up of stocks to the extent of £1,000.

13.1.2 The Profit Forecast

A principal objective of business activity is to maximize the rate of return on capital employed. Therefore, management needs to know the likely profitability (and capital employed) of alternative courses of action so that the option which appears to produce the best rate of return on capital employed can be studied further; for instance, it is necessary to prepare a cash forecast to see whether the most profitable alternative is also viable from the financial viewpoint. The period covered by the profit forecast must be considered carefully; the option which shows the greatest profit in the short term may appear less favourable in the longer term. As is the case with cash forecasts, the further into the future the forecast is projected, the less accurate it will be.

The main elements to be predicted in a profit forecast are:

1. Sales

The value of future sales depends on the number of units to be sold and their price. Once a sales forecast has been prepared, consideration can be given to whether the necessary production capacity is available. If sufficient units cannot be produced to meet expected demand, the sales price may be raised to restrict demand or, alternatively, extra capacity may be arranged; the importance of a sales forecast is that it enables plans to be formulated well in advance to overcome any foreseeable problems. Subject to the limitations imposed by the forecast available capacity of a business, a variety of combinations of selling price and resultant sales volume can be tried in order to see which gives the greatest forecast profit. In examination questions, the value of future sales may be given or may have to be calculated.

2. Cost of Goods Manufactured

In the case of a manufacturing concern, the various elements of cost incurred in production must be totalled to find the cost of goods manufactured, which is then transferred to the trading account. The costs may be broadly classified as fixed or variable. Variable costs (see Chapter 11.2.2) depend on the level of production and may be calculated on the basis of cost per unit or as a percentage of the value of production; fixed costs (see Chapter 11.2.1) do not vary over a limited range of output, and care must be taken to calculate and include depreciation on any new fixed assets.

3. Cost of Goods Sold

The volume of sales is likely to differ from purchases, in the case of a trading company, or from production in the case of a manufacturer. In either case there is a change in the level of stock; if more is sold than is produced or bought, stock levels fall. If production or purchases exceed sales, then stocks increase. Where stock levels change, the cost of goods sold is found by the familiar formula:

$$\text{Cost of Goods Sold} = \text{Opening Stock} + \text{Cost of Goods} \left\{ \begin{array}{c} \text{Purchased} \\ \text{or} \\ \text{Manufactured} \end{array} \right\} - \text{Closing Stock}$$

To apply this formula requires the valuation of opening and closing stocks, which is dealt with in Chapter 5.1.

4. Other Costs

These cover a wide range and include such items as discounts, interest charges and administration and delivery costs. They may be fixed or variable and the information given must be studied carefully to enable their calculation.

Example 13.4

Popplewell Ltd is an engineering company and the directors have decided to extend the range of items manufactured by producing a special type of steel pallet suitable for the storage of cylinders of dangerous gases. The summarized accounts of Popplewell Ltd for 19X0 are as follows:

MANUFACTURING, TRADING AND PROFIT AND LOSS ACCOUNT FOR 19X0

	£	£
Sales		1,160,000
Less: Raw materials consumed	305,200	
Manufacturing wages	246,500	
Factory overheads (depreciation £27,000)	238,300	
Cost of goods manufactured	790,000	
Opening stock of finished goods	167,000	
Closing stock of finished goods	(167,000)	
Cost of goods sold		790,000
Gross profit		370,000
Administration, selling and distribution costs		
(depreciation £10,000)		277,000
Net profit		93,000

BALANCE SHEET AT 31 DECEMBER 19X0

	£	
Fixed assets at cost		
Less: depreciation	301,000	
Stocks of raw		
materials and		
finished goods	187,000	
Debtors	73,000	
Bank	24,000	
	585,000	
Less: Trade creditors	62,000	
	523,000	
	£	
Share capital	300,000	
Reserves	223,000	
	523,000	

It is expected that existing activities will continue at a similar level during the forthcoming year, and for forecasting purposes it is to be assumed that the 19X0 results will be exactly repeated. None of the existing plant will require replacement until 19X5.

The following plans and forecasts are provided in connection with the plan to manufacture pallets.

(i) Plant and machinery costing £80,000 will be required and this will be purchased in March and paid for immediately. The plant is expected to have a five-year life and a nil scrap value at the end of that period.

(ii) The raw materials needed to manufacture 150 pallets will be purchased in March and sufficient purchases will be made in each subsequent month to replace quantities consumed. The raw materials cost per pallet is estimated at £50 and one month's credit will be obtained from suppliers.

(iii) Production will commence on 1 April 19X1 at the rate of 100 pallets each month and sales are expected to be made at a similar rate commencing 1 May 19X1. The selling price of each pallet is to be £130 and one month's credit is to be allowed to customers. No bad debts are expected to arise.

(iv) Direct wages are expected to amount to £30 per pallet, and factory overhead expenses (other than depreciation) relating specifically to this project will commence in March and will be £1,900 per month. Both wages and overheads will be paid for during the month the service is provided. There will be no increase in administration, selling and distribution costs.

Required:
(a) A forecast of cash receipts and cash payments for the new project covering each of the ten months to 31 December 19X1.

(b) A forecast profit statement for the new project for 19X1.

(c) A calculation of the bank balance of Popplewell Ltd at 31 December 19X1.

(d) A brief report, for the company's bank, on the profitability and financial implications of the new project, for which the bank has been asked to provide overdraft facilities if required.

Notes:
1. It is the company's policy to value finished stock at prime cost, i.e. raw materials and direct labour only, in its management reports.

2. Ignore work in progress, taxation, dividends and any bank interest payable.

Solution

(a)

		Cash Receipts and Payments					
	Receipts			Payments			
	Opening Balance	Sales	Plant	Raw Materials	Wages	Over-heads	Closing Balance
19X1	£	£	£	£	£	£	£
March			80,000			1,900	(81,900)
April	(81,900)			7,500	3,000	1,900	(94,300)
May	(94,300)			5,000	3,000	1,900	(104,200)
June	(104,200)	13,000		5,000	3,000	1,900	(101,100)
July	(101,100)	13,000		5,000	3,000	1,900	(98,000)
August	(98,000)	13,000		5,000	3,000	1,900	(94,900)
September	(94,900)	13,000		5,000	3,000	1,900	(91,800)
October	(91,800)	13,000		5,000	3,000	1,900	(88,700)
November	(88,700)	13,000		5,000	3,000	1,900	(85,600)
December	(85,600)	13,000		5,000	3,000	1,900	(82,500)

(b) *Forecast Profit Statement for 19X1*

	£	£
Sales		104,000
Less: Raw materials purchased	52,500	
Less: Closing stock	7,500	
	45,000	
Manufacturing wages	27,000	
Depreciation	12,000 (WI)	
Other factory overheads	19,0(0	
Cost of goods manufactured	103,000	
Less: Closing stock of finished goods	8,000 (W2)	
Cost of goods sold		95,000
Profit		9,000

Workings

W1 Compute depreciation on the straight-line basis:
£80,000 (depreciable amount) ÷ 5 (expected life) x ¾ (plant used for nine months in 19X1) = £12,000.

W2 Value stock on the prime cost basis:

Raw materials per unit	50
Direct labour per unit	30
	80 x 100 units = £8,000

(c) *Forecast Bank Balance at 31 December 19X1*

	£	£
Opening cash balance		24,000
Add: Cash flow from existing activities:		
Profit	93,000	
Depreciation	37,000	
		130,000
		154,000
Less: Deficit on new project		82,500
Closing cash balance		71,500

(d) The profit of £9,000 seems a small return on an investment in plant and working capital totalling £103,500; but in a full year the return from the new project should be significantly higher:

	£	£
Sales		156,000
Less: Materials	60,000	
Wages	36,000	
Overheads	22,800	
Depreciation	16,000	
		134,800
Net Profit		21,200

Cash generated from existing activities amounts to £130,000 per annum (profit + depreciation) or nearly £11,000 per month. It is clear that the company will require some financial support from the bank during the first few months of the project, but the facility should be liquidated well before the year end as the result of cash generated from existing and additional business activities.

Example 13.4 draws attention to the kind of distortion that can arise where the forecast covers a time period which is not typical; in this case it covers less than a year and includes heavy start-up costs. A reconciliation of the results for a full year and those of the first eight months is:

	£
Eight months' profit expressed as a proportion of a full year's predicted results (see (d)), £21,200 x $\frac{8}{12}$	14,133
Profit in 19X1 (see (b))	9,000
Shortfall	5,133
Shortfall made up as follows:	
Non-recurring start-up costs:	
March and April factory overheads: £1,900 x 2	3,800
April depreciation $\frac{£12,000}{9}$	1,333
	5,133

The sales for the first eight months of the new project bear ten months' overheads and nine months' depreciation. In future years, twelve months' expenses will be matched by twelve months' sales.

13.1.3 The Forecast Balance Sheet
It is necessary to prepare a forecast balance sheet to discover the effect of forecast profit and cash flows on the financial position of the company. The forecast balance sheet may be analysed in the same way as a factual statement which relates to the past, and the analysis may point to the need for action to avoid any shortcomings which are revealed.

The items contained in a balance sheet forecast are calculated as follows:

1. Fixed Assets
These are reported at cost, or revalued amount, less accumulated depreciation. The opening position must be established; forecast acquisitions are then added to the opening assets at cost, or revalued amount, and the forecast depreciation charge is added to the figure for accumulated depreciation to date. The cost and related

depreciation of forecast disposals are subtracted from the opening position. Where revaluations take place, the surplus is added to equity and a higher depreciation charge may result.

2. Stocks

The basis of stock valuation must be established (see Chapter 5.1). Where the valuation has already been made for the purpose of preparing the forecast for the cost of goods sold (see Example 13.4), this figure should also be used in the balance sheet.

3. Trade Debtors

These represent a number of weeks' or months' sales, and may be calculated on the basis of specific patterns of sales (see Example 13.1 above). Their level depends on the value of sales, the company's credit policy, and the willingness of customers to pay on the due date; allowance must be made for anticipated bad debts.

4. Cash and Overdrafts

This balance may be calculated in a separate cash forecast (see section 13.1.1) or may be the balancing figure in the balance sheet found after all the other values have been entered. Where it is a balancing figure, it shows the cash surplus or deficit arising from the adoption of particular plans after a period of time has elapsed, but major drawbacks are that it reveals neither the fluctuations which take place over the period of the forecast nor the maximum or minimum surplus or deficit which is likely to be encountered. A detailed cash forecast is needed to satisfy these requirements.

5. Equity

This consists of share capital and reserves. The value of share capital is adjusted for issues, redemptions, and the purchase by the company of its own shares during the period of the forecast. Reserves are of many types and may change in value as a result of, for example, a premium on the issue of shares, capitalization by a bonus issue, or the revaluation of fixed assets. The most usual change is caused by the impact on revenue reserves of the forecast profit retained or loss suffered during the forthcoming accounting period.

6. Non-equity Shares and Debentures and other Loans

The opening balance must be adjusted for any issues or redemptions which are to take place in the period of the forecast.

7. Trade Creditors

The value of trade creditors depends on purchases and the period of credit granted by suppliers (see Example 13.2 above).

8. Accruals and Prepayments

At the date of the forecast balance sheet, adjustments may be needed to match anticipated revenues with their related costs. A prepayment arises where a sum of money has been paid which provides benefits after the balance sheet date; accruals occur when benefits have been enjoyed prior to the balance sheet date but have not been paid for. Care must be taken to include dividends and taxation due at the balance sheet date.

Example 13.5

A new trading company called Fayet Ltd is to be incorporated in December 19X1, and the intention is to commence business activity on 1 January 19X2. The directors, who will also own all the shares in the new company, are considering how much to invest in their new enterprise.

The bank has agreed to provide any overdraft facilities required during the year, provided that the forecast liquidity ratio (i.e. the ratio of debtors to current liabilities) at 31 December 19X2 is not less than 1.2:1. Accordingly, the directors intend to introduce sufficient share capital on 1 January 19X2 to produce a liquidity ratio of 1.2:1 at 31 December 19X2.

Other forecasts and estimates are as follows:
1. Current liabilities at 31 December 19X2 are expected to amount to £50,000.

2. Sales will accrue evenly during the year and the debtors' balance at 31 December 19X2 will represent one-and-a-half months' sales.

3. The working capital ratio at 31 December 19X2 will be 2:1.

4. On 1 January 19X2, £100,000 will be spent on fixed assets which are expected to last for ten years and have no resale value at the end of that time.

5. Purchases of stock will occur evenly during the year and one month's credit will be received from suppliers.

6. The gross profit margin will be 33⅓% of sales.

7. Running expenses, other than depreciation, are estimated at £125,000.

Required:
The estimated trading and profit and loss account of Fayet Ltd for 19X2 and the estimated balance sheet at 31 December 19X2. The balance sheet should show clearly the share capital which would have to be raised at the outset in order to meet the bank's requirement.

Notes:
1.   Assume that a year consists of twelve months of equal length.

2.   At 31 December 19X2 current assets will consist of stocks and trade debtors. Current liabilities will consist of trade creditors and the bank overdraft.

3.   No dividends will be paid during 19X2.

4.   Ignore taxation.

Solution

Estimated Trading and Profit and Loss Account

	£
Sales (W4)	480,000
Purchases (W6)	360,000
Less: Stock	40,000
Cost of goods sold (W5)	320,000
Gross profit	160,000
Running expenses	125,000
Depreciation (W9)	10,000
Net profit	25,000
	160,000

Estimated Balance Sheet

	£	£	£
Fixed assets at cost			100,000
Less: Depreciation			10,000
			90,000
Current Assets			
Stock (W3)	40,000		
Debtors (W1)	60,000		
		100,000 (W2)	
Current Liabilities:			
Creditors (W7)	30,000		
Overdraft (W8)	20,000		
		50,000	
Net current assets			50,000
			140,000
Financed by:			
Share capital (balancing figure)			115,000
Net profit			25,000
			140,000

Workings

		£
1.	Trade debtors, 1.2 x £50,000	60,000
2.	Current assets, 2 x £50,000	100,000
3.	Stocks, £100,000 – £60,000	40,000
4.	Sales, 12/15 x 60,000	480,000
5.	Cost of goods sold, 66⅔ of sales	320,000
6.	Purchases, £320,000 + £40,000	360,000
7.	Creditors, 1/12 x £360,000	30,000
8.	Overdraft, £50,000 – £30,000	20,000
9.	Depreciation, £100,000 x 1/10	10,000

The following example requires the preparation of a forecast cash statement, profit and loss account and balance sheet. Note how these interlink; for example the forecast cash balance is used in the balance sheet, the forecast profit is added to capital, and the value of drawings in the balance sheet agrees with that in the cash forecast.

Example 13.6

The summarized final accounts of Michael, a trader, for the year ended 30 June 19X1, are as follows:

PROFIT AND LOSS ACCOUNT, YEAR ENDED 30 JUNE 19X1

	£	£
Sales		480,000
Less: Cost of goods sold		360,000
Gross profit		120,000
Less: Depreciation	10,000	
General expenses	96,000	106,000
Net profit		14,000

BALANCE SHEET AS AT 30 JUNE 19X1

	£	£
Fixed assets at cost		100,000
Less: Depreciation		30,000
		70,000
Current assets		
Stock-in-trade	45,000	
Trade debtors	40,000	
Bank	2,000	
	87,000	
Trade creditors	60,000	
Net current assets		27,000
		97,000
Capital		97,000

Michael has approached your bank for a loan to finance the acquisition of additional freehold premises. The premises are situated next door to his existing premises and occupation could be obtained on 1 October 19X1. The premises would cost £50,000 and payment would be made during the month of October. There is a heavy demand for the goods which Michael sells and he is confident that from 1 October monthly sales can be increased by 20% if the additional premises are obtained. The gross profit percentage would remain unchanged and general expenses, inclusive of an allowance for bank interest at 15%, would increase by £1,200 per month from 1 September. Michael intends to employ two sources of finance for the planned expansion:

1. He will offer customers a discount of 2% for immediate payment on all sales made from 1 October 19X1 onwards. He expects half the customers to take advantage of this offer. The remaining customers will take the same period of credit as in the previous year.

2. He has asked for a bank overdraft facility of £20,000 for the next twelve months.

   Michael expects creditors to increase in proportion to sales; the stock-in-trade balance will remain at £45,000. The depreciation charge on existing fixed assets will remain unchanged. The additional buildings will be depreciated on the straight-line basis assuming a life of 20 years; for this purpose the buildings are considered to comprise £40,000 of the planned expenditure on premises referred to above. General expenses are paid monthly for cash; Michael draws £1,000 from the business bank account each month to cover personal expenditure.

Required:
(a) Michael's estimated profit and loss account for the year ended 30 June 19X2 and estimated balance sheet at 30 June 19X2.

(b) Calculations of the estimated maximum overdraft Michael will require during the year to 30 June 19X2 and of his bank balance or overdraft at 30 June 19X2.

(c) An assessment of Michael's plans for expansion.

Notes:
1. There are no seasonal fluctuations in the level of activity in Michael's trade.

2. Purchases and sales take place evenly during the year.

3. Your calculations under (a) and (b) should be based on the assumption that the bank agrees to finance the planned expansion.

Solution

(a) *Forecast Profit and Loss Account, Year to 30 June 19X2*

	£	£
Sales		552,000 (W1)
Less: Cost of Goods Sold		414,000 (W1)
Gross profit		138,000
Depreciation	11,500 (W2)	
Discounts	4,320 (W3)	
General Expenses	108,000	
		123,820
Net Profit		14,180

Workings

W1 (£000)

	Sales	Cost of Goods sold
July-September: 480 x 1/4	120	
360 x 1/4		90
October-June: 480 x 3/4	360	
Add 360 x 20%	72	
	432	
360 x 3/4		270
Add 270 x 20%		54
		324
	552	414

W2 Depreciation:	£	£	£
Existing fixed assets			10,000
Additional buildings, (£40,000 ÷ 20) x 3/4			1,500
			11,500

W3 Discounts: 1% of £432,000 = £4,320

Forecast Balance Sheet 30 June 19X2	£	£	£
Fixed assets at cost			150,000
Less: Accumulated			
depreciation			41,500
			108,500
Current Assets:			
Stock in trade	45,000		
Debtors	24,000		
		69,000	
Current Liabilities:			
Trade creditors	72,000		
Bank overdraft	6,320		
		78,320	
Net current assets			(9,320)
			99,180
Financed by:			
Opening capital			97,000
Add: Net profit		14,180	
Less: Drawings		(12,000)	2,180
			99,180

(b) *Cash Forecast*

Month	Opening Balance	Sales Cash	Credit	Purchases	General Expenses	Drawings	Premises	Closing Balance
July	2,000		40,000	30,000	8,000	1,000		3,000
Aug.	3,000		40,000	30,000	8,000	1,000		4,000
Sept.	4,000		40,000	30,000	9,200	1,000		3,800
Oct.	3,800	23,520	40,000	30,000	9,200	1,000	50,000	(22,880)
Nov.	(22,880)	23,520	24,000	30,000	9,200	1,000		(15,560)
Dec.	(15,560)	23,520	24,000	36,000	9,200	1,000		(14,240)

The overdraft then declines at the rate of £1,320 per month until June 19X2, i.e. 14,240-(6 x 1,320) = £6,320.

(c) The forecast profit is only marginally higher than that achieved in the year to 30 June 19X1. However, the increased sales were achieved only in the last nine months of the year. In a full year:

	£	£
Sales		576,000
Less: Cost of goods sold		432,000
		144,000
Depreciation	12,000	
Discounts	5,760	
General Expenses	110,400	
		128,160
Net profit		15,840

In addition:

(1) The bank overdraft will be repaid by the end of 19X2 and interest charges will then cease.

(2) Alternatively, if possible, Michael should discontinue the practice of allowing discounts for prompt payments. Although he collects the cash, on average, a month earlier, he pays 2% (approximately 24% per annum) for this privilege.

Michael marginally exceeds the requested overdraft facility in October. The excess is only for one month and so the facility, if granted, should be in the region of £25,000. The new premises will provide one possible source of security for the overdraft.

13.1.4 The Identification of Alternatives

The forecasts so far considered have been prepared on the basis of well-formulated plans. In other circumstances, there may be a number of possible courses of action; the forecaster must clearly identify the alternatives, prepare forecasts of the likely results from each, and, if required, give advice based on these forecasts.

Example 13.7

Rowan recently won a premium bond prize of £50,000. At present he is employed as a travelling salesman with an annual income of £4,000 and fringe benefits that are worth £1,000 a year to him. His wife works as a receptionist and her salary is £2,000 per annum. He has been exploring two investment possibilities.

(i)   To invest his money in a local company. The proposal is that, with the £50,000 available, he should acquire 20,000 shares, which the firm intends to issue in order to finance a plan for expansion. The firm's managing director informs him, 'Our annual profits are at present in the region of £30,000, of which two-thirds are paid out in dividends. As a result of the expansion profits should increase by 25% all of which will be added to the current annual dividend.' At present the company's share capital consists of 80,000 shares with a nominal value of £1 each. Under this option Rowan would play no part in the management of the company.

(ii) To acquire a shop which has recently come on to the market. The cost would be £60,000 and this includes stocks to which a value of £15,000 is attached. Finance would be provided out of his winnings and by realizing some investments currently yielding a 'safe' return of 10% per annum (gross). These investments can be added to or reduced without affecting the rate of return. The following estimates are provided concerning this business.

Average annual rate of stock turnover	10
Gross profit as a percentage of sales	25%
Overhead expenses	£33,000

If this option is pursued, Rowan can either run the business with the help of his wife, both working full-time, or engage a manager at an annual salary of £8,000. Management salaries are not included in the overhead expenses shown above.

Required:
(a)   A numerical analysis of the options open to Rowan presented in a manner which will help him to make comparisons. Confine your calculations to the information given.

(b)   An indication of the alternative you would recommend on the basis of the information given.

Note:
Ignore taxation.

Solution

(a) Alternative:

1. Continue in present employment and purchase additional investments.

	£	£
Present salary		4,000
Fringe benefits		1,000
Wife's earnings		2,000
£50,000 invested at 10%		5,000
		12,000

2. Continue in present employment and purchase shares in local firm.

	£	£
Salary, fringe benefits and wife's earnings as above		7,000
Present dividend paid by firm	20,000	
Estimated increase in profits: 25% of 30,000	7,500	
Share of future dividend $^{20,000}/_{100,000}$ x	27,500	= 5,500
		12,500

3. Acquire a shop to be managed by Rowan and his wife.

	£	£
Cost of sales = 10 x 15,000	150,000	
Sales = $^{100}/_{75}$ x 150,000	200,000	
Gross profit	50,000	
Less: Overheads	33,000	
Profit		17,000
Loss of investment income: 10% of £10,000		1,000
		16,000

4. Acquire a shop and engage a manager.

	£	£
Present salary, fringe benefits and wife's earnings as in 1		7,000
Profit as in 3	16,000	
Less: Manager's salary	8,000	
		8,000
		15,000

(b) Investment in the shares of a local company may produce some appreciation in the capital value of Rowan's investment, as well as the forecast dividend, but there is considerable risk and alternative 1 seems better than alternative 2 despite the marginally lower expected return. Going into business seems attractive. There is likely to be risk in any business venture but perhaps a travelling salesman is not in the most secure employment. Provided Rowan and his wife appear likely to possess the necessary expertise, it is probably better for them to manage the shop themselves.

13.2 BUDGETING, PLANNING AND CONTROL

A budget is a financial plan based on expected future activity and it is used to control that activity. It is possible to make a number of forecasts of the financial outcome under different assumptions, and the forecast which best meets the firm's objectives, and is within its capabilities, is chosen as the budget. Management must then convert the budget into plans which are put into action. For example, if the budget requires an increase in production which needs additional capacity, management must plan its acquisition in advance so that it is available when needed. The budget gives control as responsibility for its various parts can be assigned to managers who are then responsible for them; it also gives a basis with which to compare actual results and hence evaluate managerial performance.

A firm's budget should be comprehensive and coordinated, and not simply a set of vague and unrelated hopes and wishes. By being comprehensive it covers all of the organization and so ensures that all activity is geared to achieving the budget's objective. The fact that it is coordinated means that, as long as each individual manager is seeking to fulfil his or her part of the budget, the organization as a whole is going in the right direction.

13.2.1 The Sales Budget

It is usual to start the process of budget preparation with the sales budget as the predicted volume of sales determines most of the other features of the organization, such as the production capacity to be provided. The manager responsible for sales must analyse the potential market in which the firm intends to operate during the budget period and consider, and draft answers to, such questions as:

- What products are going to be sold?

- What is the maximum size of the market?

- What portion of the market can be captured?

- Who is going to sell the products?

- In what geographical areas are the products to be sold?

- When will the products be sold?

- What price will be charged for each unit?

- How many units will be sold?

When an outline sales budget has been prepared, it is compared with the firm's resources to see if it can be met and whether it gives an adequate profit. If not, then it must be reviewed by, for example, examining the effect of charging a higher price per unit but selling fewer of them or increasing spending on advertising. At all times the budget must be realistic and achievable; it is no use assuming levels of sales which cannot be met simply to show a budgeted profit which it is obvious will not transpire in reality.

The finalized sales budget, which should be agreed with those who have to put it into operation, may be presented in a form such as:

Sales Budget for January 19X0 (000)

Area: Product	1	2	3	4	Total
A	10	20	30	40	100
B	30	10	30	40	110
C	40	10	10	10	70
Total	80	40	70	90	280

This may be aggregated with other sales budgets to give the result for the company as a whole, or further analysed to show the sales expected by each member of the sales force, whose performance can then be measured against it.

13.2.2 The Production Budget
The right quantity of goods must be available for delivery to customers at the right time, and so the amount to be produced in a period is determined by:

- the sales for that period;

- the increase or decrease in stocks during the period.

The production budget is based on the requirement to fulfil the sales budget; any increase in stock levels will require additional production, while stock reductions mean that less needs to be produced. At an early stage in the preparation of the budget the existing physical production capacity must be assessed to see if it can meet production targets, and this will be linked with the capital investment programme. The impact of production levels on the purchasing of materials and labour requirements also has to be evaluated.

Cost behaviour, as described in Chapter 11, should be considered and costs classified according to whether they are fixed or variable. This will enable, at a later stage, the budget to be 'flexed' so that it reflects the actual level of activity. For example, the budget may initially show material costs of £2,500 based on the production and sale of 100 units with a material cost of £25 each; if only 50 units are sold, the material budget should be reduced to £1,250. The adjustment of the budget in this way allows managers to be monitored on the basis of factors for which they are responsible. The fact that sales are above or below target is due to the efficiency, or otherwise, of the sales force, and so should not affect the judgement of how well the production facility is performing. On the other hand, the production manager is responsible for fulfilling the orders in accordance with the budgeted costs per unit, and so should have to account for variations in the variable cost per unit.

13.2.3 The General and Administration Budget

These costs should be monitored and controlled as carefully as production costs, and a specific manager should be given responsibility for each of them. It is possible to classify general and administrative costs according to whether they are fixed or variable; for example, a finance department manager's salary is a fixed cost while the amount of discounts allowed to credit customers for prompt payment is influenced by the value of sales made. The budgets for the variable costs can be flexed to allow for the effect of sales variations, and control over fixed costs exercised by ensuring that they are within budget and represent the most economical way of obtaining the services which they provide.

13.2.4 The Cash Budget

This is a specific cash forecast based on the finalized budgets. It brings together the results of not only sales and costs, but also capital transactions, such as the purchase of fixed assets or the issue of a debenture. By breaking the cash budget down into short intervals, usually a month, it is possible to identify anticipated cash surpluses and deficits; appropriate steps can be taken in advance to deal with them, and their consequences, in the form of interest paid or received, built into the budgets.

13.2.5 The Master Budget

Once all of the budgets have been finalized, their results are brought together into a master budget for the organization as a whole. The master budget is a forecast profit and loss account and balance sheet to which can also be added a forecast cash flow statement, and these overall budgeted results show the outcome which will transpire if all the budgets are fulfilled exactly, which in practice is exceedingly unlikely. Senior management should review the master budget to see if it shows satisfactory results; if they are not, then action should be planned and taken to improve them. This may mean going through the whole budgeting process again, but the increasing use of computers for budget preparation makes this a much less onerous task than previously.

Example 13.8

Kaplan Ltd is a well-established private company whose balance sheet at 31 December 20X2, was as follows:

20X1		20X2	
£000		£000	£000
1,250	Fixed assets at cost		1,370
450	*Less*: Accumulated depreciation		500
800			870
	Current Assets		
280	Stock	285	
302	Debtors	296	
12	Cash at bank	56	
594		637	
	Current liabilities		
128	Creditors	131	
30	Corporation tax due 30 September	35	
158		166	
436	Net current assets		471
1,236			1,341
	Financed by:		
1,000	Share capital		1,000
150	Plant replacement reserve		200
86	Retained profit		141
1,236			1,341

The profits derived from existing activities during 20X2 are expected to be repeated during the financial year to 31 December 20X3.

In addition, the directors plan to expand the company's range of business operations by selling glass conservatories imported from abroad. The following plans have been made in conjunction with relevant personnel:

1.   Advertising costs will amount to £10,000 in June 20X3 and £1,000 in each month that follows. The advertising agency is expected to allow one month's credit.

2.   Sales of conservatories to amount to £30,000 per month during the months of July September 20X3, inclusive, and £45,000 per month thereafter.

3. An initial stock of conservatories costing £60,000 will be purchased and paid for in June 20X3. Commencing July 20X3, sufficient conservatories will be purchased and paid for each month to replace items sold.

4. The sales price of conservatories is to be fixed at 50% above purchase price.

5. Customers will be required to pay 80% of the sales price on installation, and 20% one month later.

6. Installation costs are expected to be £2,000 per month during the months of July-September, inclusive, and £3,000 per month thereafter. The costs are to be paid immediately they are incurred.

7. General administration expenses, also paid immediately they are incurred, will amount to £6,000 per month commencing July.

8. Provision is to be made for corporation tax at the rate of 25% on forecast profit before tax.

Required:
(a) A reconstruction of the profit and loss appropriation account of Kaplan Ltd for 20X2.

(b) A monthly cash budget, for the new project, for each of the six months from 1 July to 31 December 20X3.

(c) A budgeted profit and loss account for the new project for the six month period to 31 December 20X3 (monthly figures are not required).

(d) A calculation of the estimated bank balance, or overdraft, of the company at 31 December 20X3.

(e) A budgeted balance sheet of the company as at 31 December 20X3.

Notes:
1. The bank has agreed to provide overdraft facilities if required.

2. Ignore bank interest payable if any.

Solution

(a) *Profit and Loss Appropriation Account for Kaplan, 20X2*

	£000
Profit before tax	140
Less: Corporation tax	35
	105
Less: Transfer to plant replacement reserve	50
Retained profit for 20X2	55
Retained profit at 1 January 20X2	86
Retained profit at 31 December 20X2	141

(b) *Cash Forecast, New Project, July-December 20X3, £000*

	July	Aug.	Sept.	Oct.	Nov.	Dec.
Sales 80%	24	24	24	36	36	36
20%	___	6	6	6	9	9
	24	30	30	42	45	45
Purchases (W1)	20	20	20	30	30	30
Advertising	10	1	1	1	1	1
Installation	2	2	2	3	3	3
General admin.	6	6	6	6	6	6
	38	29	29	40	40	40
Net increase (decrease)	(14)	1	1	2	5	5
Opening balance	(60) (W2)	(74)	(73)	(72)	(70)	(65)
Closing balance	(74)	(73)	(72)	(70)	(65)	(60)

(c) *Profit Forecast, New Project, July-December 20X3*

	£000	£000
Sales		225 (W3)
Less: Cost of sales		150 (W4)
Gross profit		75
Advertising	16	
Installation	15	
General admin	36	67
Net profit		8
Less: Taxation		2
		6

W1. Sales July-Sept: 30,000 x 100/150; Oct-Dec. 45,000 x 100/150.
W2. 60,000 (stock paid for in June).
W3. 30,000 x 3 (July-Sept. sales) + 45,000 x 3 (Oct-Dec. sales).
W4. 225,000 (sales) x 2/3.

(d)	£000	£000
Opening bank balance		56
Cash flow from existing operations:		
Profit	140	
Depreciation	50	190
		246
Less: Taxation paid	35	
Cash deficit on new project	60	95
Closing bank balance		151

(e) *Budgeted Balance Sheet at 31 December 20X3*

	£000	£000
Fixed assets at cost		1,370
Less: Accumulated depreciation		550
		820
Current Assets		
Stock	345 W5	
Debtors	305 W6	
Cash at bank	151	
	801	
Current Liabilities		
Creditors and accruals	132 W7	
Corporation tax due 30 September	37 W8	
	169	
Net current assets		632
		1,452
Financed by		
Share capital		1,000
Plant replacement reserve		200
Retained profit		252
		1,452

W5. 265 (stock existing operations) + 60 (stock new project)
W6. 296 (debtors existing operations) + 9 (debtors new projects)
W7. 131 +1 (advertising accrual)
W8. 35 (taxation existing operations) + 2 (taxation new project).

13.3 THE FINANCING DECISION

The cash forecast provides information on the expected cash position of the company, and, where a deficit is revealed, consideration must be given to the manner in which it is to be financed. Two important aspects are the size of the deficit and its expected duration. To avoid overtrading, a company should not normally use short-term sources of finance to acquire long-term assets, but the size of the investment must be judged relative to the scale of the company. A large company can make a relatively small capital investment by using short-term funds and not seriously impair a satisfactory working capital position, whereas a small company, investing a similar sum of money, would seriously deplete its working capital if it used short-term finance. A cash deficit must be funded in an appropriate manner if a firm's financial development is to be balanced; this requires the matching of a long-term deficit with long-term funds, such as share capital or debentures, while a deficit expected to last only a short time can be matched with short-term funds, such as an overdraft. The position from which a company starts is also relevant, because one with a healthy working capital position can accept a short-term deterioration but the future of a firm with existing liquidity problems would be jeopardised by any worsening (see Chapter 10 for a detailed discussion of the financial development of companies).

The cash flow patterns which result from alternative courses of action can be entered in cash flow forecasts to see which best suits the company's requirements. However, when deciding how to obtain finance, there are other factors to be considered:

1. *Security*. The ability of a company to attract finance may depend on the assets it can offer as security and the extent to which these are already pledged.

2. *Gearing*. The capital structure of the company should be developed in a balanced manner. A company with little or no gearing has the capacity to raise fixed interest loans, whereas a highly-geared company should give priority to expanding its equity capital.

3. *Ownership*. The owners of a company may be unwilling to allow it to issue new shares which are taken up by new members and, therefore, reduce their control.

4. *Cost*. Investors expect a return on their investment. Debentures and loans carry interest charges and shareholders expect dividends and capital growth. Management must weigh the relative costs of the different forms of finance available to the company.

5. *Assistance*. Some assistance towards the cost of fixed assets may be available from the government. To qualify, the assets might have to be of a specified type or be used in a designated location.

Example 13.9

Norman Berman is a trader whose draft balance sheet as at 30 June 19X2 is as follows:

BALANCE SHEET AT 30 JUNE 19X2

	£000	£000
Fixed assets at cost		89
Less: Depreciation		31
		58
Current Assets:		
Stock-in-trade	64	
Trade debtors	35	
Bank	1	
	100	
Less:		
Current Liabilities		
Trade creditors	32	
		68
		126
Capital		
Balance at 1 July 19X1		120
Add: Net profit		24
Less: Drawings		(18)
Balance at 30 June 19X2		126

There is a buoyant demand for Berman's products, and sales have increased steadily over the years. The following forecasts and estimates are made for the year ending 30 June 19X3:

1 . Forecast monthly sales are as follows:
   19X2. July-December £40,000 per month.
   19X3. January-June £45,000 per month.
       July-December £50,000 per month.

2. The gross profit margin will be 20% on sales.

3. It is Berman's policy to maintain stocks, at the end of each month, sufficient to cover the expected sales for the following two months.

4. The period of credit allowed to customers and obtained from suppliers is expected to remain the same as for the year ended 30 June 19X2, i.e. one month.

5. Berman has sufficient accommodation for the planned increase in sales, but vehicles and equipment costing £20,000 will need to be purchased and paid for in December 19X2.

6. Wages and general expenses (including an allowance for bank interest) are paid for in the month that they are incurred and will amount to £5,000 per month.

7. The depreciation charge for the year is to be £12,000.

8. Berman will withdraw £2,000 each month for personal use.

9. Berman's bank has agreed to provide any overdraft facilities required during the year ended 30 June 19X3 and will charge interest at a rate of 12% per annum.

Required:
(a) A forecast cash statement, showing the bank balance or overdraft at the end of each month, for the year ending 30 June 19X3.

(b) Berman's forecast profit and loss account for the year ending 30 June 19X3.

(c) Berman's forecast balance sheet at 30 June 19X3.

(d) A discussion of the respective merits of bank overdraft finance as compared with loan finance, in the light of Berman's requirements, assuming that he could alternatively finance the purchase of vehicles and equipment by raising a five-year loan at a fixed interest rate of 10% per annum.

Notes:
1. Ignore taxation.

2. Assume for the purpose of the question that your calculations are being made on 1 July 19X2 and that the year to 30 June 19X3 consists of twelve months of equal length.

Solution

(a) *Forecast Cash Statement*

Month	Opening Balance £000	Sales £000	Purchases £000	Vehicles £000	Wages etc. £000	Drawings £000	Closing Balance £000
July	1	35	32		5	2	(3)
Aug.	(3)	40	32		5	2	(2)
Sept.	(2)	40	32		5	2	(1)
Oct.	(1)	40	32		5	2	-
Nov.	-	40	32		5	2	1
Dec.	1	40	36*	20	5	2	(22)
Jan.	(22)	40	36*		5	2	(25)
Feb.	(25)	45	36		5	2	(23)
March	(23)	45	36		5	2	(21)
April	(21)	45	36		5	2	(19)
May	(19)	45	36		5	2	(17)
June	(17)	45	40*		5	2	(19)

*Includes additional purchases of £4,000 required to keep the stock level equal to the next two months' sales.

(b) *Forecast Profit and Loss Account*

	£000	£000
Sales		510 (W1)
Less: Cost of goods sold (80%)		408
Gross profit		102
Less: Wages and general expenses	60	
Depreciation	12	
		72
Net profit		30

W1 Sales (£40,000 x 6) + (45,000 x 6) = £510,000

(C) *Forecast Balance Sheet, 30 June, 19X3*

	£000	£000
Fixed assets at cost		109
Less: Depreciation		43
		66
Current Assets		
Stock-in-trade	80	
Trade debtors	45	
	125	
Less:		
Current Liabilities		
Trade creditors	40	
Bank overdraft	19	
	59	
Net current assets		66
		132
Financed by:		
Capital		
Balance at 1 July, 19X2		126
Add: Net profit		30
Less: Drawings		(24)
		132

(d) Berman's firm is expected to generate funds from operations totalling £42,000 (£30,000 profit + £12,000 depreciation) during the year. Of this, Berman will withdraw £24,000 and the remaining £18,000 will be used to finance an increase in working capital, defined as stock + debtors – creditors. In addition fixed assets costing £20,000 will be purchased and this expenditure converts a £1,000 bank balance, at the beginning of the year, into a £19,000 deficit at the year end. The result is that the firm is expected to rely heavily on the bank for financial support, although the forecast working capital ratio is a fairly healthy 2.1:1.

Whether Berman should seek longer-term finance for the additional fixed assets, for example, a five-year loan, depends a lot on whether there are plans for further expansion. If the rate of expansion slows down, but profit margins continue at present levels, then the bank overdraft will be reduced fairly quickly. For instance, in the early months of 19X3, before the second phase of expansion, the overdraft is expected to fall at the rate of £2,000 per month. In such circumstances the decision to raise a five-year loan might soon result in the firm being in possession of liquid resources surplus to requirements. Despite the apparently favourable rate of loan interest, the total interest payable would then significantly exceed that accruing on a declining bank overdraft. If, however, further expansion is anticipated over the next five years, it would probably be wise to raise medium-term finance at this stage.

13.4 FURTHER READING

Arnold, J. and Turley, S. (1996) *Accounting for Management Decisions*, London: Prentice Hall, Chapter 8.

Drury, C. (1997) *Management Accounting for Business Decisions*, London: International Thomson Business Press, Chapter 3.

Idowu, S. (1998) 'The concept of break-even analysis in decision making', *ACCA Students' Newsletter*, April, pp. 62-4.

Weetman, P. (1999) *Management Accounting. An Introduction*, London: Pitman, Chapter 9.

13.5 QUESTIONS

Question 13.1

The summarized trading and profit and loss account and other financial data relating to Oxenhope Ltd is as follows:

Summarized Trading and Profit and Loss Account for 1998

	£000	£000
Credit sales		18,000
Less: Variable costs: Cost of goods sold	12,600	
Fixed costs: Depreciation	1,800	
Other operating expenses	2,400	16,800
Operating profit		1,200

Other financial data at 31 December 1998

	£000
Stocks	2,100
Trade debtors	1,500
Trade creditors	1,050
Bank overdraft	90

The directors of Oxenhope Ltd are keen to increase the company's sales and profit. They issued a circular to customers in December 1998 informing them that the credit period allowed will be increased from one to two months, to take effect for all sales made from 1 April 1999 onwards. The bank has agreed to provide overdraft facilities to cover any cash requirements over the forthcoming twelve-month period.

The directors have prepared the following plans and estimates for 1999:

* The new credit terms will produce an increase in monthly sales over 1998 levels of 20% with effect from April 1999.

* The period of credit received from suppliers to remain unchanged at one month.

* It is the directors' policy to maintain stocks at a level equivalent to expected sales over the forthcoming two months.

* Other operating expenses, which include an allowance for any interest payable, will rise to £240,000 per month with effect from the month of April. These expenses are paid for, as soon as they are incurred, on a monthly basis.

Required:
(a) A cash budget showing the forecast bank balance or overdraft at the end of each month during the year to 31 December 1999. *[7 marks]*

(b) A forecast profit statement for 1999. *[5 marks]*

(c) A calculation of the extra profit resulting from the new credit policy in the year to
     31 December 1999.   *[3 marks]*

(d) A calculation of the net cash inflow from operating activities for 1999.   *[5 marks]*

Notes:

•   Assume you are making the calculations on 1 January 1999.

•   Assume that each year consists of twelve months of equal length.

•   Trading transactions occurred at an even rate during the year to 31 December 1998.

[Total – 20 marks]

Question 13.2

The forecast cash budget of Severn Ltd for the eight months to 31 May 1998 is as follows:

Monthly cash forecast, 8 months to 31 May 1998, £000

	1997			1998				
Receipts	*Oct*	*Nov*	*Dec*	*Jan*	*Feb*	*March*	*April*	*May*
Sales	100	100	110	90	70	70	70	70
Payments								
Direct materials	50	50	55	45	35	35	35	35
Direct factory labour	22	18	14	14	14	14	14	14
Factory Expenses:								
Fixed	11	11	11	11	11	11	11	11
Variable	6	7	5	4	4	4	4	4
Salesmen's commission	5	6	5	4	4	4	4	4
Fixed overheads	3	3	3	3	3	3	3	3
	97	95	93	81	71	71	71	71
Balance bt/fwd	20	23	28	45	54	53	52	51
Balance cd/fwd	23	28	45	54	53	52	51	50

The directors of Severn Ltd have recently discovered that major repairs (covered by insurance) are
required to the factory due to subsidence, and there will be no production in the months of December
1997 and January 1998. The company manufactures to meet customer orders and no stock is carried.
Therefore, no sales will take place in December 1997 and January 1998. There will be no opportunity
to recover lost sales in subsequent months.

The directors have requested overdraft facilities in case they should be required to meet any temporary
cash shortage. The following additional information is provided:

1. Customers receive, and suppliers allow, two months' credit.

2. Direct factory labour and variable factory expenses are paid in the month they are incurred.

3. Fixed factory expenses are paid one month in arrears and salesmen are paid commission based
    on deliveries made during the previous month.

4.   The depreciation charge for the six months to 31 March 1998 will amount to £24,000.

The company has taken out an insurance policy which provides for the wages of factory workers to be paid directly by the insurance company immediately production is interrupted by unforeseen events.

Required:
(a)   A calculation of the forecast profit or loss for the four-month period to 31 March 1998 assuming the dislocation of production had not occurred. A monthly forecast is not required.   *[4 marks]*

(b)   A revised monthly cash forecast for each of the four months commencing 1 December 1997 assuming no production or sales in the months of December 1997 and January 1998. *[8 marks]*

(c)   A calculation of the revised forecast profit or loss for the four-month period to March 1998 assuming no production or sales in the months of December 1997 and January 1998. A monthly forecast is not required.   *[4 marks]*

(d)   A numerical reconciliation of the profits or losses forecast to arise under (a) and (c) above.
                                                                                                                  [4 marks]

                                                                                                      [Total – 20 marks]

Question 13.3

Trevor Scapens is a trader who has approached you with a request for financial advice. The products supplied by Scapens are in popular demand. An expansion of sales is expected, based on an advertising campaign which is to be run throughout the month of December 1996. The cost of the campaign, £30,000, is to be paid immediately. Scapens suspects that these developments will result in a shortage of operating cash over the forthcoming months and requires guidance concerning how to fund the expected shortfall.

The following further forecasts and estimates are provided:

1.   *Forecast balance sheet at 31 October 1996*

	£000	£000
Fixed assets at cost		300
Less: Accumulated depreciation		250
		50
Current assets:		
Stock in trade	170	
Trade debtors	100	
Cash at bank	5	
	275	
Less: Trade creditors	85	
Net current assets		190
		240
Financed by:		
Capital		240

2.   Forecast sales are £100,000 per month during November and December 1996 and £120,000 per month during the period January 1997 to October 1997.

3. Scapens maintains stocks at a level which is sufficient to meet expected sales requirements for the next two months, i.e. the stock held at 31 October 1996 is sufficient to cover the planned sales for November and December 1996.

4. The period of credit allowed to suppliers and obtained from customers will continue to be one month. The gross profit margin is 15% on all sales.

5. Fixed assets costing £90,000 will be acquired and paid for on 1 January 1997. The depreciation charge for the year to 31 October 1997 will amount to £32,000.

6. Other outgoings (excluding interest) will amount to £11,000 per month and this figure will include monthly cash drawings by Scapens of £3,000.

Notes:
You should assume that the year to 31 October 1997 consists of twelve months of equal length. Ignore interest on any forecast deficiency for the purpose of requirements (a)-(c) below.

Required:
(a) The cash forecast for the twelve months to 31 October 1997 showing the cash balance or cash deficit at the end of each month. [6]

(b) The forecast profit and loss account for the year ending 31 October 1997. Monthly profit figures are not required. [5]

(c) The forecast balance sheet at 31 October 1997. [7]

(d) A discussion of the respective merits of the following schemes for funding the forecast deficiency:

  (i) Raise a loan of £150,000 at 10% per annum on 1 November 1996. The loan is repayable on 31 October 1998.

  (ii) Arrange overdraft facilities at 12% per annum chargeable on the balance outstanding at the end of each month.

You should support your discussion with the following calculations:

• The amounts of interest payable under each of the two schemes.

• The impact of each of the schemes on the forecast profit and loss account for the year to 31 October 1997 and the forecast balance sheet at that date. [12]

[Total marks – 30]

Question 13.4

Cox Ltd's bank overdraft facility at present amounts to £350,000. The company's bank has requested the directors to take steps to reduce the level of the overdraft to £200,000 by 30 April 1996.

The forecast accounts for the six months to 31 October 1995 contain the following information:

Profit and Loss Account: Six Months to 31 October 1995

	£
Turnover	1,200,000
Less: Cost of goods sold (variable)	720,000
Operating expenses	360,000
Depreciation (straight-line)	40,000
	1,120,000
Net profit	80,000

Balance Sheet at 31 October 1995

	£
Fixed assets at cost	500,000
Less: Accumulated depreciation	200,000
	300,000
Stock in trade	240,000
Trade debtors	200,000
	440,000
Trade creditors	120,000
Bank overdraft	350,000
	470,000
Net current liabilities	(30,000)
	270,000
Issued share capital	100,000
Retained profit	170,000
	270,000

Trading transactions take place at a constant rate during the year. All payments are made to trade creditors and received from trade debtors in the month following the date on which the purchase or sale takes place. Payments for operating expenses are made immediately they are incurred. The profit and loss account for the six months to April 1996 is expected to contain the same information as the forecast statement set out above, except for the financial effect of the alternative plans set out below.

The company's directors are considering the following ways of achieving the required reduction in the bank overdraft:

Plan A: A reduction in stock of £50,000 which would mean that, with effect from 1 November 1995, monthly sales would fall by 5%, as a result of having fewer goods available for customers. Operating expenses would fall by £2,000 per month.

Plan B: A discount of 3% to be allowed to customers who agree to pay immediately goods are supplied to them. It is estimated that half the customers would take the discount and the remainder would continue to take one month's credit.

Either alternative (A or B) would be put into effect on 1 November 1995.

That is:

*   stock would be reduced by £50,000 in November by reducing purchases (Plan A); or

*   sales in the month of November would be eligible for the 3% discount (Plan B).

Required:
(a) Separate forecast profit and loss accounts (monthly figures not required) for the six months to 30 April 1996 as a result of implementing:
    (i)   Plan A
    (ii) Plan B   [7]

(b) Identify the forecast decrease in profit, compared with the expected results for the six months to 31 October 1995, which would result from the implementation of.
    (i)   Plan A
    (ii) Plan B   [2]

(c) Select the plan (A or B) which would achieve the required reduction in the overdraft at the lower cost, and prepare:
    (i)   A monthly cash budget for the six months to 30 April 1996.
    (ii) A balance sheet at 30 April 1996.   [15]

(d) The directors have asked the bank to consider allowing a longer period to achieve the required reduction in the level of the overdraft. Assuming the company is not obliged to implement either Plan A or Plan B, calculate how long it will take to achieve the required reduction and state whether this repayment period seems reasonable.   [6]

[Total marks – 30]

Notes:
Ignore bank interest.
Assume each month consists of 30 days.

Question 13.5

The forecast accounts of Pinfold Ltd for the year to 30 June 20X1 show the following financial results which the directors are confident will be achieved:

PROFIT AND LOSS ACCOUNT

	£000
Turnover	4,800
Less: Direct materials	1,800
Direct labour and variable overheads	1,500
	3,300
Contribution	1,500
Less: Fixed overheads	1,200
Net profit	300

BALANCE SHEET

	£000
Fixed assets at cost less depreciation	1,000
Current Assets	
Stocks: Raw materials	150
Work in progress	425
Finished goods	275
Cash	50
	900
Trade creditors	(225)
Working capital	675
Total assets less current liabilities	1,675
Financed by:	
Shareholders' equity	1,675

The company's accountants are preparing the budget for the year to 30 June 20X2. There is a strong demand for the company's products and it is estimated that an increase of up to 25% in the volume of sales can be achieved, which would have consequential implications for the selling price and operating costs. The following information is provided:

1. The selling price can be increased by 11% with effect from 1 July, assuming the existing level of activity, or 2.5% if the directors decide to aim for a 25% increase in the volume of activity. All sales are made for cash.

2. Direct material costs per unit are expected to increase by 6%, due to rising prices, with effect from 1 July 20X1. However, a 25% increase in the level of activity would enable the directors to negotiate a 4% trade discount on all purchases. Materials are held in stock for one month before being transferred to production. Suppliers allow 45 days credit.

3. Direct labour and variable overheads per unit are expected to increase by 8%, with effect from 1 July 20X1, following the completion of wage negotiations presently in progress. Payments for labour and variable overheads are made on the last day of each month.

4. Fixed overheads are expected to rise by 10% for the 12 months commencing 1 July 20X1.

5. Factory processing takes two months. Production is carried out at a steady rate throughout the year. Materials are introduced at the start of processing; labour and overheads are then incurred at an even rate during the processing period.

6. Finished goods are held in stock for one month awaiting sale.

7. Stocks are matched with sales on the first in, first out (FIFO) basis. Work-in-progress and finished goods are valued on the variable (marginal) cost basis for the purpose of the management accounts.

8. Operating cash requirements will increase from £50,000 to £52,000 if activity remains at existing levels, but will rise to £65,000 if activity rises by 25%.

Required:
(a) Prepare budgeted profit and loss accounts for the year to 30 June 20X2 in the format given in the question, on the alternative assumptions that:

    (i)   the volume of sales will remain unchanged;

    (ii) the volume of sales will increase by 25%.

    Ignore changes in the value of opening and closing stocks for the purpose of the above calculations.   [8]

(b) Calculate the expected additional investment in working capital, compared with the forecast position at 30 June 20X1, as the result of implementing each of the two plans examined under (a).   [10]

(c) Compare the two plans, indicating the advantages/disadvantages to the company and paying particular attention to their relative profitability and the possible ways of financing the additional working capital requirements.   [12]

[Total marks – 30]

Notes:

(i)   Make all calculations to the nearest £000.

(ii)   Assume that a year consists of twelve months of 30 days each.

(iii) Present your answers to (a) and (b) in columnar format.

(iv)   Ignore taxation.

APPENDIX A

SOLUTIONS TO CHAPTER-END QUESTIONS

Solution 1.1

Thinker Ltd – Trading and Profit and Loss Account for the Year to 30 June 20X3

	£000	£000
Sales		11,260
Opening stock	1,250	
Purchases	9,000	
Less: Closing stock	1,375	
Cost of goods sold		8,875
Gross profit		2,385
Depreciation:		
Buildings (1,600/50)	32	
Fixtures and fittings (300-146) x 20%	31	
Salaries and commissions	750	
Heat, light, maintenance etc	700	
Rates (175-60/2)	145	
Bank interest and charges	27	
Bad and doubtful debts (35-10)	25	1,710
Net trading profit		675
Less Dividend (3,000 x 10p)		300
		375
Retained profit brought forward		2,468
Retained profit carried forward		2,843

Balance Sheet at 30 June 20X3

	£000	£000
Fixed Assets		
Land		2,100
Buildings at cost	1,600	
Less: Accumulated depreciation	132	1,468
Fixtures and fittings at cost	300	
Less: Accumulated depreciation	177	123
		3,691
Current Assets		
Stock	1,375	
Debtors (2,670-10-35)	2,625	
Prepaid rates	30	
Cash	2	
	4,032	
Current Liabilities		
Creditors	740	
Overdraft	240	
Dividend	300	
	1,280	
Working capital		2,752
		6,443
Financed by:		
Ordinary shares of £1 each		3,000
Retained profit		2,843
Revaluation reserve		600
Shareholder's equity		6,443

Solution 1.2

(a) *Balance Sheet, 31 December, 19X0*

	£	£
Fixed assets at book value		2,200
Current Assets:		
Stock in trade	2,141	
Debtors	3,219	
Prepaid expense	100	
Bank balance	821	
	6,281	
Less: Current Liabilities:		
Trade creditors	1,842	
Accrued expense	31	
	1,873	
Working capital		4,408
		6,608
Financed by: Capital (balancing figure)		6,608

(b) *Trading and Profit and Loss Account for 19X1*

	£	£
Sales		24,433 (W1)
Less: Stock in trade at 31 December 19X0	2,141	
Purchases	18,673 (W2)	
Stock in trade at 31 December 19X1	(2,648)	
Cost of goods sold		18,166
Gross profit		6,267
Less: Salaries	2,249	
Rent and rates	804 (W3)	
Lighting and heating	179 (W4)	
General expenses	1,781	
Depreciation	220	
		5,233
Net profit		1,034

Balance Sheet, 31 December 19X1

	£	£
Fixed Assets at book value, £2,200-£220		1,980
Current Assets:		
Stock in trade	2,648	
Debtors	3,388	
Prepaid expense	120	
	6,156	
Less: Current Liabilities:		
Trade creditors	1,891	
Accrued expense	42	
Bank overdraft	1,030	
	2,963	
Working Capital		3,193
		5,173
Financed by:		
Capital at 31 December, 19X0		6,608
Add: Net profit		1,034
Less: Drawings		(2,469)
		5,173

W1. Sales:	£	W2. Purchases:	£
Cash received from customers	24,264	Cash paid to suppliers	18,624
Add: Debtors at 31 December		*Add*: Creditors at 31 December	
19X1	3,388	19X1	1,891
Less: Debtors at 31 December		*Less*: Creditors at 31 December	
19X0	(3,219)	19X0	(1,842)
	24,433		18,673

W3. Rent and rates:		W4. Lighting and heating:	
Cash paid	824	Cash paid	168
Add: Prepaid at 31 December		*Add*: Accrued at 31 December	
19X0	100	19X1	42
Less: Prepaid at 31 December		*Less*: Accrued at 31 December	
19X1	(120)	19X0	(31)
	804		179

Solution 1.3

(a) *Trading and Profit and Loss Account for 20X8*

	£000	£000
Sales		368 (W1)
Less: Opening stock	63	
Purchases	221 (W2)	
Closing stock	(75)	
Cost of goods sold		209
Gross profit		159
Less: Bad debts written off	5	
Administration and distribution expenses	62	
Depreciation	42	
Development expenditure written off	8 (W3)	
Loan interest	9	126
Net profit		33

(b) *Cash account for 20X8*

	£000	£000
Opening balance		13
Receipts from customers		362
		375
Less: Payments to suppliers	214	
Administration etc.	62	
Development expenditure	11	
Purchase of fixed assets	39	
Loan repaid	69	395
Closing balance		(20)

(c) Balance Sheet at 31 December 20X8

	£000	£000
Fixed Assets		
Tangible assets at cost or revalued amount		414 (W4)
Less: Accumulated depreciation		42
		372
Intangible asset: Development expenditure		15
Current Assets		
Stock	75	
Debtors	52	
	127	
Current Liabilities		
Trade creditors	42	
Bank overdraft	20	
	62	
Net current assets		65
		452
Capital and Reserves		
Called up share capital		100
Revaluation		210 (W5)
Retained profit		142 (W6)
		452

W1. 362 (receipts) + 52 (closing debtors) + 5 (bad debts written off) − 51 (opening debtors) = 368.

W2. 214 (payments) + 42 (closing creditors) − 35 (opening creditors) = 221.

W3. 12 (brought forward) + 11 (expenditure) − 15 (carried forward) = 8.

W4. 375 (revalued amount) + 39 (purchases) = 414.

W5. 375 (revalued amount) − 165 (net book values) = 210.

W6. 109 (brought forward) + 33 (profit) = 142.

(d) The company has traded profitably during 20X8; the profit of £33,000 represents a return of 9% (33/368 x 100) on sales and 7.3% (33/452 x 100) on the closing figure for shareholders' equity. The fact that the loan has been repaid early indicates that management is confident that the company will be able to meet debts as they fall due, and this is supported by a positive figure for net current assets of £65,000 and a working capital ratio of approximately 2:1 (127/62).

The main function of the profit and loss account is to calculate the increase or decrease in shareholders' wealth during a particular accounting period. It provides a measure of the effectiveness with which management has utilized the resources available to it, and provides a basis for assessing profitability by comparison with sales and capital employed. The details contained in the profit and loss account help to explain why profits have increased or decreased when comparisons are made with results achieved during the year, or by a different business, or by comparison with pre-determined budgets. The preparation of the profit and loss account involves the exercise of subjective judgement – in the above case relating to the amount of depreciation charged and the amount of development expenditure written off – and errors made will affect the reliability of the reported profit figure.

The main merit of the cash flow statement is that it provides a record of the financial effect of all transactions undertaken during an accounting period. Whereas the profit and loss account is confined to revenue transactions, the cash flow statement also includes capital inflows and outflows. In the above example it sets out capital expenditure on fixed assets and on development. Because it focuses on 'hard cash', possible distortions resulting from incorrect measurement procedures are avoided.

Solution 1.4

Course of action	Operating profit 20X0-1	Bank balance 31 July 20X1	Working capital 31 July 20X1	Gearing ratio 31 July 20X1
	£000	£000	£000	
1	200	50	1,000	0.2:1 (W1)
2	300	50	1,000	0.19:1 (W2)
3	200	50	1,000	0.1:1 (W3)
4	200	50	1,000	0.24:1 (W4)
5	120 (W5)	260 (W6)	920 (W7)	0.21:1 (W8)
6	200	350 (W9)	1,000	0.2:1

W1. 500/2,500.

W2. 500/(2,500 + 100).

W3. 500/(2,500 + 2,500).

W4. 500/(2,500-400).

W5. Monthly sales 6,000/12 = 500.
Discount taken. June and July sales paid for in July and August respectively,
500 x 2 x 8% = 80.
Revised profit, 200-80.

W6. Bank balance becomes 50 + 210 (extra cash received in July, 250-40 (discount)).

W7. July sales, 500, outstanding at year end, less provision for discount 40 = 460 + 500 + 260 – 300.

W8. 500/(2,500-80).

W9. Creditors become 3,600/6 = 600, i.e. an increase of 300.

Solution 2.1

(a) Under HCA, capital is the cash sum raised from the shareholders at the outset. This capital is distributed among a range of business assets and the purpose of the profit measurement process is to match the cost of resources consumed against sales proceeds in order to maintain intact the money value of the shareholders' investment.

Under CPP accounting, capital invested by shareholders is regarded as a pool of purchasing power units whose value must be maintained intact so that, when the firm closes down, a sum of money possessing an equivalent amount of purchasing power can be returned to the shareholder. This outcome is achieved by charging resources against revenue at cost as adjusted for changes in a general price index.

Under CCA, capital is treated as the operating capacity of the assets purchased with the funds invested in the company. It is these assets that generate income, so nothing must be distributed until sufficient resources have been retained in the business to enable the replacement of assets which are sold or have been worn out. This outcome is achieved by charging against sales proceeds the replacement cost of goods and services consumed as the result of undertaking business activities.

(b) See section 2.2.3.

Solution 2.2

(a) *Profit and Loss Accounts 19X1*

	HCA		CPP
	£		£
Sales	20,000	120/100	24,000
	20,000		20,000
	40,000		44,000
Cost of goods sold	25,000	120/100	30,000
Gross profit	15,000		14,000
Operating expenses	6,000		6,000
Loss on holding net monetary assets, 20,000 x 20/100	–		4,000
Net profit	9,000		4,000
Dividends	9,000		9,000
Retained profit	=		(5,000)

Balance Sheets, 31 December 19X1

	HCA		CPP
	£000		£000
Plant at cost	50,000	120/100	60,000
Cash at bank (75,000-75,000+40,000-6,000)	34,000		34,000
	84,000		94,000
Share capital	75,000	120/100	90,000
Retained profit	=		(5,000)
	75,000		85,000
Proposed dividend	9,000		9,000
	84,000		94,000

(b) Four advantages to be discussed might be:

- CPP accounting measures whether the purchasing power of the shareholders' capital has been maintained intact. It does this by expressing all transactions in terms of year-end £s. It can thus be seen, in this case, that the real value of the shareholders' investment has declined by £5,000. There are two elements to this loss: the reduction in gross profit resulting from the fact that the increased cost of goods sold, expressed in year-end £s, is £1,000 more than the sales value computed on a similar basis; and a loss of purchasing power arising from holding monetary assets during the year of £4,000.

- CPP accounting is likely to provide a better measure of the value of resources which must be retained in the business in order to enable assets to be replaced, although current cost accounting would provide an even better measure. In the case of Cornwell, after the dividend has been paid out based on the HC profit figure, there will be cash in bank of just £25,000. Assuming that the replacement cost of stock has risen during this inflationary period, the company will not be able to replace all ten Grommets sold during the year.

- The restatement of asset values in terms of a stable money value provides a more meaningful basis for comparison with other companies. Similarly, provided that previous year's profits are restated in CPP terms, it is also possible to compare more realistically the current year's results with past performance.

- CPP accounting restates all £s in terms of year-end values and this avoids the mixing together of different generations of £s that occurs under historical cost accounting.

Solution 2.3

(a) A holding gain is the difference between the cost of an asset and its current (replacement) cost at the accounting date. It is important to take account of holding gains when preparing financial statements for the following two reasons:

- to ensure that assets are shown in the balance sheet at their current value, representing the real resources available to management for business purposes;

- to identify the full cost of undertaking business activity during an accounting period and thereby ensure that the reported profit figure does not include windfall gains as the result of holding assets which happen to have risen in value due to rising prices.

Consequently, the reported figure for operating profit is a better measure of managerial performance.

Figures for 'holding gains' are reflected in the profit and loss account within both the cost of sales figures and the depreciation figure in order to measure the true cost of the resources consumed during the year. In the balance sheet, tangible fixed assets and current assets are higher under CCA in order to reflect the higher replacement cost of fixed assets and stocks during a period of rising prices.

(b)

	HCA	CCA	
Net profit percentage	10/120 x 100	8.3%	
	1/120 x 100		0.8%
Total asset turnover	120:100	1.2:1	
	120:121		1:1
ROSE	10/60 x 100	16.7%	
	1/81 x 100		1.2%
Debt:equity ratio	40:60	0.7:1	
	40:81		0.5:1

(c) *Net profit percentage*: this is lower under CCA reflecting the re-statement of stocks and depreciation of fixed assets at current cost.

The upward adjustments total £9 million, which is exactly equal to the reported reduction in the net profit figure.

Note that sales remain unaltered due to the fact that they are already stated at current prices.

Total asset turnover: this ratio is significantly lower under CCA, reflecting the fact that this accounting method measures the current cost of the total resources available to management for business purposes.

Once again, the sales figure remains unchanged and so the entire reduction in the ratio is accounted for by the increase in asset value.

ROSE: this is significantly lower under CCA. The ROSE is, of course, the product of the net profit percentage and the net asset turnover. Therefore, the fall in the ROSE is a combined consequence of the causes of the reductions in the other two ratios under CCA.

Debt: equity ratio: this is lower and, therefore, more favourable under CCA. The shareholders' equity will include the figure for holding gains and, as a result, is a third higher than its HCA equivalent.

With long-term liabilities remaining unaltered under CCA, the consequence is a significant reduction in the level of gearing from 0.7:1 to 0.5:1.

Solution 2.4

(a) *Profit and loss accounts for the year to 31 December 1999*

Alternative	Production	Order	Sale	Cash
Units	2,000	1,800	1,700	1,200
	£000	£000	£000	£000
Output	200	180	170	120
Cost	*160	144	136	96
Profit	40	36	34	24

* Cost per unit, £160,000/2,000=£80

The production director has a vested interest in profit being recognized on the basis of what the factory produces, irrespective of whether there is, say, a market for the items produced.

The sales director is naturally keen to emphasise the importance of securing sales orders for items produced and would therefore favour a profit recognition process that accords primacy to that achievement.

The managing director favours profit recognition in accordance with conventional practice although there is no particular vested interest evident in this choice.

The finance director is naturally concerned with cash generation as the 'life blood' of the business and would prefer to delay profit recognition until the money is in the bank.

(b) Profit is usually recognized at the point of sale – option 3

Balance Sheet at 31 December 1999

	£000
Share capital	200
Profit	34
	234
Stock (300 x £80)	24
Debtors (500 x £100)	50
Cash (£200,000-£160,000+£120,000)	160
	234

(c) Relevant comments are:

- Revenue is recognized at the point of sale in order to comply with relevant standard accounting practice and company law. In particular, the accruals concept assumes that profit is realized when the goods or services are supplied to the customer.

- Earlier recognition of profit may be seen to contravene the prudence concept given that the production of an item does not guarantee its sale; moreover, even the receipt of an order does not give rise to a contractual obligation on the part of the potential customer until the delivery takes place.

- The supply of goods to a customer represents an identifiable economic event which has legal significance; the supply of goods to the customer gives rise to a debt which, if necessary, could be pursued in a court of law.

- A strict application of the prudence concept might lead one to suppose that the recognition of profits should be delayed until cash is received from the customer. However, the purpose of accounting is to portray economic reality and, once the goods are supplied, the receipt of the sales price is reasonably assured. If, of course, it becomes evident that the purchase price will not be received, a provision must be made for the expected bad debt.

Solution 2.5

(a) The two accounting concepts are:

- The 'going concern' concept: the enterprise will continue in operational existence for the foreseeable future. This means in particular that the profit and loss account and balance sheet assume no intention or necessity to liquidate or curtail significantly the scale of operations.

- The 'accruals' concept: revenue and costs are accrued (that is, recognized as they are earned or accrued, not as money is received or paid) and matched with one another so far as their relationship can be established or justifiably assumed, and dealt with in the profit and loss account of the period to which they relate.

(b) *Revised Balance Sheet at 31 December 1998*

	£000 Cost	£000 Depreciation	£000 Book Value
Fixed assets			
Machine 1	4,100	2,000	2,100
Machine 2	4,100	2,000	2,100
	8,200	4,000	4,200
Current assets			
Stock of product 1		600	
Stock of product 2		600	
Debtors		728	
Cash		40	
		1,968	
Current liabilities			
Creditors		1,000	
Damages accrued		20	
		1,020	
Net current assets			948
			5,148
Financed by:			
Ordinary shares of £1 each			1,000
Share premium			400
Profit and loss account balance at 1 January 1998		1,780	
Profit for 1998	500		
Adjustments: i	+2,000		
ii	−400		
iii	−100		
iv	+60		
v	−72		
vi	−20	1,968	
			3,748
			5,148

(c) Appropriate examples of the application of the accounting concepts, when calculating the balances for fixed assets set out in the balance sheet, are.

- The proposed treatment of machine 1 contravenes the going concern concept. There is no intention to liquidate the company and the machine should not be reduced to residual value.

- The proposed treatment of machine 2 contravenes the accruals concept; the year 1998 has benefited from the use of the machine and should bear a fair proportion of its depreciable amount of £4m.

Solution 2.6

(a) See section 2.3.3.

(b) See section 2.3.5.

Solution 3.1

(a) The objective of FRS 3 is to require reporting entities falling within its scope to highlight a range of important components of financial performance to aid users in understanding the performance achieved by a reporting entity in a period and to assist them in forming the basis for their assessment of future results and cash flows.

(b) 1. This is an exceptional item. The general rule is that such items should be credited or charged in arriving at the profit or loss on ordinary activities for inclusion under the statutory format heading to which they relate, in this case distribution costs. No adjustment is therefore necessary to the profit and loss account but the bad debt must be disclosed by way of a note to the accounts.

2. A profit or loss on the sale or termination of an operation should be shown separately on the face of the profit and loss account after operating profit and before interest and included under the appropriate heading of continuing or discontinued operations.

3. This enables the required distinction to be made between continued and discontinued operations in order to improve the comparability of this year's results with those of forthcoming years.

4. The change of accounting policy gives rise to the need for a depreciation charge of £6 million for 1997. The change also gives rise to a prior year adjustment of £12 million in respect of 1995/6 which must be charged against retained profits brought forward.

5. This is also an exceptional item which should be charged in arriving at the profit or loss on ordinary activities as an administrative expense in respect of continuing operations. No adjustment is therefore necessary to the profit and loss account but the restructuring costs must be disclosed by way of a note to the accounts.

(c) *Trading and Profit and Loss Account for 1997*

	Continuing £ million	Discontinued £ million	Total £ million
Sales	463	100	563
Cost of sales	280	30	310
	183	70	253
Distribution costs	45	–	45
Administration expenses (W1)	94	–	94
Operating profit	44	70	114
Profit on disposal of asset	–	10	10
Profit on ordinary activities before tax	44	80	124
Taxation			45
Retained profit			79

Reserves

	Profit and loss £million
At beginning of year	101
Prior year adjustment	–12
	89
Transfer from profit and loss account	79
At end of year	168

W1 78 (given in question) + 10 (profit on sale of distribution division to be separately disclosed) + 6 (depreciation on offices)

Solution 3.2

(a) Exceptional items are abnormal as regards their size but which result from ordinary activities of the business. An example is an abnormal charge for bad debts. Such items appear above the line in the published profit and loss account, and have to be separately disclosed.

Extraordinary items result from events outside the normal trading activity of a business; they are material in amount and not expected to recur. As such items are not associated with normal operations, they are brought into the profit and loss account (less attributable taxation) after post-tax profits arising from ordinary activities have been computed. Because of the rarity of such items, no examples are provided in the standard.

(b) *Profit and Loss Account*

	Continuing operations		Discontinued operations	Total
	Existing	*Acquisitions*		
	£m	*£m*	*£m*	*£m*
Turnover	163	41	46	250
Cost of sales	71	21	38	130
Gross profit	92	20	8	120
Administrative expenses	57	6	7	70
Distribution costs	19	2	3	24
Operating profit (loss)	16	12	(2)	26
Loss on plant	(5)			(5)
Reorganization			(7)	(7)
Profit on ordinary activities	11	12	(9)	14
Taxation				5
Profit after tax				9

(c)   The key features of FRS 3 are the separate identification of the results relating to new acquisitions during the year or operations discontinued during the year. The purpose of requiring this information is to enable improved comparability with the results from previous periods, subsequent periods and other companies. In the case of comparisons with previous periods, the relevant figures are those relating to continuing existing operations and discontinued operations. For the purpose of making comparisons with the future, the relevant results for the year to 30 September 1996 are those relating to continuing existing operations and new acquisitions.

Solution 3.3

(a) *Exceptional items.* Broadly speaking, these are items which are abnormal as regards their size but which result from the ordinary activities of the business. An example is an abnormal charge for bad debts.

Extraordinary items. These arise as a result of events outside normal trading activities; they are material in amount and not expected to recur. Because of the extreme rarity of such items, no examples are provided in FRS 3.

Prior year adjustments. These consist of:

• Material adjustments applicable to prior years arising from changes in accounting policies, e.g. where a company changes from FIFO to AVCO.

• The correction of fundamental errors made when preparing earlier years' accounts, e.g. where the directors forget to count the stocks in one of the warehouses and, as a result, materially understate profits.

(b)

(i) *Profit and Loss Account for the year ended 31 December 20X5*

	£	£
Turnover		3,620
Cost of goods sold		2,533
Gross profit		1,087
Administrative expenses		526
Distribution costs (317+90)		407
Operating profit		154
Investment income		110
Interest payable		(12)
Profit on ordinary activities before taxation		252
Tax charge	40	
Tax credits re investment income	22	62
Profit after taxation		190
Dividends: Ordinary		80
Retained profit for the year		110

(ii) *Statement of Movement on Reserves, 20X5*

	Retained profit £000	Redemption reserve £000
Balance brought forward	560	–
Prior year adjustments:		
Development expenditure written off	(88)	
Change in method of stock valuation	(24)	
Transfer to redemption reserve	(12)	12
Retained profit for the year	110	–
	546	12

Workings, £000

W1 2,105 + 102 (development expenditure) + 6 (change in method of stock valuation) + 320 (depreciation).

(iii) *Balance Sheet at 31 December 20X5*

	£000	£000
Fixed assets		
Tangible assets		
Plant and machinery at cost	2,108	
Less: Accumulated depreciation	1,320	
		788
Advance corporation tax recoverable		20
Current assets		
Stocks	321	
Debtors and prepayments	320	
Cash at bank and in hand	7	
		648
Creditors: amounts falling due within one year		
Trade creditors	126	
Current corporation tax	40	
Proposed dividend	80	
Advance corporation tax	20	
Interest payable	12	
		278
Net current assets (liabilities)		370
Total assets less current liabilities		1,178
Creditors: amounts falling due after more than one year		
10% Debentures		120
		1,058
Capital and Reserves		
Called up share capital		500
Debenture redemption reserve		12
Profit and loss account		546
		1,058

Solution 3.4

(a) Segmental reports provide for identifiable segments, figures for turnover, profit and net assets.

Segmental reports must be prepared when an entity carries on operations in different classes of business or in different geographical areas.

The purpose of segmental information is to assist the user of financial statements to do the following:

*   To appreciate more thoroughly the results and financial position of the entity by permitting a better understanding of the entity's past performance and thus a better assessment of its future prospects, and

*   To be aware of the impact that changes in significant components of a business may have on a business as a whole.

(b) *Segmental Statement (£m)*

Classes of business	Beer & Pub	Hotel business	Other drinks & leisure	Total Operations
Turnover				
Turnover	508	152	368	1,028
Profit				
Segment profit (W1)	85	45	18	148
Common costs				15
Operating profit				133
Interest				14
Published net profit				119
Net Assets				
Segment net assets (W2)	1,127	391	403	1,921
Unallocated assets (W2)				−82
Published net assets				1,839

Workings:

W1

Sales	508	152	368	
Cost of sales	316	81	287	
Administrative expenses	43	14	38	
Distribution costs	64	12	25	
	423	107	350	
Segment profit	85*	45	18	

W2

Net Assets

	Beer & Pub	Hotel	Other	Total
Fixed assets at book value	890	332	364	77
Stocks and debtors	230	84	67	–
Bank	73	15	28	12
	303	99	95	12
Less: Current liabilities	66	40	56	31
Net current assets	237	59	39	−19
10% Debentures				−140
Net assets	1,127*	391	403	−82

* excluding interest and interest bearing loans as appropriate

(c)

Accounting ratios:	Operating divisions			Competitors	
	Beer & Pub	Hotel business	Other	Dean	Clarke
	%	%	%	%	%
Operating profit percentage	16.7	29.6	4.9	13.3	40.0
Asset turnover	45.1	38.9	91	46.0	50.0
Return on assets	7.5	11.5	4.5	6.2	20.0

The following matters could be covered in the examination of the relative performance of the operating divisions of Filios Products, and the comparison of the performance of the operating divisions of Filios Products, where appropriate, with that of the competitor companies.

Brief relevant comments include:

- The best performing segment, based on the primary accounting ratio, the return on assets, is the hotel division.

- The superior performance of the hotel division is attributable to the fact that it is able to generate higher operating margins than either of the other segments, and this outweighs the fact that it has the lowest asset turnover of the three.

- In order to interpret effectively the performance of the company, the results achieved by each division need to be compared with its direct competitor.

- The beer and pub division achieved a return on assets higher than that of its competitor Dean. The beer and pub division has achieved a far higher profit margin which has more than compensated for the marginally inferior asset turnover.

- It would appear that Filios' beer and pub division pursues a policy of higher selling prices and margins while also endeavouring to maintain asset turnover.

- Filios' hotel business division performs poorly compared to its competitor, producing a return on assets of not much more than half of that achieved by Clarke. The division's profit margin and rate of asset turnover are both lower than those of its competitor.

- It would appear that the hotel business division is performing poorly both in terms of cost control and use of assets, and each of these areas requires detailed investigation.

- The third division – other drinks and leisure – is making a contribution to profit of £18 million but performance is mediocre by all measures, including a return on net assets of just 4.5%.

- The performance of each of the two divisions for which competitor information is available is not encouraging. The position is even worse when it is recognized that there are unallocated common costs of £15 million and interest of £14 million. All the indications are that Filios is not being managed in the most effective manner.

- The rate of return on assets earned by Filios Products as a whole (6.5%) is marginally better than that achieved by its competitor Dean but far below that of Clarke.

Solution 3.5

(a) Planned dividend

	£000		£000
20X4	60	20X7	72
20X5	64	20X8	76
20X6	68	20X9	80

(b)

	20X4	20X5	20X6	20X7	20X8	20X9
	£000	£000	£000	£000	£000	£000
Retained profit at 1 Jan	–	50	6	33	–	124
Profit for the year	110	20	95	30	200	(20)
Distributable profit	110	70	101	63	200	104
Dividend	60	64	68	63	76	80
Retained profit at 31 Dec	50	6	33	–	124	24

The distributable profits of a limited company are accumulated realized profits minus accumulated realized losses. In every year, except 20X7, there are sufficient accumulated profits (including profits brought forward) to enable the planned payment to be made. In 20X7 the distribution must be restricted to available profits, i.e. £63,000.

(c) Capitalization issue, £24,000.

Solution 4.1

The total revaluation deficit that is recognized in 20X-10 is £1,875,000 (£10,375,000 – £8,500,000).

If the deficit had been attributable to a consumption of economic benefits, it would have been fully charged to the profit and loss account, regardless of any existing credit to the revaluation reserve in respect of that asset. However, given the fact that the deficit is due to a general fall in property prices then it is necessary to compute the depreciated historical cost assuming the property had never been revalued.

The depreciated replacement cost would have been: £9,500,000 (£12,500,000 – [10 x £300,000]). Therefore the revaluation deficit of £1,875,000 would be recognized as follows:

• £875,000 in the statement of total recognized gains and losses – this being the amount by which the carrying value immediately before the second valuation exceeds the hypothetical carrying value had the property never been revalued in 20X5.

• £1,000,000 in the profit and loss account.

Solution 4.2

(a) (i) The current assets are reduced by £1,000,000 to reflect the cash payment and increased by £1,000,000 being the amount of the lease prepayment.

(ii) *Revised Balance Sheet of Cooper Ltd at 1 January 20X0*

	£000	£000
Fixed Assets at book value (3,210+900)		4,110
Current Assets (3,000-1,000)		2,000
		6,110
Less: Creditors payable within one year		1,600
		4,510
Less: Creditors payable in more than one year		
15% Debenture 2010	200	
Critical plc	2,210	2,410
		2,100
Financed by:		
Share capital		1,600
Retained profits		500
		2,100

(b) (i) Annual rental debited to the profit and loss account £1 million

(ii) *Workings*

	20X0 £000	20X1 £000	20X2 £000	20X3 £000
Capital outstanding, 1 Jan.	3,210	2,586	1,856	1,000
Rental paid 1 Jan.	1,000	1,000	1,000	1,000
	2,210	1,586	856	
Interest charged, 17%	376	270	144	
Capital outstanding, 31 Dec.	2,586	1,856	1,000	

Profit and loss account entries

	20X0 £000	20X1 £000	20X2 £000	20X3 £000
Depreciation charge 3,210/4	802	803	802	803
Interest charge	376	270	144	–

Balance Sheet entries 31 December

	20X0 £000	20X1 £000	20X2 £000	20X3 £000
Fixed asset at cost	3,210	3,210	3,210	3,210
Accumulated depreciation	802	1,605	2,407	3,210
	2,408	1,605	803	–
Critical plc – creditor	1,000	1,000	1,000	
Long-term liability	1,586	856		

(c) Main points for discussion:

- the treatment adopted for an operating lease under (a)(i) acknowledges the fact that the rental is a normal running cost.

- the treatment of the transaction as a finance lease under (a)(ii):
  - emphasizes the economic substance of the transaction – Cooper the true 'owner' of the machinery; and
  - avoids off balance sheet finance.

- the treatment as a finance lease affects the content of the accounts, including the figures for capital employed and reported profit, and the accounting ratios computed therefrom such as the return on capital employed and gearing

- the economic consequence of the alternative treatments is that the differential content of the accounts affects user perception of a company's financial performance and position and, therefore, the decision-making process.

Solution 4.3

(a)

Fixed Assets Cost or valuation	Property A £000	Property B £000	Plant £000
At 1 January	10,600	20,000	–
Acquisition	–	–	6,346
Revaluation adjustment	6,400	–	–
Sale	–	(20,000)	–
At 31 December	17,000	–	6,346

Depreciation			
At 1 January	2,200	4,000	–
Revaluation adjustment	(2,200)	–	–
Provided during year	1,700	–	793
Sale	–	(4,000)	–
At 31 December	1,700	–	793
Net book value	15,300	–	5,553

Revaluation reserve			
At 1 January	–	5,400	
Revaluation (17,000,000-8,400,000)	8,600	–	
Transfer to P & L reserve	–	5,400	
At 31 December	8,600	–	

Profit and Loss Account for 20X1

	£000	£000
Turnover		106,000
Cost of goods sold 75,100-1,200	73,900	
Depreciation: Property A	1,700	
Plant	793	76,393
Gross profit		29,607
Administration expenses	20,600	
Selling and distribution	3,300	23,900
Operating profit		5,707
Profit on disposal of fixed assets 25,400-16,000		9,400
Profit on ordinary activities		15,107
Less: Interest payable (6,346-1,200)x14%		720
Net profit		14,387

Balance Sheet at 31 December 20X1

Fixed Assets	£000	£000
Property		15,300
Plant		5,553
Net current assets	33,800	
Proceeds from property B	25,400	
	59,200	
Less: Bargoed creditor 6,346-1,200+720	5,866	53,334
		74,187
Capital and reserves		
Issued share capital		10,000
Revaluation reserve		8,600
Retained profit at 1 January	35,800	
Transfer from revaluation reserve	5,400	
Net profit for 20X1	14,387	55,587
		74,187

(b) Main points for discussion:

- Property A: the difference between the carrying value and the revalued amount is credited to revaluation reserve.

- Property B: the difference between sales proceeds and the carrying value is a profit arising on disposal which must be credited to the profit and loss account above the line.

- FRS 3 rules out:
  - the treatment of the profit on disposal of property B as an extraordinary item; and
  - the calculation of profit on disposal is made by comparing sales proceeds with carrying value to produce a surplus of £9.4 million. The result is that the balance previously credited to revaluation reserve (£5.4 million) is merely transferred to profit and loss reserve rather than credited to the profit and loss account.